北京大学中国语言学研究中心

早期北京话珍稀文献集成

主编 刘云

—— 西人北京话教科书汇编

分卷主编 翟赟 郭利霞 陈颖

言语声片

[英]爱德华·丹尼森·罗斯 主编

老舍 等编著

卷一

北京大学出版社
PEKING UNIVERSITY PRESS

图书在版编目(CIP)数据

言语声片. 卷一、卷二 /(朝)爱德华·丹尼森·罗斯(Edward Denison Ross)主编；老舍等编著. —影印本. —北京：北京大学出版社, 2017.9
（早期北京话珍本典籍校释与研究）
ISBN 978-7-301-28725-5

Ⅰ. ①言… Ⅱ. ①爱… ②老… Ⅲ. ①北京话—汉语史—史料 ②北京话—对外汉语教学—研究资料 Ⅳ. ①H172.1

中国版本图书馆CIP数据核字（2017）第219095号

书　　名	言语声片（影印本）（卷一、卷二）
	YANYUSHENGPIAN（YINGYIN BEN）（JUAN YI, JUAN ER）
著作责任者	［英］爱德华·丹尼森·罗斯 主编　老舍 等编著
责任编辑	任蕾
标准书号	ISBN 978-7-301-28725-5
出版发行	北京大学出版社
地　　址	北京市海淀区成府路205号　100871
网　　址	http://www.pup.cn　新浪微博：@北京大学出版社
电子信箱	zpup@pup.cn
电　　话	邮购部 62752015　发行部 62750672　编辑部 62753334
印刷者	北京虎彩文化传播有限公司
经销者	新华书店
	720毫米×1020毫米　16开本　27.5印张　188千字
	2017年9月第1版　2018年5月第2次印刷
定　　价	98.00元（全二册）

未经许可，不得以任何方式复制或抄袭本书之部分或全部内容。
版权所有，侵权必究
举报电话: 010-62752024　电子信箱: fd@pup.pku.edu.cn
图书如有印装质量问题，请与出版部联系，电话: 010-62756370

总　序

　　语言是文化的重要组成部分，也是文化的载体。语言中有历史。

　　多元一体的中华文化，体现在我国丰富的民族文化和地域文化及其语言和方言之中。

　　北京是辽金元明清五代国都（辽时为陪都），千余年来，逐渐成为中华民族所公认的政治中心。北方多个少数民族文化与汉文化在这里碰撞、融合，产生出以汉文化为主体的、带有民族文化风味的特色文化。

　　现今的北京话是我国汉语方言和地域文化中极具特色的一支，它与辽金元明四代的北京话是否有直接继承关系还不是十分清楚。但可以肯定的是，它与清代以来旗人语言文化与汉人语言文化的彼此交融有直接关系。再往前追溯，旗人与汉人语言文化的接触与交融在入关前已经十分深刻。本丛书收集整理的这些语料直接反映了清代以来北京话、京味文化的发展变化。

　　早期北京话有独特的历史传承和文化底蕴，于中华文化、历史有特别的意义。

　　一者，这一时期的北京历经满汉双语共存、双语互协而新生出的汉语方言——北京话，它最终成为我国民族共同语（普通话）的基础方言。这一过程是中华多元一体文化自然形成的诸过程之一，对于了解形成中华文化多元一体关系的具体进程有重要的价值。

　　二者，清代以来，北京曾历经数次重要的社会变动：清王朝的逐渐羸弱、八国联军的入侵、帝制覆灭和民国建立及其伴随的满汉关系变化、各路军阀的来来往往、日本侵略者的占领，等等。在这些不同的社会环境下，北京人的构成有无重要变化？北京话和京味文化是否有变化？进一步地，地域方言和文化与自身的传承性或发展性有着什么样的关系？与社会变迁有着什么样的关系？清代以至民国时期早期北京话的语料为研究语言文化自身传承性与社会的关系提供了很好的素材。

　　了解历史才能更好地把握未来。新中国成立后，北京不仅是全国的政治中心，而且是全国的文化和科研中心，新的北京话和京味文化或正在形成。什么是老北京京味文化的精华？如何传承这些精华？为把握新的地域文化形成的规律，为传承地域文化的精华，必须对过去的地域文化的特色及其形成过程进行细致的研究和理性的分析。而近几十年来，各种新的传媒形式不断涌现，外来西方文化和国内其他地域文化的冲击越来越强烈，北京地区人口流动日趋频繁，老北京人逐渐分散，老北京话已几近消失。清代以来各个重要历史时期早期北京话语料的保护整理和研究迫在眉睫。

　　"早期北京话珍本典籍校释与研究（暨早期北京话文献数字化工程）"是北京大学中国语言学研究中心研究成果，由"早期北京话珍稀文献集成""早期北京话数据库"和"早期北京话研究书系"三部分组成。"集成"收录从清中叶到民国末年反映早期北京话面貌的珍稀文献并对内容加以整理，"数据库"为研究者分析语料提供便利，"研究书系"是在上述文献和数据库基础上对早期北京话的集中研究，反映了当前相关研究的最新进展。

　　本丛书可以为语言学、历史学、社会学、民俗学、文化学等多方面的研究提供素材。

　　愿本丛书的出版为中华优秀文化的传承做出贡献！

王洪君、郭锐、刘云
2016年10月

"早期北京话珍稀文献集成"序

清民两代是北京话走向成熟的关键阶段。从汉语史的角度看,这是一个承前启后的重要时期,而成熟后的北京话又开始为当代汉民族共同语——普通话源源不断地提供着养分。蒋绍愚先生对此有着深刻的认识:"特别是清初到19世纪末这一段的汉语,虽然按分期来说是属于现代汉语而不属于近代汉语,但这一段的语言(语法,尤其是词汇)和'五四'以后的语言(通常所说的'现代汉语'就是指'五四'以后的语言)还有若干不同,研究这一段语言对于研究近代汉语是如何发展到'五四'以后的语言是很有价值的。"(《近代汉语研究概要》,北京大学出版社,2005年)然而国内的早期北京话研究并不尽如人意,在重视程度和材料发掘力度上都要落后于日本同行。自1876年至1945年间,日本汉语教学的目的语转向当时的北京话,因此留下了大批的北京话教材,这为其早期北京话研究提供了材料支撑。作为日本北京话研究的奠基者,太田辰夫先生非常重视新语料的发掘,很早就利用了《小额》《北京》等京味儿小说材料。这种治学理念得到了很好的传承,之后,日本陆续影印出版了《中国语学资料丛刊》《中国语教本类集成》《清民语料》等资料汇编,给研究带来了便利。

新材料的发掘是学术研究的源头活水。陈寅恪《〈敦煌劫余录〉序》有云:"一时代之学术,必有其新材料与新问题。取用此材料,以研求问题,则为此时代学术之新潮流。"我们的研究要想取得突破,必须打破材料桎梏。在具体思路上,一方面要拓展视野,关注"异族之故书",深度利用好朝鲜、日本、泰西诸国作者所主导编纂的早期北京话教本;另一方面,更要利用本土优势,在"吾国之旧籍"中深入挖掘,官话正音教本、满汉合璧教本、京味儿小说、曲艺剧本等新类型语料大有文章可做。在明确了思路之后,我们从2004年开始了前期的准备工作,在北京大学中国语言学研究中心的大力支持下，早期北京话的挖掘整理工作于2007年正式启动。本次推出的"早期北京话珍稀文献集成"是阶段性成果之一，总体设计上"取异族之故书与吾国之旧籍互相补正"，共分"日本北京话教科书汇编""朝鲜日据时期汉语会话书汇编""西人北京话教科书汇编""清代满汉合璧文献萃编""清代官话正音文献""十全福""清末民初京味儿小说书系""清末民初京味儿时评书系"八个系列，胪列如下：

"日本北京话教科书汇编"于日本早期北京话会话书、综合教科书、改编读物和风俗纪闻读物中精选出《燕京妇语》《四声联珠》《华语跬步》《官话指南》《改订官话指南》《亚细亚言语集》《京华事略》《北京纪闻》《北京风土编》《北京风俗问答》《北京事情》《伊苏普喻言》《搜奇新编》《今古奇观》等二十余部作品。这些教材是日本早期北京话教学活动的缩影，也是研究早期北京方言、民俗、史地问题的宝贵资料。本系列的编纂得到了日本学界的大力帮助。冰野善宽、内田庆市、太田斋、鳟泽彰夫诸先生在书影拍摄方面给予了诸多帮助。书中日语例言、日语小引的翻译得到了竹越孝先生的悉心指导，在此深表谢忱。

"朝鲜日据时期汉语会话书汇编"由韩国著名汉学家朴在渊教授和金雅瑛博士校注，收入《改正增补汉语独学》《修正独习汉语指南》《高等官话华语精选》《官话华语教范》《速修汉语自通》《速修汉语大成》《无先生速修中国语自通》《官话标准：短期速修中国语自通》《中语大全》《"内鲜满"最速成中国语自通》等十余部日据时期（1910年至1945年）朝鲜教材。这批教材既是对《老乞大》《朴通事》的传承，又深受日本早期北京话教学活动的影响。在中韩语言史、文化史研究中，日据时期是近现代过渡的重要时期，这些资料具有多方面的研究价值。

"西人北京话教科书汇编"收录了《语言自迩集》《官话类编》等十余部西人编纂教材。这些西方作者多受过语言学训练，他们用印欧语的眼光考量汉语，解释汉语语法现象，设计记音符号系统，对早期北京话语音、词汇、语法面貌的描写要比本土文献更为精准。感谢郭锐老师提供了《官话类编》《北京话语音读本》和《汉语口语初级读本》的底本，《寻津录》、《语言自迩集》（第一版、第二版）、《汉英北京官话词汇》、《华语入门》等底本由北京大学图书馆特藏部提供,谨致谢忱。《华英文义津逮》《言语声片》为笔者从海外购回,其中最为珍贵的是老舍先生在伦敦东方学院执教期间,与英国学者共同编写的教材——《言语声片》。教材共分两卷:第一卷为英文卷,用英语讲授汉语,用音标标注课文的读音;第二卷为汉字卷。《言语声片》采用先用英语导入,再学习汉字的教学方法讲授汉语口语,是世界上第一部有声汉语教材。书中汉字均由老舍先生亲笔书写,全书由老舍先生录音,共十六张唱片,京韵十足,殊为珍贵。

上述三类"异族之故书"经江蓝生、张卫东、汪维辉、张美兰、李无未、王顺洪、张西平、鲁健骥、王澧华诸先生介绍,已经进入学界视野,对北京话研究和对外汉语教学史研究产生了很大的推动作用。我们希望将更多的域外经典北京话教本引入进来,考虑到日本卷和朝鲜卷中很多抄本字迹潦草,难以辨认,而刻本、印本中也存在着大量的异体字和俗字,重排点校注释的出版形式更利于研究者利用,这也是前文"深度利用"的含义所在。

对"吾国之旧籍"挖掘整理的成果,则体现在下面五个系列中:

"清代满汉合璧文献萃编"收入《清文启蒙》《清话问答四十条》《清文指要》《续编兼汉清文指要》《庸言知旨》《满汉成语对待》《清文接字》《重刻清文虚字指南编》等十余部经典满汉合璧文献。入关以后,在汉语这一强势语言的影响下,熟习满语的满人越来越少,故雍正以降,出现了一批用当时的北京话注释翻译的满语会话书和语法书。这批教科书的目的本是教授旗人学习满语,却无意中成为了早期北京话的珍贵记录。"清代满汉合璧文献萃编"首次对这批文献进行了大规模整理,不仅对北京话溯源和满汉语言接触研究具有重要意义,也将为满语研究和满语教学创造极大便利。由于底本多为善本古籍,研究者不易见到,在北京大学图书馆古籍部和日本神户市外国语大学竹越孝教授的大力协助下,"萃编"将以重排点校加影印的形式出版。

"清代官话正音文献"收入《正音撮要》(高静亭著)和《正音咀华》(莎彝尊著)两种代表著作。雍正六年(1728),雍正谕令福建、广东两省推行官话,福建为此还专门设立了正音书馆。这一"正音"运动的直接影响就是以《正音撮要》和《正音咀华》为代表的一批官话正音教材的问世。这些书的作者或为旗人,或寓居京城多年,书中保留着大量北京话词汇和口语材料,具有极高的研究价值。沈国威先生和侯兴泉先生对底本搜集助力良多,特此致谢。

《十全福》是北京大学图书馆藏《程砚秋玉霜簃戏曲珍本》之一种,为同治元年陈金雀抄本。陈晓博士发现该传奇虽为昆腔戏,念白却多为京话,较为罕见。

以上三个系列均为古籍,且不乏善本,研究者不容易接触到,因此我们提供了影印全文。

总体来说,由于言文不一,清代的本土北京话语料数量较少。而到了清末民初,风气渐开,情况有了很大变化。彭翼仲、文实权、蔡友梅等一批北京爱国知识分子通过开办白话报来"开启民智""改良社会"。著名爱国报人彭翼仲在《京话日报》的发刊词中这样写道:"本报为输进文明、改良风俗,以开通社会多数人之智识为宗旨。故通幅概用京话,以浅显之笔,达朴实之理,纪紧要之事,务令雅俗共赏,妇稚咸宜。"在当时北京白话报刊的诸多栏目中,最受市民欢迎的当属京味儿小说连载和《益世余谭》之类的评论栏目,语言极为地道。

"清末民初京味儿小说书系"首次对以蔡友梅、冷佛、徐剑胆、儒丐、勋锐为代表的晚清民国京味儿作家群及作品进行系统挖掘和整理,从千余部京味儿小说中萃取代表作家的代表作品,并加以点校注释。该作家群活跃于清末民初,以报纸为阵地,以小说为工具,开展了一场轰轰烈烈的底层启蒙运动,为新文化运动的兴起打下了一定的群众基础,他们的作品对老舍等京味儿小说大家的创作产生了积极影响。本系列的问世亦将为文学史和思想史研究提供议题。于润琦、方梅、陈清茹、雷晓彤诸先生为本系列提供了部分底本或馆藏线索,首都图书馆历史文献阅览室、天津图书馆、国家图书馆提供了极大便利,谨致谢意!

"清末民初京味儿时评书系"则收入《益世余谭》和《益世余墨》,均系著名京味儿小说家蔡友梅在民初报章上发表的专栏时评,由日本岐阜圣德学园大学刘一之教授、矢野贺子教授校注。

这一时期存世的报载北京话语料口语化程度高,且总量庞大,但发掘和整理却殊为不易,称得上"珍稀"二字。一方面,由于报载小说等栏目的流行,外地作者也加入了京味儿小说创作行列,五花八门的笔名背后还需考证作者是否为京籍,以蔡友梅为例,其真名为蔡松龄,查明的笔名还有损、损公、退化、亦我、梅蒐、老梅、今睿等。另一方面，这些作者的作品多为急就章，文字错讹很多，并且鲜有单行本存世，老报纸残损老化的情况日益严重，整理的难度可想而知。

　　上述八个系列在某种程度上填补了相关领域的空白。由于各个系列在内容、体例、出版年代和出版形式上都存在较大的差异，我们在整理时借鉴《朝鲜时代汉语教科书丛刊续编》《〈清文指要〉汇校与语言研究》等语言类古籍的整理体例，结合各个系列自身特点和读者需求，灵活制定体例。"清末民初京味儿小说书系"和"清末民初京味儿时评书系"年代较近，读者群体更为广泛，经过多方调研和反复讨论，我们决定在整理时使用简体横排的形式，尽可能同时满足专业研究者和普通读者的需求。"清代满汉合璧文献萃编""清代官话正音文献"等系列整理时则采用繁体。"早期北京话珍稀文献集成"总计六十余册，总字数近千万字，称得上是工程浩大，由于我们能力有限，体例和校注中难免会有疏漏，加之受客观条件所限，一些拟定的重要书目本次无法收入，还望读者多多谅解。

　　"早期北京话珍稀文献集成"可以说是中日韩三国学者通力合作的结晶，得到了方方面面的帮助，我们还要感谢陆俭明、马真、蒋绍愚、江蓝生、崔希亮、方梅、张美兰、陈前瑞、赵日新、陈跃红、徐大军、张世方、李明、邓如冰、王强、陈保新诸先生的大力支持，感谢北京大学图书馆的协助以及萧群书记的热心协调。"集成"的编纂队伍以青年学者为主，经验不足，两位丛书总主编倾注了大量心血。王洪君老师不仅在经费和资料上提供保障，还积极扶掖新进，"我们搭台，你们年轻人唱戏"的话语令人倍感温暖和鼓舞。郭锐老师在经费和人员上也予以了大力支持，不仅对体例制定、底本选定等具体工作进行了细致指导，还无私地将自己发现的新材料和新课题与大家分享，令人钦佩。"集成"能够顺利出版还要特别感谢国家出版基金规划管理办公室的支持以及北京大学出版社王明舟社长、张凤珠副总编的精心策划，感谢汉语编辑室杜若明、邓晓霞、张弘泓、宋立文等老师所付出的辛劳。需要感谢的师友还有很多，在此一并致以诚挚的谢意。

　　"上穷碧落下黄泉，动手动脚找东西"，我们不奢望引领"时代学术之新潮流",惟愿能给研究者带来一些便利,免去一些奔波之苦,这也是我们向所有关心帮助过"早期北京话珍稀文献集成"的人士致以的最诚挚的谢意。

刘 云

2015年6月23日

于对外经贸大学求索楼

2016年4月19日

改定于润泽公馆

导　读

陈　颖

19世纪，西方各国在中国扩张政治势力，译员和海关公务人员学习汉语的需求大量增长，对西方各国的本土汉语教学提出了要求。《言语声片》就是在这样的时代背景下编撰而成的一部汉语教材，是观察彼时汉语本体面貌和汉语教学情况的珍贵资料。

一、《言语声片》及其编写团队

（一）灵格风（The Linguaphone Institute）

灵格风是由翻译家杰克·罗士顿（Jacques Roston）于1901年创立的语言教学机构，目前它在全球60多个国家设有语言培训中心。他们于20世纪20年代出版了一系列的语言教材，用灌制唱片的办法教发音和会话。从《言语声片》书末的广告可知，灵格风推出了会话、旅行和文学等系列教程，都有配套的教材和唱片。"旅行教程"用30篇课文学习目的国的艺术、音乐、历史和地理，有英语、法语和意大利语等版本。"文学教程"用20篇课文学习目的语国家著名作家的诗歌和散文，有英语、法语、意大利语和德语等版本。

"灵格风会话教程"系列有英语、汉语、法语、德语、意大利语、西班牙语、俄语、荷兰语、南非荷兰语、爱尔兰语、波斯语、世界语等语种，每种都是30篇课文，教材和唱片一起装在小提箱里。其中，汉语教材委托伦敦大学东方学院编写。

（二）伦敦大学东方学院（School of Oriental Studies, University of London）

1916年，伦敦大学成立了东方学院，后改名为亚非学院（School of Oriental and African Studies），是英国唯一一所专门研究亚洲，包括近东和中东以及非洲的高等教育机构。东方学院的学生年龄差异较大，学习汉语的目的各不相同，汉语水平也参差不齐。学院的汉语教学完全是因材施教，竭力满足不同学生的需求，因此缺乏系统的汉语课程安排和教材，也难以保障教学效果。《言语声片》正是在这样的教学环境中编写而成的。

《言语声片》的正式出版名称为《灵格风东方语言教程：汉语》，唱片和课本都未标明具体的出版时间，《言语声片》序言中提到：The Mandarin dialect of Pekin... which it held all through the Manchu regime and the first twelve years of the Republic, ...（北京官话是满族政权一直以来的代表和民国前十二年的代表）可见这部教材最迟从1923年起就开始编撰，老舍1924年到达英国后参与其中，负责中文部分的编写工作和录制唱片。远藤光晓认为出版时间是1930年，但编撰完成和进行录音的时间是1928年（远藤光晓，1986/2001）。也有人推测该书完成于1926年（仇志群，1993）。

《言语声片》在国际上沿用至20世纪50年代，唱片发行的范围可能比较广，也可能有不同的版本，例如在封面装帧上有差别而内容未有大的改动（舒乙，2011：272）。

（三）《言语声片》编撰团队

作为"灵格风东方语言教程"的系列教材之一，《言语声片》的编撰团队中既有英国人又有中国人，是中英两国的合编教材。

这部系列教程的主编（General Editor）是英国人Edward Denison Ross（1871—1940），他出生于伦敦，1894年获得波斯语博士学位，做过伦敦大学学院（University College London）波斯语教授，曾在不列颠博物馆为斯坦因藏品编目，作为英国情报局官员被派往伊斯坦布尔。他曾在印度穆斯林大学和加尔各答大学工作，也曾负责印度政府档案管理、担任教育部大臣。他不仅从事伊斯兰研究，对梵文、汉语和藏语也有所了解。1916年至1937年，他担任东方学院的首任院长。

语音编辑（Phonetic Editor）是英国人Arthur Lloyd James（1884—1943），他负责灵格风非欧洲语言（non-European languages）系列教材的语音工作。他在剑桥三一学院获得文学硕士学位，1920年开始先后任职于伦敦大学学院和伦敦大学东方学院，1927年担任东方学院语音系主任。他曾在BBC做广播员，后来成为BBC的语言学顾问，编撰了7本"广播英语"手册。他还发起创立了英语口语咨询委员会，先后担任顾问和秘书（Paul Carley, 2013：27—30）。

《言语声片》第一卷（英文部分）还有两位编著者Daniel Jones和Charles Otto Blagden。

Daniel Jones（1881—1967）是英国语言学家和语音学家，时任伦敦大学东方学院语音学教授。他在剑桥大学获得数学学位后，又获得了瑞士苏黎世大学博士学位。他后来对语音学产生了兴趣，曾任国际语音学会助理秘书，提出了国际音标的设想，并描述了有影响的公认发音法（斯蒂芬·R.安德森，2015：279）。

Charles Otto Blagden（1864—1949）是英国东方学家和语言学家，致力于马来语、缅甸语等语言研究。

《言语声片》第二卷（中文部分）有三位编辑。

Joseph Percy Bruce（卜道成，1861—1934）是英国浸礼会牧师。1887年来华，在山东传教办学，创办了青州神学院、山东基督教联合大学等，曾任齐鲁大学校长。1922年获伦敦大学文学博士学位，1925年任伦敦大学汉文教授（周川，2012：672）。

Evangeline Dora Edwards（1888—1957）也是英国人，其父是苏格兰长老会派遣来华的传教士。Edwards出生于中国，在中国接受过教育，曾担任奉天女子师范学堂校长。1921年被聘为伦敦大学汉学讲师，后晋升为该校远东系主任和汉学教授。主要著述有《孔子》(Confucius)《中国唐代散文文学》(Chinese Prose Literature of the Tang Period A.D. 618—906)（熊文华，2000：16）。

C. C. Shu就是中国现代著名小说家、文学家、戏剧家老舍（1899—1966）。1924年，老舍被伦敦大学东方学院聘请为中文讲师，英文名为Conlin C. Shu（舒柯林），在东方学院讲授中国语言和中国文学，1929年约满离职（舒济、郝长海、吴怀斌，2013：495）。

《言语声片》的编撰团队至少有7人，主编、语音编辑和英语编辑都有较为深厚的语言学功底，汉语编辑都有很强的汉语能力，再加上老舍这样的语言大师，编撰团队可谓专业、强大，并且分工细致、各司所长。

二、体例一览

《言语声片》教材包括16张唱片和两卷课本。

16张唱片均由老舍发音。前15张唱片录了30篇课文，每张唱片录两课。第16张是作为序篇的发音练习，录有《伊索寓言·酸葡萄》和《红楼梦》第二十五回片段。

课本是羊皮封面，烫金书边。第一卷（英文部分）共190页，第二卷（中文部分）共213页，课文的汉字系老舍毛笔手书。

（一）第一卷概况

第一卷扉页页首"灵格风东方语言教程"（Linguaphone Oriental

Language Courses)是系列教程的总名,其下署名依次为系列教程的主编Edward Denison Ross和语音编辑Arthur Lloyd James。页面正中大字Chinese表明这是系列教程的汉语卷,作者依次是Joseph Percy Bruce、Evangeline Dora Edwards和C. C. Shu。唱片发音也是C. C. Shu。页脚是灵格风的地址。有意思的是,扉页还注明了"使用国际语音学会的音标字母标音"(With Phonetic Transcription in the Alphabet of the International Phonetic Association),可见这是该书引以为傲的一大特色。

1. 序言(Preface)

主编Edward Denison Ross撰写序言,强调了这本教材的特点:

A. 留声机唱片可以弥补教师不足之缺,也能让学生反复模仿练习;

B. 国际音标记音能修补威妥玛记音法之不足;

C. 以北京官话为学习标准,能帮助学习其他方言。

2. 导论(Introduction)

导论包括三个部分:目标和方法(Aim and Method)、口语的演变(Evolution of the Spoken Language)和汉字的构造(Formation of Chinese Characters)。

目标是"让学生花最少的精力转用汉语交谈,并且发音用词准确"(enable the student with a minimum of effort to converse in Chinese intelligently and with accuracy of prounciation and idiom)。方法是使用国际音标,这样可以更有效地帮助学生掌握元音的细微区别。为了强调这一方法的有效性,还特别提到赵元任的《国语留声片课本》(*A Phonograph Course in the Chinese Language*, 1922)也使用了国际音标。

口语的演变部分强调了针对汉语四声而专门设置的声调练习,特别提出使用双音节复合词可以避免同音歧义,关注到了汉语的构词法及教学规律。

汉字的构造部分介绍了造字法，并归为三类：A. 象形和指事；B. 会意和形声；C. 其他。希望用214个部首的相关知识来解决汉字书写这一难点。

3. 汉语发音（Notes on Chinese Sounds）

这是对第16张唱片所做的说明（Explanatory of the Preliminary Record, entitled "Chinese sounds"）。

第16张唱片有两个部分，"发音练习（上）"是汉语语音的基本情况，包括首音、尾音和四声的基本字词训练，"发音练习（下）"是《伊索寓言·酸葡萄》和《红楼梦》第二十五回片段。

第一卷只对"发音练习（上）"做了详细说明，包括23个首音（21个辅音声母和半元音j、w）、39个尾音（39个韵母）、四声和音标。这个部分可以看作是非常详尽而专业科学的汉语发音指导，详细讲解了首音和尾音的发音部位和发音方法，用英语单词中对应的近似发音来帮助理解，还用到了舌面元音舌位图；讲解声调时对比了北京话和山东话的调值，用五线谱来表示与重音相关的声调高低变化；讲解音标时则对比了国际音标、威妥玛记音符号和国语记音符号，便于读者参照学习。

4. 学习指导（Directions to the Student）

第一卷的学习指导注重听说能力的训练，要求从听音辨音练起，声调是基础，包括变调，熟练之后才进入词汇和语法的学习，再回到听力练习。强调不能靠规则来学习汉语，只能多次重复记忆，还指出汉语的语序和虚词特别重要。

5. 课文文本（Transcription and Translation of the Chinese Linguaphone Records）

和第二卷汉语文本对应，偶数页为课文的国际音标注音，奇数页为对应的英语译文。（参见后文图表）

6. 课文注释（Notes）

这个部分的作用相当于教师参考用书，分别指出每篇课文的发音要点(Pronunciation)、语法构造(Grammatical Construction)和汉字(Chinese Characters)。有的课后还安排了复习(Review),例如写出课文句子的音标(第3课下)。

例如第1课上的注释包括三个部分:

发音要点共2条,指出本课有六个首音ʃ、ḅ、x、j、m、ɹ和七个尾音i、eɪ、ɛ、ɑo、ɔ、u、ǝn;提示特别注意声调练习中第三声和第四声的ju(指"忧/油/有/右"四字)元音音值因为声调的影响而有变化。

语法构造共7条,首先提出这部分涉及的主要语法点是肯定、否定和疑问,"有没有"是肯定否定并列形式表示疑问;指出在这种形式中,名词主语通常放在第一个"有"后面(练习3"有书没有"),当主语是词组时,"有没有"就整体放在主语后(练习10"笔墨有没有");依次提出了形容词、连词"也"、集合名词"笔墨"等语法知识点;最后归纳了简单句的一般语序是"A. 主语; B. 连词、时间副词或方式副词; C.动词; D. 宾语"。

汉字共4条,提示本课汉字对应的组成部首是哪些,并要求读汉字书写指导,根据汉字表学写描画部首,继而根据词汇表、参照附录表2,观察描写汉字字形。

(二)第二卷概况

1. 学习指导(Directions to the Student)

第二卷的学习指导注重书写能力的训练,强调了汉字的结构、笔画、笔顺等书写基础知识,认为将汉字拆分成部件来学习和记忆是更为有效的方法,指导学生使用附录的部首表和课文生字示例分析。

《言语声片》重视使用字典辅助汉字学习,多次提到参考字典的罗马字母注音及字形分析,附录中还列出了这些字典中的对应序号以便查找。这些参考书包括Wieger(戴遂良)《汉字》*Chinese Characters*、George Durand Wilder(万卓志)和James Henry Ingram(盈亨利)《汉字解析》

Analysis of Chinese Characters、Frank Herring Chalfant（方法敛）《中国早期文字》*Early Chinese Writing*、William Edward Soothill（苏慧廉）《四千常用汉字学生袖珍词典》*The Student's Four thousand 字 and General Pocket Dictionary* 和 Courtenay Hughes Fenn（芳泰瑞）《五千汉字字典》*The Five Thousand Dictionary* 等。

2. 发音练习（Chinese Sounds）

因第一卷"汉语发音"已用英语详细解释了发音并标明了国际音标，第二卷的这一部分就只有汉字没有注音。"发音练习上"是基本语音训练，包括23个首音字、40个尾音字（编者认为"日"和"志吃诗"的元音不同，故单独列出）、10组同音节四声字（低/敌/底/地）、6组和重音相关的双音节词（风光/山河/乡长/公断）、2组和位置相关的变调练习（不多/不是）。"发音练习下"包括《伊索寓言·酸葡萄》和《红楼梦》第二十五回片段，均为从右至左竖行书写。

3. 课文（Chinese Text）

从版块设置来看，30课课文可以分为起步、初级、中级和高级四个阶段。

1—10课既是语音阶段又是起步阶段，每课均上下两部分，各自设置生字（Vocabularies）、词语（Compound Words and Expressions）、声调练习（Tone Practice）和练习（Exercise）四个版块。从第10课第2部分开始取消声调练习版块，其余安排不变，因此可将11—15课视为初级阶段。

16—28课为中级阶段，统一给出生字后再分为两部分。第一部分设置词语和练习两个版块，第二部分设置词语和会话（Conversation）两个版块。

29和30课为高级阶段，不再分上下两部分，统一给出生字和词语，然后是长篇语料。第29课是寓言故事《阿剌伯人和他的骆驼》，第30课是关于新闻时事的会话。

4. 附录1（Appendix I）部首表（The Radicals）

用英文和汉字两个表格逐个分析214个部首。

英文表包括威妥玛式注音、解释意义、汉字构造类别（导论中划分出的A、B、C三类）和字形解释：

No.	Wade's Spelling.	Meaning.	Class of Formation	Remarks.
75.	Mu⁴	Tree. Wood	A	A tree with its branches and roots.[W., 119, A; I., 22; C, 97.]

汉字表包括楷书形体、笔顺和小篆形体：

5. 附录2（Appendix II）1至4课汉字分析（Analysis of Characters in Lessons 1 to 4）

列表详细分析了1至4课的75个汉字。包括威妥玛拼音、部首表对应序号、苏慧廉字典的对应序号、字形类别和详尽分析备注。如第1课上的"有"字：

No.	Wade's Spelling.	No. of Radical.	No. of Phonetic in Soothill.	Class of Formation.	Remarks.
5.	Yu³	74	184	B	*The moon* and *the right hand.* The original meaning is *the moon's phases* presenting the appearance of being partly covered by the hand. *To be* and *to have* are borrowed meanings. [W., 46, H; I., 43.]

6. 汉字索引（Chinese Index）

将全书统一编号的947个生字按214部首重新排列，并标明在课文中的序号。如第5个部首是"乙"，下有"乙、九、也、乾"等字，"九"字的序号是61，可以根据这个序号迅速找到该字在第4课上这个部分。

7. 英文索引（English index）

将全书字词的对译英文按A至Z的顺序排列，如 Cabin 870, 28^4，指序号870"舱"字在第28课出现，包含在该课的第4个词语（船舱）中。

三、特　点

（一）循序渐进的教学理念

《言语声片》是为零起点学习者编写的速成式教材，所以不注重语言知识的讲解，而是强调反复练习，注重对学习进度的全盘考虑和协调。

从总体的版块设计上看，起步、初级、中级、高级阶段之间的版块安排并非一刀切，而是有部分穿插过渡，体现出循序渐进。

从生字编排上看，1—15课将生字分散到上下两个部分，每个部分约15个生字，让学生逐步适应汉字的学习。从第16课开始，生字不再分上下部分，集中给出，大约每课50字，和中级学习水平相适应。

从练习编排上看，1—15课都有单句练习，16—27课的上部分是单句形式的练习，下部分是二至四人的会话，教学中可以安排分角色朗读等等，可以看作是练习的另一种形式。28课上下两部分均为会话，29课是一篇故事，30课仍为会话。这样，28课又显示出从中级向高级过渡的性质。

（二）精选语料"一物多用"

《言语声片》非常重视声调练习，除了9课下和10课下，1—10课每课都有安排，遵循了"单音节—多音节—变调—重音—轻声"的习得顺序，由易到难，步步推进。

第1课安排单音节的同声韵四声练习（书熟属树，先闲险线），第2课就安排三音节的数量名词组四声练习，从同词组的数词四声练习（三本书/十本书/五本书/六本书）到与不同的指量词组合的名词四声练习（这本书/这个人/那管笔/那块墨），初步接触了变调；第3课练习三音节、四音节的数词变调（五十块钱/十五块钱，三十三/五十三/六十三），涉及不同语序造成的变调；第4课练习五音节、七音节数词变调（三百七十八/五百八十三/四百八十五，三千七百五十九/五千九百四十六/六千四百七十八），难度逐步提高；第5课下的四组16词安排更为巧妙，既考虑了双音节词的两个音节各为四声，又选择了口语中使用频率极高的动宾词组：

iv.	v.	vi.	vii.
交书	拿书	买书	卖书
交钱	拿钱	买钱	卖钱
交笔	拿笔	买笔	卖笔
交墨	拿墨	买墨	卖墨

对刚刚接触到汉语语音，还在适应感知阶段的学习者来说，词语的学习既是必须的，又有一定的负担。《言语声片》第1课上有3个词语，第1课下有4个词语，这是课文组句的必需内容。第2课上就没有安排专门的词语版块，将其合并到了声调练习中，既保证了该课知识点数量词的训练量，又减轻了初学者的学习负担。

（三）听说优先，读写结合

全书第一卷为英文卷，第二卷才是汉字文本，这和很多汉语教科书的编排方式不同。比如狄考文《官话类编》（1892）是上下栏中英对照，上栏汉字，下栏英语解释；英安仁《官话汇编》（1916）是左右页中英对照。这样的版式安排体现出口语和书面语齐头并进的教学思想。但《言语声片》和威妥玛《寻津录》（1859）一样，都是先用英语导入，再学习汉字。

第一卷学习指导明确提出，学习的顺序是"听力—单词—语法注释—

听练习—读课文—看译文":1. 从听力开始。7. 听熟了发音以后,转而学习词汇表,弄懂单词的含义,再仔细读语法结构的注释。8. 掌握语法注释之后,再听练习。重复,直到你不看文本也能听懂句子的意思。9. 再读整个文本的第一部分,重复几次。足够熟悉之后,看着译文重复。

第一卷每篇课文都是音标(Transcription)和英文(Translation)对照。

第二卷学习指导都是针对汉字书写的,前提条件是"第一课口语掌握好了再转向汉语文本"。即便是最后一课的生字也都全部注音并按四声排列,可见编者高度重视口语发音训练。

	第一卷		第二卷
	音标	英文	
生字	35. thaɪ	35. terrace, slab.	35.台 tái
词语	3. 'jaŋ'chiɛn	3. dollars	3.洋钱
声调操练	ii. ˌwuˈʃɪˌkhuai ˌchiɛn	ii. fifty dollars.	ii.五十块钱
练习	2. ˉtha ˌɪ ˌɔax ˌnɛɪ ˋnɑˌgɘˌnu ˌxɔax	2. He is a good man. That man is good.	2.他是好人。那个人好。

(四)口语特色,话题编排

作为汉语口语速成教材,且将标准定为"北京官话",选词用语非常考究。考虑到学习者可能接触到非官话方言,所以北京方言土语词并不算太多。但也有不少当时的口语词,到今天已不再使用。

课文	今天的说法	课文	今天的说法	课文	今天的说法
不甚么(第10课上)	不太	拢总(第15课上)	全部	末末了(第20课上)	最后
就手(第28课上)	顺手	定规(第13课下)	决定	多咱(第13课下)	什么时候
上半天(第13课下)	上午	下半天(第13课下)	下午	凑手(第16课下)	合适可用

全书安排的话题包括了日常生活的多个方面，比如打电话（第16课）、卖水果（第17课）、遇友（第18课）、火车站（第19课）、游戏（第20课）、看小说（第21课）、贺友人结婚（第22课）、邮政局（第23课）、银行（第24课）、洋服庄（第25课）、烟铺和卖糖的（第26课）、旅馆（第27课）、江上（第28课上）、商业谈话（第28课下），涉及买卖地产、运费税捐、游历、车票、篮球、骑马、讨论小说、婚俗、挂号信、汇票、布料等内容。

四、价　值

（一）保存了珍贵的语音资料

《言语声片》的配套唱片全部发音由老舍先生完成，现存于北京的老舍纪念馆。听老舍先生朗读课文，可以发现百年前的汉语共同语面貌和今天有不少差别。

词汇表中，"了"有liǎo、le、la三个读音，"啦"也有la和le两个读音，"了""啦"的用法都是过去助词（past auxiliary），如："我所看入了liao神啦la。""早叫二妹妹拿去了liao。"（第21课下）"呢"不读ne而读ni，如："为什么不早说呢ni？"（第15课下）"着"不读zhe而读zhuo："竟靠着zhuo他夫人办事。"（第18课上）"还"不读hái而读huán："先生还huán吃不吃？还huán吃。"（第8课下）"些"不读xiē而读xiě，以及不完全儿化（"反正不是远道儿"的"儿"是独立音节）等现象，和今天的北京话有所不同。结合同时代的其他语料，可以看到这些读法和记法如实地反映了当时的语言实际面貌（郭锐、陈颖、刘云，2017；陈颖，2016），是非常珍贵的文献材料。

（二）反映了当时的民风时事

民国时期的社会生活跟今天颇不相同，《言语声片》围绕生活话题安排练习和会话，反映了百年前的民风时事。比如谈论烟铺时提到了黄丝烟、水烟、叶子烟、吕宋烟和"三炮台"(第26课下)。"三炮台"是英美烟草公司(British American Tobacco Company)在中国推出的高级卷烟。"昔日抽烟用木杆白铜锅,抽关东大烟叶,今则换用纸烟,且非三炮台、政府牌不御矣。"(李家瑞,1937:2)"北京人民于纸烟一项颇讲究。上海之上流社会,以三炮台为应酬品者,北京则视若平常。"(胡朴安,1988:5)又如新式婚礼只有点心和茶水,没有晚饭,会话中特别提出这一点,说明这一风俗尚未普及,新娘从女子师范学校毕业这一身份也很引人关注(第22课下),可以看出当时新旧观念风俗更替的社会面貌。

其他诸如各种生活日常读来也颇有趣味。比如交通工具"东洋车"就是人力两轮车,因从日本传入故名(第22课上),当时的日常用品"卫生衣",就是带绒毛的秋冬内衣(第25课下),寄普通信件和挂号信件不在同一个地方(第23课下),内阁总辞职的事件(第30课)更是民国乱世的真实写照。

(三)科学的语言认识观及教学观念

《言语声片》的编写者都是具有专业素养的语言学家,包括在语音学领域颇有建树的人才、具有较强汉语能力的教师和高超汉语口语运用能力的母语者。因此,这部教材是在科学的语言观和教学观指导下编写而成,对今天的汉语教材编写也不无启发和借鉴意义。

"序言"中明确提出以北京官话为标准:"这时候的北京官话方言在官方圈子中的独家地位并不安稳,尽管它是满族政权一直以来的代表和民国前十二年的代表,但它的地位从来没有被其他方言明确侵占过。对那些前往中国的人来说,无论他们在中国将要面对和学习多少方言,这本教程都将成为他们最初的导论和预备训练。不管其他方言有多少跟北京官话不同的声音和声调,也不管他们的句法和措辞跟我们的思考方式有多么不同,但他们的句法和北京官话是一样的。一个人只要掌握了简单短句的语序,他就能容易地学会一种新方言。"这里提到编写教材时选用的语言标准问题,在社会动荡的大变革时代并非易事却又至关重要。威妥玛《寻津录》(1859)是第一部正式明确以北京官话为标准的汉语口语教材,其在当世的价值和对后世的意义都因此而不可小觑。《言语声片》进一步提出了汉语内部各方言语法的一致性,北京官话能够跨越方言障碍、具有"共同语"性质,因此学习北京官话对于将要游历中国的学习者有极大的便利。

《言语声片》高度重视声调,"序言"说:"这种陌生语言的语音飘忽不定,非常难学。汉语声调只有被强加到耳朵里以后才能模仿,只能靠不断地听,才能抓住它们之间的细微差别。"在"导论"中进而提到:"声调普遍不准确是汉语说得不好的一个标志。"抓对了学习难点,再用各种手段帮助学习者熟悉并逐步掌握声调,比如利用五线谱讲解和安排精心编排的各式练习,都可以看出《言语声片》对口语和发音的重视。

"导论"还提到:"音节zhe、zhen、zhang中的元音,威妥玛和其他标音法都用了一个符号ê,通常认为,当ê后面跟着n或ng时音值会有所改变,只要提醒学生这一点就够了。然而,从教学的目的出发,应该用音标符号表示出元音之间的细微区别,避免增加额外的规则,这是一条语音学原则。"同一个元音音位的不同音值变化,也是学习者的难点,虽然使用不同音标符号在某种程度上增加了学习者的负担,但在口语优先的编写原则之下,这是帮助学习者准确发音的有效手段。

由于时代背景和教学条件所限,《言语声片》也有不尽如人意的地方,比如生词量的分布不尽均衡,汉字教学显得不够系统,也较为简单。但其运用留声机进行汉语教学的先进方法,以及科学的语言观和教学理念,使之具有不可替代的历史价值和极高的参考借鉴意义。

参考文献

陈　颖（2016）朝鲜时代后期汉语教科书的"咧"，《四川师范大学学报》第5期。

郭　锐，陈　颖，刘　云（2017）从早期北京话材料看虚词"了"的读音变化，《中国语文》第3期。

韩　笑（2015）《伦敦大学英中合编〈言语声片〉研究》，硕士学位论文，上海师范大学。

胡朴安（1988）《中华全国风俗志》，河北人民出版社。

李家瑞（1937）《北平风俗类征》，上海艺文出版社。

刘小湘（1992）我国对外汉语教学的珍贵遗产——试论老舍在伦敦期间的汉语教学，《世界汉语教学》第3期。

宁恩承（1999）老舍在英国，《百年回首》，东北大学出版社。

仇志群（1993）老舍参加编写录制的国语唱片教材，《语文建设》第8期。

舒　济、郝长海、吴怀斌（2013）老舍年谱，《老舍全集19》，人民文学出版社。

舒　乙（1986）《老舍》，人民出版社。

舒　乙（1999）《老舍的第一部学术专著》，《北京晚报》，1月29日。

舒　乙（2011）老舍在英国，《崇文集三编——中央文史研究馆馆员文选》，中华书局。

斯蒂芬·R.安德森[美]（2015）《二十世纪音系学》，商务印书馆。

吴婷婷（2012）《老舍参编〈言语声片〉研究》，硕士学位论文，中山大学。

熊文华（2000）《英国的汉学研究》，《汉学研究 第5集》，中华书局。

远藤光晓[日]（1986/2001）老舍のleとliao，《中国音韵学论集》，白帝社。

张西平（2009）《世界汉语教育史》，商务印书馆 。

周　川（2012）《中国近现代高等教育人物辞典》，福建教育出版社。

Paul Carley（2013）Arthur Lloyd James and English pronunciation for foreign learners, Phonetics Teaching and Learning Conference, London.

School of Oriental and African Studies (SOAS) Archives, University of London. https://archiveshub.jisc.ac.uk

Linguaphone Oriental Language Courses.

General Editor: Sir E. DENISON ROSS, C.I.E., Ph.D., Director, School of Oriental Studies, University of London.

Phonetic Editor: A. LLOYD JAMES, M.A., Reader in Phonetics, School of Oriental Studies, University of London.

CHINESE

by

J. PERCY BRUCE, M.A., D.Lit., Professor of Chinese, School of Oriental Studies, University of London.

E. DORA EDWARDS, M.A., Lecturer in Chinese, School of Oriental Studies, University of London.

C. C. SHU, Lecturer in Chinese, School of Oriental Studies, University of London.

Spoken by
C. C. SHU, Lecturer in Chinese, School of Oriental Studies, University of London.

With Phonetic Transcription in the Alphabet of the International Phonetic Association.

VOL. I

First Edition.

THE LINGUAPHONE INSTITUTE,
24-27, HIGH HOLBORN, LONDON, W.C.1,
ENGLAND.

PREFACE.

The value of gramophone records, especially the Linguaphone courses, is now universally recognised in connection with the learning of familiar European languages such as French, German, Italian and Spanish; the value of a course in Chinese is for a variety of reasons even more greatly to be appreciated. In the first place, Chinese teachers outside London are difficult to come by, while the elusiveness of the sounds of this unfamiliar language renders it one of the most difficult to learn; for Chinese tones cannot be imitated until they have been impressed on the ear, and it is only by the constant hearing of them that their subtle differences can be grasped. Constant repetition is exactly what the Linguaphone is able to provide to an extent that would certainly wear out the patience of the ordinary teacher.

Apart from the tones the actual sounds of Chinese syllables are too strange to be fittingly recorded in Latin characters; the famous system of transliteration invented by Sir Thomas Wade cannot probably be improved on as far as Englishmen are concerned, but at the same time no Englishman could obtain any idea of many of the Chinese sounds were he to study Wade without a teacher. The Linguaphone course now offered to the public therefore fills a very real want, and there is nothing to prevent a man of ordinary intelligence obtaining a very approximate notion of how to pronounce Chinese if he gives himself the trouble of going through these lessons over and over again. He, at any rate, will avoid the pitfall of learning to pronounce wrongly, which is the common result of most self-study.

The Mandarin dialect of Pekin does not at the moment enjoy that exclusive position in official circles which it held all through the Manchu régime and the first twelve years of the Republic, but its place has not been definitely usurped by any other dialect, and for persons proceeding to China the present course constitutes a first class introduction and preliminary training whatever may be the dialect he finds he has to learn on arriving in China; however much the sounds and tones of such a dialect may differ from Pekin Mandarin, the syntax and the turn of phrase so unfamiliar to our way of thinking, is the same, and having mastered the order of words in simple phrases he will readily pick up a new dialect.

E. DENISON ROSS.

CONTENTS.

Introduction	5
Notes on Chinese Sounds	11
Directions to the Student	25
Transcription and Translation of the Chinese Linguaphone Records	27-159
Notes on Lessons	160-190

PLAN OF THE LESSONS.

Chinese Sounds.	Pt. I. Initials. Finals. The Four Tones	...	28
	Pt. II. Examples of the Mandarin Style	...	34
Lesson 1.	Pt. I. Affirmation, Negation and Interrogation	...	40
,, 1.	,, II. Personal Pronouns. Sign of the Plural	...	42
,, 2.	,, I. Numerals and Classifiers...		44
,, 2.	,, II. The Verb *to be*. Negatives. The Possessive ...		46
,, 3.	,, I. The Adjective as Predicate		48
,, 3.	,, II. The Interrogative Pronoun *what?* ɖɪ with Adjectives. Compound Numerals		50
,, 4.	,, I. The Interrogative *how many?* Compound Numerals		52
,, 4.	,, II. Interrogative Personal Pronouns. ɖɪ with Verbs. The ordinal ɖi. Compound Numerals...	...	54
,, 5.	,, I. Adverbs of place. Prepositions		56
,, 5.	,, II. Auxiliaries. Reduplication of Verbs and Adjectives		58
,, 6.	,, I. The Reflexive Pronoun. The Dative. Topic: The Lesson		60
,, 6.	,, II. Past and future Time. The Lesson	...	62
,, 7.	,, I. Honorific terms. A Visitor		64
,, 7.	,, II. The Imperative. Enclitics. The Household...		66
,, 8.	,, I. khʌ·i as Subjunctive and Imperative. More Prepositions. The Household		68
,, 8.	,, II. Continuation of Part I.		70
,, 9.	,, I. Probability. The Participle ɖʒɔ. The Household		72
,, 9.	,, II. The Interrogative *why?* Noun suffixes. Business Management		74
,, 10.	,, I. Similarity and Difference. Distance		76
,, 10.	,, II. The Suffix thou. The Imperative ba. Money. Buying and Selling		78

Lesson				Page
Lesson 11.	Pt. I.	The Comparative	... ...	80
,, 11.	,, II.	The Superlative	... ...	
,, 12.	,, I.	The passive. The Family	... ...	84
,, 12.	II.	The Prepositions *before*, and *after* or *behind*. The Family	... ...	86
,, 13.	,, I.	Time	... ...	88
,, 13.	,, II.	Time	... ...	90
,, 14.	,, I.	The Conditional Mood	... ...	92
,, 14.	,, II.	Alternation. Necessity. Emphatic Imperative. Accounts	... ...	94
,, 15.	,, I.	Distributive and Collective Adjectives. Connectives. The Weather	... ...	96
,, 15.	,, II.	The Subjunctive. Conjunctions. The Seasons		98
,, 16.	,, I.	Possibility and Impossibility	... ...	110
,, 16.	,, II.	At the Telephone	... ...	102
,, 17.	,, I.	Totality. Emphasis	... ...	104
,, 17.	,, II.	Selling Fruits	... ...	106
,, 18.	,, I.	The Optative. Willingness	... ...	108
,, 18.	,, II.	Meeting a Friend	... ...	110
,, 19.	,, I.	Totality. The Tailor (Chinese clothes)	... ...	112
,, 19.	,, II.	At the Station	... ...	114
,, 20.	,, I.	Sequence of Time. Frequency	... ...	116
,, 20.	,, II.	Sport	... ...	118
,, 21.	,, I.	Geographical Terms	... ...	120
,, 21.	,, II.	Reading a Novel	... ...	122
,, 22.	,, I.	Modes of Transport	... ...	124
,, 22.	,, II.	A Wedding	... ...	126
,, 23.	,, I.	Health	... ...	128
,, 23.	,, II.	At the Post Office	... ...	130
,, 24.	,, I.	Emphatic Prohibition	... ...	132
,, 24.	,, II.	The Bank	... ...	134
,, 25.	,, I.	Double Negatives	... ...	136
,, 25.	,, II.	The Tailor (Western Clothes)	... ...	138
,, 26.	,, I.	Trades	... ...	140
,, 26.	,, II.	Tobacconist and Confectioner	... ...	142
,, 27.	,, I.	Uncertainty. Travel	... ...	144
,, 27.	,, II.	The Hotel	... ...	146
,, 28.	,, I.	By the River	... ...	148
,, 28.	,, II.	A Conversation between two Merchants	...	150
,, 29.		An Arab and his Camel	... ...	152
,, 30.		News	... ...	155

INTRODUCTION.

1.—*Aim and Method.*

The aim of this course is to enable the student with a minimum of effort to converse in Chinese intelligently and with accuracy of pronunciation and idiom. It differs in some respects from its predecessors. On the one hand it is less ambitious than Wade's *Tzu Êrh Chi*, Mateer's *Mandarin Lessons* or Baller's *Primer*, and on the other hand it is not a mere book of sentences. Starting from Lesson 1, Part I, in the vocabulary of which there are only eight words and which treats of only one idiom, the course proceeds by easy steps on to the last Lesson, which is a conversation on Politics; and in all includes a vocabulary of nearly 1,000 words.

Lessons 1–15 are arranged from the point of view of grammatical construction. Part II of Lessons 16–27, and the whole of Lessons 28–30 are conversations prepared by Mr. Shu, Lecturer in Chinese at the School of Oriental Studies. They introduce the student to modern Chinese modes of thought as well as to their expression in modern Chinese speech.

The transcription is in the International Phonetic Alphabet as the most effective instrument of expressing sounds for the purpose of language study. It is what is known as a " narrow " transcription ; e.g. it takes into account minor differences in pronunciation which a " broad " transcription—reading them as modifications of one sound through the influence of other sounds in the immediate context—would represent by a single letter with a rule to cover the cases in which the sound is modified.

It may be freely admitted that for general literary purposes the broader transcription is to be preferred as less cumbersome, but for pedagogic purposes in the initial stages of language study the narrow transcription has decided advantages ; and from this point of view, inasmuch as the course is primarily intended for beginners, it is desirable that rules should be avoided as much as possible and the transcription itself suggest even minor differences in pronunciation. For example, for the vowel sound in the syllables dʒɤ, dʒən and dʒʌŋ Wade and others use one letter *ê*, and it is regarded as sufficient to remind the student that when the *ê* is followed by n or ng its quality is modified. From the pedagogic point of view, however, it is a sound principle to make the symbol express the vowel-sound closely in each case, and so avoid the necessity of recalling a rule.

The same motive has been the determining factor in the decision to use the symbols ḅ, ḍ, g̊, dz, dʒ, ǰ, to represent the devoiced unaspirated sounds corresponding to the aspirates ph, th, kh, tsh, tʃh, ch. For the beginner learning to speak Pekinese there are two pitfalls which he has to avoid. On the one hand he is in danger of voicing the six sounds referred to, and on the other of aspirating them. To a French student the latter would probably be no danger at all, but to the English student if the letters p, t, k, etc., are used the danger is very considerable, and the error is far more disastrous than it would be if he voiced them, because it leads to confusion with words which have the aspirated sounds, whereas the error of voicing sounds which should be devoiced, while it means bad pronunciation does not result in the speaker being misunderstood, for the simple reason that the devoiced sounds do not exist in Pekinese. The contrary would be the case in Ningpo or the Wu dialects because in those dialects there are the three classes, the voiced b, etc., the unaspirated p, etc., and the aspirated ph, etc. It may be added that in Pekinese the devoicing is not uniform. Prof. Guernier says that the sounds change to b, d, g, etc., before certain vowels, and it is doubtful whether they are devoiced in any but initial positions. It is a question, therefore, whether strict accuracy would not require that the letters should be changed in certain words in certain positions to correspond with the linguistic facts. Under all the circumstances it seems simpler and less confusing to the beginner to use the symbols ḅ, ḍ, g̊, etc., which it is interesting to note, so expert a phonetician, and one with such experience as a practical teacher of spoken Chinese as Mr. Chao Yüan-rên, also adopts in his Phonograph course.[1] The fact is that the sounds in question are neither b, d, g, etc., nor p, t, k, etc., as spoken in English, so that to the English student neither symbol suggests strictly accurate pronunciation, whereas the ḅ, ḍ, g̊, etc., while they suggest an approximation to the b, d, g, etc., at the same time suggest that they are different from them, which is just what the beginner needs to bear in mind.

2.—*Evolution of the Spoken Language.*

In Giles' dictionary there are 13,848 different Chinese words of which approximately 4,000 are used in common speech. In Pekinese colloquial there are not more than about 420 distinct syllable-sounds. From these figures the poverty of the language in respect of sounds, and the great possibilities of confusion will be apparent. Several devices have been adopted in the course of the centuries to avoid this confusion. These devices have been described in considerable detail by Professor Karlgren in his *Sound and Symbol in Chinese*, which the student is recommended to read.

---

[1] A Phonograph Course in the Chinese National Language.

One of the most obvious of the " devices " referred to is the use of tones, by which it is possible to multiply the 420 sound-syllables by the number of tones in which they are uttered. In Pekinese there are four such tones, so that it is possible that sound-syllables otherwise alike may have four different tones and each represent a different word. The tone, indeed, is an integral part of the word, and although in unstressed positions it is considerably modified and modified also by its relation to the tones of other words in the immediate context, yet to give a false tone in a stressed position will often lead to disastrous mistakes, as will readily be seen from the examples given in the Record " Chinese Sounds " and in Lesson 1. It should be added that even when there is no fear of misunderstanding the word the fact remains that a general inaccuracy in tones is the mark of a poor speaker.

Attention to tones, therefore, is of great importance, and for this reason tone practice is made a special feature of this course. Illustrations of the four tones and their modification by stress or position are given in the Record on Chinese Sounds ; and the very first lesson, with its four nouns, one in each of the four tones, is so constructed as itself to constitute a lesson in tones. The vocabularies are arranged in tabular form according to tones so as to impress the tone of each word on the visual memory. In the notes attention is called to variations in tone and explanations given ; and in the first 10 lessons exercises in Tone Practice are provided so as to furnish tone-drill in all finals in all degrees of stress.*

Finally, in the Text accompanying the Record on Chinese Sounds methods of recording tones are described and illustrated. There is thus provided sufficient ear-training, and practice in recording, to enable the student to become an efficient speaker in this respect.

A second device described by Karlgren in his little book as adopted to avoid the ambiguity which would otherwise result from the paucity of sounds, is the use of two-word combinations. The possibilities of ambiguity which exist when single words are used to express single ideas are very much reduced when compounds of two words are used. Four classes of such two-word combinations may be mentioned here : i. Synonym compounds in which the two words are synonymous in meaning ; as ˋjɛn ʹthaɪ (L. 3, Pt. I), *an ink-slab*, in which ˋjɛn and ʹthaɪ are two distinct words each of which means an ink-slab or slab. Thus, while ˋjɛn or ʹthaɪ by itself might be easily confused with other words of the same sound, the combination ˋjɛn ʹthaɪ is much less liable to misunderstanding.

---

* This last is the plan adopted by Chao Yüan-rên in his book. In this course, however, the exercises are spread over several lessons so as to make them less wearisome and more easily assimilated.

ii. A second class of words are formed by the combination of two ideas, similar to the logical combinations in the formation of characters (v. p. 9). Thus, ⁻ɕiɛn, *before*, and ⁻ʃʌŋ, *to be born*, are joined together in colloquial to form the word ⁻ɕiɛn·ʃʌŋ, *a teacher*.

iii. Compounds of the verb with its object; as, ˋniɛn⁻ʃu, *to read*. The word ˋniɛn is *to read*, and ⁻ʃu is *a book*. Whereas in English we should say simply *to read*, in colloquial Chinese the idea is expressed by saying *to read books*. Attention will be called in the Lessons to words of this type.

iv. Another class consists of combinations of opposites to form abstract nouns; e.g., ˋdɑ, *large*, and ˎɕiɑo, *small*. Other modes of combination will be noted as they occur in the Lessons.

It has been said that these two-word combinations have arisen from the necessity of differentiating two words of the same sound, but with different meanings. The same necessity applies to a phonetic transcription. What is necessary for the ear in hearing is necessary also for the eye in reading. In the case of the Chinese characters which are essentially pictographs there is no difficulty, because every word is written differently from every other. In the case of a phonetic transliteration, however, it is otherwise. It is as necessary that these two-word combinations should be joined up in writing as that they should be joined up in speaking. This plan, therefore, has been adopted in these Lessons.

3.—*Formation of Chinese Characters.*

In the preceding paragraph the student has been introduced to the methods adopted to express thought in speech, and to the different classes of word-compounds which have resulted therefrom. A somewhat analogous process has been at work in the development of the written language. It is hardly necessary to point out that Chinese written symbols are ideographic. In the earliest stage in their growth they were pictures of concrete objects; e.g.

with the branches above and roots below. From such a beginnng Chinese writing has developed by stages until there are now something like 40,000 symbols, more than 13,000 of which have such currency that it is found necessary to include them in Giles' Chinese-English Dictionary. Chinese scholars classify them in six classes—four of which are classified according to their formation, representing roughly successive stages in their development. First, the true pictures of concrete objects as stated above. Second, pictures, or combinations of pictures, indicative of things or processes in nature; e.g. 本 *trunk of a tree*, i.e. the part of the 木 *tree* above the 一 earth. Third, logical compounds, in which such pictures were combined together to represent abstract ideas; e.g. 好 *good*, composed of 女 *woman* and 子 *child*.

Notwithstanding the large number of characters it was possible to create by the methods of combination in Classes 2 and 3, they were not sufficient to meet the need of a prolific literature, and a further development resulted which allowed for indefinite expansion by the creation of a fourth class, viz., phonetic compounds, which were composed of two elements, the one a character the sound of which approximately represented the pronunciation of the new compound, and the other a primitive giving a clue to its meaning by indicating the class of ideas to which it belonged. Thus, 記 *to remember*, is composed of 己 pronounced ži, and 言 meaning *words;* 紀 *to record*, composed of 己 ži, and 糸 *silk*, the material used for writing; 忌 *jealous*, of ži, and 心 *the heart*.*

Classes 5 and 6 consisted of characters with extended and borrowed meanings respectively. They do not concern the structure of the characters and need not detain us. Classes 1 and 2, both pictographs, are often difficult to distinguish. In this book, in the Radical Table and Analysis of Characters given in the Appendices, they are combined in one class represented by the letter A. Classes 3 and 4 are represented by the letters B. and C. respectively.

In the Radical Table referred to in the preceding paragraph the formation of each Radical is shown with its ancient form, and with brief notes on its significance. The Phonetics, though

---

* For fuller information on this subject see Karlgren's little book, already mentioned, *Chinese Characters*, by L. Wieger, and *Analysis of Chinese Characters*, by Wilder and Ingram.

not of such vital importance as the Radicals are nevertheless important; and the student will find it helpful to note them as they occur. In the *Pocket Dictionary* by W. E. Soothill the 4,000 most common characters are classified under 888 such Phonetics. If the student refers to almost any one of these he will find it interesting to compare the characters of the group and to notice how they have approximately the same sound but different meanings according to their respective Radicals.

In the course of time the whole number of characters was classified under 214 primitives or *mother-characters*, as they are termed in Chinese, but by foreigners commonly called Radicals. Dictionaries are arranged on this basis so that any particular character must be looked for under its " Radical." A fact to be noted is that every character which is not itself a Radical may be analyzed into two or more of these 214 Radicals. The student, therefore, will appreciate their importance. If he can readily recognize them and write them, he will have mastered the problem of the written language.

NOTES ON CHINESE SOUNDS.

[Explanatory of the Preliminary Record, entitled " Chinese Sounds."]

The Chinese language has often been styled monosyllabic. It has been objected that the term is not strictly accurate, because there are such sounds as liaŋ and lyə which ought to be regarded as words of two syllables ; but the union of the two vowels in these words is so close that they may not unreasonably be looked upon as semi-diphthongs, and they are not many, so that with this qualification the language may still be regarded as monosyllabic. The syllables in Pekinese are with a few exceptions open. The exceptions are words ending in one of the two nasals n and ŋ, and the fricative ɹ. In Nankinese, and in non-Mandarin dialects, there are others which have the glottal stop, but they are in what is called the Entering Tone (see below) which does not exist in pure Pekinese.

From time immemorial Chinese linguistic scholars have analysed the syllable sounds of their language into initials and finals. As the syllables are open, with the exception of those mentioned in the preceding paragraph, the finals are all vowels, with the addition in certain cases of a nasal or fricative ending. Similarly the initials, with two or three exceptions, are all consonants. It is convenient, therefore, to follow this division. In the Record the initials and finals as they occur in Pekinese are produced, and corresponding lists given in the Transcription.

While, however, it is convenient to follow the Chinese analysis of sound-syllables into initials and finals it will be helpful to take careful note from the phonetic point of view of the consonants and vowels of which they are composed.

I. INITIALS.

Phoneticians classify consonants (1) as plosive, nasal, lateral, fricative and affricative, according to the manner of their production ; (2) as bi-labial, dental, retroflex, palatal and velar, according to the place of their articulation ; and (3) as voiced and devoiced, aspirated and unaspirated, according to the presence or absence of the vibration of the vocal chords, and the presence or absence of aspiration, respectively. Table I shows the Initials of Pekinese syllable-sounds arranged according to this classification. The initials on the Record are in the same order, so that the student will be able to follow the table with the ear.

(Note : The whole syllable-sound, the final as well as the initial, is given in the Record in order that the full value of the initial may be heard. The finals are in brackets. The words selected are all in the 4th Tone so as not to confuse the student by difference of sound due to tone.)

TABLE I.

*Initials classified according to the mode of their production.

		Voiced.	Voiceless.	Devoiced unaspirated.	Devoiced aspirated.	
1.	Plosive—Bi-Labial	...	...	ˋb̥(a)	...	1.
2.	,, Bi-Labial	...	...	...	ˋph(a)	2.
3.	Plosive—Dental	...	...	ˋd̥(a)	...	3.
4.	,, Dental	...	...	...	ˋth(a)	4.
5.	Plosive—Velar	...	...	ˋg̥(u)	...	5.
6.	,, Velar	...	...	...	ˋkh(u)	6.
7.	Nasal—Bi-Labial	ˋm(a)	...	...	...	7.
8.	,, Dental	ˋn(u)	...	...	...	8.
9.	Lateral—Dental	ˋl(a)	...	...	...	9.
10.	Fricative—Labio-Dental	...	ˋf(u)	...	...	10.
11.	,, Dental	...	ˋs(u)	...	...	11.
12.	,, Retroflex	ˋɹ(u)	...	...	...	12.
13.	,, Retroflex	...	ˋʃ(u)	...	...	13.
14.	,, Palatal	...	ˋɕ(i)	...	...	14.
15.	,, Velar	...	ˋx(u)	...	...	15.
16.	Affricative—Dental	...	...	ˋd̥z(aɪ)	...	16.
17.	,, Dental	...	...	...	ˋtsh(ai)	17.
18.	,, Retroflex	...	...	ˋd̥ʒ(u)	...	18.
19.	,, Retroflex	...	...	...	ˋtʃh(u)	19.
20.	,, Palatal	...	...	ˋɟ̊(i)	...	20.
21.	,, Palatal	...	...	...	ˋch(i)	21.
22.	Semi-Vowels—Bi-Labial	ˋw(u)	...	...	...	22.
23.	,, Palatal	ˋj(a)	...	...	...	23.

Attention to the pronunciation of the devoiced b̥, d̥, g̥, d̥z, d̥ʒ, ɟ̊, and to the aspirated p, t, k, ts, tʃ, c, is of great importance if the student wishes to speak with a pure enunciation. The difference between voiced and devoiced may be detected by the student if he pronounces the sound z with a sizzle and then passes into the s-sound. He will notice in the former case a vibration of the vocal chords which ceases when changed to the s-sound. The former is voiced, the latter voiceless.

---

* See note on page 27.

The Chinese consonants represented in Wade's system as p, t, k, ts, ch, and in the Standard Romanization system by b, d, g, dz, dj, except in medial positions, are different on the one hand from the English p, t, k, ts, ch, which are aspirated, and on the other hand, from the English b, d, g, dz, dʒ, ɟ, which are voiced ; they approximate rather to the French p, t, k, ts tʃ, and the Italian c. They may be represented either as unaspirated p, t, k, ts, tʃ, c, or as devoiced b̥, d̥, g̊, d̥z, d̥ʒ, ɟ̊.[1]

The aspirates ph, th, kh, tsh, tʃh, ch, are more strongly aspirated than the English letters p, t, k, ts, tʃ. It is as if the letter h were inserted after the consonant as in the following expressions :
    ph as in *u*p **h**ill.   tsh as in *i*ts **h**o*t*.
    th as in *a*t **h**ome.   tʃh as in *c*at*c*h **h**old.
    kh as in *d*ar**k** **h**ole.   ch as in *ea*ch **h**eel.

Notice that the palatal consonants ɟ and ch (N.B. ch is the aspirated form of the Italian c) are produced somewhat differently from the dʒ and tʃh, with which they are often confused. The latter occur only before back vowels and the former only before the front vowels i and y (Wade's ü). The influence of these vowels is to palatalize the consonants ; that is, the consonants are produced with the highest part of the tongue further back than in the case of the dʒ and tʃh, which are dentals. In wide areas outside Peking the ɟ and ch class of sounds splits into two classes—one g̊ and kh and the other d̥z and tsh ; that is, the one a class of velar sounds and the other dentals. In Pekin they have approximated to a middle position, viz. palatal. It will be convenient to many students to be able readily to distinguish between those which become g̊ and kh, and those which become d̥z and tsh. As a help in this direction the letters in the latter case are thickened in the vocabularies.

The ɹ calls for some comment The sound has been variously represented by j (French), which in the I.P.A. is ʒ, and by r. Mateer says truly that the Chinese sound is somewhat between the two, or perhaps it would be more accurate to say a combination of the two, and might be represented by jr (ʒɹ). Some Chinese speakers tend more in the direction of the ʒ, but much more widely, and particularly outside Peking itself, the sound approximates more closely to the r. It is, however, never rattled as by many English and Scotch people. It is produced with the tip of the tongue curled up, and is better represented by the retroflex ɹ as in the International Phonetic Alphabet.

---

[1] Cf. A Phonograph Course, etc., by Chao Yüan-rên, pp. 2-3.

The letters w and j are used to represent the semi-vowels when functioning as consonants. Some writers have adopted the letters u and i for this purpose. But there is a decided difference in the Chinese sounds when functioning as consonants compared with when they are functioning as vowels, and it is better to represent them differently.

The ʃ is a fricative, approximating to the English sh but produced with the tip of the tongue slightly curled up; i.e. in a retroflex position.

The initial ç (Wade's hs) is a peculiarly characteristic Chinese sound. It approximates to the German ich, but is produced a little more forward on the palate, and often ends in almost a pure s. Like the ɟ and ch it occurs only before the front vowels i and y (Wade's ü), and like them the class splits into two classes in wide areas outside Peking; viz. h, as in the English word *hew*, and s as in *seam*. In Pekinese they have approximated to a position between the two, the ç being produced with the highest part of the tongue farther back than in the case of the dental s, and farther forward than the h sound referred to. In words in which the initial changes to the s sound the ç is thickened, so that anyone changing to another variety of Mandarin will know which becomes h and which s.

The x is stronger and more guttural than the English h. It is similar to the German ch with the back pronunciation as in *machen*, or the Scotch ch in *loch*, but is produced farther back on the tongue.

The initials m, n, l, f, s, approximate closely to the English sounds represented by these letters.

2. FINALS.

Vowel sounds are classified (1) as front, back and middle, according to the position of the highest part of the tongue when the particular sound is produced; (2) as open, half open, half close and close, according to the space left open between the tongue and palate; (3) as unrounded and rounded, according to the lip position. Table II shows the finals of Pekinese syllable-sounds arranged according to this classification. The Table also shows the diphthongs, and combinations of vowels or diphthongs with i and u. The initials are in brackets. Tables III and IV are diagrams showing the position of the tongue in the formation of the vowels.

15
TABLE II.

Finals classified according to the mode of their production.

	Pure vowels and diphthongs.	With i, y, or u prefixed	With n, ŋ, or ɹ endings	With i, u or y prefixed and nasal ending.	
1. Front unrounded, close	ˋ(b̥)i	...	...	...	1.
2. Front rounded, close	ˋ(l)y	...	...	...	2.
3. Front rounded, close	...	...	ˋ(ɕ)yn	...	3.
4. Front unrounded, close	...	...	ˋ(ɕ)ɪn	...	4.
5. Front unrounded, close	...	...	ˋ(m)ɪŋ	...	5.
6. Front unrounded, half close	ˋ(f)eɪ	...	...	...	6.
7. Front unrounded, half close	...	ˋ(ʃ)ueɪ	...	...	7.
8. Front unrounded, half open	ˋ(j)ɛ	...	...	...	8.
9. Front unrounded, half open	...	ˋ(m)iɛ	...	...	9.
10. Front unrounded, half open	...	...	...	ˋ(m)iɛn	10.
11. Front unrounded, open	...	...	ˋ(f)an	...	11.
12 Front unrounded, open	...	...	...	ˋ(x)uan	12
13. Front unrounded, open	...	...	...	ˋ(ɟ̊)yan	13.
14. Front unrounded, open	ˋ(m)aɪ	...	...	...	14.
15. Front unrounded, open	...	ˋ(kh)uaɪ	...	...	15
16. Back unrounded, open	ˋ(d̥ʒ)ɑ	...	...	...	16.
17. Back unrounded, open	...	...	ˋ(f)ɑŋ	...	17.
18 Back unrounded, open	...	ˋ(g̊)uɑ	...	...	18.
19. Back unrounded, open	...	...	...	ˋ(kh)uɑŋ	19.
20. Back unrounded, open	ˋ(ɕ)iɑ	...	...	...	20.
21 Back unrounded, open	...	...	...	ˋ(ɕ)iɑŋ	21.
22. Back unrounded, half open	ˋ(n)ao	...	...	...	22.
23. Back unrounded, half open	...	ˋ(m)iao	...	...	23.
24. Back unrounded, half open	ˋ(kh)ʌ	...	...	...	24.
25. Back unrounded, half open	...	...	ˋ(b̥)ʌŋ	...	25.
26. Back unrounded, half open	...	...	ˋʌɹ	...	26.
27. Back rounded, half open	ˋ(m)ɔ	...	...	...	27.
28. Back rounded, half open	...	ˋ(x)uɔ	...	...	28.
29 Back rounded, half close	ˋ(ʃ)ou	...	...	...	29.
30. Back rounded, half close	ˋ(d̥ʒ)ɤ	...	...	...	30.
31. Back rounded, close	ˋ(d̥)u	...	...	...	31.
32. Back rounded, close	...	...	ˋ(ʃ)un	...	32.
33. Back rounded, close	...	...	ˋ(d̥)uŋ	...	33.
34. Back rounded, close	...	ˋ(l)iu	...	...	34.
35. Back rounded, close	...	...	...	ˋ(ɕ)iuŋ	35.
36. Back unrounded, close	ˋ(s)ɯ	...	...	...	36.
37. Middle unrounded, half open	...	...	ˋ(m)ən	...	37.
38. Middle unrounded, half open	...	ˋ(j)yə	...	...	38.
39. Apical unrounded, half open	ˋ(d̥ʒ)ɹ	...	...	...	39.
[Apical unrounded, half open]	[ˋɹ][1]	...	...	...	

[1] This final, though the same as 39, is given on the Record because of its peculiarity as following the initial ɹ. See remarks p. 17.

TABLES III AND IV.

Diagrams illustrating the Vowel and Diphthong Sounds of Mandarin Chinese as pronounced on the Records.

The black spots indicate the positions of the eight Cardinal Vowels as recognised by the International Phonetic Association. The circles and dotted lines represent Chinese vowel sounds in so far as they differ from the Cardinal Vowels. They indicate the average pronunciation of the vowel phonemes, most of which vary in pronunciation according to the sounds in their vicinity. The Finals n and ŋ, for example, often influence the preceding vowels in a marked degree.

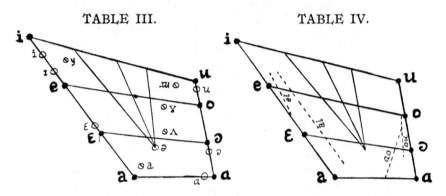

TABLE III.   TABLE IV.

Many of the vowel sounds approximate to English sounds. For example :—

The front vowels, i, ɪ, ɛ, as in English *pique*, *pin*, *yet*, respectively.

The back vowels, ɑ, u, as in *father* and *rule* respectively, but before ŋ, as in laŋ, the ɑ narrows, and so approximates towards the sound of o in the English word *long* (see below). The a is like the North English or Scotch pronunciation of a in *man*. The diphthongs eɪ, aɪ, and ou are pronounced very nearly as the italicized letters in wh*ey*, *ai*sle, and s*ou*l.

The diphthong ɑo approximates to ou in *loud*, but is produced farther back, thus giving more prominence to the sound of the ɑ.

Note that the i in miɛ, miɛn, ɕia, ɕiaŋ, miɑo, and like syllables, is unaccented, the stress falling on the vowel or diphthong following ; but it is nevertheless distinct, whereas in the syllables ʃueɪ, xuan, khuaŋ, khuaɪ, ʐuɔ, xuɔ, the u is merged more closely into the following vowel, though in some syllables, such as d̥ueɪ, it is more prominent.

The mixed vowel ə in mən is like the English e in *open*. It occurs also as an open syllable in mə, a contracted form of mɔ when in unstressed positions.

The ɹ which is used to represent the retroflex initial, is also used to represent the apical vowel in the finals dʒɹ, tʃhɹ, ʃɹ. The nearest approach to these sounds in English is in the first syllable of the words *giraffe, chirrup,* and *cheroot,* respectively. The apical ɹ occurs also in a word ɹ, *sun,* which stands by itself, there being no other word of the same sound in the language. If the syllable-sound were fully represented it would be ɹɹ representing the initial ɹ and the final ɹ. It is here contracted to the single ɹ.

The non-English vowel-sounds call for special attention from the English student. The simplest of them is the front vowel y which approximates to the French u, or the German ü. It is produced with rounded lips. Let the student keep his lips in the position in which he would pronounce the vowel sound u, (the English oo) and, instead of pronouncing u try to pronounce i (the English ee), and he will find that he has produced the sound symbolized by y. This vowel like i and u, is joined with other vowels in such close union as to form what may be termed semi-diphthongs ; as in jyə and jyan.

The sound represented by ɯ is the converse of y ; it is a back vowel with unrounded lips. It is produced by spreading the lips as if to pronounce i (ee), and, while the lips are in this position, trying to pronounce the u (oo).

The ʌ and ɤ are, like the above, back vowels with unrounded lips. They are produced by spreading the lips and, while they are in that position, trying to produce the sounds ɔ and ou respectively. Thus, ʌ, ɤ, and ɯ, are the unrounded forms of ɔ, ou, and u.

The student will notice the effect of the nasals on the vowel sounds preceding them. The case of ɑ being modified so that it approximates to o in *long* has been cited. There are other instances. The n following the y and u produce the same effect as if a short ɪ sound were inserted after the y, and a short ə after the u ; thus : cyɪn, ʃuən. In the finals ɪn, ɪŋ, an, ʌŋ, uŋ, there is no modification of the vowel by the nasal ending.

B

3. THE FOUR TONES.

A.—Single Sound-syllables in the Four Tones.

The examples given in the Record show how sounds otherwise alike have four different tones, and represent as many different words, differences often being of a somewhat humorous nature; e.g. ⁻ma is *a frog*, while ˌma is *a horse*.

In Lesson **1** the Tone Practice exercise contains other instances of this characteristic of the Chinese Language.

The Four Tones are called by Chinese:—
1. The Upper Level Tone.
2. The Lower Level Tone.
3. The Rising Tone.
4. The Falling Tone.

By foreigners, and by many modern Chinese, they are called respectively the First, Second, Third and Fourth Tones.

Originally there were eight tones, as is evidenced by other dialects, such as Cantonese. They were:—
1. The Upper Level Tone.
2. The Lower Level Tone.
3. The Upper Rising Tone.
4. The Lower Rising Tone.
5. The Upper Falling Tone.
6. The Lower Falling Tone.
7. The Upper Entering Tone.
8. The Lower Entering Tone.

In Pekinese, however, there has been a process of assimilation in the tones as well as in the consonant and vowel sounds. It will be noticed that 7 and 8 have disappeared altogether, and that the distinction between Upper and Lower is lost in the case of the Rising and Falling Tones. In Pekinese they are prevailingly Lower in the former and Upper in the latter. In other forms of Mandarin the reverse is the case. For example, in the Shantung tones, which are substantially the same as the Tientsin tones, the 3rd tone starts where the Pekinese 3rd stops, and goes upward in the same direction. It is possibly the old Upper Rising Tone.

Similarly the Tientsin 4th starts downward in the same direction as the Peking 4th but begins where the latter leaves off. The student will notice in this connection the low pitch of the Tientsin 1st as compared with the Pekinese. The 2nd Tone in both cases is interesting. It is called the Lower Level, but it is not level at all; it is rising in the one case and falling in the other. In all probability the original level tone, being short in its duration, and therefore staccato, could not remain level, and in the one case took an upward, and in the other a downward turn.

TABLE V.

Peking and Shantung Tones.

Peking Tones.	1st Tone.	2nd Tone.	3rd Tone.	4th Tone.
	▬	／	﹄	＼

Shantung Tones	1st Tone.	2nd Tone.	3rd Tone.	4th Tone.
	▬	＼	／	＼

TABLE VI.

Musical representation of Peking tones.

The following is a musical representation (prepared by Mr. A. Lloyd James), of the four Peking Tones as produced on the " Chinese Sounds " Record at the rate of 84 revolutions per minute. It must be remembered that there is considerable variety—within essential unity—in the pronunciation of a given Tone by different speakers, and even by the same speaker at different times and in different connections. The pronunciation as here recorded, however, may be taken as typical.

B.—Tones in relation to Stress.

It will be noticed by carefully listening to the Tones as produced from the Record that they differ in three particulars, viz. direction, pitch and duration. They vary, however, considerably as affected by stress and the position of the sounds concerned.

There is an intimate relation between Tone and Stress, so intimate that sometimes what is taken to be stress is really high or low pitch. In the main there are three varieties of Tones as thus affected :—

(i.) Tones in which the direction, pitch and duration of the **original, or etymological,** tone are retained.

(ii.) Tones in which the word practically becomes toneless; that is, the duration is disregarded, the pitch modified and the direction changed. In some cases the direction changes from the monotone of the 1st to the falling direction of the 4th. In other cases it changes from that of a rising tone like the 2nd and 3rd, or falling tone like the 4th, to a level tone like the first. In other cases again, such as in the particles and classifiers, it has no regular direction at all.

(iii.) Tones in which the direction of the etymological tone is retained, but the pitch is modified and duration is disregarded.

Class 1 are found in fully stressed words unless modified by position. Class 2 are found in words like the possessive particle, the particles generally, most of the classifiers, and in monotonic two-word combinations. Class 3 are found in words in which the stress is secondary but not altogether absent, such as two-syllable combinations, in some of which the first word is stressed and the second only partially so, and in others *vice versâ*. Examples of Classes 1 and 2 are given in the record and the tone characteristics are indicated in the Transcription. Other examples of these modifications, and of Class 3 will be found in the two passages in Part II of this Lesson on Chinese Sounds, as well as in the Lessons in the main body of the work. For example in Passage (1) the phrases ˌɕy˞ dɔ and ˈdʒɪˋdɑo are examples of Class 2.

C.—*Tones Modified by Position.*

The tone of a word is also modified through the influence of the tone of an adjacent word, especially of one that follows the word concerned.

(i.) The most outstanding instance of such modification through the influence of a following tone is that of the 3rd Tone, which varies in three or more different ways. In the examples given in the record, it will be noted that :—

(1) When followed by another 3rd tone it is raised to the middle position, as shown in the first and second examples. (Note: In the 2nd example the ˌɕy is unaccented and therefore the series counts as two.) (2) When there are three 3rd tones in succession, the last of which is stressed, they are in three positions in descending scale as shown in the third example. If the first is stressed, it may be in the highest position or it may be in the middle position, and the second and third in the highest and lowest positions respectively, as in L. 1, S. 12. (3) When there are four consecutive 3rd

tones, the first of the four is in the middle and the other alternate between the middle and low positions as in L. 1, S. 5, 28. The 5th third tone in each of the sentences referred to begins a new clause, and is in the normal position.

(ii.) The case of the negative ˋb̬u is peculiar. Its etymological tone is the 4th, and before the 1st, 2nd and 3rd tones it is retained, but before another 4th tone it changes to the 2nd tone. This is specially noticeable in the common phrase ʹb̬u ˋʃʌ, *it is not*.

4. TONE MARKING AND TONE GRAPHS.

It is desirable that the student should not only train the ear to recognise tones correctly and quickly, but also practice recording them. This may be done in various ways.

(1) In the Transcription of the first of the two passages in the "Chinese Sounds" Record, Section 3 [The Four Tones], see p. 34, shows the most exact and complete method of recording, which is the method adopted in Lessons 1–4. Each mark precedes the syllable, and shows the direction, pitch and stress of the tone. The direction is shown by the mark itself. The pitch is shown by the position of the mark in one of the three positions, upper, middle and lower. In fully stressed syllables, where the full etymological tone occurs, a thick mark is used; in syllables with a weak stress, in which the tone though weak still retains the direction of the etymological tone, a thin mark is used; in unstressed syllables in which the tone has lost its original direction, or in which its original direction is negligible, a thick dot is used.

(2) The above method may be varied by substituting tone-graphs, in which the tone marks are written as above, but in a kind of musical stave, instead of before each word. This method is useful when the subject matter is already transcribed; or when it is desired to record the tones only, without any transcription In the former case the graph is written above the transcription. An example of this method is given in Lesson 3, Note 20. page 160.

(3) After some practice the student will find himself instinctively giving the tones as correctly as need be in unstressed positions, and that he needs only to mark the tone of the stressed syllables. It is in fact desirable that after a certain amount of ear training the student should disregard the individual tone of all but stressed syllables, and concentrate his attention on rhythm and the intonation of the sentence as a whole. This is the method adopted in the second of the two passages in the "Chinese Sounds" Record (p.36.) and in Lesson 5 and after. It is desirable, however, that he should notice and mark for himself the pitch of the tones of the stressed syllables.

Note that the tone-marking in the transcription both of the "Chinese Sounds" Record and of the Lessons, represents the tones as pronounced by the speaker in these records. Another speaker, however, might pronounce them with more or less variation. The same speaker, even, might vary them somewhat on another occasion though recording precisely the same passages. This fact must be borne in mind by the student, namely, that the essential constants, if they may be so termed, are combined with considerable variation. The intonation, therefore, as here recorded should be regarded not necessarily as the only accurate intonation in every shade of variation, but as an intonation which is itself accurate, and which not only can be safely followed, but should be slavishly imitated by the student if he in his turn is to obtain accuracy and fluency in the use of tones.

Students who, after learning Pekinese, go to some other part of the country, will find the facility thus acquired especially useful, because, though the tones vary in different localities they vary for the most part consistently ; that is, the intonation of all words in the First Tone is the same, and similarly with the other three tones. Even when the number of tones is increased the student will find some sort of rule by which they vary ; so that with a trained ear, and facility in recording, he will find that he can adapt himself to the new conditions quite easily.

5. WADE'S ROMANIZATION AND THE NATIONAL PHONETIC SCRIPT.

Most of the Chinese-English Dictionaries use Wade's Romanization to represent the pronunciation of the Chinese Characters. It is desirable therefore that the student should familiarize himself with this system, and with the help of the following comparative table he will quickly acquire facility in its use. It will be an advantage to some also to be acquainted with the Chinese National Phonetic Script, adopted a few years ago by the Chinese Government in order to promote uniformity in the pronunciation of Mandarin. This will be found in a third column, the initial or final being given by itself, and by its side, the combination of both as in the other two columns. Both tables follow the order in the Record : *Chinese Sounds, Part I.*

Note.—The Tones are indicated in Wade's system by figures after the words, and in the National Phonetic Script by a dot or comma at one of the corners of the symbol ; thus :—

23

	1st Tone.	2nd Tone.	3rd Tone.	4th Tone.
I.P.A.	⁻b̥a	´b̥a	ˌb̥a	ˋb̥a
Wade	pa¹	pa²	pa³	pa⁴
N.P.S.	.ㄅ丫	,ㄅ丫	ˇㄅ丫	ㄅ丫·

TABLE VII.

1. *Initials in Wade and the National Phonetic Script.*

I.P.A.	Wade.	N.P.S.		I.P.A.	Wade.	N.P.S.	
1. ˋb̥a	pa⁴	ㄅ	ㄅ丫·	13. ˋʃu	shu⁴	ㄕ	ㄕㄨ·
2. ˋpha	p'a⁴	ㄆ	ㄆ丫·	14. ˋɕi	hsi⁴	ㄒ	ㄒㄧ·
3. ˋd̥a	ta⁴	ㄉ	ㄉ丫·	15. ˋxu	hu⁴	ㄏ	ㄏㄨ·
4. ˋtha	t'a⁴	ㄊ	ㄊ丫·	16. ˋd̥zaɪ	tsai⁴	ㄗ	ㄗㄞ·
5. ˋg̊u	ku⁴	ㄍ	ㄍㄨ·	17. ˋtshaɪ	ts'ai⁴	ㄘ	ㄘㄞ·
6. ˋkhu	k'u⁴	ㄎ	ㄎㄨ·	18. ˋd̥ʒu	tsu⁴	ㄓ	ㄓㄨ·
7. ˋma	ma⁴	ㄇ	ㄇ丫·	19. ˋtʃhu	ts'u⁴	ㄔ	ㄔㄨ·
8. ˋna	na⁴	ㄋ	ㄋ丫·	20. ˋɟ̊i	chi⁴	ㄐ	ㄐㄧ·
9. ˋla	la⁴	ㄌ	ㄌ丫·	21. ˋchi	ch'i⁴	ㄑ	ㄑㄧ·
10. ˋfu	fu⁴	ㄈ	ㄈㄨ·	22. ˋwu	wu⁴	ㄨ	ㄨ·
11. ˋsu	su⁴	ㄙ	ㄙㄨ·	23. ˋja	ya⁴	ㄧ	ㄧ丫·
12. ˋʒu	ju⁴	ㄖ	ㄖㄨ·				

TABLE VIII.

2. *Finals in Wade and the National Phonetic Script.*

I.P.A.	Wade.	N.P.S.		I.P.A.	Wade.	N.P.S.	
1. ˋbi	pi⁴	一	ㄅㄧ˙	20. ˋɕiɑ	hsia⁴	ㄒㄚ	ㄒㄧㄚ˙
[ˋʃui]	[shui⁴]			21. ˋɕiaŋ	hsiang⁴	ㄒㄤ	ㄒㄧㄤ˙
2. ˋly	lü⁴	ㄩ	ㄌㄩ˙	22. ˋnɑo	nao⁴	ㄠ	ㄋㄠ˙
3. ˋɕyn	hsün⁴	ㄩㄣ	ㄒㄩㄣ˙	23. ˋmiɑo	miao⁴	ㄧㄠ	ㄇㄧㄠ˙
4. ˋɕɪn	hsin⁴	ㄧㄣ	ㄒㄧㄣ˙	24. ˋkhʌ	k'ê⁴	ㄜ	ㄎㄜ˙
5. ˋmɪŋ	ming⁴	ㄧㄥ	ㄇㄧㄥ˙	25. ˋbʌŋ	pêng⁴	ㄥ	ㄅㄥ˙
6. ˋfeɪ	fei⁴	ㄟ	ㄈㄟ˙	26. ˋʌɹ	êrh⁴	ㄦ	ㄦ˙
7. ˋʃueɪ	suei⁴	ㄨㄟ	ㄙㄨㄟ˙	27. ˋmɔ	mo⁴	ㄛ	ㄇㄛ˙
8. ˋjɛ	yeh⁴	ㄝ	ㄧㄝ˙	28. ˋxuɔ	huo⁴	ㄨㄛ	ㄏㄨㄛ˙
[ˋjɛn]	yen⁴	ㄧㄢ	ㄧㄢ˙	29. ˋʃou	shou⁴	ㄡ	ㄕㄡ˙
9. ˋmiɛ	mieh⁴	ㄧㄝ	ㄇㄧㄝ˙	30. ˋdʒɤ	chê⁴	ㄜ	ㄓㄜ˙
10. ˋmiɛn	mien⁴	ㄧㄢ	ㄇㄧㄢ˙	31. ˋdu	tu⁴	ㄨ	ㄉㄨ˙
11. ˋfan	fan⁴	ㄢ	ㄈㄢ˙	32. ˋʃun	shun⁴	ㄨㄣ	ㄕㄨㄣ˙
12. ˋxuan	huan⁴	ㄨㄢ	ㄏㄨㄢ˙	33. ˋduŋ	tung⁴	ㄨㄥ	ㄉㄨㄥ˙
13. ˋɟyan	chüan⁴	ㄩㄢ	ㄐㄩㄢ˙	34. ˋliu	liu⁴	ㄧㄡ	ㄌㄧㄡ˙
14. ˋmaɪ	mai⁴	ㄞ	ㄇㄞ˙	35. ˉciuŋ	hsiung¹	ㄩㄥ	ㄒㄧㄩㄥ˙
15. ˋkhuaɪ	k'uai⁴	ㄨㄞ	ㄎㄨㄞ˙	36. ˋsɯ	ssŭ⁴	ㄙ*	ㄙ˙
16. ˋdʒɑ	cha⁴	ㄚ	ㄓㄚ˙	[ˋɡə]	kê⁴	ㄜ	ㄍㄜ˙
17. ˋfaŋ	fang⁴	ㄤ	ㄈㄤ˙	37. ˋmən	mên⁴	ㄣ	ㄇㄣ˙
18. ˋɡuɑ	kua⁴	ㄨㄚ	ㄍㄨㄚ˙	38. ˋjyə	yüeh⁴	ㄩㄝ	ㄩㄝ˙
19. ˋkhuaŋ	k'uang⁴	ㄨㄤ	ㄎㄨㄤ˙	39. ˋdʒɪ	chih⁴	ㄓ*	ㄓ˙
				ˋɹ	jih⁴	ㄖ	ㄖ˙

* Not written after the initial as it is simply vocalization.

Directions to the Student.

1. Begin by listening, with the Transcription before you, to the Vocabulary as produced by the Record of Lesson 1, Part I. Repeat this several times. Notice the initials and finals enumerated in the Notes (p. 160). Read carefully the description of them in the Notes on the " Chinese Sounds " Record, Part I, (p. 11), and compare it with the sounds themselves as produced by that Record as well as the Record of this Lesson. At this stage, while referring to the Translation for the meanings of words so as to follow the Record intelligently, the student is advised to concentrate on listening to the pronunciation.

2 Note that in Part I there are four nouns, one in each tone. The selection is made in order to provide in these early lessons as much tone practice as possible.

3. Repeat the Tone Practice several times, until the " chime " becomes fixed in the memory. N.B.—The meanings of the words in this part of the lesson are not to be learned; they are simply to show the importance of correctness of tones in ordinary speech. The words which occur in the Vocabulary are in black type.

4. Turn next to the Exercise, and listen to the first three sentences several times, using them as tone practice. Pay special attention to stress. Remember that rhythm is more important than tones, for the simple reason that it includes both tones and stress.

5. Repeat the rest of the Exercise several times and note carefully the modifications of tones due to position or weakness of stress (see pp. 19, 20). These modifications are indicated by the tone-markings in the Transcription.

6. Notice particularly the sequence of pitches in a series of 3rd Tones. In S. 1, in the expression ⌐ju⌐bi, the first of the two 3rd Tones is raised to the middle position. In S. 12 there are two series of three 3rd Tones each, in the first of which the order of the tones is middle, high, low, whereas in the second they are in descending sequence. The latter is more normal, the former being due to the influence of the question. In S. 5 there is a series of four 3rd Tones in middle and low positions alternately, which is the normal type of sequence. (See pp. 20, 21).

7. When the ear has become thoroughly familiar with the pronunciation and rhythm turn to the Vocabulary again and note the meaning of each word. Then carefully read the Notes on Grammatical Construction.

N.B.—The notes are not given as rules to be learned, but simply by way of explanation. Chinese is not to be learned by rules but by repetition of correct forms of speech.

8. When the Notes on Grammatical Construction have been grasped listen again to the Exercise with the Translation before you. Repeat this until you can follow the meaning of the sentences as you listen to the Record without the aid of the Translation.

9. Next read the whole of Part I from the Transcription. Repeat this several times. When sufficiently familiar with it, repeat it with the Translation before you.

10. Follow the order here suggested throughout the Lessons. Remember that in learning to speak Chinese the secret of success lies in memoriter work. Every sentence should be learned so that it rolls off the tongue by itself when once started. *Automaticity* should be the student's watchword.

11. Note also that in Chinese there is no such thing as Inflexion or Conjugation. A particular word may be a Verb, Noun or Adjective; it may be Singular or Plural, and of any Gender, though a few modern innovations are now being introduced which will be referred to later. In so far as is necessary the differences indicated by such functions as Inflexion and Conjugation are shown by the use of a few Auxiliary words, or, more generally, by the order of the words in the sentence. Attention to this word-order is of the first importance.

Transcription and Translation

of the

Chinese Linguaphone Records

The following Transcription in the International Phonetic Alphabet was considered and adopted by a committee composed of:—

The General Editor, Sir E. Denison Ross.

Professor Daniel Jones, Professor of Phonetics at University College, University of London.

The Phonetic Editor, Mr. A. Lloyd James.

Dr. C. Otto Blagden, Reader in Malay at the School of Oriental Studies, University of London.

And the Authors.

Transcription.   Chinese Sounds.   Part I.

⁻fɑ⁻jɪn ˋliɛn ʹɕi. ˋʃaŋ.

1. ˳ʃou ⁻jɪn [Initials].

1. ˋb̥(ɑ)	9. ˋl(ɑ)	16. ˋd̥z(aɪ)
2. ˋph(ɑ)	10. ˋf(u)	17. ˋtsh(aɪ)
3. ˋd̥(ɑ)	11. ˋs(u)	18. ˋd̥ʒ(u)
4. ˋth(ɑ)	12. ˋɹ(u)	19. ˋtʃh(u)
5. ˋg̥(u)	13. ˋʃ(u)	20. ˋɟ̥(i)
6. ˋkh(u)	14. ˋɕ(i)	21. ˋch(i)
7. ˋm(ɑ)	15. ˋx(u)	22. ˋw(u)
8. ˋn(u)		23. ˋj(ɑ)

2. ˳wɛɪ ⁻jɪn [Finals].

1. ˋ(b̥)i	11. ˋ(f)an	22. ˋ(n)ao	31. ˋ(d̥)u
2. ˋ(l)y	12. ˋ(x)uan	23. ˋ(m)iao	32. ˋ(ʃ)un
3. ˋ(ɕ)yn	13. ˋ(ɟ̥)yan	24. ˋ(kh)ʌ	33. ˋ(d̥)uŋ
4. ˋ(ɕ)in	14. ˋ(m)ai	25. ˋ(b̥)ʌŋ	34. ˋ(l)iu
5. ˋ(m)iŋ	15. ˋ(kh)uai	26. ˋʌɹ	35. ⁻(ɕ)iuŋ
6. ˋ(f)ei	16. ˋ(d̥ʒ)a	27. ˋ(m)ɔ	36. ˋ(s)ɯ
7. ˋ(ʃ)uei	17. ˋ(f)aŋ	28. ˋ(x)uɔ	37. ˋ(m)ən
8. ˋ(j)ɛ	18. ˋ(g̥)ua	29. ˋ(ʃ)ou	38. ˋ(j)yə
9. ˋ(m)iɛ	19. ˋ(kh)uaŋ	30. ˋ(d̥ʒ)ɤ	39. ˋ(d̥ʒ)r
10. ˋ(m)iɛn	20. ˋ(ɕ)ia		ˋɹ
	21. ˋ(ɕ)iaŋ		

Translation. Chinese Sounds. Part I.

1. INITIALS.

1. Imperative particle
2. to fear
3. great
4. couch
5. firm
6. treasury
7. revile
8. anger
9. winter sacrifice
10. father
11. tell
12. enter
13. forgive
14. theatricals
15. door
16. at
17. vegetables
18. dwell
19. a place
20. remember
21. air
22. thing
23. surprise

2. FINALS.

1. must
2. laws
3. teach
4. faith
5. command
6. spend
7. customs duty
8. estate
9. destroy
10. face
11. rice
12. to exchange
13. scroll
14. sell
15. quick
16. artful
17. put down
18. suspend
19. a desert
20. down
21. funds
22. bustle
23. mysterious
24. lesson
25. burst
26. two
27. end
28. merchandise
29. animal
30. this
31. measure
32. favourable
33. freeze
34. six
35. elder brother
36. four
37. depressed
38. moon
39. purpose, sun

Transcription. Chinese Sounds. Part I (*cont.*).

3. ʽsɯ ⁻ʃʌŋ [The Four Tones].

[A. Single Sound-Syllables in the Four Tones.]

(i.)	⁻ɖi	ʹɖi	ˌɖi	ʽɖi
(ii.)	⁻thi	ʹthi	ˌthi	ʽthi
(iii.)	⁻j̊y	ʹj̊y	ˌj̊y	ʽj̊y
(iv.)	⁻mɑ	ʹmɑ	ˌmɑ	ʽmɑ
(v.)	⁻ɹɑŋ	ʹɹɑŋ	ˌɹɑŋ	ʽɹɑŋ
(vi.)	⁻g̊ʌ	ʹg̊ʌ	ˌg̊ʌ	ʽg̊ʌ
(vii.)	⁻d̥ʒɤ	ʹd̥ʒɤ	ˌd̥ʒɤ	ʽd̥ʒɤ
(viii.)	⁻tshɯ	ʹtshɯ	ˌtshɯ	ʽtshɯ
(ix.)	⁻fən	ʹfən	ˌfən	ʽfən
(x.)	⁻tʃhɹ	ʹtʃhɹ	ˌtʃhɹ	ʽtʃhɹ

Translation. Chinese Sounds. Part I (*cont.*).

[A. Single Sound Syllables in the Four Tones].

(i) low, oppose, under, the earth.

(ii) ladder, mention, body, substitute.

(iii) dwell, office, raise, sentence.

(iv) nurse, hemp, horse, curse.

(v) wrangle, kernel, plunder, yielding.

(vi) elder brother, pattern, a surname, each.

(vii) to cover, a despatch, aux. particle, wise.

(viii) blemish, kind, this, second.

(ix) command, burn, powder, anger.

(x) eat, grasp, foot-measure, flesh-colour.

Transcription. Chinese Sounds. Part I (*cont.*).

[B. Tones in Relation to Stress.]

(i.) ⁻fʌŋ ⁻g̊uaŋ ; ⁻ʃan ′xʌ ; ⁻ɕiaŋ ˌdʒaŋ ; ⁻g̊uŋ ˎduan.

′xuŋ ⁻xua ; ′chyn ˌtshən ; ′liɛn ˌʃu ; ′thaɪ ˎi̥ao.

ˌɕiaŋ ⁻i̥a ; ˌlao ′niaŋ ; ⁻liaŋ ˌguaŋ ; ˌbao ˎg̊ueɪ.

ˎfaŋ ⁻ɕɪn ; ˎdʒʌŋ ′chiɛn ; ˎkhuaɪ ˌdzou ; ˎxaɪ ˎpha.

(ii.) ˎly·dɪ ; ˎmu·thou ; ˌdzou·lə ; ′naˎchy.

    [⁻dɪ]   [′thou]   [ˌlə]

    ˌda·fa ; ˎli·chiɛn ; ⁻ʃou·bi ; ′meɪ·g̊ueɪ

    [⁻fa]   [′chiɛn]   [ˌbi]   [ˎg̊ueɪ]

[C. Tones Modified by Position.]

(i.) ′waŋ ˌɕiɛn·ʃʌŋ ˌʃuɔ, ⁻tha ′mɪŋ·thiɛn ⁻ɕy ˌdzou.

   ˌtha ⁻ɕiuŋ·di ˌʃuɔ, ⁻tha ˌjɛ ⁻ɕy ˌdzou.

   ⁻tha·mən ˎJʌ·ʃɪ ˌdzou, ⁻wɔ ˌjɛ·ɕy ˌdzou.

(ii.) ˎbu⁻dɔ, ˎbu′nʌŋ, ˎbuˌxao ;

    ′bu ˎʃɪ, ′bu ˎda, ′bu ˎjuŋ.

Translation. Chinese Sounds. Part I (*cont.*).

[B. Tones in Relation to Stress].

(i) custom ; mountains and rivers ; village elder ; give judgment. saffron ; body of ministers ; related to ; carry a sedan chair. home-sick ; old lady ; two Kuang provinces ; valuable. easy in mind ; earn money ; go quickly ; afraid.

(ii) green ; wood ; gone ; take away. send ; interest ; hand-writing ; a rose.

[C. Tones Modified by Position].

(i) Mr. Wang says he may go to-morrow.
His brother says he also may go.
If they go, I too may go.

(ii) not many ; not able ; not good.
it is not ; not large ; not needed.

Transcription. Chinese Sounds. Part II.

‾fɑ‾jɪn ˋliɛn ⁄ ɕi. ˋɕiɑ

(i.) *‾i ˌsɔ ˋjy ′jɛn. ˋsuɑn ′phu ˳thɑo

‾i•gə ˌxən ˏɔ•ɖɪ ′xu•li ˋlu ˋ gŭɔ ‾i ˋ dzɔ ′phu•thɑo ˋjyɑn, ˋkhɑn•ʄiɛn ˌɐy‾ɖɔ ˋju ′ʃou ˋju ˳xɑo ˋkhɑn•ɖɪ ′phu•thɑo ‾gɑo‾gɑo •əɪ•dɪ •dzaɪ ˋʄiɑ ′ʃɑŋ ′ʧhueɪ•dʒɔ. ‾thɑ •ʄiu ˌwɑŋ ˌchi ˋthiɑo, ˌkhʌ•ʃɪ, ′dʒɪ ˋɖɑo ‾thɑ ‾ɖu ˋthiɑo ′fɑ•lə, ‾i ˳gə ′phu•thɑo ⁄ xuɑn ʃɪ ⁄meɪ‾ʧɪ•ɖʒɑo. ˳ɖɑo ˋmɔ ˋmɔ ˌliɑo ˌthɑ ˌʃuɔ ˳lə : ′ʃueɪ ˋaɪ ˋjɑo ′ʃueɪ ˋjɑo, ⁻wɔ ˌfɑn ˋdʒʌŋ ˋbu ˳guɑn ˳lə, ˋdʒɤ ′bu ˋguɔ ˋʃɪ ˳ɕiɛ ′meɪ ′ʃou ˳dɪ ˋsuɑn ′phu ˋthɑo.

Translation. Chinese Sounds. Part II.

(1) ÆSOP'S FABLES.—THE SOUR GRAPES.

A fox very hungry, chanced to come into a vineyard, where hung branches of charming ripe grapes, but nailed up to a trellis so high that he leaped till he quite tired himself, without being able to reach one of them. At last, " Let who will take them," said he, " they are but green and sour, so I'll even let them alone."

Transcription. Chinese Sounds. Part II (*cont.*).

(ii.) ʻxuŋ ʻlou ˋmʌŋ. ˋd̬i ˋʌɪʻʃɪ˻wu ʻxueɪ.

ˋd̬ʒɤ· fanˋxou,ˋkhan·liao ˻liaŋ·phiɛn ˉʃu, ʻju ʻthuŋ *d̬zɯˉi̯yan d̬ʌŋ ˋd̬zɔ·liao ˉi·xuə·ɹ ˉd̬ʒən·ɕiɛn ; ˻d̬zuŋ ˋmən ˋmən·b̬u ˉʃu, ˉi·thuŋ ˋb̬u· ɕɪŋ ˉt̬ʃhu·laɪ, khan ʻthɪŋ ʻchiɛn tshaɪ ˋb̬ʌŋ·t̬ʃhu·d̬ɪ ˉɕɪn˻sun ; b̬u ˒i̯yə ˉt̬ʃhu·liao ˋjyan ʻmən. ʻlaɪ·d̬ao ʻjyan·d̬ʒuŋ, ˋsɯ ˋwaŋ ʻwu ʻɹən, ʻweɪ i̯iɛn ˉxua ˉg̬uaŋ ˻niao˻jy ; ɕɪn ˋb̬u ˋb̬iɛn waŋ *ʻi·xuŋ ˋjyan laɪ. ˻d̬ʒɪ i̯iɛn ˻i̯i·g̬ə ˉja·thou ˻waɪ˻ʃueɪ, ˉd̬u ˋd̬zaɪ·xueɪ ʻlaŋ·ʃaŋ khan ˋxua·meɪ ˻ɕi˻d̬zao nɪ. ˋthɪŋ·i̯iɛn ʻfaŋ·neɪ ˋɕiao ʃʌŋ, ʻjyan· laɪ ʃɪ *˻li·g̬uŋ ʻtshaɪ, *ˋfʌŋ˻i̯iɛ, *ˋb̬ao ˉt̬ʃhaɪ, ˉd̬u d̬zaɪ ˋd̬ʒɤ·li. ˉi· i̯iɛn tha ˉi̯ɪn·laɪ, d̬u ˋɕiao d̬ao : ˋd̬ʒɤ b̬u ˋju ʻlaɪ·liao ˻liaŋ·g̬ə ? *ˋd̬aɪ ˋjy ˋɕiao ˋd̬ao : ˉi̯ɪn·ɹ ʻchi·chyan, ʻʃueɪ ɕia ˻thiɛ·d̬zɯ ˻chɪŋ·d̬ɪ ? *ˋfʌŋ·i̯iɛ ˋd̬ao : ˻wɔ ʻchiɛn·ɹ ˻d̬a·fa ʻɹən suŋ ˻liaŋ· phɪŋ ˋt̬ʃha·jɛ jy ˉg̬u·niaŋ, ˻khʌ ʻxuan ˻xao ma ? *ˋd̬aɪ·jy ˋd̬ao

Translation. Chinese Sounds. Part II (*cont.*).

(ii) THE DREAM OF THE RED CHAMBER. Chap. 25.

That day, after food, having read a few pages and done a little needle-work with Tzŭ Chüan, they were both depressed and came out together to look at the new shoots springing up in front of the house, and without meaning to they strayed out of the courtyard gate. When they came into the garden there was no one in sight in any direction, and nothing but the beauty of flowers and the chirping of birds. They strolled on towards the I Hung Courtyard. Here there were only a few maids drawing water, all on the verandah watching a thrush take a bath. From inside the house came the sound of laughter, and behold Li Kung-ts'ai, Miss Feng and Pao Ch'ai were all there. As soon as they saw them come in they all laughed and said, "Well, if there aren't two more come!" Tai Yü said laughing, "Now we are all here; who sent out the invitations?" Miss Feng replied, "I sent a messenger with two jars of tea to you two days ago; was it all right?"

Tai Yŭ replied, "I had quite forgotten. Many thanks for thinking of it."

Transcription. Chinese Sounds. Part II (*cont.*).

wɔ ˋdʒʌŋ ˋwaŋ·lə ; ⁻d̬o·ɕiɛ ˌɕiaŋ·dʒɔ. *ˋb̬ao·jy ˋd̬ao: wɔ ʹtʃhaŋ·liao ˋb̬u˰xao, ˋb̬u·dʒɪ ʹb̬iɛ ɪən ʹtʃhaŋ·liao ʹdzə·mə·jaŋ. *ˋb̬ao⁻tʃhaɪ ˋd̬ao: ˋweɪ d̬ao ˰xao, ˌdʒɪ·ʃɪ ʹmeɪ ʃən ʹjɛn·sɤ. *ˋfʌŋ·ɉiɛ ˋd̬ao: ˋna ʃɪ *⁻ɕyan·lɔ ʹg̬uɔ ˋg̬uŋ·d̬ɪ ; ˌwɔ ʹtʃhaŋ·lə ˌjɛ b̬uʹȷ̊yə ʃən˰xao, ʹxuan b̬uʹɪu ˌwɔ·mən ʹtʃhaŋ ⁻tʃhɪ·d̬ɪ nɪ! *ˋd̬aɪ·jy ˋd̬ao: ˌwɔ ⁻tʃhɪ·dʒɔ ˰xao, ˋb̬u⁻dʒɪ ˌni·mən·d̬ɪ ʹphi·weɪ ʃɪ ˌdzə·məˋjaŋ·d̬ɪ. *ˋb̬ao·jy ˋd̬ao: ˌni ⁻ʃuɔ ˰xao, b̬a ˌwɔ·d̬ɪ d̬u ʹna·liaoˋchy ⁻tʃhɪ b̬a! *⁻fʌŋ·ɉiɛ ˋd̬ao: wɔ ˋna·li xuan ⁻d̬o·dʒɔ nɪ! *ˋd̬aɪ·jy ˋd̬ao: ˌwɔ ɉiaó ˌja·thou ˌchy·chy. *ˋfʌŋ·ɉiɛ ˋd̬ao: ʹb̬u·juŋ, ˌwɔ ˌd̬a·fa ʹɪən ˋsuŋ·laɪ ; wɔ ʹmɪŋ·ɪ ʹxuan ju ⁻i·ʃɪ ʹchiu ni, ⁻i·thuŋ ˋɉiao ɪən ˋsuŋ·laɪ. *ʹlɪn ˋd̬aɪ·jy ⁻thɪŋ·liao, ˋɕiao d̬ao: ˌni·mən ⁻thɪŋ·thɪŋ ; ˋdʒɤ ʃɪ ⁻tʃhɪ·liao ⁻tha ɉia ⁻i·dɪɛn·dzɯ ʹtʃha·jɛ ɉiu ˌʃɪ·xuan·chiʹɪən laɪ·lɔ.

Translation. Chinese Sounds. Part II (*cont.*).

Pao Yü said: " I tasted it, but didn't like it. I don't know what the others thought of it."

Pao Ch'ai replied: " It tasted alright, but it hadn't much colour.

Miss Feng remarked, " It was Siam tribute (tea). I didn't like the taste of it either. It is not as good as we drink ordinarily." Tai Yü said : " I enjoyed it. I don't know what is the matter with your appetites."

Pao Yü answered, " You are right. Take all mine away and drink it."

Miss Feng said, " I still have quite a lot." " I'll send a slave-girl to fetch it away," said Tai Yu.

" There is no need," answered Miss Feng, " I'll send a messenger with it. There is another request I want to make to you to-morrow and the man can attend to both matters at once." Lin Tai-yü heard, and said, laughing, " Just listen. Over a mere matter of drinking a little tea given by someone else we begin to summon (employ) servants."

Transcription. Lesson 1. Part I.

\di ˉi \khʌ. ˈʃaŋ.

VOCABULARIES.

1st Tone.	2nd Tone.	3rd Tone.	4th Tone.
1. ˉʃu	2. ˈɪən	4. ˌb̥i	8. ˋmɔ
	3. ˈmeɪ	5. ˌjəu [ˌju]	
		6. ˌxɑo	
		7. ˌjɛ	

COMPOUND WORDS AND EXPRESSIONS.

[The thick tone-mark indicates the stressed syllables.]

1. ˌb̥i ˋmɔ   2. ˈmeɪ ˌjəu   3. ˌjəu ˈmeɪ ˌjəu

TONE PRACTICE.

[The words in **black** letters are those which occur in this lesson.]

	i.	ii.	iii.	iv.	v.	vi.
1st Tone	ˉ**ʃu**	ˉb̥i	ˉxɑo	ˉjɛ	ˉju	ˉmɔ
2nd Tone	ˈʃu	ˈb̥i	ˈxɑo	ˈjɛ	ˈju	ˈmɔ
3rd Tone	ˌʃu	ˌ**b̥i**	ˌ**xɑo**	ˌ**jɛ**	ˌ**jəu**	ˌmɔ
4th Tone	ˋʃu	ˋb̥i	ˋxɑo	ˋjɛ	ˋjəu	ˋ**mɔ**

EXERCISE.

1. ˌju ˉʃu, ˌju ˈɪen, ˌju ˌb̥i, ˌju ˋmɔ. 2. ˈmeɪˌju ˉʃu, ˈmeɪ ˌju ˈɪen, ˈmeɪˌju ˌb̥i, ˈmeɪˌju ˋmɔ. 3. ˌju ˉʃu ˋmeɪˌju? ˌju ˈɪen ˋmeɪˌju? ˌju ˌb̥i ˈmeɪˌju? ˌju ˋmɔ ˈmeɪ ˌju? 4. ˌju ˌb̥i ˋmɔ ˈmeɪˌju? ˈmeɪ ˌju. 5. ˌju ˌxɑo ˉʃu, ˌjɛ ˌju ˌxɑo ˌb̥i ˌxɑo ˋmɔ. 6. ˌxɑo ˈɪen ˌju ˈmeɪ ˌju? ˌju.

7. ˌju ˉʃu ˈmeɪˌju? ˌju ˉʃu. 8. ˌju ˌb̥i ˈmeɪˌju? ˈmeɪˌju ˌb̥i. 9. ˌju ˋmɔ ˈmeɪ ˌju? ˈmeɪˌju. 10. ˌb̥i ˋmɔ ˌju ˈmeɪˌju? ˌju ˌb̥i, ˈmeɪˌju ˋmɔ. 11. ˌju ˌxɑo ˉʃu ˈmeɪˌju? ˌju. 12. ˌju ˉxɑo ˌb̥i ˈmeɪˌju? ˉju ˌxɑo ˌb̥i, ˌjɛ ˌju ˌxɑo ˋmɔ. 13. ˌju ˌxɑo ˈɪen ˈmeɪˌju? ˌju ˌxɑo ˈɪen. 14. ˌxɑo ˌb̥i ˋmɔ, ˌju ˈmeɪˌju? ˌxɑo ˌb̥i ˋmɔ ˌju.

Translation. Lesson 1. Part I.

VOCABULARIES.

1st Tone.	2nd Tone.	3rd Tone.	4th Tone.
1. book.	2. man, person.	4. pen.	8. ink.
	3. not.	5. there is (are), to have.	
		6. good.	
		7. also.	

COMPOUND WORDS AND EXPRESSIONS.

1. pen and ink, stationery. 2. there is not. 3. is there?

TONE PRACTICE.

	i.	ii.	iii.	iv.	v.	vi.
1st Tone.	**book.**	oppress.	plant.	choke.	sad.	touch.
2nd Tone.	ripe.	nose.	trifling.	father.	oil.	bread.
3rd Tone.	belong.	**pen.**	**good.**	**also.**	**to have.**	last.
4th Tone.	tree.	poor.	mark.	night.	right hand.	**ink.**

EXERCISE.

1. There are books (here), there are people, there are pens, and there is ink. 2. There are no books, no people, no pens, and no ink (here). 3. Are there any books (here)? Are there any people? Are there pens? Is there ink? 4. Is there any stationery (here)? There is none. 5. There are good books (here), there are also good pens and good ink. 6. Are there any good people? There are.

7. Are there any books? There are books. 8. Are there any pens? There are no pens. 9. Is there any ink? There is none. 10. Are there pens and ink? There are pens, (but) no ink. 11. Are there good books? There are. 12. Are there good pens? There are good pens, and there is also good ink. 13. Are there any good people? There are good people. 14. Is there any good stationery? There is (some) good stationery.

Transcription. Lesson 1. Part II.
\di ⁻i \khʌ. ˋɕia

VOCABULARIES.

1st Tone.	2nd Tone.	3rd Tone.	4th Tone.
9. ⁻tha	12. ´mən	14. ˌwɔ	
10. ⁻ɕiɛn	13. ´chiɛn	15. ˌni	
11. ⁻ʃʌŋ		16.* ˌli	

COMPOUND WORDS AND EXPRESSIONS.

4. ˌwɔ´mən   5. ˌni ´mən   6. ⁻tha ˌmən   7. ⁻ɕiɛn-ʃʌŋ

TONE PRACTICE.

[The words in **black** letters are those which occur in this lesson.]

	vii.	viii.	ix.	x.
1st *Tone*	⁻**ɕiɛn**	⁻ʃʌŋ	⁻chiɛn	⁻ni
2nd *Tone*	´ɕiɛn	´ʃʌŋ	´**chiɛn**	´ni
3rd *Tone*	ˌɕiɛn	ˌʃʌŋ	ˌchiɛn	ˌni
4th *Tone*	ˋɕiɛn	ˋʃʌŋ	ˋchiɛn	ˋni

EXERCISE.

15. ˌwɔ ˌju ⁻ʃu, ⁻ɕiɛn-ʃʌŋ ˌju ˌmeɪ ˌju? 16. *ˌli ⁻ɕiɛn-ʃʌŋ ´meɪ-ju ˌxao ˋmɔ. 17. ˌni ˌju ˋmɔ, ⁻tha ˌju ˌmeɪ ˌju? 18. ˌni ˌmən ˌju ⁻ʃu, ⁻tha ´mən ´meɪ ˌju. 19. ˌwɔ ˌmən ´meɪ ju ´chiɛn, ˌni ˌmən ˌju ˌmeɪ ju? 20. ⁻tha ˌmən ˌju ˌxao ˋmɔ, ´meɪ ju ˌxao ˌb̥i.

21. ´tha ˌju ˌb̥i ˋmɔ, ⁻ɕiɛn-ʃʌŋ ˌju ˌmeɪ ju? ˌwɔ ˌju ˌb̥i ˋmɔ. 22. ˌni ˌju ˌb̥i, ⁻tha ˌju ˌmeɪ ju? ⁻tha ´meɪ ju ˌb̥i. 23. *ˌli ⁻ɕiɛn-ʃʌŋ ˌju ˌxao ˌb̥i ˌmeɪ ju? *ˌli ⁻ɕiɛn-ʃʌŋ ˌju ˌxao ˌb̥i, ´meɪ ju ˌxao ˋmɔ. 24. ˌni ˌju ˌxao ˋmɔ ˌmeɪ ju? ˌju, ⁻ɕiɛn-ʃʌŋ ˌju ˌmeɪ ju? 25. ⁻tha ˌmən ˌju ⁻ʃu, ˌni ˌmən ˌju ˌmeɪ ju? ˌwɔ ˌmən ˌju ˌxao ⁻ʃu. 26. ˌni ˌmən ˌju ˋmɔ, ⁻tha ˌmən ˌju ˌmeɪ ju? ⁻tha ˌmən ´meɪ ju ˌxao ˋmɔ. 27. ˌwɔ ˌmən ˌju ´chiɛn, ˌni ˌmən ˌju ˌmeɪ ju? ˌwɔ ˌmən ˌju ˌchiɛn. 28. ˌwɔ ˌmən ˌju ⁻ʃu, ˌju ˌb̥i, ˌju ˋmɔ; ⁻tha ˌmən ˌju ˌmeɪ ju? ⁻tha ˌmən ˌju ˌxao ⁻ʃu, ˌjɛ ˌju ˌxao ˌb̥i, ˌxao ˋmɔ.

---

* The asterisk before a word indicates that the word is a proper name.

Translation. Lesson 1. Part II.

VOCABULARIES.

1st Tone.	2nd Tone.	3rd Tone,	4th Tone.
9. he, she.	12. sign of the plural.	14. I.	
10. before.	13. money, cash.	15. you (sing.)	
11. born.		16. plum, a surname.	

COMPOUND WORDS AND EXPRESSIONS.

4. we.   5. you (pl.)   6. they.   7. teacher, sir, Mr.

TONE PRACTICE.

	vii	viii	ix	x.
1st Tone.	**before.**	**born.**	humble.	interrog. part.
2nd Tone.	leisure.	rope.	**money.**	mud.
3rd Tone.	danger.	province.	shallow.	you (sing.).
4th Tone.	thread.	holy.	lead (the metal).	foolish.

EXERCISE.

15. I have books; have you, sir? 16. Mr. Li has no good ink. 17. You have ink; has he? 18. You (pl.) have books, (but) they have none. 19. We have no money; have you? 20. They have good ink, (but) no good pens.

21. He has pen and ink; have you, sir? I have pen and ink. 22. You have a pen; has he? He has no pen. 23. Has Mr. Li a good pen? Mr. Li has a good pen, but no good ink. 24. Have you good ink? I have; have you, sir? 25. They have books; have you (pl.) any? We have good books. 26. You (pl.) have ink; have they any? They have no good ink. 27. We have money; have you? We have money. 28. We have books, we have pens, and we have ink; have they? They have good books, and they also have good pens and good ink.

Transcription. Lesson 2. Part I.

\di ˋʌɪ \khʌ. ˋʃaŋ.

VOCABULARIES.

1st Tone.	2nd Tone.	3rd Tone.	4th Tone,
17. san	18. ʃɪ	20. wu	23. liu
	19. nɪn	21. bən	24. g̊ʌ [g̊ə]
		22. g̊uan	25. khuaɪ

TONE PRACTICE.

[Note : In unstressed syllables a thick dot is used to indicate pitch.]

i.
¯san ˌbən -ʃu
¯san·g̊ə ʹɪən
¯san·g̊uan ˌbi
¯san·khuaɪ \mɔ

ii.
ʹʃɪ ˌbən -ʃu
ʹʃɪ·g̊ə ʹɪən
ʹʃɪ·g̊uan ˌbi
ʹʃɪ·khuaɪ \mɔ

iii.
ˌwu ˌbən -ʃu
ˌwu·g̊ə ʹɪən
ˌwu·g̊uan ˌbi
ˌwu·khuaɪ \mɔ

iv.
ˋliu ˌbən -ʃu
ˋliu·g̊ə ʹɪən
ˋliu·g̊uan ˌbi
ˋliu·khuaɪ \mɔ

EXERCISE.

1. ˌju ¯san·g̊ə ʹɪən. 2. ˌju ʹʃɪ·g̊uan ˌbi. 3. ˌwɔ ˌju ˌwu ˌbən -ʃu. 4. ¯tha ˌju ˋliu·g̊uan ˌbi. 5. * li ¯ɕiɛn·ʃʌŋ ˌju ¯san ·khuaɪ ˌxao \mɔ. 6. ¯tha·mən ˌju ˋliu·khuaɪ ʹchiɛn.

7. ¯ɕiɛn·ʃʌŋ ˌju ¯ʃu ·meɪ ˌju? ˌwɔ ˌju ¯san ˌbən -ʃu. 8. ¯tha ¯ju ˌbi ·meɪ ˌju? ¯tha ˌju ˌwu·g̊uan ˌbi. 9. ʹnɪn ˌju ˋmɔ ˌmeɪ ˌju? ˌwɔ ˌju ˋliu·khuaɪ \mɔ. 10. ¯tha ˌju·meɪ ˌju? ¯tha ˌju ˌxao ˌbi, ˌxao \mɔ. 11. ʹnɪn ˌju ʹchiɛn ·meɪ ˌju? ˌwɔ ˌju ¯san·khuaɪ ʹchiɛn. 12. ˌni·mən ˌju ˌbi ·meɪ ˌju? ˌwɔ·mən ˌju ˋliu·g̊uan ˌxao ˌbi. 13. ¯tha·mən ˌwu·g̊ə ʹɪən ˌju ¯ʃu ·meɪ ˌju? ¯tha·mən ˌju ʹʃɪ ˌbən -ʃu.

Translation. Lesson 2. Part I.

VOCABULARIES.

1st Tone.	2nd Tone.	3rd Tone.	4th Tone.
17. three.	18. ten.	20. five.	23. six.
	19. you (polite).	21. volume, classifier of books.	24. general classifier.
		22. tube, c. of pens.	25. piece, cake, c. of ink.

TONE PRACTICE.

i.	ii.	iii.	iv.
three books.	ten books.	five books.	six books.
three people.	ten people.	five people.	six people.
three pens.	ten pens.	five pens.	six pens.
three cakes of ink.	ten cakes of ink.	five cakes of ink.	six cakes of ink.

EXERCISE.

1. There are three people (here). 2. There are ten pens (here). 3. I have five books. 4. He has six pens. 5. Mr. Li has three cakes of good ink. 6. They have six dollars.

7. Have you any books, sir? I have three books. 8. Has he pens? He has five pens. 9. Have you ink? I have six cakes of ink. 10. Has he any? He has good pens and good ink. 11. Have you any money? I have three dollars. 12. Have you (pl.) any pens? We have six good pens. 13. Have those five people any books.? They have ten books.

Transcription. Lesson 2. Part II.

\di ˋʌɪ \khʌ. ˋɕia.

VOCABULARIES.

1st Tone.	2nd Tone.	3rd Tone.	4th Tone.
26. ḍi [dɪ]		27. ɕiao	29. ʃɪ
		28. ɕiɛ	30. dʒɤ
			31. na
			32. ḍa
			33. ḅu

COMPOUND WORDS AND EXPRESSIONS.

1. ˋʃɪ 2. ʹḅu ˅ʃɪ 3. ˋʃɪ·ḅu˅ʃɪ

TONE PRACTICE.

```
        v                          vi
   ▁wɔ·ḍɪ                    ▁wɔ·mən·ḍɪ
   ▁ni·ḍɪ                    ▁ni·mən·ḍɪ
   ⁻tha·ḍɪ                   ⁻tha mən ḍɪ

        vii                        viii
   ˋdʒɤ ḅən ⁻ʃu              ˋna ɕiɛ ⁻ʃu
   ˋdʒɤ ğə ⁄ɪən              ˋna ɕiɛ ⁄ɪən
   ˋna ğuan ▁ḅi              ˋdʒɤ ɕiɛ ▁ḅi
   ˋna·khuai ˋmɔ             ˋdʒɤ ɕiɛ ˋmɔ
```

EXERCISE.

14. ˋdʒɤ ·ʃɪ ▁ḅi, ˋna ʃɪ ˋmɔ. 15. ˋdʒɤ ʹḅu·ʃɪ ▁ḅi, ˋna ʹḅu ʃɪ ˋmɔ. 16. ˋdʒɤ ·ʃɪ ▁wɔ·ḍɪ ʹchiɛn, ·ʃɪ·ḅu·ʃɪ? 17. ˋna ·ʃɪ ▁ni·mən·ḍɪ ⁻ʃu ·ḅu·ʃɪ? 18. ˋdʒɤ ɕiɛ ʹchiɛn ·ʃɪ ▁ni·ḍɪ, ·ʃɪ ▁wɔ·ḍɪ? 19. ʹḅu ·ʃɪ ▁wɔ·ḍɪ, jɛ ʹḅu·ʃɪ ▁ni·ḍɪ, ·ʃɪ ⁻tha·ḍɪ. 20. ˋdʒɤ·ğə ⁄ɪən ju ˋmɔ ·meɪ ju? ▁ju. 21. ˋna·ğə ⁄ɪən ju·meɪ ju? ˋna·ğə ⁄ɪən ⊣jɛ ▁ju. 22. ˋdʒɤ ·ʃɪ ▁xao ˋmɔ ·ḅu·ʃɪ? ˋʃɪ, ˋʃɪ ▁xao ▁mɔ. 23. ˋdʒɤ ·ʃɪ * ▁li ⁻ɕiɛn-ʃʌŋ·ḍɪ ▁ḅi ʹḅu·ʃɪ? ʹḅu·ʃɪ, ˋʃɪ ▁wɔ·ḍɪ ▁ḅi. 24. ˋna·guan ▁ḅi ·ʃɪ ⁻tha·ḍɪ ·ḅu·ʃɪ? ʹḅu·ʃɪ, ˋna·ğuan ▁ḅi jɛ ·ʃɪ ▁wɔ·ḍɪ. 25. ⁻tha ·mən ju ⊣ɕiao ▁ḅi ·meɪ ju? ⁻tha·mən ju ⊣ɕiao ▁ḅi, ⊣jɛ ju ˋda ▁ḅi.

Translation. Lesson 2. Part II.

VOCABULARIES.

1st Tone.	2nd Tone.	3rd Tone	4th Tone.
26. sign of possessive.		27. small.	29. it is, yes.
		28. some.	30. this.
			31. that.
			32. large.
			33. not.

COMPOUND WORDS AND EXPRESSIONS.

1. yes.   2. no.   3. is it ?

TONE PRACTICE.

v.	vi.	vii.	viii.
my.	our.	this book.	those books.
your.	your.	this person.	those people.
his.	their.	that pen.	these pens.
		that cake of ink.	these cakes of ink.

EXERCISE.

14. This is a pen, that is ink.   15. This is not a pen, that is not ink.   16. This is my money, is it not ?   17. Are those your (pl.) books?   18. Is this money yours or mine ?   19. It is not mine, nor is it yours, it is his.   20. Has this person any ink ?   He (*or* she) has.   21. Has that person any ?   That person has some also.   22. Is this good ink ?   Yes, it is good ink.   23. Is this Mr. Li's pen ?   No, it is my pen.   24. Is that pen his ?   No, that pen is also mine.   25. Have they any small pens.?   They have small pens, and also large pens.

Transcription. Lesson 3. Part I.
ḍi ⁻san khʌ. ˋʃaŋ.

VOCABULARIES.

1st Tone.	2nd Tone.	3rd Tone.	4th Tone.
34. ḍʒaŋ	35. thaɪ	38. ḍʒɪ	43. jɛn
[ma]*	36. thuŋ	39. xən	44. weɪ
	37. jaŋ	40. ʂi	
	[ʌɪ]†	41. liaŋ	
		42. ḍzɯ	
		[ʃao]‡	

COMPOUND WORDS AND EXPRESSIONS.

1. ˍḍʒɪˍḅi   2. ˋjɛn·thaɪ   3. ˊjaŋ ˊchiɛn   4. ˊthuŋˍḍzɤ·ɪ

TONE PRACTICE.

i.
san·ʃɪˑḍʒaŋ ˍḍʒɪ
/ʃɪ ⁻san·ḍʒaŋ ˍḍʒɪ

ii.
ˍwuˑʃɪ·khuai ˏchiɛn
ˊʃɪ ˍwuˑkhuai ˏchiɛn

iii.
ˋliu·ʃɪˑğə ˏɪən
/ʃɪ ˋliuˑğə ˏɪən

iv.
ˍwɔ ju ⁻wu ˍğuan ˍḅi
ˍni·ḍɪ ˍḅi ˍxən ˍxao
⁻tha·ḍɪ ˍḍʒɪ ˍxən ˍʃao

EXERCISE.

1. ˋḍʒɤ ·ʃɪ ˍxao ⁻ʃu. ˋḍʒɤˑḅən ⁻ʃu ˍxao. 2. ⁻tha ·ʃɪ ˍxao ˏɪən. ˋna·ğə ˏɪən ˍxao. 3. ˍwɔ ju ˍxao ˍḅi. wɔ·ḍɪ ⁻ḅi ˍxao. 4. ˊḍʒɤ ·ʃɪ ˍxao ˋmɔ. ˋḍʒɤ·khuaɪ ˋmɔ ˍxao. 5. ˋḍʒɤ·ğə ˋḍa, ˋna·ğə ˍɕiao· 6. ˋḍʒɤ·khuaɪ ˋjɛn·thai ⁻xən ˍɕiao, ˋna ·liaŋˏkhuaɪ jɛ ·ḅu ˋḍa. 7. ˍwɔ·ḍɪ ⁻ḅi ˍxao, ⁻tha·ḍɪ ˍḅi ˋḅu ˍxao, ˊnɪn·ḍɪ ˍxaoˑḅu ˍxao? 8. ˋḍʒɤˑɕiɛ ˍḍʒɪˍḅi ˍxən ˍxao. 9. ˋḍʒɤ·weɪ ⁻ɕiɛn·ʃʌŋ ju ˊʃɪ ˍwu ḅən ⁻ʃu, ˋna·wei ⁻ɕiɛn·ʃʌŋ ˍju ˍwu ˊʃɪˍḅən. 10. ⁻tha·ḍɪ ˋmɔ ˍxaoˑḅu ˍxao? ⁻tha·ḍɪ ˋmɔ ˍxən ˋḅu ˍxao. 11. ˋna ʂi·ḍʒaŋ ˍḍʒɪ ˍxao ˑma? ˋna ʂi ˑḍʒaŋ ˍḍʒɪ ˋḅu ˍxən ˍxao. 12. ⁻ɕiɛn·ʃʌŋ·ḍɪ ˋjɛn·thai ˋḍa, ·ʃɪ ·ḅu·ʃɪ? ˋʃɪ, ˍxən ˋḍa. 13. ˊnɪn ju ˊchiɛn ˑmei ju? ˍwɔ ju ˊjaŋ ˏchiɛn, ˍjɛ ˍju ˊthuŋˍḍzɤ·ɪ.

---
* This word is recorded in the Vocabulary of Part II, v. 48.
† This word is recorded in the Vocabulary of Less. 5, Part I, v. 81.
‡ This word is recorded in the Vocabulary of Less. 4, Part I, v. 63.

Translation. Lesson 3. Part I.

VOCABULARIES.

1st Tone.	2nd Tone.	3rd Tone.	4th Tone.
34. sheet, cl. of paper, a surname. [interrog. particle.]*	35. terrace, slab. 36. copper. 37. foreign. [son, an enclitic particle.]*	38. paper. 39. very. 40. few, how many? 41. two. 42. son, [an enclitic particle.]*	43. ink-slab. 44. position, c. of persons.

COMPOUND WORDS AND EXPRESSIONS.

1. stationery. 2. ink-slab. 3. dollars. 4. copper cash.

TONE PRACTICE.

i.	ii.	iii.	iv.
thirty sheets of paper. thirteen sheets of paper.	fifty dollars. fifteen dollars.	sixty people. sixteen people.	I have five pens. Your pen is very good. He has very little paper.

EXERCISE.

1. This is a good book. This book is good. 2. He is a good man. That man is good. 3. I have a good pen. My pen is good. 4. This is good ink. This cake of ink is good. 5. This is large, that is small. 6. This ink-slab is very small; those two are also not large. 7. My pen is good, his pen is not good, is yours good? 8. This stationery is very good. 9. This gentlemen has fifteen books, that gentleman has fifty volumes. 10. Is his ink good? His ink is very poor. 11. Are those few sheets of paper good? Those few sheets of paper are not very good. 12. Your ink-slab is large, sir, is it not? Yes, very large. 13. Have you any money? I have some dollars, and also some coppers.

---

* See footnote on Transcription page.   D

Transcription. Lesson 3. Part II.

\ɖi ⁻saŋ \khʌ. ʻɕia.

VOCABULARIES.

1st Tone.	2nd Tone.	3rd Tone.	4th Tone.
45. ɕiaŋ	50. ʃən		53. i̥ao
46. ɖuŋ	51. xʌ		
47. ɕi	52. jyan		
48. mɔ [mɑ] [mə]			
49. i			

COMPOUND WORDS AND EXPRESSIONS.

5. ⁻ɖuŋ ˌɕi 6. ⁻i ˌɕie 7. ʻthuŋ ˌjyan 8. ˌʃə·mə

TONE PRACTICE.

v.	vi.	vii.
⁻san·ʃɪ ⁻san	⁻san·ʃɪ ˌwu	⁻san ʃɪ ʻliu
ˌwu·ʃɪ⁻san	ˌwu·ʃɪ ˌwu	ˌwu·ʃɪʻliu
ʻliu ʃɪ ˌsan	ʻliu ʃɪ ˌwu	ʻliu·ʃɪʻliu

EXERCISE.

14. \ɖʒɤ ·ʃɪ ˌʃə·mə? 15. ʻna ·ʃɪ ˌʃə·mə ⁻ɖuŋ·ɕi? 16. ʻna ⁻i ˌɕie ⁻ɕiaŋ ˌdzɯ, ˌju ʻɖa·ɖɪ, ˌju ˌɕiao·ɖɪ. 17. ʻɖʒɤ ʃi ʻɖʒaŋ ˌɖʒɪ, ⁻ju ˌxao·ɖɪ, ˌju ʻbu ˌxao·ɖɪ. 18. ˌwɔ ˌju ʻliu ·ʃɪ ⁻san·jyan ˌchien, ˌje ˌju ⁻i ˌɕie ʻthuŋ ˌjyan. 19. ʻɖʒɤ ⁻i ˌɕie ⁻ɖuŋ·ɕi ·ʃɪ ˌʃə·mə? ʻɖʒɤ ⁻i ˌɕie ⁻ɖuŋ·ɕi ·ʃɪ ⁻ʃu. 20. ʻna ˌɕie ⁻ɖuŋ·ɕi i̥ao ˌʃə·mə? ʻna ˌɕie ⁻ɖuŋ·ɕi i̥ao ˌɖʒɪ ˌbi. 21. ʻɖʒɤ·ɡə ˌxʌ·ɖzɯ ˌxao ʻbu ˌxao? ˌxao; ʻna ˌliaŋ ·ɡə ʻɖa·ɖɪ ˌje ˌxao. 22. ʻna ˌɕie ˌmɔ ˌju ˌxao·ɖɪ ʻma? ˌju ⁻san·ʃɪ ˌwu·khuai ˌxao·ɖɪ, ˌju ˌwu·ʃɪ ʻliu·khuai ʻbu ˌxao·ɖɪ.

Translation. Lesson 3. Part II.

VOCABULARIES.

1st Tone.	2nd Tone.	3rd Tone.	4th Tone.
45. box.	50. what ? very.		53. to call, to name.
46. East.	51. box (small).		
47. West.	52. dollar.		
48. interrog. part.			
49. one.			

COMPOUND WORDS AND EXPRESSIONS.

5. things.   6. several.   7. copper cash.   8. what ?

TONE PRACTICE.

v.	vi.	vii.
thirty-three.	thirty-five.	thirty-six.
fifty-three.	fifty-five.	fifty-six.
sixty-three.	sixty-five.	sixty-six.

EXERCISE.

14. What is this ?* 15. What is that thing ?† 16. Some of that lot of boxes are large, and some are small. 17. Some of these few sheets of paper are good, and some are not good. 18. I have sixty-three dollars, and also some copper cash. 19. What are all these things ? These things are books. 20. What are those things called ? Those things are called paper and pens. 21. Is this box good ? Yes ; those two large ones are also good. 22. Are any of those cakes of ink good ? There are thirty-five cakes which are good, and fifty-six cakes which are not good.

---

* *or*, What are these ?   † *or*, What are those things ?

Transcription. Lesson 4. Part I.

\di ˈsɯ \khʌ. ˈʃaŋ.

VOCABULARIES.

1st Tone.	2nd Tone.	3rd Tone.	4th Tone.
54. chi	59. mao	61. ʃ̥iu	64. ʌɪ
55. b̥a	60. lɪŋ	62. b̥aɪ	65. sɯ
56. d̥ɔ		63. ʃao	
57. fən			
58. d̥ʒɪ			

COMPOUND EXPRESSION.

1. ⁻d̥ɔ ˌʃao

TONE PRACTICE.

i.
⁻i, ˋʌɪ, ⁻san, ˋsɯ, ˌwu, ˋliu,
⁻chi, ⁻b̥a, ˌʃ̥iu, ˊʃɪ.

ii.
⁻san ˌb̥aɪ ⁻chi·ʃɪ ⁻b̥a.
ˌwu ˌb̥aɪ ⁻b̥a·ʃɪ ⁻san.
ˋsɯ ˌb̥aɪ ⁻b̥a·ʃɪ ˌwu.

iii.
⁻chi ·b̥aɪ ˌwu·ʃɪˋsɯ.
⁻ʃ̥iu·b̥aɪ ˌwu·ʃɪ ˌʃ̥iu.
ˋliu·b̥aɪ ˌʃ̥iu·ʃɪ ˌwu.

iv.
⁻b̥a ˌb̥aɪ ˋsɯ·ʃɪ ˌwu.
ˌwu ˌb̥aɪ ˋʌɪ·ʃˊliu.
ˌʌɪ ˌb̥aɪ ˋliu·ʃˌsɯ.

EXERCISE.

1. ˌju ⁻d̥ɔ ʃao ˊɪən? 2. ⁻ɕiɛn·ʃʌŋ ˌju ⁻ʃ̥i·g̊uan ˌb̥i? 3. ⁻tha ·mən ˌju ˋsɯ ʃɪ ˌwu ˌb̥ən ⁻ʃu, ⁻chi·ʃɪ ⁻b̥a·g̊uan ˌb̥i, ˋʌɪ·ʃɪ ʃ̥iu ·khuaɪ ˋmɔ. 4. *⁻d̥ʒaŋ ⁻ɕiɛn·ʃʌŋ ˌju ⁻b̥a·b̥aɪ ˌwu·ʃɪ ˋsɯ·jyan ˌchiɛn. 5. ˌwɔ ˌju ˊʃɪ·khuaɪ ⁻san ˌmao ˋlıu·fən ˌchiɛn. 6. ˌju ˌwu·b̥aɪ ·lıŋ ⁻chi·g̊ə ˌɪən. 7. ⁻ni ˌju ʃ̥i·d̥ʒɪ ˌb̥i? ˌwɔ ˌju ˋsɯ·d̥ʒɪ. 8. *⁻d̥ʒaŋ ⁻ɕiɛn ʃʌŋ ˌju ⁻d̥ɔ ʃao ⁻ʃu? ˌju ⁻i·b̥aɪ ·lıŋ ˋliu·b̥ən ʃu. 9. ˋd̥ʒɤ·wei ˌju ⁻d̥ɔ ʃao ˌchiɛn? ⁻tha ˌju ⁻b̥a·khuaɪ ·lıŋ ⁻san·fən ˊjaŋ ˌchiɛn.

Translation. Lesson 4. Part I.

VOCABULARIES.

1st Tone.	2nd Tone.	3rd Tone.	4th Tone.
54. seven.	59. 10 cents.	61. nine.	64. two.
55. eight.	60. fraction.	62. hundred.	65. four.
56. many.		63. few, how many?	
57. cent (tenth).			
58. branch, c. of pens and pencils.			

COMPOUND EXPRESSION.

1. How many?

TONE PRACTICE.

i.	ii.	iii.	iv.
1. 1; 2; 3; 4; 5; 6; 7; 8; 9; 10.	378.	754.	845.
	583.	959.	526.
	485.	695.	264.

EXERCISE.

1. How many people are there? 2. How many pens have you, sir? 3. They have 45 books, 78 pens, 29 cakes of ink. 4. Mr. Chang has 854 dollars. 5. I have 10 dollars and 36 cents. 6. There are 507 people (here). 7. How many pens have you? I have four. 8. How many books has Mr. Chang? He has 106 volumes. 9. How much money has this (gentleman)? He has 8 dollars and 3 cents.

Transcription. Lesson 4. Part II.

\di 'sɯ \khʌ. 'ɕia.

VOCABULARIES.

1st Tone.	2nd Tone.	3rd Tone.	4th Tone.
66. chiɛn	69. ʃui [ʃueɪ]	70. ɕiɛ	71. jao
67. ʃʌŋ			72. dzɯ
68. chiɛn			73. wan
			74. diao
			75. di

COMPOUND WORDS AND EXPRESSIONS.

2. ′ʃui·dɪ [′ʃueɪ·dɪ]   3. ‿ɕiɛ‵dzɯ   4. ‾chiɛn‗bi

TONE PRACTICE.

v.

‾san·chiɛn ‾chi·baɪ ‿wu·ʃɪ‚ĵiu.
‿wu·chiɛn ‿ĵiu‚baɪ \sɯ·ʃɪ\liu.
\liu·chiɛn \sɯ‚baɪ ‾chi·ʃɪ‿ba.

vi.

\sɯ·wan ‿wu·chiɛn ‿ĵiu·baɪ ‿wu.
‾ba·wan \sɯ·chiɛn \ʌɪ‚baɪ \liu.
‿ĵiu·wan ‾san·chiɛn ‾chi‚baɪ ‑ba.

EXERCISE.

10. ′bu·jao \dʒɤ‚gə, \jao \na‚gə. 11. \dʒɤ‚gə ‾chiɛn‗bi ·jao·bu ·jao? 12. \dʒɤ ‿liaŋ·weɪ ‾ɕiɛn·ʃʌŋ ·ʃɪ ′ʃueɪ? 13. ‿wɔ ·jao ‿ɕiɛ\dzɯ. 14. \dʒɤ\dʒɪ ‿bi ·ʃɪ ′ʃueɪ·dɪ? 15. ‿ju ‿wu·wan ‾san·chiɛn ‾chi·baɪ ⁄jyan. 16. *‾dʒaŋ ‑ɕiɛn·ʃʌŋ ju ‾ba ·chiɛn ‾wu ·baɪ lɪŋ ‾chi·diao ⁄chiɛn. 17. ‾ʃu ·ʃɪ ·di‾i ·ʃʌŋ; ′chiɛn ·ʃɪ ·di\ʌɪ ʃʌŋ; ‗bi ·ʃɪ ·di‾san ʃʌŋ; \mɔ ·ʃɪ ·di\sɯ ʃʌŋ. 18. ‗ni \jao ′ʃə·mə? ‿wɔ ·jao ‾dʒɪ‿bi ‿ɕiɛ\dzɯ. 19. \jao ′chiɛn ·bu·jao? ′bu·jao ⁄chiɛn, ‿wɔ ju ‾i‚ɕiɛ. 20. \na·weɪ ‾ɕiɛn·ʃʌŋ ·ʃɪ ⁄ʃueɪ? \na ·ʃɪ *‾dʒaŋ ‑ɕiɛn·ʃʌŋ. 21. \dʒɤ ·ʃɪ ′ʃueɪ·dɪ ⁄chiɛn? \na ·ʃɪ ‿wɔ·dɪ ⁄chiɛn. 22. \na‚ɕiɛ \dzɯ · ʃɪ ‾ɕiɛn·ʃʌŋ ‿ɕiɛ·dɪ ·ma? ′bu·ʃɪ ‿wɔ ‿ɕiɛ·dɪ, ·ʃɪ *‿li ‾ɕiɛn·ʃʌŋ ‿ɕiɛ‚dɪ.

Translation. Lesson 4. Part II.

VOCABULARIES.

1st Tone.	2nd Tone.	3rd Tone.	4th Tone.
66. thousand.	69. who ?	70. write.	71. want, future aux.
67. tone, sound.			72. words(written)
68. lead (the metal).			73. ten thousand.
			74. to suspend, string of cash.
			75. s. of ordinal numeral.

COMPOUND WORDS AND EXPRESSIONS.

2. whose ?   3. write.   4. lead pencil.

TONE PRACTICE.

v.	vi.
3,759.	45,950.
5,946.	84,260.
6,478.	93,780.

EXERCISE.

10. I do not want this, I want that. 11. Do you want this pencil? 12. Who are these two gentlemen? 13. I want to do some writing. 14. Whose is this pen? 15. There are 53,700 dollars. 16. Mr. Chang has 8,507 *tiao* of cash. 17. ʃu is the first tone, chien is the second, ƀi the third, and mɔ the fourth. 18. What do you want? I want paper and pens to write with. 19. Do (you) want any money? (I) do not want any money, I have some. 20. Who is that gentleman? That is Mr. Chang. 21. Whose money is this? That is my money. 22. Are those characters your writing, sir? They are not my writing; they were written by Mr. Li.

Transcription. Lesson 5. Part I.

\di ˌwu ˈkhʌ. ˈʃaŋ.

VOCABULARIES.

1st Tone.	2nd Tone.	3rd Tone.	4th Tone.
76. ʃuɔ	81. ʌɪ	83. li	84. ɕɪn
77. ḅiɛn	82. faŋ	83a. [na]	85. niɛn
78. d̦u			86. xua
79. ʄia			87. waɪ
80. fʌŋ			88. d̦uɛɪ
			89. d̦zaɪ

COMPOUND WORDS AND EXPRESSIONS.

1. \niɛn⁻ʃu
2. ⁻ʃuɔ\xua
3. \waɪ ḅiɛn
4. ˌli·ḅiɛn
5. \d̦ӡɤ ḷi
6. \na ḷi
7. ˌna ḷi
8. \d̦ӡɤ ʌɪ
9. \na ʌɪ
10. ˌna·ʌɪ
11. \d̦ӡɤ ḅiɛn
12. \na ḅiɛn
13. ˌna·ḅiɛn

TONE PRACTICE.

i.	ii.	iii.
·d̦zaɪ\d̦ӡɤ ḷi	·d̦zaɪ\na ḷi	·d̦zaɪ⁻na·li
·d̦zaɪ\d̦ӡɤ ʌɪ	·d̦zaɪ\na ʌɪ	·d̦zaɪˌna·ʌɪ
·d̦zaɪ\d̦ӡɤ ḅiɛn	·d̦zaɪ\na ḅiɛn	·d̦zaɪˌna·ḅiɛn

EXERCISE.

[Note: The thin dot is used as a hyphen. See Note 2.]

1. \na ˌʄi·weɪ ⁻ɕiɛn·ʃʌŋ ⁻d̦u d̦zaɪ\d̦ӡɤ·ɪ. 2. *ˌli ⁻ɕiɛn·ʃʌŋ d̦zaɪ⁻ʃuˈfaŋ·li ɕiɛ\ɕɪn. 3. *⁻d̦ӡaŋ ⁻ɕiɛn·ʃʌŋ d̦zaɪ⁻ʄia niɛn⁻ʃu. 4. d̦zaɪ\waɪ·ḅiɛn ju ⁻i·ɕiɛ ˈɪən ʃuɔ\xua. 5. \d̦ӡɤ ʃɪ ⁻i·weɪ niɛn ⁻ʃu·d̦ɪ ˈɪən. 6. ˌli·ḅiɛn ʃuɔ\xua·d̦ɪ ʃɪ ˈʃueɪ? 7. wɔ ˌɕiɛ·d̦ɪ \na·fʌŋ \ɕɪn d̦zaɪˌna·ɪ? 8. \na ⁻san·weɪ ⁻ɕiɛn·ʃʌŋ d̦zaɪ\d̦ӡɤ·ḅiɛn ma? ⁻tha·mən \ḅu d̦zaɪ\d̦ӡɤ·ḅiɛn, ⁻d̦u d̦zaɪ\na·ḅiɛn. 9. ˌwɔ·d̦ɪ ⁻chiɛn·ḅi d̦zaɪˌna·li? ˌni·d̦ɪ ⁻chiɛn·ḅi d̦zaɪ\na·li. 10. ˌwɔ ⁻ʃuɔ·d̦ɪ \xua \d̦ueɪ·ḅu \d̦ueɪ? ⁻ɕiɛn·ʃʌŋ ⁻ʃuɔ·d̦ɪ \xua d̦u \d̦ueɪ. 11. ˌju ɕɪnˈfʌŋ meiˌju? ˌju; d̦zaɪ\d̦ӡɤ·li.

Translation. Lesson 5. Part I.

VOCABULARIES.

1st Tone.	2nd Tone.	3rd Tone.	4th Tone.
76. say.	81. son, an enclitic particle.	83. in.	84. letter.
77. side.		83a. [where ?]	85. read.
78. all.			86. words (spoken).
79. home.	82. house, a room.		87. outside.
80. to seal, c. of letter.			88. correct.
			89. at, to be at.

COMPOUND WORDS AND EXPRESSIONS.

1. read.	5. here	8. here.	11. here.
2. speak.	6. there.	9. there.	12. there
3. outside.	7. where ?	10. where ?	13. where ?
4. inside.			

TONE PRACTICE.

i.	ii.	iii.
here.	there.	where ?
here.	there.	where ?
here.	there.	where ?

EXERCISE.

1. Those few gentlemen are all here. 2. Mr. Li is in the study writing a letter. 3. Mr. Chang is at home studying. 4. Outside there are a lot of people talking. 5. This is a scholar. 6. Who is that talking indoors? 7. Where is that letter which I wrote ? 8. Are those 3 gentlemen here ? They are not, they are all over there. 9. Where is my pencil ? Your pencil is there. 10. Is what I say correct ? What you say, sir, is all correct. 11. Are there any envelopes ? Yes ; they are here.

Transcription. Lesson 5. Part II.

\di ˌwu \khʌ. ˋɕia.

VOCABULARIES.

1st Tone.	2nd Tone.	3rd Tone.	4th Tone.
90. thɪŋ.	91. dɣ	92. chɪŋ.	96. khan.
	[də] [deɪ].	93. diɛn.	97. ʝiɛn.
		94. sɔ.	98. wən.
		95. liɑo	99. khuaɪ.
		[lə] [lɑ].	100. man.
			101. g̊ou.
			102. g̊ɑo.
			103. su.

COMPOUND WORDS AND EXPRESSIONS.

14. ˋkhan·ʝiɛn 17. ˉthɪŋ·ʝiɛn 20. ˋkhuaɪ·i·diɛn 23. [ˋkhan·də
15. ˋkhan·khan 18. ˋg̊ɑo·su 21. ˋman ˋman·dɪ   ˋʝiɛn]
16. ˋkhan·i·khan 19. ɕɪn ˉfʌŋ 22. ˋkhuaɪ ˋkhuaɪ· 24. [ˉthɪŋ·də
                                     dɪ   ˋʝiɛn]

TONE PRACTICE.

iv.	v.	vi.	vii.
ˉʝiɑo ˉʃu	ˊnɑ ˉʃu	ˌmaɪ ˉʃu	ˋmaɪ ˉʃu
ˍʝiɑo ˊchiɛn	ˊnɑ ˊchiɛn	ˌmaɪ ˊchiɛn	ˋmaɪ ˊchiɛn
ˍʝiɑo ˌbi	ˊnɑ ˌbi	ˌmaɪ ˌbi	ˋmaɪ ˌbi
ˍʝiɑo ˎmɔ	ˊnɑ ˋmɔ	ˌmaɪ ˋmɔ	ˋmaɪ ˋmɔ

EXERCISE.

12. ˋkhan·də ˋʝiɛn ˋkhan·bu ˋʝiɛn ? ˋkhan·də ˋʝiɛn. 13. ˉthɪŋ· ʝiɛn·liɑo ma ? ˊmeɪ ˉthɪŋ·ʝiɛn. 14. ni ˋʝɑo ˋkhan bu·ʝɑo ˋkhan ? wɔ ˋʝɑo ˋkhan. 15. ˍwɔ ˍɕiɛ·dɪ ˋdʒɣ·ɕiɛ ˋdzɯ, ˍchɪŋ ˉɕiɛn·ʃʌŋ· mən ˋkhan·i ˋkhan. 16. ˍchɪŋ ˉɕiɛn·ʃʌŋ man ˋman·dɪ ˍʃuɔ. 17. ˍchɪŋ ˉɕiɛn·ʃʌŋ ˋkhuaɪ·i·diɛn ˋniɛn. 18. ˉtha ˋg̊ɑo·su ˍwɔ, ˋnɑ·ɕiɛ ˉʃu bu ˋg̊ou. 19. ˍwɔ ˍɕiɛ·dɪ ˋnɑ·ɕiɛ ˋdzɯ, ni ˋkhan·ʝiɛn·liɑo ma ? ˋkhan·ʝiɛn·liɑo. 20. ˍwɔ·dɪ ˋxua ni ˉthɪŋ·də ˋʝiɛn ˉthɪŋ·bu ˋʝiɛn ? ˉthɪŋ·bu ˋʝiɛn. 21. chɪŋ ˋwən, ˋdʒɣ ʃɪ ˊʃə·mə ˋdzɯ ? wɔ ˋkhan· khan; ˋdʒɣ ʃɪ ˋg̊ɑo ˋdzɯ. 22. ˋdʒɣ·ɕiɛ ˊchiɛn ˋg̊ou·bu ˋg̊ou ? ˋg̊ou· lə. 23. ˍli·biɛn ju ˊɹən meɪ ˍju ? wɔ ˋwən·i ˋwən.

Translation. Lesson 5. Part II.

VOCABULARIES.

1st Tone.	2nd Tone.	3rd Tone.	4th Tone
90. listen.	91. obtain, potential auxiliary.	92. to request.	96. to look.
		93. a point, a little.	97. perceive.
		94. sign of the relative.	98. ask.
		95. past aux., sign of complete action.	99. quick, quickly.
			100. slow, slowly.
			101. enough.
			102. tell
			103. relate.

COMPOUND WORDS AND EXPRESSIONS.

14. to see.
15. to look and see.
16. to have a look.
17. to hear.
18. to tell.
19. an envelope.
20. a little more quickly.
21. slowly.
22. quickly.
23. [can see.]
24. [can hear.]

TONE PRACTICE.

iv.	v.	vi.	vii.
to hand a book.	to take a book.	to buy books.	to sell books.
to hand money.	to take money.	to buy money.	to sell money.
to hand a pen.	to take a pen.	to buy pens.	to sell pens.
to hand ink.	to take ink.	to buy ink.	to sell ink.

EXERCISE.

12. Can you see? I can see. 13. Have you heard? I have not heard. 14. Do you want to look or not? I want to look. 15. Please, gentlemen, have a look at these characters which I have written. 16. Please, sir, speak slowly. 17. Please, sir, read a little faster. 18. He tells me that those books are not enough. 19. Have you seen those characters which I wrote? I have seen them. 20. Can you hear what I say? I cannot hear (what you say). 21. May I ask what is this character? Let me have a look. This is the character " ğao "? 22. Is this money enough? It is enough. 23. Is there anyone indoors? I will enquire.

Transcription. Lesson 6. Part I.

˅di ˅liu ˅khʌ. ˈʂaŋ.

VOCABULARIES.

1st Tone.	2nd Tone.	3rd Tone.	4th Tone.
104. sɯ.	106. mɪŋ.	110. ɖuŋ.	114. ɹən.
105. ɕɪn.	107. ḅaɪ.	111. ɕiao.	115. xueɪ.
	108. nan.	112. g̊eɪ.	116. i.
	109. ʃɹ.	113. ɟ̊i.	117. ɟ̊y.
			118. ɖzɯ.
			119. ʧhu.

COMPOUND WORDS AND EXPRESSIONS.

1. ˈmɪŋ·ḅaɪ
2. ˌɖuŋ·ɖə
3. ˌɕiao·ɖə
4. ˈʃɹ˅ɖzɯ
5. ˅ɹəɹ·ʃɹ
6. ˅ɹən·ɖə
7. ˌɕiɛ·g̊ə
8. ˅ɖzɯˌɟ̊i
9. ˅i.sɯ
10. ˈnan·ʧhu

TONE PRACTICE.

i.	ii.	iii.	iv.	v.
ˉtha·ɖɪ	ˉɟ̊ia·li	ˉʃuɔ·liao	ˉɖao·ɖzɯ	ˉɖɔ·mə
ˈḅaɪ·ɖɪ	ˈʧhʌŋ·li	ˈlaɪ·liao	ˈfaŋ·ɖzɯ	ˈʃə·mə
ˌju·ɖɪ	ˉna·li	ˉɖzou·liao	ˌli·ɖzɯ	ˌɖzə·mə
˅ʃɹ.ɖɪ	˅na.li	˅ɟ̊iɛn.liao	˅mao.ɖzɯ	˅ɖʒɤ.mə

EXERCISE.

1. ˈmɪŋ·ḅaɪ ḅu ˈmɪŋ·ḅaɪ? ˌɖuŋ·ɖə ḅu ˌɖuŋ·ɖə? ˌɕiao·ɖə ḅu ˌɕiao·ɖə? 2. ˅ɖʒɤ ʃɹ ˈʃə·mə ˅i·sɯ? ˌwɔ ˅ḅu ˌɕiao·ɖə. 3. ˅ɖʒɤ·g̊ə ˅ɖzɯ ni ˅xueɪ ɕiɛ ḅu ˅xueɪ ˌɕiɛ? 4. ˅ɖʒɤ·ɟ̊y ˅xua ni ˌɖuŋ·ḅu ˌɖuŋ? ˉwɔ ˌɖuŋ·ɖə. 5. ˅ɖʒɤ·ɕiɛ ˅ɖzɯ ni ˅ɹən·ʃɹ ḅu ˅ɹən·ʃɹ? ˅ɹən·ʃɹ ˌɕiɛ·g̊ə. 6. ˅na·g̊ə ˈɹən ˈʃɹ˅ɖzɯ ḅu ˈʃɹ˅ɖzɯ? tha ˈʃɹ ˅ɖzɯ ḅu ˌʃao. 7. ˅na·weɪ ˉɕiɛn·ʃʌŋ ni ˅ɹəɹ·ɖə ma? 8. ˉtha ˅ɖzɯ·ɟ̊i ˉʃuɔ tha ḅu ˈmɪŋ·ḅaɪ ni·ɹ̥ ˅i·sɯ. 9. ni ḅu ˈmɪŋ·ḅaɪ tha ˉɕɪn·li·ɖɪ ˈnan·ʧhu, ˉwɔ ˌg̊eɪ ni ɹaɹ̥ ˉʃuɔ·i ˉʃuɔ.

Translation. Lesson 6. Part I.

VOCABULARIES.

1st Tone.	2nd Tone.	3rd Tone.	4th Tone.
104. thought.	106. clear.	110. understand.	114. recognise.
105. mind, heart.	107. white.	111. know, understand.	115. able.
	108. difficult.	112. give, sign of dative.	116. meaning.
	109. recognize.	113. self.	117. sentence.
			118. self.
			119. a place.

COMPOUND WORDS AND EXPRESSIONS.

1. understand.
2. understand.
3. understand.
4. educated.
5. recognise.
6. recognise.
7. some.
8. self.
9. thought, meaning.
10. difficulty

TONE PRACTICE.

i.	ii.	iii.	iv.	v.
his.	at home.	have said.	knife.	how much ?
white.	in the city.	has come.	house.	what ?
what I have.	where ?	has gone.	plum.	how ?
yes.	there.	has seen.	hat.	thus.

EXERCISE.

1. Do you understand? (Three modes of expression). 2. What is the meaning of this? I do not know. 3. Can you write this character? 4. Do you understand this sentence? I understand it. 5. Do you recognise these characters? I recognise several. 6. Is that man educated? He is very well educated. 7. Do you know that gentleman? 8. He says himself he does not understand what you mean. 9. You do not understand the difficulties he has in his mind; I will explain them to you.

Transcription. Lesson 6. Part II.

\di `liu \khʌ. `ɕia.

VOCABULARIES.

1st Tone.	2nd Tone.	3rd Tone.	4th Tone.
120. chɪŋ.	124. wan.	127. tʃhu.	130. ɕiao.
121. jɪn.	125. ɕyə.	128. khou.	131. khʌ.
122. ʝɪŋ.	126. ɕi.	129. i.	132. b̥iɛn.
123. wən.			133. d̥zaɪ.
			134. ʝ̊iu.
			135. d̥zʌŋ.
			136. ʝ̊iao.

COMPOUND WORDS AND EXPRESSIONS.

11. ⁻ʃʌŋ·jɪn   13. ′ɕyə·ʃʌŋ   15. ˌi⁻ʝɪŋ   17. ′ɕyə`ɕiao
12. ⁻chɪŋ·tʃhu   14. ˌkhou·jɪn   16. ˌliaŋ`b̥iɛn   18. ⁻wən·ɕi

TONE PRACTICE.

vi.	vii.	viii.	ix.
⁻ɕiɛn −ʃʌŋ	⁻ʃu /fu	⁻chɪŋ ˌtʃhu	⁻thɪŋ \ʝ̊iɛn
′mɪŋ −thiɛn	′nan /weɪ	′laɪ ˌwaŋ	′lɪŋ \sueɪ
ˌb̥eɪ −b̥iɛn	ˌli /thou	⁻ɕiaŋ ˌni	ˌdzɯ \li
\i −sɯ	\jɛn /thaɪ	\d̥zɯ ˌʝ̊i	\g̊ao \su

EXERCISE.

10. `d̥zɤ·b̥ən ⁻ʃu ju ⁻san·ʃɪ `khʌ, ˌwɔ ˌi·ʝ̊ɪŋ ′ɕyə·liao ˌxao·ʝ̊i`khʌ. 11. khan′wan·liao `d̥zɤ i`khʌ, ʝ̊iu `khan d̥i⁻chi khʌ. 12. `d̥zɤ i`khʌ ˌxən·nan ′ɕyə, `na i`khʌ ˌjɛ d̥eɪ ⁻wən·ɕi ⁻wən·ɕi. 13. ni ⁻ʃuɔ·d̥ɪ `xua wɔ ′mei thɪŋ′mɪŋ·b̥aɪ, chɪŋ `d̥zaɪ ʃuɔ i`b̥iɛn. 14. ˌni ˌɕiɛ·wan `na·ɕiɛ `d̥zɯ, ˌwɔ \jao `khan·i`khan. 15. `na·weɪ ′ɕyə·ʃʌŋ·d̥ɪ ˌkhou·jɪn xən `d̥zʌŋ. 16. ⁻tha·d̥ɪ ⁻ʃʌŋ·jɪn xən ˌxao, ⁻ʃuɔ·d̥ɪ `xua jɛ ⁻chɪŋ·tʃhu. 17. ⁻ɕiɛn·ʃʌŋ ˌi·ʝ̊ɪŋ `ʝ̊iao·lə ˌʝ̊i `khʌ? 18. `na·g̊ə ′ɕyə·ɕiao·d̥ɪ ′ɕyə·ʃʌŋ ˌxən⁻d̥ɔ, ⁻ɕiɛn·ʃʌŋ ˌjɛ b̥uˌʃao.

Translation. Lesson 6. Part II.

VOCABULARIES.

1st Tone.	2nd Tone.	3rd Tone.	4th Tone.
120. pure.	124. finish.	127. clear.	130. school house.
121. sound.	125. learn.	128. mouth.	131. lesson.
122. past.	126. practice.	129. already.	132. a time.
123. warm, to review or practice.			133. again.
			134. then.
			135. correct.
			136. teach.

COMPOUND WORDS AND EXPRESSIONS.

11. voice.	13. scholar.	15. already.	17. school.
12. distinct.	14. pronunciation.	16. twice.	18. practice.

TONE PRACTICE.

vi.	vii.	viii.	ix.
teacher.	comfortable.	clear.	hear.
to-morrow.	worry.	intercourse.	fragments.
north side.	inside.	I think of you.	seeds.
meaning.	ink-slab.	oneself.	tell.

EXERCISE.

10. This book contains thirty lessons, I have already learned several lessons. 11. When (we) have finished reading this lesson, (we) will read the seventh. 12. This lesson is very difficult to learn, that lesson must also be practised. 13. I do not understand what you say, please say it over again. 14. When you have written those characters, I want to see them. 15. That student's pronunciation is very correct. 16. His voice is very good, and what he says is distinct. 17. How many lessons has the teacher taught up till now? 18. The number of scholars in that school is very large, and the number of teachers is not small either.

Transcription. Lesson 7. Part I.

ˌdi ˉchi ˌkhʌ. ˈʃaŋ.

VOCABULARIES.

1st Tone.	2nd Tone.	3rd Tone.	4th Tone.
137. g̊uan.	143. g̊uɔ.	145. ɟ̊iaŋ.	147. d̥zɔ.
138. d̥ʒuŋ.	144. laɪ.	146. d̥ʌŋ.	148. g̊uɔ.
139. jɪŋ.			149. ɕɪŋ.
140. thɪŋ.			150. g̊ueɪ.
141. a.			151. ɟ̊iɛn.
142. la [lə].			152. b̥i.
			153. khʌ.

COMPOUNDS WORDS AND EXPRESSIONS.

1. *ˉd̥ʒuŋˈg̊uɔ   3. ˉg̊uanˈxua   5. ˌxaoˉthɪŋ   7. ˈkhʌˉthɪŋ
2. *ˉjɪŋˈg̊uɔ   4. ˌxaoˈkhan   6. ˈkhʌ·ɹən   8. ˈg̊uɔˌɟ̊iaŋ

TONE PRACTICE.

i.	ii.	iii.	iv.
ˌd̥ao ˉɟ̊ia	ˈɕia ˉʃuaŋ	ˈd̥zueɪ ˉg̊ao	ˌthaɪ ˉd̥ɔ
ˉfa ˊja	ˌxən ˊmaŋ	ˌma ˊtshao	ˉd̥ʒuŋ ˊg̊uɔ
ˈchɪ ˌma	ˈg̊uɔ ˌɟ̊iaŋ	ˈthaɪ ˌɕiao	ˈʃɪ ˌwɔ
ˉʃuɔ ˋxua	ˉi ˈjaŋ	ˊxuan ˈjao	ˌchɪŋ ˈd̥zɔ

EXERCISE.

1. laɪ ˈkhʌ liao. ˊlaɪ·liao ˈkhʌ lə. ˈkhʌ ˊlaɪ·liao. 2. ˌchɪŋ d̥zaɪ·ˈkhʌˉthɪŋ·li ˈd̥zɔ·iˈd̥zɔ. 3. ˉɕiɛn·ʃʌŋ g̊ueɪ ˈɕɪŋ? ˈɟ̊iɛn ɕɪŋ *ˌli. 4. *ˌli ˉɕiɛn·ʃʌŋ ˌxao a? ˌxao; ˉɕiɛn·ʃʌŋ ˌxao? 5. ˌchɪŋ ˈd̥zɔ, ˌchɪŋ ˈd̥zɔ. 6. ˈg̊ueɪˊg̊uɔ ʃɪ ˌnaˊg̊uɔ? ˈb̥iˊg̊uɔ ʃɪ*ˉjɪŋ·g̊uɔ. 7. ˉɕiɛn·ʃʌŋ ˈxueɪ ʃuɔ *ˉd̥ʒuŋ·g̊uɔ ˈxua ma? ˊb̥u d̥a ˈxueɪ. 8. ˉɕiɛn·ʃʌŋ d̥i ˉg̊uan·xua xən ˌxao. (Ans.) ˈg̊uɔˌɟ̊iaŋ, ˈg̊uɔˌɟ̊iaŋ. 9. *ˉjɪŋ·g̊uɔ·d̥i ˉʃu ˈg̊ueɪ; *ˉd̥ʒuŋ·g̊uɔ·d̥i ˉʃu ˈɟ̊iɛn·iˌd̥iɛn. 10. ˊlaɪ·liao ˌliaŋ·weɪ ˈkhʌ·ɹən, jao ˈɟ̊iɛn ni. 11. ˌchɪŋ ˉtha·mən d̥zaɪˈkhʌˉthɪŋ·li ˌd̥ʌŋ·iˌd̥ʌŋ. 12. ˈna·weɪ ˊɕyə·ʃʌŋ ɕɪŋ ˊʃə·mə? ˉtha ɕɪŋ *ˉd̥ʒaŋ.

Translation. Lesson 7. Part I.

VOCABULARIES.

1st Tone.	2nd Tone.	3rd Tone.	4th Tone.
137. an official, a Mandarin.	143. kingdom, a state.	145. to praise.	147. sit.
138. middle.	144. come.	146. wait.	148. to pass.
139. flourishing.			149. surname.
140. hall.			150. dear, honourable
141. honorific particle.			151. cheap, humble.
142. past auxiliary.			152. unworthy.
			153. guest.

COMPOUND WORDS AND EXPRESSIONS.

1. China.
2. England.
3. Mandarin language.
4. beautiful, (to see).
5. beautiful, (to hear).
6. guest.
7. guest-hall.
8. over complimentary.

TONE PRACTICE.

i.	ii.	iii.	iv.
arrive home.	fall of frost.	very high.	too many.
to sprout.	very busy.	manger.	China.
ride a horse.	over complimentary.	too small.	it is I.
speak.	one kind, the same.	to want more.	please be seated.

EXERCISE.

1. A guest has come. A guest has come. The guest has come. 2. Ask him to take a seat in the guest-hall, 3. What is your name, sir? My name is Li. 4. How do you do, Mr. Li? I am well; how do you do, sir? 5. Please be seated. 6. Of what nationality are you? I am English. 7. Can you speak Chinese, sir? Not very well. 8. Your Mandarin, sir, is very good. (Ans.) You are too complimentary. 9. English books are expensive, Chinese books are somewhat cheaper. 10. Two guests have arrived and they want to see you. 11. Ask them to wait a little in the guest-hall. 12. What is that student's name? His name is Chang.

Transcription. Lesson 7. Part II.

˻di ˉchi ˻khʌ. ˋɕia.

VOCABULARIES.

1st Tone.	2nd Tone.	3rd Tone.	4th Tone.
154. wu.	160. tʃha.	166. wan.	169. faŋ.
155. g̊ʌ.	161. d̦iɛ.	167. b̦a.	170. chy.
156. xʌ.	162. na.	168. xuɔ.	
157. tʃha.	163. phan.		
158. d̦ao.	164. ʃao.		
159. ȷ̊ia.	165. nʌŋ.		
159a. [b̦a].			

COMPOUND WORDS AND EXPRESSIONS.

9. ′na ′laɪ
10. ′na ˋchy
11. ′na·liao ˋchy
12. ′tʃha ˍwan
13. ˉȷ̊ia·xuɔ

TONE PRACTICE.

v.	vi.	vii.	viii.
ˋd̦a ˉd̦ʒou	ˉtʃhun ˉchiu	ˉd̦ʒuaŋ ˉtshun	ˋʃaŋ ˉd̦uŋ
′tshuŋ ′thou	ˍwu ′fu	ˍwu ′lun	′phɪn ′chiuŋ
˧xao ˍd̦zou	ˋg̊uɔ ˍwu	˧jyn ˍd̦ʒun	˧luŋ ˍd̦zuŋ
ˉg̊ao ˋʃou	ˉʃu ˋphu	′b̦u ˋʃun	ˉchɪŋ ˋd̦ʒuŋ

EXERCISE.

13. ′nʌŋ·b̦u ′nʌŋ? ˋb̦u ′nʌŋ. ′nʌŋ. 14. ni ′nʌŋ chy b̦u ′nʌŋ ˋchy? ˋb̦u·nʌŋ ˋchy. 15. d̦zaɪ ˋna·g̊ə ′ɕyə·ɕiao ′nʌŋ·b̦u ′nʌŋ ɕyə *ˉd̦ʒuŋ·g̊uɔ ˋxua? ′nʌŋ ′ɕyə. 16. ′na ˉsan·g̊ə ′phan·d̦zɯ ′laɪ. 17. ˉb̦a ˋd̦ʒɤ ȷ̊i·g̊ə ′d̦iɛ·d̦zɯ ′na·liao ˋchy. 18. ˉb̦a ˋd̦ʒɤ·ɕiɛ ˍwan ˋfaŋ d̦zaɪ ˉɕi·wu·li. 19. ˉb̦a ˋna·ɕiɛ ′tʃha·wan ˉd̦u jao ′na ′laɪ. 20. ˋʃao·d̦zɯ ˉtʃha·d̦zɯ ′na·laɪ·liao ma? d̦u ′na·laɪ·liao. 21. ˋd̦ʒɤ ȷ̊i·b̦a ˉd̦ao·d̦zɯ ′b̦u·jao ˉg̊ʌ d̦zaɪ ˋd̦ʒɤ·ɪ; ˉd̦u jao ′na·chy. 22. khan ′wan·liao ˋd̦ʒɤ i ˋkhʌ, wɔ ˋȷ̊iu xʌ ′tʃha. 23. ′na liaŋ·wan ′tʃha chy, ˉg̊ʌ d̦zaɪ ˋkhʌ ˉthɪŋ·li. 24. ˉb̦a ˋd̦ʒɤ·ɕiɛ ˉȷ̊ia·xuɔ, ˋfaŋ d̦zaɪ ˉd̦uŋ·wu·li.

Translation. Lesson 7. Part II.

VOCABULARIES.

1st Tone.	2nd Tone.	3rd Tone.	4th Tone.
154. a room.	160. tea.	166. bowl.	169. to place, put down.
155. to place.	161. small plate.	167. c. of chairs, knives, jugs, &c. (in 1st Tone, to grasp).	170. go.
156. to drink.	162. take.		
157. fork.	163. plate.		
158. knife.	164. spoon.		
159. tools.	165. able.	168. tools.	
159a. [to grasp, cf. 167].			

COMPOUND WORDS AND EXPRESSIONS.

9. bring.
10. take away.
11. take away.
12. tea-cup.
13. furniture, implements, utensils.

TONE PRACTICE.

v.	vi.	vii.	viii.
continent.	spring and autumn.	villages.	to go east.
from the beginning.	the five beatitudes.	the five relationships.	poor.
good for travelling.	afternoon.	authorize.	altogether.
great age.	bookshop.	unfavourable.	weight.

EXERCISE.

13. Can you? I cannot. I can. 14. Can you go or not? I cannot go. 15. Is it possible to study Chinese in that school? It is possible. 16. Bring three plates. 17. Take away these few small plates. 18. Put these bowls in the West room. 19. Bring all those tea cups. 20. Have you brought the spoons and forks? They have all been brought. 21. Do not put these few knives here; take them all away. 22. When I have finished reading this lesson I am going to have tea. 23. Take two cups of tea and put them in the guest room. 24. Put these things in the East room.

Transcription. Lesson 8. Part I.

\di ⁻bɑ \khʌ. ˋʃaŋ.

VOCABULARIES.

1st Tone.	2nd Tone.	3rd Tone.	4th Tone.
171. dʒɔ.	174. tʃhuaŋ.	178. i.	182. ʃaŋ.
172. ȷ̈iaŋ.	175. phaŋ.	179. khʌ.	183. ɕia.
173. faŋ.	176. xu.	180. i.	184. dao.
	177. tʃhu.	181. di.	185. di.
			186. tʃhɤ.
			187. wɔ.

COMPOUND WORDS AND EXPRESSIONS.

1. \ʃaŋˊfaŋ
2. ˊtʃhuˌfaŋ
3. ˋwɔˌfaŋ
4. ˌphaŋˊb̥iɛn
5. ˌdiˑɕia
6. ˋdiˑɕia
7. ⁻ȷ̈iaŋˋjao
8. ˌkhʌˑi
9. ˊtʃhuˑdʒɯ
10. ˋdiˑfaŋ
11. ˊtʃhaˊxu
12. ˋfaŋˑɕia
13. ˋtʃhɤ\chy
14. ˊlaɪˋdao

TONE PRACTICE.

i.	ii.	iii.
⁻chɪŋ ⁻thaɪ	\ɕiɛn ⁻guan	ˌȷ̈iu ⁻b̥eɪ
ˊtshaɪ ˊlaɪ	⁻d̥uŋ ˊnan	ˊmən ˊmeɪ
ˌxɑo ˌd̥aɪ	ˌfan ˌwan	ˌnan ˌb̥eɪ
ˊliaŋ ˋkhuaɪ	-tʃhr \fan	ˌɕiao ˋmeɪ

iv.	v.
\d̥ao ⁻chi	\b̥u ⁻tʃhɪ
\b̥u ˊli	ˋdʒʌŋ ˊdʒɪ
-chiɛn ˌb̥i	ˌmaɪ ˌdʒɪ
-thiɛn ˌdi	ˊʃɪ \ʃɪ

EXERCISE.

1. ˌkhʌˑi b̥uˌkhʌˑi? ˋb̥uˌkhʌˑi. ˌkhʌˑi. 2. ˋdʒɤˑɕiɛ ⁻d̥uŋˑɕi, jao ⁻gʌ dzaɪ ˊʃəˑmə ˋdiˑfaŋ? 3. ˋʃaŋˊfaŋˑli ju ⁻sanˑdʒaŋ ⁻dʒɔˑdzɯ, ⁻dʒɔˑdzɯ ˊphaŋˑb̥iɛn ju ˋliuˑb̥a ˌiˑdzɯ. 4. ˊnaˑiˑb̥a ˊtʃhaˊxu laɪ, ˋfaŋ dzaɪ⁻dʒɔˑdzɯ\ʃaŋ. 5. ˋdʒɤˑɕiɛ ⁻d̥uŋˑɕi ˌkhʌˑi ˋfaŋˑɕia. 6. ⁻b̥a ˊtʃhuaŋˑdiˋɕiaˑdɪ ⁻d̥uŋˑɕi, ⁻d̥u jao ˊnaˑlaɪ. 7. ˋdʒɔˑdzɯˑˋʃaŋˑdi ⁻d̥aoˑdzɯ ⁻tʃhaˑdzɯ, ˌkhʌˑi ˋtʃhɤˑchy. 8. \wɔˊfaŋˑdɪ ˌiˑdzɯ xɑo ˋdzɔ. 9. ˋnaˑɕiɛ ⁻d̥uŋˑɕi ˌkhʌˑi ˋfaŋ dzaɪˋdiˑɕia ma? ˋb̥u ˌkhʌˑi. 10. ⁻b̥a ˋdʒɤˑɕiɛ ⁻ȷ̈iaˑxuɔ ⁻gʌ dzaɪˑtʃhuˊfaŋˑli, ˌkhʌˑiˊb̥u ˌkhʌˑi? ˌkhʌˑiˑdɪ. 11. ˋna liaŋˑweɪ ⁻ɕiɛnˑʃaŋ ⁻ȷ̈iaŋ ˊlaɪˑdao. 12. ⁻tha ju xənˋdaˑdɪ ˊfaŋˑdzɯ; ˌwɔˑdɪ ˊfaŋˑdzɯ ˊb̥uˋda.

Translation. Lesson 8. Part I.

VOCABULARIES.

1st Tone.	2nd Tone.	3rd Tone.	4th Tone.
171. table.	174. couch, divan.	178. chair.	182. upon, above.
172. about to.	175. side.	179. able.	183. below, down.
173. a place.	176. kettle, jug.	180. to use.	184. arrive.
	177. kitchen.	181. below, under	185. earth.
			186. clear away.
			187. to sleep.

COMPOUND WORDS AND EXPRESSIONS.

1. upper room.
2. kitchen.
3. bedroom.
4. beside.
5. below, underneath.
6. on the ground.
7. about to.
8. able, may.
9. a cook.
10. a place.
11. tea-pot.
12. put down.
13. clear away.
14. arrive.

TONE PRACTICE.

i.	ii.	iii.	iv.	v.
moss.	district magistrate.	winecup.	at the appointed time.	not to eat.
just come.	south-east.	eyebrow.	not far out.	straight.
good and bad.	rice-bowl.	north and south.	lead pencil.	buy paper.
two pieces.	eat food.	younger sister.	universe.	actual fact.

EXERCISE.

1. Will it do? It will not do. It will do. 2. Where do you want these things put? 3. In the upper room there are three tables, and by the side of the tables there are six chairs. 4. Bring a tea-pot and put it on the table. 5. Put these things down. 6. Bring all the things that are under the couch. 7. Clear away the knives and forks that are on the table. 8. The chairs in the bedroom are comfortable. 9. Will it do to put those things on the floor? It will not do. 10. Will it do to put these things in the kitchen? It will do. 11. Those two gentlemen are just about to arrive. 12. He has a very large house, my house is not large.

Transcription. Lesson 8. Part II.

\di ⁻ba \khʌ. ˋɕia.

VOCABULARIES.

1st Tone.	2nd Tone.	3rd Tone.	4th Tone.
188. tʃhɪ.	193. liaŋ.	195. ʃueɪ.	199. fan.
189. ğan.	194. xuan.	196. ɕi.	200. ʝɪŋ.
190. khaɪ.		197. liɛn.	201. ɪʌ.
191. ʃɪ.		198. ƃan.	202. fu.
192. tsha.			203. ɖʌŋ.

COMPOUND WORDS AND EXPRESSIONS.

15. ⁻tʃhɪˋfan   17. ⁻ʃɪ·fu   19. ˌƃanˋɖʌŋ
16. -fan⁻thɪŋ   18. ˋɖa·ʃɪ·fu   20. ⁻ğan·ʝɪŋ

TONE PRACTICE.

vi.	vii.	viiii.	ix.
-ƃa ⁻jin	ˌxao ⁻thɪŋ	ˌʃaŋ ⁻ʝiɛ	ˌxao ⁻thiɛn
ʹfeɪ ʹchin	ʹchi ˌchɪŋ	ˌwan ʹɖiɛ	ʹjaŋ ʹchiɛn
ˌjao ˌʝin	⁻ʃan ˌɖɪŋ	-ʃʌŋ ˌthiɛ	-i ˌɖiɛn
ˌɕiɛ ˋɕin	⁻thiɛn ˋmɪŋ	-i ˋchiɛ	-i ˋphiɛn

EXERCISE.

13. ʹna ˋɪʌ·ʃueɪ ʹlaɪ, ˌwɕ ˋjao ɕiˌliɛn. 14. ⁻khaɪ·ʃueɪ ˋkhuaɪ ʹlaɪ·lə. 15. ʹliaŋ·ʃueɪ ˌi·ʝɪŋ ʹna ʹlaɪ·liao. 16. ʹna i·xu ⁻wən·ʃueɪ ʹlaɪ. 17. ˋfan ˌxao·lə. ˋfan xuan ʹmeɪ·xao. 18. ʹtʃha ʹliaŋ·lə, na ˋɪʌ·ɖɪ laɪ. 19. ⁻ɕiɛn·ʃʌŋ xuan ⁻tʃhɪ·ƃu⁻tʃhɪ? xuan ⁻tʃhɪ. ˋƃu· tʃhɪ·liao. 20. ʹxuan ju ⁻khaɪˌʃueɪ, ni ˋjao·ƃuˋjao? ʹxuan ˋjao. ƃuˋjao·liao. 21. ⁻ƃa ˋɖʒɤ·ɕiɛ ʹphan·ɖzɯ ˌɕi·iˌɕi. 22. ˋɖʒɤ·ɕiɛ ˌƃan·ɖʌŋ ƃu ⁻ğan·ʝɪŋ, ˌkhʌ.i ⁻tsha·i⁻tsha. 23. ˌkhʌ.i ˋwən·wən ʹtʃhu·ɖzɯ fan ʹɖɤ·lə ma? xuan ʹmeɪʹɖɤ. 24. ˋɖa·ʃɪ·fu ⁻ʃuɔ, fan ʹɖɤ·lə; chɪŋ ⁻ɕiɛn·ʃʌŋ ⁻tʃhɪˋfan.

Translation. Lesson 8. Part II.

VOCABULARIES.

1st Tone.	2nd Tone.	3rd Tone.	4th Tone.
188. eat.	193. cool.	195. water.	199. rice, food.
189. dry.	194. still, yet.	196. to wash.	200. pure.
190. to open, to boil.		197. face.	201. hot.
191. teacher.		198. board, stool.	202. teacher, superintendent.
192. to rub, to polish.			203. stool.

COMPOUND WORDS AND EXPRESSIONS.

15. eat
16. dining-room.
17. teacher, title of servant or artisan.
18. head servant, a cook.
19. stool.
20. clean.

TONE PRACTICE.

vi.	vii.	viii.	ix.
the eight notes of the scale.	good to hear.	to go on to the street.	a fine day.
birds.	the seven emotions	cups and saucers.	dollars.
important.	crest of a hill.	cast iron.	a little.
write a letter.	Divine Will.	all.	a slice.

EXERCISE.

13. Bring some hot water; I want to wash my face. 14. Boiling water will be here soon. 15. The cold water has already been brought. 16. Bring a jug of warm water. 17. Dinner (or other meal) is ready. Dinner is not yet ready. 18. The tea is cold, bring some hot. 19. Will you take some more to eat, sir? Yes, I will take some more. I do not want any (more.) 20. There is still some boiling water left, do you want any (more)? I do want some more. I do not want any (more). 21. Wash these plates. 22. These stools are not clean; give them a polish. 23. Ask the cook if dinner is ready. It is not yet ready. 24. The cook says that dinner is ready, will you please dine, sir.

Transcription. Lesson 9. Part I.

\ḍi ˌʝiu \khʌ. \ʃaŋ.

VOCABULARIES.

1st Tone.	2nd Tone.	3rd Tone.	4th Tone.
204. ḍʒɪ.	205. thiao.	213. sao.	216. ʃɪ.
	206. ḍʒɔ.	214. ḍʒou.	217. ḍao.
	207. liu.	215. ʃɪ.	218. g̊aɪ.
	208. xʌ.		219. tshɔ.
	209. ɕɪŋ.		220. juŋ.
	210. tshuŋ.		
	211. thou.		
	212. waŋ.		

COMPOUND WORDS AND EXPRESSIONS.

1. ⁻ḍʒɪ·ḍao　3. ⁻tshuŋ ⸝ thou　5. \juŋ·ḍʒɔ　7. \ḍa \g̊aɪ
2. ′xʌ \ʃɪ　4. ′thiao·ḍʒou　6. \juŋ·ḅu·ḍʒɔ

TONE PRACTICE.

i.	ii.	iii.	iv.
\ḅi ⁻ɕy	\g̊uɔ ⁻ʝyn	ˌḅu ⁻chyə	\ḍa ⁻chyan
′chi ′ly	⁻xeɪ ⸝jyn	\ḍa ⸝ɕyə	ˌḅən ⸝jyan
\ɕia ˌjy	\ḅu ˌjyn	\ɕia ˌɕyə	⁻thiao ˌɕyan
′thuŋ \chy	ˌg̊u \ɕyn	ˌman \jyə	ˌma \ʝyan

EXERCISE.

1. ⁻ḍʒɪ·ḍao \ḅu·ḍʒɪ \ḍao? \ḅu·ḍʒɪ \ḍao. ⁻ḍʒɪ·ḍao. 2. \ḍʒɤ·ɕiɛ ⁻ʝia·xuɔ \ḅu·xao ˌʃɪ. 3. \ḍʒɤ·ɕiɛ ′phan·ḍzɯ ′xʌ·ʃɪ ḅu ′xʌ·ʃɪ? 4. ′ḅu·juŋ \na·ɕiɛ ˌwan lə, ˌkhʌ·i \na·chy. 5. ni ⁻ʃuɔ·ḍɪ ḅu ⁻chɪŋ·tʃhu, ˌkhʌ·i ′tshuŋ′thou \ḍzaɪ ⁻ʃuɔ. 6. \ḍʒɤ·ɕiɛ ⁻ʃu ni \juŋ·ḍə′ḍʒɔ \juŋ·bu′ḍʒɔ. 7. na ′thiao·ḍʒou ′laɪ, ˌsao·sao \ḍʒɤ·g̊ə ⁻wu·ḍzɯ. 8. ḅu \tshɔ, \na·ɕiɛ ⁻ʃu ⁻du \ḍzaɪ·ʃu′faŋ·li. 9. \ḍʒɤ·g̊uan ˌḅi ′ɕiŋ·ḅu′ɕɪŋ? \ḅu′ɕɪŋ, na ˌxao·ḍɪ ′laɪ. 10. ni \jao·ḍɪ \na·ɕiɛ ⁻ʝia·xuɔ ⁻du \ḍzaɪ·tʃhu′faŋ·li, ′ni ⁻ḍʒɪ·ḍao \ḅu·ḍʒɪ \ḍao? wɔ ⁻ḍʒɪ·ḍao·liao. 11. *′waŋ ⁻ɕien·ʃʌŋ \ḍzaɪ·ʃu′faŋ·li ma? wɔ \ḅu·ḍʒɪ \ḍao; \ḍa \g̊aɪ \ḍzaɪ \na·li nɪ. 12. fan ⁻thɪŋ·li ju ′ḍiɛ·ḍzɯ ˌwan ma? ḍa \g̊aɪ ˌju.

Translation. Lesson 9. Part I.

VOCABULARIES.

1st Tone.	2nd Tone.	3rd Tone.	4th Tone.
204. know.	205. broom.	213. to sweep.	216. pattern.
	206. pres. participle (aux.).	214. broom.	217, say, reason
		215. employ.	218. probably.
	207. to keep.		219. incorrect.
	208. with.		220. to use.
	209. go, do.		
	210. from.		
	211. head.		
	212. prince, a surname.		

COMPOUND WORDS AND EXPRESSIONS.

1. know.
2. suitable.
3. from the beginning.
4. broom.
5. needed.
6. not needed.
7. probably.

TONE PRACTICE.

i.	ii.	iii.	iv.
must.	head of the state.	fill a vacancy.	complete collection
to ride a donkey.	dark clouds.	college.	origin.
to rain.	to refuse.	to snow.	to select.
to go together.	ancient teaching.	full moon.	a stable.

EXERCISE.

1. Do you know? I do not know. I know. 2. These things are inconvenient to use. 3. Are these plates suitable? 4. We do not need those bowls. Take them away. 5. You are not speaking clearly, say it over again from the beginning. 6. Do you need these books? 7. Bring a broom and sweep this room. 8. You are correct, those books are all in the library. 9. Will this pen do? No; bring [me] a good one. 10. Those things you want are all in the kitchen; do you know? I know. 11. Is Mr. Wang in the library? I do not know; probably he is there. 12. Are there cups and saucers in the dining room? Probably there are.

Transcription. Lesson 9. Part II.

ˎdi ˌȡiu ˎkhʌ. ˋɕia.

VOCABULARIES.

1st Tone.	2nd Tone.	3rd Tone.	4th Tone.
221. ni [nɪ].	224. chɪŋ.	227. ȡzən.	231. ḅan.
222. jɪn.	225. maŋ.	228. ȡɪn.	232. weɪ.
223. ḍaŋ.	226. jyan.	229. fa.	233. ȡiɛn.
223a. [fa].		230. thɔ.	234. ʃr.
			235. ʃun.
			236. jaŋ.

COMPOUND WORDS AND EXPRESSIONS.

8. ˌɕiao⁻ɕɪn
9. ⁻jɪn·weɪ
10. ʹjyanʹlaɪ
11. ˌḅənʹlaɪ
12. ˋʃɪ·chɪŋ
13. ˌȡzə·mə
14. ˌȡzə·məˋjaŋ
15. ˋjaoˌȡɪn
16. ˌxao·tʃhu
17. ˋḅan·fa
18. ˋweɪʹʃə·mə
19. ˋȡʒə·mə
20. ˋna·mə
21. ⁻ḍo·mə
22. ˌthɔ·ḍaŋ
23. ˋʃun·ḍaŋ
24. ˋȡʒɤ·jaŋ
25. ˋna·jaŋ

EXERCISE.

13. ˋȡʒɤ ʃɪ weɪʹʃə·mə? ˋna ʃɪ weɪʹʃə·mə? 14. ˋna·ḡə ʹḅu·jao ˌȡɪn. 15. ˌli·thou ju ʹnan·tʃhu, jao ˌɕiao·ɕɪn ˋḅan. 16. ˋna·ȡiɛn ˋʃɪ·chɪŋ xənˋʃun·ḍaŋ, ˌxaoˋḅan. 17. ˋȡʒɤ·ȡiɛn ˋʃɪ·chɪŋ jaoˌȡɪn, ni ˌȡzə·mə ˋḅan nɪ? 18. ˋna·ȡiɛn ˋʃɪ tha ˋḅan·ḍɪ ˌȡzə·məˋjaŋ? 19. ˌni weɪʹʃə·mə ˋna·jaŋ ˋḅan nɪ? 20. ˋna·ȡiɛn ˋʃɪ ni ˋḅan·ḍɪ xənˌthɔ·ḍaŋ. 21. ˋna·ḡə ˋḅan·fa ˋmeɪ·ju ˌxao·tʃhu. 22. ˋȡʒɤ·ȡiɛn ˋʃɪ ˌḅənʹlaɪ ˌxən nanˋḅan. 23. ⁻tha weɪʹʃə·mə ḅuˋchy? ⁻jɪn·weɪ ⁻tha xənʹmaŋ. 24. ˋna·ḡə ⁻ɕiaŋ·ḍzɯ ⁻ḍo·mə ˋḍa? ˋȡiu·ʃɪ ˋȡʒɤ·mə ˋḍa. 25. ˌwɔ meɪˋchy ⁻jɪn·weɪ ⁻tha meɪˋȡiao wɔ ˋchy. 26. ʹjyan·laɪ ˋȡʒɤ·ȡiɛn ˋʃɪ·chɪŋ ˋḅu·xaoˋḅan.

Translation. Lesson 9. Part II.

VOCABULARIES.

1st Tone.	2nd Tone.	3rd Tone.	4th Tone.
221. interrog. particle.	224. feelings.	227. how.	231. manage.
222. a cause.	225. busy.	228. urgent.	232. because.
223. right, correct	226. origin.	229. law.	233. c. of affairs.
223a. [method].		230. satisfactory.	234. affairs.
			235. favourable.
			236. a sort, a kind.

COMPOUND WORDS AND EXPRESSIONS.

8. be careful.
9. because.
10. originally.
11. originally.
12. affairs.
13. how?
14. in what way?
15. important.
16. a benefit.
17. method of management.
18. why?
19. in this way, to this extent.
20. in that way, to that extent
21. how much?
22. satisfactory.
23. smoothly.
24. thus, in this way.
25. in that way.

EXERCISE.

13. Why is this? Why is that? 14. That does not matter. 15. There are difficulties in (this affair); you must be careful how you manage it. 16. That affair goes very smoothly; it is easy to manage. 17. This matter is important; how do you propose to manage it? 18. How has he managed that affair? 19. Why do you manage (it) in that way? 20. You have managed that affair very satisfactorily. 21. There is no good in that way of managing it. 22. This affair in itself is very difficult to manage. 23. Why does he not go? Because he is very busy. 24. How large is that box? It is just this size. 25. I have not gone, because he did not tell me to go. 26. This affair was awkward to manage from the start.

Transcription. Lesson 10. Part I.

˻di ˈʃɿ ˻khʌ. ˋʃaŋ.

VOCABULARIES.

1st Tone.	2nd Tone.	3rd Tone.	4th Tone.
237. g̈uan.	243. mən.	247. b̦eɪ.	251. b̦i.
238. ɕiaŋ.	244. nan.	248. sɔ.	252. lu.
239. ʝɪŋ.	245. li.	249. li.	253. ʝɪn.
240. thuŋ.	246. g̈ʌ.	250. jyan.	254. dʒu.
241. dʒou.			255. tʃha.
242. tʃhɤ.			

COMPOUND WORDS AND EXPRESSIONS.

1. ˉkhaɪ·khaɪ
2. ˉg̈uan·ʃaŋ
3. ˉi˻jaŋ
4. ˋtʃha·b̦uˈli
5. ˋtʃha·b̦uˉdɔ
6. ˋb̦uˈli
7. ˈb̦u˻d̦a·li
8. ˉɕiaŋˈg̈ʌ
9. *˻b̦eɪˉʝɪŋ
9a. *ˈnan-ʝɪŋ
10. *ˉthuŋ·dʒou

TONE PRACTICE.

i.	ii.	iii.	iv.
ˉʝyan ˉdʒɯ	˻dʒɔ ˉtʃhɤ	ˋɹən ˉdʒən	˗g̈ua ˉfʌŋ
ˈən ˻tshɯ	ˉtʃhɤ ˈdʒɤ	ˋg̈ʌ ˈɹən	˻b̦u ˈnʌŋ
ˋb̦u ˗sɯ	ˈnan ˗ʃɤ	ˋliu ˻b̦ən	ˉthiɛn ˻lʌŋ
˗ɕiɛ ˻dʒɯ	ˋg̈uan ˻tʃhɤ	ˉfa ˋmən	ˋɕia ˋʃʌŋ

EXERCISE.

1. ˉkhaɪ·khaɪ ˈmən. ˉg̈uan·ʃaŋ ˈmən. ˋb̦i·ʃaŋ ˈmən. ˗sɔ·ʃaŋ ˈmən. 2. ˋna ˻liaŋ·g̈ə ˈtʃha·wan ˋb̦u·i˻jaŋ. 3. ˋdʒɤ ˻liaŋ·g̈ə ˈɹən·d̦ɪ ˋi·sɯ ˈtʃha·b̦uˉdɔ i˻jaŋ. 4. ˋdʒɤ·g̈ə ˋd̦i·faŋ li ˋna·g̈ə ˋd̦i·faŋ ˉdɔ·mə ˻jyan. 5. tshuŋ ˋdʒɤ·li d̦ao ˋna·li ˋb̦u˻jyan ; ju ˋliu·ʃɹ ˉd̦ɔ li ˋd̦i. 6. ˋna·g̈ə ˋd̦i·faŋ xən ˋʝɪn, ʃɹ·b̦u·ʃɹ? ˈb̦uˋtshɔ, li ˋdʒɤ·li ˈb̦u·g̈uɔ ˉb̦a·li ˋlu. 7. tshuŋ *˻b̦eɪˉʝɪŋ d̦ao *ˉthuŋ·dʒou ˋb̦uˈʃə·mə ˻jyan. 8. ˉtha ˉʃuɔ·d̦ɪ b̦uˈli. 9. ˋna·g̈ə ˈɹən·d̦ɪ ˋi·sɯ ˈb̦u·d̦aˈli. 10. ˋna ˻liaŋ·g̈ə ˋd̦i·faŋ ɕiaŋˈg̈ʌ ˉdɔ·mə ˻jyan? 11. *ˉdʒaŋ ˉɕiɛn·ʃaŋ ʃɹ dʒɔˉtʃhɤ ˈlaɪ·d̦ɪ. 12. ˉtha·mən ˋdʒu dʒaɪ ˈʃə·mə ˋd̦i·faŋ? 13. ˉɕiɛn·ʃaŋ g̈ueɪ ˋtʃhu? ˋb̦i tʃhu ʃɹ *ˈnanˉʝɪŋ. 14. ˻ni·d̦i ˋb̦an·fa xʌ ˉtha·d̦ɪ ˋb̦an·fa ˋtʃha·b̦uˈli i˻jaŋ.

Translation. Lesson 10. Part I.

VOCABULARIES.

i.	ii.	iii.	iv.
237. shut, to bolt.	243. door.	247. north.	252. to close.
238. mutual.	244. south.	248. lock.	252. road.
239. the capital.	245. distant from.	249. mile (Chinese).	253. near.
240. general, to penetrate.	246. separate.	250. distant.	254. dwell.
241. district, city.			255. different.
242. vehicle.			

COMPOUND WORDS AND EXPRESSIONS.

1. open.
2. shut.
3. the same.
4. not very different.
5. not very different.
6. not far wrong.
7. not very far wrong.
8. separate.
9. Peking.
9a. Nanking.
10. T'ungchou.

TONE PRACTICE.

i.	ii.	iii.	iv.
subscribe money.	ride in a cart.	acknowledge the truth.	the wind is blowing.
kindness.	cart rut.	each person.	unable.
will not die.	difficult to part with.	six volumes.	cold weather.
write.	connected.	to be melancholy.	surplus.

EXERCISE.

1. Open the door. Bolt the door. Close the door. Lock the door. 2. Those two tea cups are not the same. 3. The meaning of what these two people say is much the same. 4. How far is this place from that? 5. It is not very far from here to that place; it is sixty odd li. 6. That place is very near, is it not? You are right, it is not more than eight li from here. 7. From Peking to T'ungchou is not very far. 8. What he says is not far wrong. 9. That man's meaning is not very far out. 10. How far apart are those two places? 11. Mr. Chang came by cart. 12. Where do they live? 13. Where is your home, sir? My home is at Nanking. 14. Your plan is much the same as his.

Transcription. Lesson 10. Part II.

\di ′ʃɪ \khʌ. ′ɕia.

VOCABULARIES.

1st Tone.	2nd Tone.	3rd Tone.	4th Tone.
256. ʝiɛ.	258. ʃɪ.	259. maɪ.	260. maɪ.
257. ʃaŋ.		259a. [ʃaŋ].	261. phu.
			262. mu.
			263. dzɔ.
			264. ʝia.
			265. diɛn.
			266. ba.
			267. ʝiɛ.

COMPOUND WORDS AND EXPRESSIONS.

11. ˎmaɪ ˋmaɪ
12. ˋfan ˋdiɛn
13. ′ʝaŋ ′chiɛn
14. ˋʝia·chiɛn
15. ′ʃɪ ˋdzaɪ
16. ˋmu·thou.

EXERCISE.

15. ˎmaɪ·bu ˎmaɪ? ˋmaɪ·bu ˋmaɪ? 16. ⁻tha ʃɪ dzɔ ˎmaɪ· ˋmaɪ·dɪ ′ɹən. 17. ⁻tha ʃɪ ⁻ʃaŋ·ʝiɛ·di ′ɹən. 18. ˎni ʃaŋ ˎna·ɹ ˋchy? ˎʃaŋ ⁻ʝiɛ chy. 19. ˎʃaŋ ⁻ʝiɛ chy dzɔ ′ʃə·mə nɪ? ˎmaɪ ⁻duŋ·ɕɪ chy. 20. ˋdʒɤ·ɡə⁻di·faŋ·dɪ ˎmaɪ ˋmaɪ xən ˋda. 21. ˋda⁻ʝiɛ·ʃaŋ·dɪ ˋphu·dzɯ xən⁻dɔ. 22. ⁻tha ˋjao·dɪ ˋʝia·chiɛn xən ˋda. 23. ˋna·ɡə ′faŋ·dzɯ ′ʃɪ·dzaɪ ˎxao, ˎmaɪ·dɪ xən ˋɡueɪ ma? 24. ⁻tha sɔ ˋmaɪ· dɪ ˋna·dʒaŋ ′tʃhuaŋ ʃɪ ˋmu·thou·dɪ. 25. ˋna ˎliaŋ·ba ˎi·dzɯ ˎjɛ ʃɪ ˋmu·thou ˋdzɔ·dɪ. 26. ˋna ⁻i·ɡə ′tʃha·wan ʃɪ ⁻i·khuaɪ ⁻san·mao chiɛn ˎmaɪ·dɪ. 27. ˋda⁻ʝiɛ·ʃaŋ·dɪ ˋfan ˋdiɛn xən ˋɡueɪ. 28. ˎɕiao· ɕɪn ba, ′bu·jao ˋban ˋtshɔ·liao. 29. ⁻tha bu ˎmaɪ ⁻jin·weɪ ′meɪ·ju ′chiɛn.

Translation. Lesson 10. Part II.

VOCABULARY.

1st Tone.	2nd Tone.	3rd Tone.	4th Tone.
256. street.	258. real.	259. buy.	260. sell.
257. commerce.		259a. [go to]	261. shop.
			262. wood, tree.
			263. make, do.
			264. price.
			265. inn, shop.
			266. to finish, imperative particle.
			267. world.

COMPOUND WORDS AND EXPRESSIONS.

11. trade.
12. restaurant, hotel
13. dollars.
14. price.
15. really.
16. wood.

EXERCISE.

15. Will you buy? Will you sell? 16. He is a tradesman. 17. He is a merchant. 18. Where are you going? I am going on to the street. 19. What are you going on to the street to do? I am going to buy some things. 20. There is a great deal of business in this place. 21. There are a great many shops in the High Street. 22. He is asking a very big price. 23. That is certainly a fine house; was it very dear? 24. That couch he sold is a wooden one. 25. Those two chairs are also made of wood. 26. That tea cup was bought for $1.30. 28. The restaurants in the High Street are very dear. 28. Be careful, do not make a mistake in managing (that affair) 29. He does not buy because he has no money.

Transcription. Lesson 11. Part I.

ˋdi ´ʃɪ⁻i ˋkhʌ. ˋʃaŋ.

VOCABULARIES.

1st Tone.	2nd Tone.	3rd Tone.	4th Tone.
268. tʃhuaŋ.	271. chiaŋ.	277. ḅi.	280. x̥u.
269. xua.	272. ḅiɛ.	278. g̊an.	281. ḁ̊ia.
270. ḓʒən.	273. ɪu.	279. san.	282. ḁao.
	274. ʃɪ.	279a. [sɔ].	283. g̊ʌŋ.
	275. jyan.		284. ḁ̊iao.
	276. phən.		

COMPOUND WORDS AND EXPRESSIONS.

1. ˋjao·ʃɪ
2. ʃuˋɟ̥ia·dzɯ
3. ⁻tʃhuaŋ·xu
4. xuaˊjuan
5. xuaˊphən
6. ˌḅiˌɟ̥iao
7. ˌɟ̥iaoˌḅi
8. ˋḅuˊɪu
9. ˌg̊an·ḅuˋʃaŋ
9a. [ˊʃɪ·ḓzaɪ]

EXERCISE.

1. ˋdʒɤ·g̊ə ⁻ɕiaŋ·dzɯ ḅi ˋna·g̊ə ⁻ɕiaŋ·dzɯ ˋda. 2. ˋdʒɤ·g̊ə ˋjao·ʃɪ ˌɟ̥iao·ḅi ˋna·g̊ə ˋjao·ʃɪ xaoˌʃɪ. 3. ˋdʒɤ·ɟ̥iɛn ˋʃɪ ˌɟ̥iao·ḅi ˋna·ɟ̥iɛn ˋʃɪ ˋg̊ʌŋ ḅu·xaoˋḅan. 4. ⁻duŋ·wu ⁻ɕɪ·wu ⁻du ˋḅu·ɪu ˌḅeɪ·wu ˌxao. 5. ˋna·g̊ə ʃuˋɟ̥ia·dzɯ xuan ˋḅu·ɪu ḅuˌmaɪ ˌxao. 6. ⁻ɕi·ḅiɛn·dɪ ⁻tʃhuaŋ·xu ˌg̊an·ḅu·ʃaŋ ⁻duŋ·ḅiɛn·dɪ ˋda. 7. ˋdʒɤ·g̊ə ˌfa·dzɯ ḅi ⁻na·g̊ə ˌfa·dzɯ ˊchiaŋ. 8. ˋdʒɤ·ɕiɛ ⁻xua ˌxao; ⁻ɕi ˊjyan·dzɯ·dɪ ⁻xua ˋg̊ʌŋˌxao. 9. ˌɕiao·ɕɪn ˋḅa; ˊḅiɛ ˋtshɔ·liao. 10. ˋna·ḅa ˌsan ⁻dʒən ˌxao, ˌmaɪ ḅa. 11. ˋna·g̊ə ˊɪən xən ˋʃɪ·ḓzaɪ. 12. ˋna ˌliaŋ·sɔ ˊfaŋ·dzɯ, ˌna i·sɔ ˌxao nɪ, ˌkhʌ·i ˌḅi·ɟ̥iao ˌḅi·ɟ̥iao. 13. ˊnan·ɟ̥iɛˋʃaŋ·dɪ ˊfaŋ·dzɯ, ḅi ˌḅeɪ·ɟ̥iɛˋʃaŋ·dɪ ˋda. 14. ⁻duŋ·ḅiɛn·dɪ ⁻xua·jyan xaoˋkhan, ˌli·ḅiɛn·dɪ ⁻xua xən ⁻dɔ. 15. ˌwɔ khan ˋdʒɤ·g̊ə ˊjyan·dzɯ ˊmeɪ·ju ˋna·g̊ə ˌxao. 16. ˋdʒɤ i·g̊ə ʃuˋɟ̥ia·dzɯ ḅi ˋna i·g̊ə ˋda·dɪ ⁻dɔ·lə.

Translation. Lesson 11. Part I.

VOCABULARIES.

1st Tone.	2nd Tone.	3rd Tone.	4th Tone.
268. window.	271. excellent.	277. compare.	280. door.
269. flower.	272. do not, another	278. pursue.	281. frame.
270. true.	273. like, as.	279. umbrella.	282. key.
	274. key.	279a.[c.of houses].	283. still more.
	275. garden.		284. compare.
	276. basin.		

COMPOUND WORDS AND EXPRESSIONS.

1. key.
2. book shelves.
3. window.
4. flower garden.
5. flower pot.
6. compare.
7. compared wuth.
8. not equal to.
9. unable to do, overtake, not equal to.
9a. [real, sincere].

EXERCISE.

1. This box is larger than that one. 2. This key is a better fit than that one. 3. This affair is still more difficult to manage than that one. 4. The north room is better than both the east and west rooms. 5. You had still better not buy those book shelves. 6. The west window is not so large as the east window. 7. This plan is better than that one. 8. These flowers are fine, but those in the west garden are still finer. 9. Take care, don't make a mistake. 10. That umbrella is excellent, buy it. 11. That man is very sincere. 12. Compare those two houses and see which is the better. 13. The house in South Street is larger than the one in North Street. 14. The east garden is beautiful ; there are a great many flowers in it. 15. I do not think this garden is so beautiful as that one. 16. This book-case is very much larger than that one.

Transcription. Lesson 11. Part II.

ˋdi ʹʃɪ ˉi ˋkhʌ. ˋɕia.

VOCABULARIES.

1st Tone.	2nd Tone.	3rd Tone.	4th Tone.
285. tʃhu.	288. phʌŋ.	289. ju.	296. ʝɪn.
286. fa.		290. dzou.	297. pha.
287. ḅaŋ.		291. khuŋ.	298. ḍʒɪ.
		292. ʃu.	299. thaɪ.
		293. ḍɪŋ.	300. jyə.
		294. ḅi.	301. dzueɪ.
		295. tshɯ.	302. ḍʒu.

COMPOUND WORDS AND EXPRESSIONS.

10. ˋʝɪn·laɪ 14. ʹna·ʝɪn ʹlaɪ 18. ʹphʌŋ·ju 22. ˌkhuŋˋpha·
11. ˉtʃhu·chy 15. ʹnaˉtʃhu·laɪ 19. ˉɕiaŋˌxao 23. ʹjyəˉfa
12. ˋʝɪn·chy 16. ʹnaˋʝɪn·chy 20. ˞ḅi ˌtshɯ
13. ˉtʃhu·laɪ 17. ʹnaˉtʃhu·chy 21. ˉḅaŋ·ḍʒu

EXERCISE.

17. ˉtha·mən du ˉtʃu·chy·liao. 18. ˌchɪŋ *ˌliˉɕiɛn·ʃʌŋ ˋʝɪn·laɪ 19. ˋna ˞ʝi·ḅən ˉʃu ˋna·ʝɪn ˋchy·liao. 20. *ˉdʒaŋ ˉɕiɛn·ʃʌŋ dzaɪ ˉwu·lɪ, ˋʝiu·jao ˉtʃhu·laɪ. 21. ˋnaʃɪtha ˋdzɯ ˌʝi ˋdzɔ·dɪ ˋʃɪ. 22. ˋna·ʝiɛn ˋʃɪ ˌkhuŋ·pha tha ˋdzɯ ˌʝi ˋḅu·nʌŋ ˋḅan ; ˌni deɪ ˉḅaŋ· ḍʒu ˉtha. 23. ˉtha jao ʃaŋ *ˌḅeɪ·ʝɪŋ ˋchy, ˋʝiu khuaɪ ˌdzou·lə. 24. ˌwɔ·dɪ ʹphʌŋ·ju ʹlaɪ·liao. 25. ˋna ˌliaŋ·ḡə ʹɹən ˌḅɪ·tshɯ ˌxən ɕiaŋˌxao. 26. ˉtha ˉdʒɪˉdɔ ḡeɪ ˋliu·ʃɪ·khuaɪ ʹchiɛn. 27. ˋna ˌʝi·ḡə ʹxʌ·dzɯ dzueɪˋda·dɪ ˉdɔ·mən ˋda? 28. ˋna·ḡə ˌfa·dzɯ ˌdɪŋ ˌxao, ˌkhʌ·i ˋna·jaŋ ˋḅan. 29. ˋdʒɤ ˌliaŋ·ḅa ˌi·dzɯ thaɪˋda. 30. ˋna ˌɕiɛ·ḡə ˋxʌ·dzɯ, ʃu ˋna i·ḡə ˌɕiao·dɪ ˌxao. 31. ˌni chy ˌḡeɪ wɔ ˌmaɪ i·dʒaŋ ˉdʒɔ·dzɯ, jyəˌɕiao jyəˌxao. 32. ˌkhuŋ·pha ˋna·ʝiɛn ˋʃɪ ˋjyə·faḍɪ ˋḅu·xao ˋḅan lə. 33. ʹxuan·ʃɪ dzou ˋda· ḍao ˌxao, ˌɕiaoˋḍao ˉdʒən·nanˌdzou. 34. ˋdʒɪˌʃao ˌdeɪ chy ˉsan·ḡə ʹɹən. 35. ʹlaɪ·liao ˉi·ɕiɛ ʹɹən, ˉtha·mən du ˋʝin·chy·lə.

Translation. Lesson 11. Part II.

VOCABULARIES.

1st Tone.	2nd Tone.	3rd Tone.	4th Tone.
285. go out.	288. friend.	289. friend.	296. enter.
286. put forth.		290. go.	297. fear.
287. help.		291. fear.	298. most.
		292. belong to.	299. extremely.
		293. very.	300. all the more.
		294. that.	301. most.
		295. this.	302. help.

COMPOUND WORDS AND EXPRESSIONS.

10. come in.	14. bring in.	18. friend.	22. fear, lest.
11. go out.	15. bring out.	19. friendly.	23. all the more.
12. go in.	16. take in.	20. mutual.	
13. come out.	17. take out.	21. to help.	

EXERCISE.

17. They have all gone out. 18. Ask Mr. Li to come in. 19. Those books have been taken in. 20. Mr. Chang is indoors, he is coming out presently. 21. That was done by himself. 22. I am afraid he cannot manage that affair by himself, you must help him. 23. He is going to Peking; he will soon have started. 24. My friend has come. 25. Those two people are great friends. 26. The most he will give is $60. 27. How large is the largest of those cases? 28. That plan is splendid, manage (the affair) in that way. 29. These two chairs are too large. 30. Of those cases the small one is the best. 31. Go and buy a table for me; the smaller the better. 32. I fear that affair will be all the more difficult to manage. 33. You had better go by the main road, the small roads are very difficult to travel. 34. At the least three men must go. 35. Several people have arrived, they have all gone in.

Transcription. Lesson 12. Part I.

`di /ʃɪ `ʌɪ `khʌ. `ʃaŋ.

VOCABULARIES.

1st Tone.	2nd Tone.	3rd Tone.	4th Tone.
303. chɪn.	308. nan.	312. ny̥.	316. ʝi.
304. ɕiuŋ.	309. niɛn.	313. ʝiɛ.	317. sueɪ.
305. dʒuaŋ.	310. g̊ʌ.	314. mu.	318. meɪ.
306. ʝia.	311. xuɔ.	315. lao.	319. fu.
307. g̊ʌ.			320. di.
			321. chi.
			322. dʒuŋ.
			322a.[ʃao].

COMPOUND WORDS AND EXPRESSIONS.

1. `fu·chɪn
2. ˌmu·chɪn
3. `fu ˌmu
4. ⁻g̊ʌ·g̊ʌ
5. ⁻ɕiuŋ·di
6. `di·ɕiuŋ
7. ˌʝiɛˌʝiɛ
8. `meɪ·meɪ
9. ˌʝiɛ`meɪ
10. `thaɪ·thaɪ
11. ′niɛn·ʝi
12. tʃhu′g̊ʌ
13. ⁻chɪn·chi

EXERCISE.

1. *ˌli`thaɪ·thaɪ dzaɪ⁻ʝia ma? `dzaɪ⁻ʝia. 2. `fu ˌmu xuan·`dzaɪ ma? xuan`dzaɪ. 3. ⁻tha·dɪ `di·ɕiuŋ ˌʝiɛ`meɪ ⁻du dzaɪ⁻ʝia. 4. `dzaɪ tha ⁻ʝia·li, ′nan⁻ny̥ˌlao`ʃao, ju `ʌɪ·ʃɪ·khou ′ɪən. 5. ˌwɔ·dɪ `fu·chɪn `ʝiao wo `chy. 6. ⁻tha·dɪ ˌmu·chɪn ′niɛn·ʝi xən `da. 7. ju ⁻i·weɪ lao `thaɪ·thaɪ ′laɪ·lə. 8. ˌwɔ·dɪ `meɪ·meɪ ⁻ʝia·chy·liao. 9. ˌni·dɪ ⁻g̊ʌ·g̊ʌ ʃaŋ ˌna·ɪ `chy·lə? 10. ⁻tha·dɪ `fu ˌmu xuan`dzaɪ ma? ⁻tha·dɪ `fu ˌmu du ′bu`dzaɪ·lə. 11. ˌni·dɪ ⁻ɕiuŋ·di ⁻do·mə·da ′niɛn·ʝi? ⁻tha ʃɪ `ʌɪ·ʃɪ⁻san sueɪ. 12. ˌwo ju `di·ɕiuŋ ⁻san·g̊ə, ′xuan ju ⁻san·g̊ə ˌʝiɛ·meɪ. 13. ⁻tha·dɪ `da·g̊ʌ dzɔ ˌmaɪ`maɪ, ⁻tha·dɪ `ʌɪ·g̊ʌ dʒuŋ`di, ⁻tha `dzɯˌʝi ʃɪ ʝiao⁻ʃu. 14. ⁻tha·dɪ ˌʝiɛ·meɪ ⁻tʃhu·liao·′g̊ʌ meɪˌju? 15. ⁻tha·dɪ ˌʝiɛ·ʝiɛ ⁻tʃu·liao′g̊ʌ; tha ˌliaŋ·g̊ə `meɪ·meɪ xuan ′meɪˌju. 16. *ˌli·lao⁻san·dɪ ⁻chɪn·chi ′laɪ·lə, ˌkhʌ·ʃɪ khuaɪ ˌdzou·lə.

Translation. Lesson 12. Part I.

VOCABULARIES.

1st Tone.	2nd Tone.	3rd Tone.	4th Tone.
303. related.	308. male.	312. woman.	316. record.
304. elder brother	309. year.	313. elder sister.	317. year, harvest.
305. farmhouse.	310. women's rooms.	314. mother.	318. younger sister.
306. to sow, to plant.	311. living, work.	315. old.	319. father.
307. elder brother.			320. younger brother.
			321. relations.
			322. to sow.
			322a. [young, junior].

COMPOUND WORDS AND EXPRESSIONS.

1. father.
2. mother.
3. parents.
4. elder brother.
5. younger brother.
6. brothers.
7. elder sister.
8. younger sister.
9. sisters.
10. lady.
11. age.
12. marry.
13. relations.

EXERCISE.

1. Is Mrs. Li at home? She is at home. 21. Are your parents still living? They are still living. 3. His brothers and sisters are all at home. 4. Altogether, old and young, male and female, there are twenty people in his family. 5. My father told me to go. 6. His mother is very aged. 7. An old lady has arrived. 8. My younger sister has gone home. 9. Where has your elder brother gone? 10. Are his parents still living? His parents are both dead. 11. How old is your younger brother? He is 23 years old. 12. I have three brothers, and also three sisters. 13. His eldest brother is in business, his second brother is a farmer, and he himself is a school teacher. 14. Are his sisters married? 15. His eldest sister is married, but his two younger sisters are not yet married. 16. The third Mr. Li's wife's relations have come, but they will soon have gone away (again).

Transcription. Lesson 12. Part II.

ˋdi ˊʃɪˋʌɪ ˋkhʌ. ˋɕia.

VOCABULARIES.

1st Tone.	2nd Tone.	3rd Tone.	4th Tone.
323. g̊uaŋ.	327. chiɛn.	333. jɛn.	336. d̥an.
324. d̥an.	328. xaɪ.	334. d̥ʒɪ.	337. thou.
325. g̊u.	329. niaŋ.	335. ʃou.	338. g̊u.
326. g̊uei.	330. jɛ.		339. b̥eɪ.
	331. ʃu.		340. hou.
	332. tshaɪ.		341. ɕiao.
			342. g̊an.

COMPOUND WORDS AND EXPRESSIONS.

14. ˋthou ⁻g̊uaŋ
15. ˌjɛnˊchiɛn
16. ˋb̥eɪˋhou
17. ˋɕiao·ʃun
18. ˌg̊anˌj̊ɪn·d̥ɪ
19. ˌb̥ən·fən
20. ˌd̥aˊjɛ
21. ˋʃao·jɛ
22. ⁻g̊ueɪ·ny
23. ⁻g̊u·niaŋ
24. ⁻t͡ʃhuˊmən
25. ˊmənˌkhou
26. ˊb̥iɛ·d̥ɪ
27. ˊtshaɪ·g̊an

EXERCISE.

17. ˋd̥ʒɤ·g̊ə ⁻t͡ʃhuaŋ·xu ˋb̥u·thou⁻g̊uaŋ. 18. ⁻g̊uaŋ ni ˋd̥zɯ·j̊i ˊlaɪ·lə ma? 19. wɔ ⁻g̊uaŋ ⁻d̥ʒɪˋd̥ao tha ⁻t͡ʃhu·liaoˊmən. 20. ˋb̥u khʌ ⁻d̥an g̊u ˌjɛnˊchiɛn, ˊb̥u·g̊u b̥eɪˋxou. 21. tha ˋd̥an ˌmaɪ ˋd̥ʒɤ iˋjaŋ, ˋb̥uˌmaɪ ˊb̥iɛ·d̥ɪ. 22. ˊnvŋ ˋb̥an b̥uˊnʌŋ ˋb̥an, na ⁻d̥an khan ⁻tha·d̥ɪ ˊtshaɪ·g̊an ˌd̥zə·məˋjaŋ. 23. tha ˊlaɪ·d̥ao mənˌkhou, j̊iu ˋju ˌd̥zou·lə. 24. ˋna·j̊iɛn ˋʃɪ jao g̊anˌj̊ɪn·d̥ɪ ˋb̥an. 25. ⁻tha ju ˌliaŋ·g̊ə ˋʃao·jɛ, ˊxuan ju ⁻san·g̊ə ⁻g̊ueɪ·ny. 26. ˋd̥ʒɤ·ɕiɛ ˌlaoˊniaŋ·men, ˊtshuŋˌxɛn jyan·d̥ɪ ˊlaɪ. 27. *ˌli d̥aˊjɛ·d̥ɪ ⁻g̊u·niaŋ ˋj̊iaŋ·jao t͡ʃhuˊg̊ʌ. 28. ⁻tha·d̥ɪ ˋfuˌmu ⁻d̥u ʃɪ ˊniɛn·j̊i xənˋd̥a, ju ⁻b̥a·ʃɪ·d̥ɔ ˋsueɪ. 29. ˌwɔ·d̥ɪ ˋʌɪ ⁻ʃu ⁻g̊uaŋ ju ⁻i·g̊ə ˊxaɪ·d̥zɯ, ˊxuan·ʃɪ ⁻i·g̊ə ⁻g̊u·niaŋ. 30. ⁻tha·d̥ɪ ˊxaɪ·d̥zɯ ʃɪ xənˋɕiao·ʃun, ˋʃɪ·d̥zaɪ ʃou ˌb̥ən·fən. 31. ˋd̥ʒɤ·g̊ə ˊxaɪ·d̥zɯ ˌj̊iˋsueɪ? ⁻j̊ɪn·niɛn ˌwuˋsueɪ. 32. ˊb̥u·d̥an ʃɪ ˋna·jaŋ, ⁻tha xuan ⁻ʃuɔ ⁻tha b̥uˊnʌŋ ˋchy. 33. ˌwɔ·d̥ɪ ˊchiɛn b̥uˋg̊ou, ˌd̥ʒɪ ju ˊʃɪ·j̊iˋkhuaɪ.

Translation. Lesson 12. Part II.

VOCABULARIES.

1st Tone.	2nd Tone.	3rd Tone.	4th Tone.
323. light, only.	327. before.	333. eye.	336. only, but.
324. only.	328. child.	334. only, but.	337. penetrate.
325. aunt.	329. mother, woman.	335. to guard.	338. to regard.
326. girl.	330. father.		339. the back.
	331. uncle.		340. after.
	332. talent.		341. filial.
			342. ability.

COMPOUND WORDS AND EXPRESSIONS.

14. clear.
15. in front.
16. behind.
17. obedient.
18. as quickly as possible.
19. duty.
20. uncle.
21. son.
22. daughter.
23. young woman
24. go out.
25. doorway.
26. another.
27. ability.

EXERCISE.

17. This window is not clear. 18. Have you come by yourself? 19. I only know that he has left home. 20. Do not look only at what is in front of you, and lose sight of what is behind you. 21. He will only buy this kind, he will not buy any other. 22. Whether he can manage it or not depends simply on what sort of ability he has. 23. He came to the door, and immediately went away again. 24. Manage that affair as quickly as possible. 25. He has two sons and also three daughters. 26. These old women have come a very long distance. 27. Uncle Li's daughter is about to be married. 28. His parents are both very old, they are over eighty. 29. My second uncle has only one child, a daughter. 30. His children are very obedient and industrious. 31. How old is this child? Five years old this year. 32. Not only so, he says also that he cannot go. 33. My money is not enough, I have only ten dollars or so.

Transcription. Lesson 13. Part I.

`di /ʃɪˉsan `khʌ. `ʃaŋ.

VOCABULARIES.

1st Tone.	2nd Tone.	3rd Tone.	4th Tone.
343. tʃhu.	348. tʃhaŋ.	352. chi.	355. ɪ.
344. dzan.	349. dzɔ.	353. dzɔ.	356. xou.
345. thiɛn.	350. ʃr.	354. dʒu.	357. ɕiɛn.
346. ğaŋ.	351. tshaɪ.		358. ju.
347. ĵɪn.			

COMPOUND WORDS AND EXPRESSIONS.

1. ′ʃɪ·xou
2. ˌĵi ⁄ ʃɪ
3. ˉdɔ·dzan
4. ˉfaŋ ⁄ tshaɪ
5. ˉğaŋ ⁄ tshaɪ
6. dɑŋˉtʃhu
7. ˉĵɪn·thiɛn
8. ′dzɔ·thɛin
9. ′chiɛn·thiɛn
10. ′mɪŋ·thiɛn
11. `xou·thiɛn
12. dɑ′chiɛn·thiɛn
13. dɑ`xou·thiɛn
13a. [`ɕiɛn·dzaɪ]
13b. [ˌchi·laɪ]

EXERCISE.

1. ˉthɑ ʃɪ ˉɕiɛn ′laɪ·dɪ, ˌwɔ ʃɪ `xou ′laɪ·dɪ. 2. ˉthɑ ʃɪ ′dzɔ·thiɛn ′laɪ·dɪ, ˌwɔ ʃɪ ′chiɛn·thiɛn ′laɪ·dɪ. 3. ′mɪŋ·thiɛn ni ′ʃə·mə ′ʃɪ·xou ˌchi·laɪ? 4. dɑ`xou·thiɛn ˉthɑ jɑo ′xueɪ·laɪ. 5. `xou·thiɛn wɔ `chy ba `nɑ·ɕiɛ ˉʃu ′nɑ·xueɪ ′laɪ. 6. ni ˉĵɪn·thiɛn ′ʃə·mə ′ʃɪ·xou ˌdzou? 7. dɑŋˉtʃhu thɑ ʃuɔ `jɑo, `ɕiɛn`dzaɪ ′bu·jɑo·lə. 8. *ˌliˉɕiɛn·ʃʌŋ ˉfaŋ·tshaɪ ˉtʃhu·chy·liɑo. 9. ni ′laɪ·dɪ ′ʃɪ·xou thɑ ′tshaɪ ′laɪ. 10. ˌwɔ ʃɪ dɑ′chiɛn·thiɛn ′laɪ·dɪ. 11. ˉthɑ ʃɪ ˌmaɪ`maɪ ′ɪən, thɑ `tʃhaŋ laɪ ˌdʒɤ·ɪ dʒɔ ˌmaɪ·maɪ. 12. `nɑ·ğə `di·faŋ xən ˌjyan, ˌkhuŋ·phɑ `xou·thiɛn ′xueɪ·ḇu ′laɪ. 13. ˌdʒu·ɪən `dzɔ dzaɪ`ju·biɛn, `khʌ·ɪən `dzɔ dzaɪ ˌdzɔ·biɛn. 14. ˉthɑ ˌi·ĵɪŋ ˌdzou·liɑo ˌliɑŋ·thiɛn, `dʒɤ ĵiu khuaɪ `dɑo·liɑo. 15. wɔ ˉğaŋ·tshaɪ ˉʃuɔ·dɪ `xuɑ, ni ˉthɪŋ ′mɪŋ·ḇaɪ·liɑo mɑ? 16. ˉthɑ ˌĵi·ʃɪ ′xueɪ·laɪ? `dzaɪ dʌŋ ˉsan·thiɛn ĵiu ′xueɪ·laɪ·liɑo.

Translation. Lesson 13. Part I.

VOCABULARIES.

1st Tone.	2nd Tone.	3rd Tone.	4th Tone,
343. beginning.	348. constantly.	352. arise.	355. sun, day.
344. length of time	349. yesterday.	353. left.	356. time.
345. heaven, day.	350. time, season.	354. master, host.	357. now.
346. just now.	351. just now.		358. right hand.
347. now.			

COMPOUND WORDS AND EXPRESSIONS.

1. time.
2. when?
3. when?
4. just now.
5. just now.
6. at the beginning.
7. to-day.
8. yesterday.
9. the day before yesterday.
10. to-morrow.
11. the day after to-morrow.
12. two days ago.
13. two days hence.
13a. [now].
13b. [rise].

EXERCISE.

1. He came first, I came later. 2. He came yesterday, I came the day before yesterday. 3. At what time do you rise to-morrow? 4. He is coming back two days hence. 5. The day after to-morrow I will go and bring back those books. 6. At what time to-day do you go? 7. At first he said he wanted it, now he does not want it. 8. Mr. Li has just gone out. 9. He came just after you did. 10. I came three days ago. 11. He is a merchant and constantly comes here on business. 12. That place is a long way off, I am afraid I cannot get back by the day after to-morrow. 13. The host sits on the right hand, and the guest on the left. 14. He has already been gone two days, he will soon be at his destination now. 15. Did you understand what I just said? 16. When is he coming back? He will be back in three days.

Transcription. Lesson 13. Part II.

ˋdi ˊʃɪˉsan ˋkhʌ. ˋɕia.

VOCABULARIES.

1st Tone.	2nd Tone.	3rd Tone.	4th Tone.
359. xeɪ.	364. tʃhən.	365. wu.	369. jɛ.
360. ǧueɪ.		366. ʃaŋ.	370. dɪŋ.
361. dʒuŋ.		367. wan.	371. chiɛ.
362. ɕɪŋ.		368. dzao.	372. ban.
363. chi.		[368a. lʌŋ]	373. khʌ.
			374. jyə.
			375. la.

COMPOUND WORDS AND EXPRESSIONS.

14. ˌdzao·tʃhən
15. ˉʃaŋˌwu
16. ˌwan·ʃaŋ
17. ˋʃaŋ·ḅan·ˉthiɛn
18. ˋɕia·ḅan·ˋthiɛn
19. ˋǧuɔˌʃaŋ
20. ˊḅaɪ·thiɛn
21. ˋjɛ·li
22. ˊmɪŋ·niɛn
23. ˊchiɛn·niɛn
24. ˉɕiŋˉchi
25. ˋdʒʌŋ·jyə
26. ˋla·jyə
27. ˋʃaŋ·jyə
28. ˋdɪŋ·ǧueɪ
29. ˉiˋchiɛ
29a. [ˉtshuŋ ˊchiɛn]

EXERCISE.

17. ˉǰɪn·thiɛn tha ˊlaɪ·dɪ ˌdzao, ˉwɔ ˌwan·lə. 18. ˌdzao·tʃhən chi ˊlaɪ·dɪ ˊʃɪ·xou xən ˊliaŋ. 19. ˊḅaɪ·thiɛn xən ˋɪʌ, ˌwan·ʃaŋ tshaɪ ˊliaŋ·iˌdiɛn, ˋjɛ·li xənˌlʌŋ. 20. ˉtha ˉchi·diɛn ˉdʒuŋ ˌchi·laɪ, ˉḅa·diɛn ˋḅan dʒuŋ tʃhɪ ˌdzao ˋfan. 21. ʃɪ ˋʌɪ·diɛn ˉsan ˋkhʌ tʃhɪ ˌʃaŋ ˋfan, ˌwan·ʃaŋ ˉḅa·diɛn tʃhɪ ˌwan ˋfan. 22. ˌʃaŋ·jyə ˉtha ʃaŋ ˌḅeɪ·ḅiɛn ˋchy·liao, dao ˉḅa·jyə ˊtshaɪ nʌŋ ˊxueɪ·laɪ. 23. ˌwɔ ʃɪ ˊchiɛn·niɛn ˊlaɪ·dɪ, ˊmɪŋ·niɛn jao ˊxueɪ·chy. 24. *ˌliˉɕiɛn·ʃʌŋ ʃɪ ˋdʒʌŋ·jyə ˊlaɪ·dɪ, ˋla·jyə jao ˌdzou. 25. ˋdao ˉɕiŋ·chiˉsan ˌʃaŋ·wu ˌwɔ ǰiu ˌdzou. 26. ˋǧʌ·ɹən jao ˋdzuɪ·ǰi ˋdɪŋ·ǧueɪ ˉdɔ·dzan ˌdzou. 27. ˉtha ˊlaɪ·dɪ xənˌwan, ˉthiɛn ˌi·ǰɪŋ ˉxeɪ·lə. 28. ˋɕiɛn·dzaɪ ˋchy xən ˊnan, ˋdzaɪ ˌdʌŋ ˉi·ǧə ˉɕɪŋ·chi wɔ ˌkhʌ·i ˋchy. 29. ˉtha ˋdzɔ·dɪ ˋʃɪ ˉdu ˌxao. 30. ǧuɔˌʃaŋ ˉtha jao ʃaŋˉǰiɛ, ˌwan·ʃaŋ ˊxueɪ·laɪ. 31. ˊmɪŋ·thiɛn ˋʃaŋ·ḅanˉthiɛn, ˉtha ǰiu ˊlaɪ. 32. ˉǰɪn·thiɛn ˋɕia·ḅanˉthiɛn, ˌwɔ jao ˌdzou.

Translation. Lesson 13. Part II.

VOCABULARIES.

1st Tone.	2nd Tone.	3rd Tone.	4th Tone.
359. black.	364. morning.	365. 11.0 a.m. to 1 p.m.	369. night.
360. rule.			370. fixed.
361. bell.		366. noon.	371. to slice.
362. star.		367. evening, late.	372. half.
363. set time.		368. early.	373. quarter.
		[368a. cold]	374. moon, month.
			375. winter.

COMPOUND WORDS AND EXPRESSIONS.

14. morning.	18. afternoon.	22. next year.	26. 12th month.
15. noon.	19. afternoon.	23. the year before last.	27. last month.
16. evening.	20. daytime.		28. decide.
17. morning.	21. in the night.	24. a week.	29. all
		25. 1st month.	29a.[formerly].

EXERCISE.

17. To-day he came early. I was late. 18. In the morning when we get up it is very cold. 19. It is very hot in the day time, in the evening it is a little cooler, and at night it is very cold. 20. He rises at seven o'clock, and breakfasts at half past eight. 21. At a quarter to one he lunches, and dines at eight o'clock in the evening. 22. Last month he went North, he will not be back until the eighth month. 23. I came the year before last and return next year. 24. Mr. Li came in the first month; he will go in the last month of the year. 25. I shall go on Wednesday at noon. 26. Let everyone decide for himself when he will go. 27. He arrived very late, it was already dark. 28. It is very difficult to go just now, but I can go in a week's time. 29. Everything he does he does well. 30. In the afternoon he is going out, he will be back in the evening. 31. He will come to-morrow morning. 32. I shall start this afternoon.

Transcription. Lesson 14. Part I.

ˋd̦i ʹʃɿˋsɯ ˋkhʌ. ˋʃaŋ.

VOCABULARIES.

1st Tone.	2nd Tone.	3rd Tone.	4th Tone.
376. ɕy.	385. thaɪ.	388. d̦zuŋ.	389. ɹʌ.
377. jɪŋ.	386. tʃhən.		390. wu.
378. g̦aɪ.	387. wu.		391. b̦i.
379. b̦an.			392. suŋ.
380. d̦uan.			393. d̦ʒuŋ.
381. thiao.			
382. chɪŋ.			
383. feɪ.			
384. d̦an.			

COMPOUND WORDS AND EXPRESSIONS.

1. ˋɹʌ·ʃɿ
2. ˋb̦i ˉɕy
3. ˋb̦iˋjao
4. ˋb̦i˳d̦eɪ
5. ˋwuˋb̦i
6. ˴d̦zuŋ˳d̦eɪ
7. ˉiˋd̦an
8. ˉjɪŋˉg̦aɪ
9. ˉd̦anˉd̦aŋ
10. ˳khʌˋʃɿ
11. ʹwuˉfeɪ

EXERCISE.

1. ˉtha ˋɹʌ·ʃɿ ʹb̦uˋchy, ˳ni ˋb̦i·ɕy ˋd̦zɯ·d̦̥i ˋchy. 2. ˉtha b̦u·ʹnʌŋ xən˳wan·liao, g̦an ˳ʃaŋ·wu ˋb̦i ʹnʌŋ ʹlaɪ·d̦ao. 3. *˳liˉɕiɛn·ʃʌŋ ʹlaɪ·d̦ɪ ʹʃɿ·xou ni ˋb̦i·d̦eɪ ˋg̦ao·su ˳wɔ. 4. ˋjao b̦a ˉɕi·wu˳li·d̦ɪ ˉd̦̥ia·xuɔ ˉb̦an d̦ao ˉd̦uŋ·wu·li ˋchy. 5. ˋd̦̥iao ˳liaŋ·g̦ə ʹɹən b̦a ˋna·d̦ʒaŋ ˉd̦zɔ·d̦ʒɯ ʹthaɪ d̦ao ˋʃaŋ·faŋ ˋchy. 6. ˉb̦a ˋd̦ʒɤ·fʌŋ ˋɕin ˋsuŋ g̦eɪ *ˉd̦ʒaŋˉɕiɛn·ʃʌŋ. 7. ʹna ˉsan wan ʹtʃha, ˉd̦uan d̦ao khʌ·ˉthɪŋ·li ˋchy. 8. ˋɹʌ ˋb̦u ˳ʃɿ ˋd̦ʒɤ·g̦ə d̦̥iu ˋb̦i·jao ˳ʃɿ ˋna·g̦ə. 9. ˳chɪŋ tha ʹmɪŋ·thiɛn ˋwu·b̦i ˳d̦zao laɪ. 10. ʹd̦̥iao ɹən ˉthiao ˉi·d̦an ˳ʃueɪ laɪ. 11. ˋna ʃɿ ˳xao ˋʃɿ, ˉjɪŋˉg̦aɪ ˋna·jaŋ ˋb̦an. 12. ˳ni ˳d̦zuŋ·d̦eɪ ˳ɕiao·ɕɪn, ˋna·d̦̥iɛn ˋʃɿ ˳xən nanˋb̦an. 13. ˋd̦ʒɤ·g̦ə ˉd̦an·d̦zɯ ˳xən ʹtʃhən, ˳khuŋ·pha ˳ni ˉthiao·b̦u˳liao. 14. ˋna·g̦ə ˋʃɿ·chɪŋ ˳xən ˋd̦a, wɔ ˉd̦an·d̦aŋ·b̦u ˳liao. 15. ˳ni ˋb̦uˉjɪŋˉg̦aɪ d̦zɔ ˋna·jaŋ·d̦ɪ ˋʃɿ. 16. ˳wɔ ˉjɪŋˉg̦aɪ ˳d̦zao ˋchy, ˳khʌ·ʃɿ ˳xən ʹmaŋ, ˋchy·b̦u ˳liao. 17. ʹwu·feɪ ʃɿ tha ˋb̦u·fən chɪŋ ˋd̦ʒuŋ, ˋd̦̥iu·ʃɿ·liao.

Translation. Lesson 14. Part I.

VOCABULARIES.

1st Tone.	2nd Tone.	3rd Tone.	4th Tone.
376. must.	385. carry, (by two people on shoulders.).	388. must.	389. if.
377. ought.			390. business, must
378. ought.			391. must.
379. remove.	386. heavy, to sink.		392. escort, take, send.
380. carry (with hands).	387. not.		
381. carry (on a pole).			393. heavy.
382. light.			
383. not.			
384. carry (on shoulder).			

COMPOUND WORDS AND EXPRESSIONS.

1. if.
2. must.
3. must.
4. must.
5. must.
6. must.
7. a pair of buckets.
8. ought.
9. endure, bear responsibility.
10. but.
11. merely.

EXERCISE.

1. If he does not go, you will have to go yourself. 2. He cannot be very late, he will certainly be here by noon. 3. Be sure you tell me when Mr. Li comes. 4. Move the furniture of the west room into the east room. 5. Call two men to carry that table to the upper room. 6. Take this letter to Mr. Chang. 7. Take three cups of tea into the guest room. 8. If you do not use this, then you must use that. 9. Ask him to be sure and come early to-morrow. 10. Tell someone to bring two buckets of water. 11. That is a good thing, and that is the way in which it ought be managed. 12. You must be careful, that is a very difficult matter. 13. This load is very heavy, I am afraid you cannot carry it. 14. That is a very big affair, I cannot take the responsibility. 15. You ought not to do that sort of thing. 16. I ought to have gone before now, but I have been very busy and found it impossible to go. 17. It is simply that he does not distinguish between what is important and what is unimportant.

Transcription. Lesson 14. Part II.

ˋdi ʹʃɿˋsɯ ˋkhʌ. ˋɕia.

VOCABULARIES.

394. d͡ʒɿ.
395. tʃhu.
396. tshun.
397. waŋ.
398. ʝiɛn.
399. ʃʌŋ.
400. ɕy.
401. ʃou.
401a.[ʃu].
402. suan.
403. d͡ʒaŋ.
404. ʃu.
405. feɪ.
406. ʃou.
407. xuan.
408. chiɛn.
409. phiɑo.
410. xuɔ.

COMPOUND WORDS AND EXPRESSIONS.

12. ˋxuɔ·ʃɿ
13. ˌɕy⁻d̥o
14. ˋsuanˋd͡ʒaŋ
15. ˋɕia⸝tshun
16. ˌɕiaˋchiɛn
17. ˎʝɪŋʹtshun
18. ˎʝɪŋˋchiɛn
19. ⁻ʝiɛnˌʃʌŋ
20. ˌwaŋˋfeɪ
21. ⁻ʃuˌʃu
22. ˋsuan·suan
23. ⁻d͡ʒɿˋchy
24. ʹtʃhu·liɑo
25. ˋd͡ʒaŋˌbən·d͡zɯ
26. ˋɕiɛnʹchiɛn
27. ⁻d͡ʒɿˋphiɑo
27a. [ˋʝi·ɹan, v. L. 15.19]

EXERCISE.

18. ˋxuɔ·ʃɿ ˌniˋchy, ˋxuɔ·ʃɿ ˌwɔˋchy, ⁻d̥u b̥uʹʃə·məˋjɑo·ʝɪn.
19. ˋna·g̊ə ˋb̥an·fa ˌjɛ·ɕyʹɕɪŋ. 20. ʹmɪŋ·thiɛn ⁻tha ɕyʹlaɪ, khʌ ˌjɛ·ɕyˋb̥u·laɪ. 21. ju ˌɕy⁻d̥oʹɹan d͡zaɪ⁻ʝiɛ·ʃaŋˋmaɪ ⁻d̥uŋ·ɕi. 22. ʹlaɪ·b̥a, ˌkhʌ·iʹxɔ ˌwɔ suanˋd͡ʒaŋ. 23. ˋɕiaʹtshun ⁻d̥ɔ·ʃɑoʹchiɛn? 24. ˋɕiaˋchiɛn ⁻d̥ɔ·ʃɑoʹchiɛn? 25. ˎʝɪŋʹtshun ⁻d̥ɔ·ʃɑoʹchiɛn? 26. ⁻ʃou·li tshun ⁻d̥ɔ·ʃɑoʹchiɛn? 27. ʹtʃhu⁻d͡ʒɿˋɕiaʹtshun ˋʌɪ·b̥aɪ⁻san·ʃɿ·khuaɪʹjaŋʹchiɛn. 28. ˌtʃhu˰d͡ʒɿˋɕiaˋchiɛn ˌsɯ·ʃɿˋsɯ·khuaɪ ˌwuʹmɑo. 29. ˌbənʹjyə ˌwɔ·mənˋxuaʹchiɛnˋxua·d̥ɪ ˌʃɑo·iˌd̥iɛn. 30. wɔ ˋsuan·d̥ə ˋd̥ueɪ·b̥uˋd̥ueɪ? ʹb̥u·d̥aˋd̥ueɪ, ⁻khʌ·iˋd͡zaɪ ˌʃu iˋb̥iɛn. 31. ˌni·d̥ɪʹchiɛn ˋʝi·ɹan b̥u⁻d̥o, ni ⁻jɪŋ·g̊aɪ ˌjiɛn·ʃʌŋ iˌd̥iɛn, ˋb̥u·khʌ ˌwaŋˋfeɪ. 32. ⁻ʃou·d̥ɪʹchiɛn ˌkhʌ·i ˋʃu·ʃu. ⁻d͡ʒɿ tʃhu·d̥ɪʹchiɛn ˌkhʌ·i ˋsuan·suan. 33. ʹtʃhu·liɑo ˋd͡ʒɤ·ɕiɛ ˋd͡ʒaŋˌbən·d͡zɯ. ⁻d̥u ˌkhʌ·ɪʹna·chy. 34. ʹnaˋd͡ʒɤ·g̊ə ˋphiɑo, chy ˋxuan ˋɕiɛnʹchiɛn. 35. ˌkhʌ·ɪ ⁻ʃuɔ·ʃuɔ ˌni jɑo ⁻d͡ʒɹ ⁻d̥ɔ·ʃɑoʹchiɛn, wɔ ˌkhʌ·i ˌg̊eɪ ni ⁻khaɪ g̊ə ⁻d͡ʒɿˋphiɑo.

Translation. Lesson 14. Part II.

VOCABULARIES.

394. a branch, to pay.
395. exclude, deduct.
396. preserve, keep.
397. useless.
398. sparing.
399. surplus.
400. promise, perhaps.
401. hand.
401a. [to count].
402. reckon.
403. account.
404. number, to count.
405. spend.
406. receive.
407. exchange.
408. owe.
409. bank note, cheque.
410. whether, or.

COMPOUND WORDS AND EXPRESSIONS.

12. whether, or.
13. very many.
14. reckon account.
15. balance to credit.
16. balance to debit.
17. nett balance to credit.
18. nett balance to debit.
19. economical.
20. wasteful.
21. add up.
22. reckon.
23. send a remittance, pay, draw out money
24. deduct.
25. account book.
26. ready cash.
27. cheque.
27a. [since, seeing that]

EXERCISE.

18. Whether you go or I go does not matter very much. 19. That way of settling it may do. 20. He may come to-morrow, but then he may not come. 21. There are a lot of people on the street selling things. 22. Come and let us reckon up our account. 23. What is the balance to credit? 24. What is the balance to debit? 25. What is the nett balance to credit? 26. How much is there in hand? 27. There is a nett balance of $230 to credit. 28. There is a nett balance to debit of $44.50. 29. This month our expenditure has been somewhat less. 30. Have I reckoned it correctly? Not quite correctly, add it up again. 31. Seeing that your means are so limited you ought to be more economical and not waste your money. 32. Add up the receipts and reckon the expenditure. 33. You can take everything away except these account books. 34. Take this note and cash it. 35. Tell me how much you want to draw and I will write a cheque for you.

Transcription. Lesson 15. Part I.

ˋdi ʹʃɪ‿wu ˋkhʌ. ˋʃaŋ.

VOCABULARIES.

1st Tone.	2nd Tone.	3rd Tone	4th Tone.
411. fʌŋ.	417. ḅao.	423. jy.	428. chi.
412. g̈ua.	418. jyn.	424. ɕyə.	429. ḍuŋ.
413. ʃuaŋ.	419. fʌŋ.	425. luŋ.	430. g̈ʌ.
414. jɪn.	420. fan.	426. meɪ.	431. d͡ʒuŋ.
415. chɪŋ.	421. thuŋ.	427. tshaɪ.	432. san.
416. ḅɪŋ.	422. xʌ.		

COMPOUND WORDS AND EXPRESSIONS.

1. ˉthiɛn·chi
2. ˉjɪn ˉthiɛn
3. ˋɕia‿jy
4. ˉchɪŋˉthiɛn
5. ˋḍuŋˉḅɪŋ
6. ˉg̈uaˉfʌŋ
7. ˋɕiaˉʃuaŋ
8. ˉḅɪŋʹliaŋ
9. ʹjynˌtshaɪ
10. ˌmeɪʹfʌŋ
11. ʹthuŋˉɕɪn
12. ʹxʌˋi
13. ˋḍaˉg̊ia
14. ˧luŋ‿d͡ʒuŋ
15. ˉjɪŋˉḍaŋ
16. ˉiˋkhuaɪ·ɪ

EXERCISE.

1. ˋg̈ʌ·ɪən ju ˋg̈ʌ·ɪən·ḍɪ ʹnan·t͡ʃhu. 2. ˉtha ˌmeɪ·thiɛn ˉt͡ʃhu·chy ˋḅanˋʃɪ. 3. ˉg̊ɪn·ɪ ˉjɪnˉthiɛn, ˉg̊iaŋ·jao ˋɕia‿jy. 4. ˋʃaŋ·niɛn ˋla·jyə ˋɕia·liao ʹḅao·d͡zɯ. 5. ʹchiɛn·thiɛn ˋɕiaˋḍa‿ɕyə. 6. ˌmeɪ ʹfʌŋ ˋchy·ḍɪ ˋʃɪ·xou tha ˧d͡ʒuŋ ju ʹnan·t͡ʃhu. 7. ˋd͡ʒuŋ·ɪən ˉḍu ʃɪ ʹthuŋˉɕɪnʹxʌˋi. 8. ʹfanˋʃɪ ˋḍa·g̊ia ʹthuŋˉɕɪn ʃɪ ˌxən ˋjao‿g̊ɪn·dɪ. 9. ˌni ˉjɪŋˉḍaŋ ˌḍʌŋ ˉtha ʹlaɪ, ʹxʌ nɪ ˋthuŋ ˋchy. 10. ˌni ʃɪ ˉg̊iao tha ʹxʌ ni ˉi·khuaɪ·ɪ ˋchy ma? 11. ˉchɪŋ·liao ˉthiɛn lə. 12. ˉg̊ɪn·thiɛn ʹmeɪ ḍuŋˉḅɪŋ. 13. ʹd͡zɔ·thiɛn ˉg̈ua·ḍa ˉfʌŋ. 14. ˉg̊ɪn·thiɛn ˉchɪŋ·t͡ʃhən ˋɕia·liao ˉʃuaŋ. 15. ˧luŋ‿d͡ʒuŋ ju ˉḍɔ·ʃao ʹɪən d͡zaɪˋna·li? 16. ˋd͡ʒɤ·ɕiɛ ˌʃueɪ ˉḅɪŋʹliaŋ, ˌkhʌ·i xuan ˋɪʌ·ḍɪ laɪ. 17. ʹjyn·tshaɪ ˉḍu ˋsanˉkhaɪ·liao. 18. ˉg̊ɪn·niɛn·ḍɪ ˉthiɛn·chi xənˋʃun·ḍaŋ.

Translation. Lesson 15. Part I.

VOCABULARIES.

1st Tone.	2nd Tone.	3rd Tone.	4th Tone.
411. wind.	417. hail.	423. rain.	428. air.
412. to blow.	418. clouds.	424. snow.	429. freeze.
413. frost (white).	419. to meet.	425. collect.	430. each.
414. dark.	420. all.	426. every.	431. all.
415. clear.	421. together.	427. clouds.	432. scatter.
416. ice.	422. with.		

COMPOUND WORDS AND EXPRESSIONS.

1. weather.
2. dull day.
3. to rain.
4. clear sky.
5. freeze.
6. wind blowing.
7. fall of white frost.
8. ice cold.
9. clouds.
10. every time.
11. of one mind.
12. of one purpose.
13. the whole company.
14. all together.
15. ought.
16. together.

EXERCISE.

1. Every one has his own difficulties. 2. He goes out every day to do his business. 3. It is a dull day to-day, it is going to rain. 4. In the last month of last year it hailed. 5. The day before yesterday there was a heavy fall of snow. 6. Every time he goes he is sure to have difficulties. 7. All are of one mind and purpose. 8. In everything it is very important to be agreed. 9. You should wait for him to come, and go with you. 10. Have you told him to go with you? 11. The sky has cleared. 12. There is no frost to-day. 13. Yesterday there was a heavy wind. 14. Early this morning there was a white frost. 15. All together how many people are there there? 16. This water is ice-cold, change it for some hot. 17. The clouds have all scattered. 18. The weather this year has been very favourable.

G

Transcription. Lesson 15. Part II.

ˋɖi ˊʃɿˌwu ˋkhʌ. ˋɕia.

VOCABULARIES.

1st Tone.	2nd Tone.	3rd Tone.	4th Tone.
433. tʃhun.	437. ɿan.	441. nuan.	442. ʝ̊i.
434. chiu.	438. ɿʌŋ.		443. ɕia.
435. ɖuŋ.	439. ʌɿ.		444. chyə.
436. xu.	440. sueɿ.		445. ʝ̊i.
			446. g̊u.

COMPOUND WORDS AND EXPRESSIONS.

17. ⁻sueɿ·ɿan
18. ˋb̥i·ɿan
19. ˋʝ̊i·ɿan
20. ⁻xu·ɿan
21. ˋg̊u·ɿan
22. ˊɿʌŋ·ɿan
23. ˊxuan·ʃɿ
24. ⁻ɖan·ʃɿ
25. ˊɿan·ʌɿ
26. ˌɖʒɿ·ʃɿ
27. ˋchyə·ʃɿ
28. ˌchi ˊɕɿŋ
29. ˊɿan ˋxou
30. ⁻¹jy ˌʃueɿ
31. ⁻tʃhun·thiɛn
32. ˋɕia·thiɛn
23. ⁻chiu·thiɛn
34. ⁻ɖuŋ·thiɛn
35. *ˊnan⁻ʝ̊ɿŋ
[see L. 10, c. 9a.]

EXERCISE.

19. ⁻sueɿ·ɿan xən ˋg̊ueɿ, wɔ ˊxuan·ʃɿ jao ˌmaɿ. 20. tha ⁻sueɿ·ɿan ⁻ʃuɔ ʃɿ ˋchy, ˊɿan·ʌɿ ˌɖao·ʃaŋ ˋb̥u·xao ˌdzou, ˊmeɿ·fa ˋchy. 21. ˌwɔ ʃuɔ ˋna·g̊ə ˋʃɿ ˋb̥u·ɿu ˊb̥u·b̥an ˌxao, ˌkhʌ·ʃɿ ⁻tha ˊɿʌŋ·ɿan jao ˋb̥an. 22. ˋna·g̊ə ˋb̥an·fa ˋb̥u·b̥i·ɿan ˌxao. 23. *ˌli⁻ ɕiɛn·ʃʌŋ ˌju·i ʃaŋ *ˊnan·ʝ̊ɿŋ ˋchy, ⁻ɖan·ʃɿ ˋɕiɛn·dzaɿ ju ˋʃɿ, ˌdzou·b̥u·liao. 24. ni ˋʝ̊i·ɿan ju ˋna·g̊ə ˋi·sɯ, weɿˊʃə·mə b̥u ˌdzao ⁻ʃuɔ nɿ? 25. ⁻tha ⁻g̊aŋ·jao chi ˊɕɿŋ, ⁻xu·ɿan ˌju ɿən laɿ ˋʝ̊iao tha, ˊmeɿ ˌdzou ˌliao. 26. ˋna·g̊ə ˊfaŋ·dzɯ ˋg̊u·ɿan ʃɿ ˌxao, ˌɖʒɿ·ʃɿ ˌwɔ ˌmaɿ·b̥u ˌchi. 27. ⁻tha ˋɕiɛn ˋdzaɿ jao ˋʝ̊iɛn ˌni, ɿan ˋxou tha dzaɿ ˋʝ̊iɛn *ˊwaŋ ⁻ɕiɛn·ʃʌŋ. 28. ˋna ˋg̊u·ɿan ʃɿ ˌxao ˋʃɿ, ˌkhʌ·ʃɿ ˌxən nan ˋb̥an. 29. ˌwɔ ˌb̥ən·laɿ ˊdzɔ·thiɛn ˋjao ˌg̊eɿ ⁻tha ɕiɛ ˋɕɿn, ˌkhʌ·ʃɿ ˋwaŋ·lə. 30. ⁻i ˊniɛn ju ˋsɯ ˋʝ̊i, ˌʝ̊iu·ʃɿ ⁻tʃhun, ˋɕia, ⁻chiu, ⁻ɖuŋ. 31. ⁻ɖuŋ·thiɛn xən ˌlʌŋ, ˋɕia·thiɛn xən ˋɿʌ. 32. ⁻tʃhun·thiɛn ⁻chiu·thiɛn ⁻ɖu ʃɿ ˋb̥u ˌlʌŋ ˊb̥u ˋɿʌ. 33. ⁻tʃhun·thiɛn ⁻chiu·thiɛn ⁻¹jy xən ˌʃao, ˋɕia·thiɛn·ɖi ⁻¹jy·ʃueɿ xən ⁻ɖɔ. 34. ⁻ɖuŋ·thiɛn ɕia ˌɕyə ɕia ˊb̥ao·dzɯ, ˋcia·thiɛn ⁻¹jɛ ju ˊʃɿ·xou ɕia ˊb̥ao·dzɯ. 35. ⁻ʝ̊ɿn·thiɛn ⁻fʌŋ xən ˋɖa, ˋchyə·ʃɿ ˋb̥u ˌlʌŋ.

Translation. Lesson 15. Part II.

VOCABULARIES.

1st Tone.	2nd Tone.	3rd Tone.	4th Tone.
433. spring.	437. but.	441. warm.	442. season.
434. autumn.	438. still.		443. summer.
435. winter.	439. and yet.		444. but.
436. suddenly.	440. although.		445. since.
			446. certain.

COMPOUND WORDS AND EXPRESSIONS.

17. although.
18. must.
19. since, seeing that.
20. suddenly.
21. certainly.
22. nevertheless.
23. but, still.
24. only (but).
25. but.
26. only (but).
27. but still.
28. to start on journey.
29. afterwards.
30. rain (noun).
31. spring.
32. summer.
33. autumn.
34. winter.
35. Nanking, [see L.10, c.9a].

EXERCISE.

19. Although it is very dear, I still want to buy it. 20. Although he said he would go, the roads were bad and it was impossible. 21. I said it would be better not to do anything in that matter, but he still means to undertake it. 22. That way of settling it will not necessarily turn out well. 23. Mr. Li has it in mind to go to Nanking, but just now he has business which prevents him going. 24. Seeing that you had that idea why did you not speak of it sooner ? 25. He was just going to start, when suddenly someone came for him and he did not go. 26. That house it is true is excellent, but the price is beyond me. 27. He will see you now, later he will see Mr. Wang. 28. That is undoubtedly a good thing, but difficult to arrange. 29. My original intention was to write to him yesterday, but I forgot. 30. There are four seasons in the year, spring, summer, autumn, winter. 31. In the winter it is very cold, and in the summer it is very hot. 32. In the spring and autumn it is neither hot nor cold. 33. In spring and autumn there is very little rain, in the summer the rain-fall is very heavy. 34. In the winter there is snow and hail, in the summer also there is hail at times. 35. There is a very heavy wind to-day, but it is not cold.

Transcription. Lesson 16.

VOCABULARY.

1st Tone.	2nd Tone.	3rd Tone.	4th Tone.
Pt.II.459. ǧuŋ	Pt.I.447. nɔ	Pt.I.453. ɕiaŋ	Pt.I.455. ḍuŋ
460. fu	448. ni	454. chiɛ	456. ju
461. tha	449. ʝ̊i	Pt.II.473. ḍʒao	457. mu
462. ʃan	450. sueɪ	474. ma	458. ḅiɛn
463. khuŋ	451. rən	475. mu	Pt.II.477. weɪ
463a. na	452. phɪŋ	476. ḍa	478. ḍiɛn
463b. ḍɪŋ	Pt.II.464. ʝ̊y	476a. ʝ̊ia	479. ḍʒɪ
	465. ḍʒaɪ	476b. ḅɪŋ	480. ʝ̊y
	466. lun		481. i
	467. jaŋ		482. ɐy
	468. ḍza		483. fu
	469. than		484. ʃueɪ
	470. ruŋ		485. ʝ̊yə
	471. chyan		486. tshou
	472. ḍza		487. jyan
	472a. ɕiaŋ		487a. i

Transcription of Part I.

`ḍi  ´ʃɪ`liu `khʌ.  `ʃaŋ.

COMPOUND WORDS AND EXPRESSIONS.

1. ´ʌɪ‿chiɛ   3. ¯i`ḍɪŋ   5. ´mu`ɕia   7. ´sueɪ`ḅiɛn
2. ´niɛn¯chɪŋ   4. `ʝ̊iɛn·ʃɪ   6. ⌐ḍʒɪ‿ǧuan   8. `ɹən´phɪŋ

EXERCISE.

1. ¯i·thiɛn pha tha ‿ǧan·ḅu`ḍao. 2. `ḍʒɤ·ɕiɛ ¯ʝ̊ia·xuɔ xen´ʧhən, wɔ `ḍzɯ·ʝ̊i ´nɔ·ḅu`ḍuŋ. 3. ¯ʝ̊in·thiɛn `ḍao·ʃaŋ ´ni xən¯ḍɔ; ¯ʧhɤ·ḍzɯ ‿ḍzou·ḅu‿liao. 4. ¯san·thiɛn ¯i·ḍɪŋ ´laɪ·ḅu´ʝ̊i. 5. ¯tha xən ´niɛn¯chɪŋ, ´ʌɪ‿chiɛ `na·ʝ̊iɛn `ʃɪ·chɪŋ ´ju xən´nan, tha `ḍzɯ‿ʝ̊i ¯i·ḍɪŋ `ḅan·ḅu‿liao. 6. ¯i·ǧə ´ɹən·dɪ ´ʝ̊iɛn·ʃɪ ‿ḍzuŋ ju `khan·ḅu `ḍao·dɪ `ḍi·faŋ. 7. ‿wɔ ´mu`ɕia ‿ɕiaŋ·ḅu·chi´laɪ. 8. ‿ni ɕiaŋ `chy ‿ḍʒɪ‿ǧuan `chy. 9. ´ḅu·juŋ ‿dʌŋ·ḍʒɔ ‿wɔ·mən, `ǧʌ·ɹən ´sueɪ`ḅiɛn ḅa. 10. `ɹən·phɪŋ ¯tha ‿ḍzə·mən ¯ʃuɔ, wɔ ´ḅu`chy.

Translation. Lesson 16.

VOCABULARY.

1st Tone.	2nd Tone.	3rd Tone.	4th Tone.
	Pt.I. 447. move	Pt.I. 453. think	Pt.I. 455. move
Pt. II. 459. work	448. mud.	454. moreover	456. and, also
460. husband	449. attain, reach, also	Pt.II. 473. seek	457. eye
461. she	450. follow	474. horse	458. convenient
462. hill	451. allow	475. acre.	Pt.II. 477. exclamatory particle
463. empty, vacant.	452. according to	476. beat.	
463a. euphonic particle	Pt.II. 464. office	476a. first of the ten stems	478. electricity
463b. fourth of the ten stems	465. residence	476b. third of the ten stems	479. will, determination
	466. natural relationships		480. according to
	467. sun		481. easy
	468. we		482. continue, succeed, join
	469. to chat		483. double, again
	470. allow		484. sleep
	471. all		485. feel
	472. miscellaneous		486. collect, make up
	472a. detail		487. willing
			487a. second of ten stems

Translation of Part I.

COMPOUND WORDS AND EXPRESSIONS.
1. moreover, also.
2. young.
3. certain.
4. experience.
5. at present.
6. simply.
7. follow one's convenience.
8. allow, at liberty

EXERCISE.
1. I am afraid he cannot get there in a day. 2. These pieces of furniture are very heavy, I cannot move them by myself. 3. The roads are very muddy to-day, the carts cannot get along. 4. It cannot possibly be done in three days. 5. He is very young, and moreover that affair is very difficult; it is quite certain that he cannot manage it by himself. 6. A single person's judgment must fail in some respects. 7. For the moment I cannot recall it. 8. If you want to go, you may as well go. 9. You need not wait for us, let each suit his own convenience. 10. Let him say what he likes, I shall not go.

Transcription. Lesson 16. Part II.

ˋȡi ˊʃɿˋliu ˋkhʌ. ˋɕia.

˒ȡɑ ˋȡiɛn ˋxuɑ.

COMPOUND WORDS AND EXPRESSIONS.

9. ˊdzɑ·mən 13. ˋȡi·mu 17. ˒ʃou·ɕy 21. ˋjyan·i
10. ˉfu·ɹən 14. ˊɹuŋ·i 18. feɪˊʧhaŋ 22. ˋtshou˒ʃou
11. ˊthan·than 15. ˉi̯ˊlaɪ 19. ˋfu·dzɑ 23. ˊɕiaŋ·ɕi
12. ˉi̯ɪn·laɪ 16. ˋʌɪˊlaɪ 20. ˒ȡɑ·ȡiɛn ˋxuɑ 24. ˉɡ̊uŋ·fu

CONVERSATION.

˒i̯iɑ. ˋweɪ, ˉɕi·i̯y, ˉi˒wuˋliuˋʌɪ.
ˋi. ˒ju ɹən ˋi̯iɑo, ˒ȡʌŋ·i˒ȡʌŋ.
˒i̯iɑ. ˋweɪ, ˋdʒɤ ʃɿ *ˉɕiˊchʌŋˉfaŋˊdʒaɪ ma?
˒b̥ɪŋ. ˋʃɿ, dʒɑo ˒na iˋweɪ?
˒i̯iɑ. *ˉdʒaŋ·dʒɯˊliaŋ ˋjɑo xʌ *ˉfaŋ·dʒɿˊlunˉɕiɛn·ʃʌŋ ʃuɔˋxuɑ.
˒b̥ɪŋ. ˋʃɿ, ˒ȡʌŋ·i˒ȡʌŋ.
ˉȡɪŋ. ˋweɪ, *ȡʑmˊliaŋ ma? ˒wɔ ʃɿ *dʒɿˊlun. ni dzaɪ ˒nɑ·ɹ nɑ?
˒i̯iɑ. ˒wɔ dzaɪ *ˉdʒʌŋ·jaŋˊmən ȡɑˉi̯iɛ ˒maɪˉȡuŋ·ɕi nɑ. wɔ ˉʃuɔ, ˊdzɔ·thiɛn ˊdzɑ·mən ˊthan·ȡi ˋnɑ·i̯iɛn ˋʃɿ, ni ˋb̥an·liɑo meɪ˒ju?
ˉȡɪŋ. wɔ ˊdzɔ·thiɛn ˒wan·ʃaŋ ȡɑo *˒maˉɕiɛn·ʃʌŋ ˋnɑ·li ˋchy·liɑo. tha ˊmeɪ dzaɪˉi̯iɑ, wɔ xʌˉtha·ȡiˉfu·ɹən ˊthan·liɑo iˊthan. i̯y ˉtha ˉʃuɔ, ˉi̯ɪn·laɪ ˋȡi·mu·ȡi ˋʃɿ·chɪŋ ˒xən b̥uˊɹuŋ·i ˋb̥an nɪ.
˒i̯iɑ. ˒dzə·mə nɪ?
ˉȡɪŋ. ˉi·laɪ ʃɿ ˉɕi·ʃan·ȡɪ ˉkhuŋˋȡi ˉʧha·b̥uˉdɔ chyan ˋmaɪ ɡ̊eɪ ˋɡ̊ʌ ɕyəˋɕiɑo liɑo. ˋʌɪ·laɪ ʃɿ ˒maɪˋȡi·ȡɪ ˊʃou·ɕy ˉfeɪ. ˊʧaŋ·ȡɪ ˋfu·dzɑ. ˊdzɔ·thiɛn wɔ ˋkhuaɪ ʃueɪˋi̯iɑo·ȡɪ ˋʃɿ·xou, *˒maˉɕiɛn·ʃʌŋ ˒ɡ̊eɪ wɔ ȡɑˋȡiɛn, ˉtha ˒i̯ɛ ɹɿ ˊdʒə·mə ˉʃuɔ. tha ˉʃuɔ, ni ˋʌ·ʃɿ b̥uˊmaŋ, tha ˒xən ˋjyan·i man ˋman·ȡɪ ˋthi ni ˒dʒɑo·i˒dʒɑo. ni ˋʌ·ʃɿ ˋɕiɛn·dzaɪ i̯iu ˋjɑo, ˒khʌ·ʃɿ ˊʃɿ·dzaɪ ˊmeɪ·ju tshou˒ʃou·ȡɪ ˋȡi.
˒i̯iɑ. *ˋdʒɿ·lun; ni ˉi̯ɪn·thiɛn ˋɕia·b̥anˉthiɛn ˋȡɑo ˒wɔ ˉi̯iɑ laɪ, ˒wɔ·mən dzaɪ ˊɕiaŋ·ɕi ˊthan·iˊthan ˒xɑo·b̥u˒xɑo? ni ˋȡɑ·ɡ̊aɪ ju ˉɡ̊uŋ·fu b̥a?
ˉȡɪŋ. ˒xɑo b̥a! ˋɕia·b̥anˉthiɛn ˋi̯iɛn.

Translation. Lesson 16. Part II.

At the Telephone.

COMPOUND WORDS AND EXPRESSIONS.

9. we
10. wife
11. chat.
12. recently.
13. land
14. easy.
15. firstly.
16. secondly.
17. process, methods.
18. unusual.
19. miscellaneous.
20. to telephone.
21. wish
22. available.
23. careful, detail.
24. leisure.

CONVERSATION.

A. Hello. West 1526.

B. The line is engaged. Wait a little.

A. Hello. Is that Mr. Fang's of West City?

C. Yes. Whom do you want?

A. Chang Tzŭ-liang wants to speak to Mr. Fang Chih-lun.

C. All right. Hold the line please.

D. Hello, is that Tzŭ-liang? I am Chih-lun. Where are you?

A. I am in Cheng Yang Men High Street, making some purchases. I say; have you managed that affair we talked about yesterday?

D. Last evening I called on Mr. Ma. He was not at home but I had a talk with his wife. According to her, the land business just now is very difficult to put through.

A. How is that?

D. To begin with, nearly all the vacant land at the Western Hills has been sold to the Schools. In the second place, the process of buying land is very complicated. Last night, as I was just going to bed, Mr. Ma himself rang me up. He said the same thing. He said if you are not in a hurry, he will be glad quietly to keep his eye open for you, but if you must have it at once, then really there is no such land available (at present).

A. Chih-lun, come along to my house this afternoon, so that we can talk the matter over more in detail, will you? You are not busy I suppose?

D. Righto. Will see you this afternoon.

Transcription. Lesson 17.

VOCABULARY.

1st Tone.	2nd Tone.	3rd Tone.	4th Tone.
Pt.I.488. jɛn	Pt.I.489. xueɪ	Pt.I.491. ǰɪn	Pt.I.493. ʃr
Pt.II.496. ǰiao	490. ǰi	492. man	494. jɛn
497. ǰɪn	Pt.II.506. xʌ	Pt.II.515. g̊aŋ	495. i
498. wɑ	507. tʃhʌŋ	516. xaɪ	Pt.II.517. khuʌŋ
499. ǰyan	508. li		518. jyn
500. ɕiaŋ	509. phɪn		519. ʃueɪ
501. jɑ	[phɪŋ]		520. g̊uan
502. g̊uŋ	510. ju		521. li
503. ma	511. luŋ		522. ǰiɛn
504. g̊uŋ	512. thao		523. jy
505. ɕɪn	513. thaŋ		524. b̥eɪ
	514. ʃou		525. ɕiɛ

Transcription of Part I.

ˋdi ´ʃɪˉchi ˋkhʌ. ˋʃaŋ.

COMPOUND WORDS AND EXPRESSIONS.

1. ´ʃɪ·jɛn   3. ˋdzaɪˉsan   5. ˉfaŋˋbiɛn
2. ˉʃaŋ·i   4. ˋd̥ao⌣di

EXERCISE.

1. ⌣wɔ ´ʃɪ·ʃɪ·d̥zaɪˋdzaɪ·d̥ɪ ˉʃuɔ b̥a. 2. ˉʃuɔ·d̥ɪ ´mɪŋ·mɪŋ·b̥aɪ ´b̥aɪ·d̥ɪ tshaɪ ⌣xɑo. 3. ni ˋʌ·ʃɪ ´b̥uˋɕin, ⌣khʌ·i ´ʃɪ·jɛn ´ʃɪ·jɛn. 4. ˋɕiɛnˋd̥zaɪ ´xuan ju ⌣wɔ·d̥ɪ ´fu·chɪn, wɔ ˋb̥i·d̥eɪ xueɪˉǰia·chy ˉʃaŋ·i ˉʃaŋ·i, ´tshaɪ nʌŋ ˋd̥iŋ·g̊ueɪ. 5. wɔ ˋd̥zaɪˉsan ˋwən tha, ˋd̥ao ⌣d̥i meɪ ˋwən·tʃhu´laɪ. 6. ⌣wɔ·mən d̥zaɪˋna·li ´ǰ̊i ˉfaŋ·b̥iɛn. 7. *´waŋˉɕiɛn·ʃʌŋ d̥zaɪ ˋxou·ǰiɛ·ʃaŋ ⌣ǰɪn ˉd̥uŋ·thou ˋd̥ʒu. 8. ⌣man ˉthiɛn ˉd̥u ʃɪ ˉxeɪ ´jyn·tshaɪ, ʃɪ ˋjao ɕia⌣jy·d̥ɪ ˋjaŋ·d̥zɯ. 9. ⌣man ˉwu·d̥zɯ ˉd̥u ʃɪˉjɛn.

Translation. Lesson 17.

VOCABULARY.

1st Tone.	2nd Tone.	3rd Tone.	4th Tone.
Pt.I.488. smoke	Pt.I.489. return.	491. extreme.	493. to test, try.
Pt.II.496. banana.	490. very.	492. full.	494. examine.
497. catty.	Pt.II.506. what.	Pt.II.515. lagoon	495. discuss.
498. final particle.	507. complete.	516. sea.	Pt.II.517. more, moreover.
499. contribute.	508. pear.		518. transport.
500. fragrant.	509. apple.		519. duty, tax.
501. final particle.	510. by, from.		520. jar, pot.
502. merit.	511. dragon.		521. lichi.
503. interrog. part.	512. peach.		522. comfits
504. public, just.	513. a kind of pear.		523. beforehand
505. new.	514. ripe.		524. prepare.
			525. thank

Translation of Part I.

COMPOUND WORDS AND EXPRESSIONS.

1. try, to test.
2. discuss, consult.
3. again and again, repeatedly.
4. after all.
5. convenient.

EXERCISE.

1. I am talking of facts. 2. It would be well to make yourself perfectly clear. 3. If you do not believe it, try (for yourself). 4. There is my father, I must go home and consult him before I can decide. 5. I have asked him several times, but still have not succeeded in getting anything out of him. 6. We found it very comfortable there. 7. Mr. Wang lives at the extreme East end of the North Street. 8. The sky is all clouded over, it looks as if we shall have heavy rain. 9. The room is full of smoke.

Transcription. Lesson 17. Part II.

ˋdi ˊʃɿ⁻chi ˋkhʌ. ˋɕia.

ˋmaɪ ˧ʃueɪ ˧g̑uɔ.

COMPOUND WORDS AND EXPRESSIONS.

6. ɕiaŋ⁻ǰiao 11. ˊʃou ˋthou· 16. ⁻g̑uŋ·d̑ao 23. ˋd̑a·mi ˊthao
7. ˋkhuaŋ˳chiɛ   liao   17. ˊb̑aɪ·li   24. xaɪ ˊthaŋ
8. ˋjyn ˋfeɪ   12. ˊwu·lun   18. ˊphiŋ·g̑uɔ   25. ˋjy·b̑eɪ
9. ˧ʃueɪ⁻ǰyan 13. ɹu ˊxʌ   19. ˋg̑uan·thou 26. [˧ʃueɪ˳g̑uɔ]
10. ˊtshuŋ ˊchiɛn 14. ˋtshou·xʌ 20. *⁻ɕiaŋ˳g̑aŋ
                15. ʧhʌŋ⁻g̑uŋ   21. ˊluŋ˳jɛn
                                22. ˋli·d̑ʒɿ

CONVERSATION.

˧ǰia. chiŋ ˋwən, ˋd̑ʒɤ·g̑ə ɕiaŋ⁻ǰiao ˋmaɪ ⁻d̑ɔ·ʃao ˊchiɛn i⁻ǰɪn ni?
ˋi. ˋʌɪ·mao ˊchiɛn i⁻ǰɪn, ɕiɛn·ʃʌŋ.
˧ǰia. ɕiaŋ⁻ǰiao ʃɿ b̑u ˋtshɔ, ˳khʌ·ʃɿ ˆʌɪ·mao ˊchiɛn i⁻ǰɪn ˳ju
     d̑ə·ɹ thaɪ ˋg̑ueɪ liao, ˋkhuaŋ·chiɛ ˋɕiɛn ˋd̑ʒaɪ·d̑ɪ ˋd̑ʒʌŋ ʃɿ ɕiaŋ
     ⁻ǰiao ˋǰiɛn·d̑ɪ ˊʃɿ·xou.
ˋi. ⁻ɕiɛn·ʃʌŋ, ni ˋb̑u·d̑ʒɿ ˋd̑ao wa, ɕiɛn ˋd̑ʒaɪ·d̑ɪ ˋjyn ˋfeɪ xʌ ˧ʃueɪ
     ⁻ǰyan ⁻d̑u b̑i ˊtshuŋ·chiɛn ˋd̑ʒuŋ liao, ˳wɔ·mən ˳jɛ ˊmeɪ·ju
     ˳fa·d̑zɯ b̑u ˋmaɪ g̑ueɪ·i˳d̑iɛn. ˋd̑ʒaɪ⁻ʃuɔ, ˋd̑ʒɤ ʃɿ ˊʃou ˋthou
     liao·d̑ɪ ɕiaŋ⁻ǰiao.
˧ǰia. ˊwu·lun ɹu ˊxʌ, ˳jɛ b̑u⁻ǰɪŋ·d̑aŋ ˋd̑ʒə·mə ˋg̑ueɪ ja.
ˋi. ˳xao b̑a, ⁻ɕiɛn·ʃʌŋ d̑ɔ ˳maɪ i⁻ɕiɛ, ˳wɔ ǰiɛn ˋmaɪ i˳d̑iɛn, liaŋ·
     ˋtshou·xʌ, ˳maɪ ˋmaɪ ˋb̑u·ʃɿ ˋǰiu ʧhʌŋ⁻g̑uŋ·liao ma?
     g̑eɪ ⁻ɕiɛn·ʃɪŋ ⁻san ǰɪn b̑a, ˋsuan ni ⁻i·mao ⁻b̑a·fən i⁻ǰɪn,
     ˋd̑ʒɤ ⁻g̑uŋ·d̑ao·b̑u⁻g̑uŋ·d̑ao?
˧ǰia. ˳xao, ˋǰiu·ʃɿ ˋd̑ʒɤ·mə ˋb̑an b̑a. ni ⁻d̑ʒən xueɪ d̑zɔ ˳maɪ ˋmaɪ
     ja!
ˋi. ˊxuan jao ˊb̑iɛ·d̑ɪ ma, ⁻ɕiɛn·ʃʌŋ? ˳wɔ·d̑ɪ ˋd̑a ˊb̑aɪ ˊli xʌ
     *⁻ʃan·d̑uŋ ˊphin·g̑uɔ ⁻d̑u ʃɿ ˋd̑ɪŋ xao·d̑ɪ ⁻d̑uŋ·ɕi, ˋǰia·chiɛn
     ˳jɛ b̑u ˋg̑ueɪ. ˋg̑ʌ ˋjaŋ·d̑ɪ ˋg̑uan·thou ⁻d̑u ʃɿ ⁻ɕɪn ju *⁻ɕiaŋ
     ˳g̑aŋ˳laɪ·d̑ɪ; ˋli·d̑ʒɿ ˊluŋ˳jɛn, xʌ ˋd̑a·mi ˊthao, d̑u ˳ju.
˧ǰia. ˳ni ju ˋd̑zɯ·ǰi ˋd̑zɔ·d̑ɪ ˋmi·ǰiɛn xaɪ ˊthaŋ meɪ·ju?
ˋi. ˋd̑ueɪ·b̑u˳chi. ˳wɔ·mən ˋɕiɛn ˋd̑ʒaɪ ˊb̑u ˋjy·b̑eɪ ˋna·g̑ə,
     ⁻jɪn·weɪ ⁻thiɛn·chi ˊxuan thaɪ ˋɹʌ, ⁻g̑ʌ·b̑u ˋd̑ʒu.
˧ǰia. ˳xao, d̑zaɪ ˋǰiɛn b̑a.
ˋi. ˋɕiɛ·ɕiɛ ⁻ɕiɛn·ʃʌŋ.

Translation. Lesson 17. Part II.

Selling Fruits.

COMPOUND WORDS AND EXPRESSIONS.

6. banana.
7. how much more.
8. freightage.
9. customs duty.
10. formerly.
11. perfectly ripe
12. no matter, not to speak of.
13. how?
14. collect, meet.
15. finish work.
16. just.
17. bartlet pears.
18. apple.
19. tinned goods.
20. Hong Kong.
21. lung yen, dragon's eyes (a fruit).
22. lichi.
23. honey peaches
24. a small apple.
25. prepare.
26. [fruits generally].

EXERCISE.

A. Please, how much do you charge for a catty of these bananas?
B. Twenty cents a catty, sir.
A. They are not bad bananas, but twenty cents a catty is rather dear, and bananas ought to be cheap at this time of the year.
B. Sir, you do not know. Now-a-days the expenses of transportation and the customs duties are both heavier than they used to be. So we are compelled to ask higher prices.
A. Anyway they ought not to be that price.
B. All right, you buy more and I will sell them cheaper, and complete the bargain. If I give you three catties and charge you 18 cents for a catty, will that be a fair deal?
A. Agreed; we will settle it that way. You certainly know how to do business.
B. Anything else, sir? My large white pears and Shantung apples are of the best, and not dear either. All sorts of tinned fruit have just arrived from Hongkong. Li Chi, Lung Yen and large Honey Peaches, we have them all here.
A. Have you got Preserved Cherries put up by yourself?
B. Sorry. We are not preparing them just now, as it is still too hot to keep them.
A. All right. Good-bye.
B. Thank you, sir.

Transcription. Lesson 18.

VOCABULARY.

1st Tone.	2nd Tone.	3rd Tone.	4th Tone.
Pt.I.526. ba	Pt.I.528. ḍa	Pt.I.530. ğan	Pt.I.535. xuɑ
527. xuan	529. jyn	531. bao	536. xən
Pt.II.538. xɑ	Pt.II.546. wu	532. thao	537. miɛn
539. dʒɪ	547. ʃr	533. ɕi	Pt.II.556. ʃɤ
540. ou	548. jy	534. dʒun	557. fu
541. dʒou	549. ḍu	Pt.II.555. meɪ	558. jy
542. ḍa	550. ɕɪŋ		559. waŋ
543. tshueɪ	551. tʃhuan		560. jɛ
544. ǰi	552. ɕi		561. baɪ
545. an	553. jɪŋ		561a. jy
	554. bɔ		

Transcription of Part I.

ˋḍi ´ʃɪ⁻ba ˋkhʌ. ˋʃaŋ.

COMPOUND WORDS AND EXPRESSIONS.

1. ˏdʒu·i
2. ´xueɪ·ḍa
3. faŋ⁻ɕɪn
4. ´ḍa·jɪŋ
5. dʒuŋˋi

EXERCISE.

1. ⁻tha ´xueɪ·ḍa ⁻ʃuɔ tha ˏxən ˋjyan·i ˋchy. 2. faŋ⁻ɕɪn ba, ˏwɔ ğan ˏbao ⁻tha bu´nʌŋ bu´ḍa·jɪŋ. 3. ˋdʒɤ·dʒaŋ ⁻xua wɔ ˋkhan· dʒɔ ˏxən dʒuŋˋi. 4. wɔ ´ʃɪ·dʒaɪ ˏɕiaŋ ni. 5. ˏxən bu ´nʌŋ ´tʃhaŋ ǰiɛnˋmiɛn tshaɪ ˏxao. 5. tha ⁻ba·bu ˋdɤ thao ˏni·mən ḍa⁻ǰia·ḍɪ ˏɕi·xuan. 6. ⁻tha dʒun ˋchy, ˋǰiu·ʃɪ ˋɕiɛn ˋdʒaɪ ´jyn·bu·tʃhu ⁻ğuŋ·fu ´laɪ. 7. ˏwɔ ⁻dʒɯ·ǰi bu´nʌŋ ˋḍɪŋ ⁻ğueɪ, ⁻chɪŋ ˏni ˋthi wɔ ´na ğə ´dʒu·i. 8. ˋna·ğə ´rən ˏlao ´meɪ·ju ´dʒu·i, ǰɪŋ ˋkhao·dʒɔ tha ⁻fu·rən ban ˋʃɪ. 9. tha ˋdzɔ·thiɛn ⁻jɪŋ·ɕy·liao, ⁻khʌ·ʃɪ ˏǰɪn thiɛn ˋdzao·tʃhən, ˋǰiɛn·liao ´na·ğə ⁻phʌŋ·ju, ˋtha ju ˋbu ˏkhən·lə. 10. ˏwɔ ˏḍa·suan ´ɕyə ´ǰi·ǰy ⁻jɪŋ´wən, ˋbu·dʒɪ ´ḍao ⁻ɕiɛn·ʃʌŋ ´meɪ·thiɛn nʌŋ ´jyn ·ḍiɛn ⁻ğuŋ·fu ˋǰiao wɔ bu´nʌŋ.

Translation. Lesson 18.

VOCABULARY.

1st Tone.	2nd Tone.	3rd Tone.	4th Tone.
Pt.I. 526. sign of optative.	Pt.I. 528. reply.	Pt.I. 530. dare.	Pt.I. 535. draw, mark.
527. rejoice, happy.	529. equal, even, divide equally.	531. protect, guarantee.	536. hate.
Pt.II. 538. expletive part.	Pt.II. 546. a surname.	532. seek.	537. face.
539. sign of genitive.	547. a thing, a file of ten.	533. happy.	Pt.II. 556. village.
540. Europe.	548. at, in.	534. permit, exactly.	557. rich.
541. continent.	549. read.	Pt.II. 555. beautiful.	558. surplus.
542. take passage.	550. form.		559. hope.
543. to urge.	551. boat.		560. estate profession.
544. machine.	552. hope.		561. ruin, destroy.
545. peace.	553. to scheme, to plan.		561a. to meet.
	554. father's elder brother.		

Translation of Part I.

COMPOUND WORDS AND EXPRESSIONS.

1. opinion, purpose.
2. reply, answer to.
3. make the mind easy.
4. reply, assent.
5. to like.

EXERCISE.

1. He replied that he was very willing to go. 2. Be easy in your mind, I guarantee that he can do no other than consent. 3. I think this picture is perfect. 4. I have wanted you badly, I would give anything to meet you constantly. 5. He would do anything to please you all. 6. He will certainly go, but just now he cannot find the time. 7. I cannot make up my mind, please decide for me. 8. That man has no mind of his own, he just leans upon his wife in all he does. 9. Yesterday he agreed, but this morning he met a friend, and now he is not willing. 10. I am planning to study a little English, I wonder whether you could find time to teach me, sir?

Transcription. Lesson 18. Part II.

`ɖi ´ʃɿ¯ba `khʌ. `ɕia.
`jy ˳ju.

COMPOUND WORDS AND EXPRESSIONS.

6. ¯dʐɿ·ʃɿ   10. ɖa´tʃhuan   14. ¯ʝi·xueɪ   18. ˳bən·dʐɔ   22. `bien·fan
7. ɖu¯ʃu   11. `fu·jy      15. ˳ɖa·suan    19. ¯ʝɪŋ·jɛn   23. `ɕia·wu
8. `ʃɤ·xueɪ      12. ´ɕi·waŋ     16. `ʃɿ·jɛ   20. ´tʃhʌŋ`baɪ 24. ¯faŋ·bien
9. ´chɪŋ·ɕɪŋ   13. i`xou   17. ¯ʝɪŋ·jɪŋ   21. ´jɪŋ¯ʃaŋ   25. ˳chɪŋ¯an
                                                                26. [`jy˳ju]
                                                                27. [´bɔ˳mu

CONVERSATION.

˳ʝia. xa¯xa! *´wu ¯ɕiɛn·ʃʌŋ ´ʃə·mə ´ʃɿ·xou xueɪ´laɪ·ɖɪ?
`i.   wɔ ´dzɔ·thiɛn ´tshaɪ xueɪ´laɪ·ɖɪ. ˳wɔ·mən ju ˳wu·niɛn meɪ
      `ʝiɛn·lə.
˳ʝia. khʌ`bu·ʃɿ. `dzaɪ *˳meɪ·ɡuɔ ´dʐə·mə ˳ʝi·niɛn i´ɖɪŋ ´ɖɤ·liao
      bu˳ʃao·ɖɪ ¯ɕɪn ¯dʐɿ·ʃɿ ba!
`i.   `bu·ɡan ¯ʃuɔ! ´bu·ɡuɔ jy ´ɖu¯ʃu·dʐɿ ´waɪ, ´tʃhaŋ ɖao `ɡʌ`tʃhu
      chy `khan·khan, ¯ɖɔ·ʃao ´mɪŋ·baɪ ¯i·ɕiɛ `ʃɤ·xueɪ`ʃaŋ·ɖɪ
      ´chɪŋ·ɕɪŋ.
˳ʝia. ˳jɛ ɖao *¯ou·dʐou `chy·liao ma?
`i.   ´meɪ·ju nɪ! ˳bən ɕiaŋ xueɪ´ɡuɔ·ɖɪ `ʃɿ·xou ɖa´tʃhuan ɖao
      *¯ou·dʐou `chy, `xou·laɪ, ¯jɪn·weɪ ˳ʃou·li bu `fu·jy, ´ju ¯ɖa·
      dʐɔ lao ˳mu·chɪn ˳ɕiɛ·ɕɪn ¯tshueɪ wɔ `khuaɪ xueɪ¯ʝia, ˳sɔ·i
      ʝiu ´meɪ´ɖɤ `chy. ´ɕi·waŋ i`xou ju ¯ʝi·xueɪ `dzaɪ `chy ba.
˳ʝia. ¯ʝi·xueɪ ¯i·ɖɪŋ ˳ju. `ɕiɛn`dzaɪ ˳ɖa·suan`dzɔ ɕiɛ ´ʃə·mə `ʃɿ·jɛ
      nɪ?
`i.   ˳ɖa·suan ¯ʝɪŋ·jɪŋ ɡə ˳ɕiao ˳maɪ`maɪ, ˳bən·dʐɔ ´dʐɤ ʝi ´niɛn
      dzaɪ `waɪ·ɡuɔ ´ɖɤ·laɪ·ɖɪ ¯ʝɪŋ·jɛn `ʃɿ·i`ʃɿ; ´tʃhʌŋ`baɪ bu˳ɡan
      ʃuɔ.
˳ʝia. ´jɪŋ¯ʃaŋ ʃɿ ˳xao `ʃɿ. ˳wɔ ¯ʃuɔ, ˳ʝi·ʃɿ ju ¯ɡuŋ·fu ɖao¯ʝia·li¯tʃhɿ
      ɡə `bien`fan nɪ? ˳lao `thaɪ·thaɪ ˳xən ɕiaŋ `khan·khan ni.
`i.   ´mɪŋ·thiɛn `ɕia·wu `liu·ɖiɛn ¯ɖjuŋ ¯faŋ·bienbu¯fan·bien?
      wɔ `dʐaŋ ɕiaŋ `chy ɡeɪ ´bɔ·mu chɪŋ¯an.
˳ʝia. ˳xao, `ʝiu ´dʐə·mə ban. ´mɪŋ·thiɛn `ʝiɛn.
`i.   ´mɪŋ·thiɛn `ʝiɛn.

Translation. Lesson 18. Part II.

Meeting a Friend.

COMPOUND WORDS AND EXPRESSIONS.

6. experience.
7. read.
8. society.
9. conditions, circumstances.
10. take passage in a boat.
11. surplus wealth.
12. hope.
13. afterwards
14. opportunity
15. reckon.
16. employment, affairs.
17. to trade.
18. taking as a basis
19. experience.
20. success and failure.
21. set up in business.
22. ordinary food.
23. afternoon
24. convenient.
25. salute, greet.
26. [to meet a friend].
27. [aunt].

CONVERSATION.

A. Hallo, Mr. Fu! When did you come back?

B. I just came back yesterday. It is five years since we met!

A. Yes, it is. You must have learned a great deal these few years you have been America.

B. I don't know about that. I can only say that, besides what I have learned from my studies, I have frequently visited different places, and I learned something of [American] social life.

A. Did you go to Europe, too?

B. No. I originally intended to go to Europe on my way home. Afterwards (I found) I had not enough money, and then my mother wrote urging me to come home at once. So I could not go. I hope I shall have a chance to go sometime later.

A. You will be sure to have a chance [sometime]. What are you going to do now?

B. I want to start a small business, and try out what I have learned abroad. Whether it will be successful or not I can't tell yet.

A. To set up in business is a good idea. I say, when will you be free to come and have a meal with us? My mother is very anxious to see you.

B. Will it be convenient to-morrow afternoon at 6 o'clock? I was wanting to pay my respects to her.

A. All right. Let it be that way, we will see you to-morrow.

B. See you to-morrow.

Transcription. Lesson 19.

VOCABULARIES.

1st Tone.	2nd Tone.	3rd Tone.	4th Tone.
Pt.I.562. i	Pt.I.568. tshaɪ	Pt.I.581. d̥zɯ	Pt.I.585. xɑo
563. ɕɪŋ	569. fʌŋ	582. chiɛn	586. d̥uan
564. ʃən	570. fu	583. ɑo	587. b̥u
565. tshu	571. jɛn	584. d̥ʒun	588. liɑo
566. ʃɑŋ	572. i	Pt.II.597. xuɔ	589. sɤ
567. g̊ən	573. tʃhou	598. ʒ̊i	Pt.II.599. d̥ʒan
Pt.II.590. ʒ̊ɪn	574. xuŋ		600. b̥eɪ
591. ʒ̊ia	575. **chi**		601. g̊uŋ
592. fʌŋ	576. lan		602. thɤ
593. juŋ	577. tshaɪ		[d̥ɤ]
	578. phi		603. tshɯ
	579. miɛn		604. fʌŋ
	580. ʒ̊ia		605. lyə
	Pt.II.594. thɪŋ		606. d̥aɪ
	595. jɑo		607. b̥aŋ
	596. lɪŋ		

Transcription of Part I.

`d̥i /ʃɪ‿jiu `khʌ. `ʃɑŋ.

COMPOUND WORDS AND EXPRESSIONS.

1. ′tshaɪ·fʌŋ
2. `d̥zɯ·xɑo
3. ⁻i·fu
4. ⁻i·ʃɑŋ
5. ′jɛn·sɤ
6. ′ʃɪ⁻ɕɪŋ
7. ′chi′chyan
8. `ʃɑŋ‿d̥ʌŋ
9. ′tshaɪ·liɑo
10. ⁻ɕiuŋ′thaɪ
11. ′phi‿ɑo
12. ′miɛn‿ɑo
13. ′ʒ̊ia·i⁻ʃɑŋ
14. ⁻d̥an·i·ʃɑŋ
15. ‿d̥ʒun‿b̥ɑo
16. ′phiɛn·i

EXERCISE.

′chiɛn ʒ̊iɛ ‿ju g̊ə ′tshaɪ·fʌŋ ′phu, `d̥zɯ·xɑo ʃɪ *′thuŋ ′xʌ. ⁻tha `d̥zɔ·d̥ɪ ⁻i·fu, `jaŋ·d̥zɯ xʌ ′jɛn·sɤ ⁻d̥u xən ′ʃɪ⁻ɕɪŋ.
⁻tha·d̥ɪ ′tʃhou`d̥uan ju ′xuŋ·d̥ɪ, ju ‿d̥zɯ·d̥ɪ, ju ⁻chɪŋ·d̥ɪ; ‿chiɛn·d̥ɪ ⁻ʃən·d̥ɪ ⁻d̥u xən ′chi·chyan. ⁻tha·d̥ɪ ′lan·b̥u, ′wu·lun ʃɪ ⁻tshu·d̥ɪ ʃɪ `ɕi·d̥ɪ, ⁻d̥u ʃɪ `ʃɑŋ·d̥ɑŋ ′tshaɪ liɑo.
⁻ɕiuŋ′thaɪ `jɑo ‿maɪ `phi‿ɑo ′miɛn‿ɑo, `xuɔ·ʃɪ ′ʒ̊ia·i⁻ʃɑŋ ⁻d̥an·i⁻ʃɑŋ, g̊ən ⁻tha ‿maɪ, ‿d̥ʒun‿b̥ɑo ′phiɛn·i.

Translation. Lesson 19.

VOCABULARY.

1st Tone.	2nd Tone.	3rd Tone.	4th Tone.
Pt.I.562 clothes.	Pt.I.568. cut out, cut.	Pt.I.581. purple	Pt.I.585. a sign, name.
563. arise.	569. sew.	582. slight, shallow.	586. satin.
564. deep, very.	570. clothes.	583. overcoat, quilted coat	587. cloth.
565. coarse.	571. colour.	584. grant, allow.	588. material.
566. clothes.	572. suitable.	Pt. II.597. fire.	589. colour
567. follow, from.	573. silk.	598. to push.	Pt.II.599. stand.
Pt.II.590. ford.	574. red.		600. double.
591. add to.	575. even, adjust.		601. all, collectively.
592. flourishing.	576. blue.		602. special.
593. to crowd.	577. material.		603. a time.
	578. skin.		604. receive.
	579. cotton		605. outline, define.
	580. double, lined.		606. lead, carry.
	Pt.II.594. stop.		607. a pound.
	595. shake.		
	596. bell.		

Translation of Part I.

COMPOUND WORDS AND EXPRESSIONS.

1. tailor.
2. shop-sign, style of firm.
3. clothes.
4. clothes.
5. colour.
6. up-to date, fashionable.
7. complete.
8. first class, finest quality.
9. materials.
10. eminent brother, term of respect.
11. fur coat.
12. wadded coat.
13. lined clothes.
14. unlined clothes.
15. guarantee.
16. cheap.

EXERCISE.

On South Street there is a tailor, his sign is T'ung Ho. The clothes he makes are up-to-date in style and colour.

His silks and satins are red, purple, and grey, and in all shades; his blue cloth, whether coarse or fine, is all of the best quality.

If you, my friend, want to buy a fur coat or wadded gown, or if you want lined or single garments, buy from him, and you will certainly find it pay you.

Transcription. Lesson 19. Part II.

ʼdi ˊʃɪ ʝiu ˋkhʌ. ˋɕia.
‿xuɔ ˉtʃhɣ ˋdʒan.

COMPOUND WORDS AND EXPRESSIONS.

17. [‿xuɔˉtʃhɣ ˋdʒan]
18. *ˉthiɛn·ɪn
19. iˋbeɪ
20. iˋǵuŋ
21. ˋda ʼjaŋ
22. ˋɕiɛn ʼjaŋ
23. ˋdʒan ʼthaɪ
24. ˉkhaɪ ˉtʃhɣ
25. *ˉfʌŋ thaɪ
26. ˋthɣ ʼbiɛ
27. ˋkhuaɪ ˉtʃhɣ
28. *ˋfʌŋ thiɛn
29. ˉthuŋ ˉtʃhɣ
30. ˋlyə ʼweɪ
31. ˉjuŋ·ʝi
32. ˋman ˉtʃhɣ
33. ʼɕɪŋ·li
34. ˋǵuɔ baŋ
35. ʼfan ˉtʃhɣ

CONVERSATION.

‿ʝia. *ˉthiɛn·ʝɪn·dɪ ˉsan·dʌŋ ˋphiao ˉdɔ·ʃao ʼchiɛn ?
ˋi ˉi·khuaɪ ˉchi·mao ‿wu.
‿ʝia. ˋʌɪ·dʌŋ nɪ ?
ˋi. ˉdɔ ˉʝia iˋbeɪ.
‿ʝia. ‿chɪŋ ‿ǵeɪ wɔ ‿liaŋ·dʒaŋ ˋʌɪ·dʌŋ ˋphiao ; ˉi ˋǵuŋ ʃɪ ?
ˋi. ˉchi·khuaɪ ˋda ʼjaŋ.
‿ʝia. ˋdʒɣ ʃɪ iˉdʒaŋ ʼʃɪ·khuaɪ ʼchiɛn·dɪ ˋphiao·dzɯ, chɪŋ ‿dʒao ǵeɪ ‿wɔ ˉsan·khuaɪ ɕiɛn ʼjaŋ ba.
‿ʝia. ‿chɪŋ ˋwən, dao *ˉthiɛn·ʝɪn ˋchy·dɪ ˉtʃhɣ dzaɪ ‿na·ǵə ˋdʒan thaɪ ˉkhaɪ ?
‿bɪŋ. ˋdzaɪ diˉsan ˋdʒan ʼthaɪ.
‿ʝia. ʼʃə·mə ʼʃɪ·xou khaɪ ˉtʃhɣ ?
‿bɪŋ. ˉsan·diɛn ʼʃɪ ‿wu·fən, ˋɕiɛn ˋdzaɪ ‿i·ʝɪŋ ʃɪ ˉsan·diɛn ˉba·fən la.
‿ʝia. ˉtʃhɣ ˉdu dzaɪ ‿na·li ʼthɪŋ nɪ ?
‿bɪŋ. ‿dʒɪ dzaɪ *ˉfʌŋ·thaɪ ʼthɪŋ ‿wu·fən ˉdʒuŋ, ˉjɪn·weɪ ˋdʒɣ ʃɪ ˋthɣ ʼbiɛ khuaɪ ˉtʃhɣ.
‿ʝia. ˋjɛ·li ju ˋju *ˉthiɛn·ʝɪn ʼxueɪ·laɪ·dɪ khuaɪ ˉtʃhɣ meɪ ‿ju ?
‿bɪŋ. ju ˉi tshɯ, ʃɪ ˋju *ˉfʌŋ·thiɛn ɕia ʼlaɪ·dɪ ˉthuŋ·tʃhɣ. ʼbu·ǵuɔ ˉtʃhɣ ʃaŋ ˋlyə·weɪ ‿juŋ·ʝi i ‿diɛn ; ˋbu·ɪu ˋdzɔ ˉba·diɛn· ˋʌɪ·ʃɪ ˉfən·dɪ ˋman·tʃhɣ, ˉtʃhɣ ʃaŋ ʼɪən ʝi bu ˉdɔ, dao ˉʝɪŋ·dɪ ˉʃɪ·xou, ʼjɛ ‿bu xən ‿wan.
‿ʝia. ‿wɔ·mən·dɪ ʼɕɪŋ·li ˋjuŋ ˋǵuɔ baŋ bu ˋjuŋ ?
ˉbɪŋ. ˋdʒə·mə ‿ɕiao·dɪ ˉɕiaŋ·dzɯ, ‿ni·mən ‿khʌ·i ˋdzɯ·ʝi ˋdaɪ dʒɔ, ʼbu·juŋ ‿da ʼɕɪŋ·li ˋphiao liao.
ˉʝia. ˉtʃhɣ·ʃaŋ ju ˋfan ˉtʃhɣ meɪ ‿ju ?
‿bɪŋ. ju ʃɪ ‿ju, khʌ·ʃɪ ˋɕiɛn ˋdzaɪ ˉi·ʝɪŋ ˋǵuɔ·liao ˉkhaɪ ‿fan·dɪ ʼʃɪ·xou·lə, ‿ni·mən ‿dɪŋ ‿xao ˋdzaɪ·dʒan ʼthaɪ·ʃaŋ ‿maɪ ɕiɛ ‿diɛn·ɕɪn ˋdaɪ·dʒɔ.
‿ʝia. ‿a ! ʼjao ʼlɪŋ liao ! ˋkhuaɪ ʃaŋ ˉtʃhɣ ba !

Translation. Lesson 19. Part II
At the Station.

COMPOUND WORDS AND EXPRESSIONS.

17. [station].
18. Tientsin, (a place).
19. double.
20. altogether.
21. dollars.
22. silver money.
23. station platform.
24. start.
25. Feng-t'ai.
26. special.
27. fast trains, express.
28. Feng-t'ien
29. through train, express.
30. rather, somewhat.
31. crowded.
32. slow train.
33. luggage.
34. to weigh luggage.
35. restaurant car.

CONVERSATION.

A. What is the third class fare to Tientsin?

B. One dollar and 75 cents.

A. What is it second class?

B. Just double.

A. Please give me a second class ticket. How much?

B. Seven dollars.

A. This is a ten dollar bill, please give me three dollars change in silver

A. Please tell me which is the platform for the Tientsin train?

C. No. 3 platform.

A. What time does the train start?

C. 3.15. It is already eight minutes past three.

A. Where does the train stop?

C. It is the special express, and only stops five minutes at Fengtai.

A. Is there an express train back from Tientsin in the night?

C. There is a through train from Mukden, but it is rather crowded. You had better take the 8.20 slow train. There are not many people on it, and therefore it is not very late arriving at Peking.

A. Is it necessary to weigh our luggage?

C. A small case like this you can carry with you. You need not buy a luggage ticket.

A. Is there a restaurant car?

C. Yes, but it is past the dinner time now. You had better get something on the platform and carry it with you.

A. Hallo! There goes the bell! Get in quickly.

Transcription. Lesson 20.

VOCABULARIES.

1st Tone.	2nd Tone.	3rd Tone.	4th Tone.
Pt.I.608. ɕiaŋ	Pt.I.610. lɪŋ	Pt.I.612. lia	Pt.I.615. ɕiaŋ
609. ǰiao	611. tʃhʌŋ	613. ʃɤ	616. li.
Pt.II.619. ɕiao	Pt.II.622. ju	614. ly	617. tshaɪ
620. ǰi	623. lan	Pt.II 628. chiɛn	618. mɔ
621. ǰyn	624. chiu	629. tʃhaŋ	Pt.II.632. ǰi
	625. ju	630. waŋ	633. ɕi
	626. chi	631. ǯuan	634. ǯzɔ
	627. chi		635. aɪ
			636. ɕiaŋ
			637. liɛ
			638. bɪŋ
			639. ǯueɪ

Transcription of Part I.

ˋǯi ˋʌɪˊʃɪ ˋkhʌ. ˋʃaŋ.

COMPOUND WORDS AND EXPRESSIONS.

1. ˋtshuŋˊlaɪ
2. ⁻ɕiɛnˊchiɛn
3. ⁻ɕiaŋˋɕia
4. ˌǯzaoˊniɛn
5. ˊlɪŋ˽ʃɤ
6. ˋɕiaŋˊlaɪ
7. ˽ǯzao˽i
8. ˋliˊʃɪ
9. ˊʃɪˋkhʌ
10. ˊliu⁻ɕɪn
11. ˊthan⁻ɕɪn
12. ˌlyˋtshɯ
13. ˌlaoˋʃɪ
14. ˋmɔ·mɔ ˌliao

EXERCISE.

˽wɔ ˊtshuŋˊlaɪ meɪˋchy·ǥuɔ. 2. ⁻tha ⁻ɕiɛnˊchiɛn ˋǯzu ǯzaɪ ⁻ɕiaŋˋɕia. 3. ˽wɔ·mən ˽lia ˽ǯzao·niɛn ˋǯzɔ·ǥuɔ ˊlɪŋ·ʃɤ. 4. ⁻tha ˋɕiaŋˊlaɪ ˋǯzu ǯzaɪ ˊtʃhʌŋ˽li. 5. ˽wɔ ˊxuan meɪ⁻ʃuɔ, tha ˽ǯzao·i ⁻ǯzɪ·ǯao·liao. 6. ˋǯzaɪ tha meɪˊlaɪ iˊchiɛn, ni ⁻jiŋ·ǥaɪ ˋjy·ʙeɪ ˽xao. 7. ⁻tha ʙa ⁻ǯuŋ·ɕi ˋǰiao ǥeɪ ˽wɔ, ˋliˊʃɪ ǰiu ˊxueɪ·chy·liao. 8. ˽wɔ ⁻tʃhu·chy ˽maɪ i·ǯiɛn ˋtshaɪ, ǰiu ˊxueɪ·laɪ. 9. ˽ni ˋjao ˊʃɪˋkhʌ ˊliu⁻ɕɪn. 10. ⁻tha ˊtʃhaŋ·tʃhaŋ ʃaŋ ˋǯzɤ·li ˊlaɪ⁻than⁻ɕɪn. 11. ˽wɔ ˽lyˋtshɯ ˽ǯzao tha, ˽lao·ʃɪ ˽ǯzao·ʙuˊǯzao. 12. ˋmɔ·mɔ ˽liao wɔ ⁻ǯa·jɪŋ·liao ⁻tha.

Translation. Lesson 20.

VOCABULARY.

1st Tone.	2nd Tone.	3rd Tone.	4th Tone.
Pt.I.608. country.	Pt.I.610. neighbour.	Pt.I.612. two.	Pt.I.615. towards.
609. give to.	611. city, town.	613. cottage, rest.	616. stand.
Pt.II.619. dissipate.	Pt.II.622. swim, ramble.	614. frequently, repeatedly.	617. vegetable.
620. rouse, stimulate.	623. basket.	Pt.II.628. send.	618. at last, afterwards.
621. military.	624. ball.	629. arena, field.	Pt.II.632. help.
	625. still more.	630. net.	633. play.
	626. he, she, it, his, this, that.	631. short.	634. do, make.
	627. ride.		635. to love.
			636. like.
			637. ardent.
			638. illness.
			639. a company, a group.

Translation of Part I.

COMPOUND WORDS AND EXPRESSIONS.

1. formerly.
2. formerly.
3. country, in the.
4. in former years.
5. neighbour.
6. formerly.
7. previously, already.
8. at once, immediately.
9. incessantly.
10. careful.
11. converse.
12. frequently, often.
13. on all occasions.
14. afterwards, after all.

EXERCISE.

1. Up till now I have not been. 2. He formerly lived in the country. 3. We two were neighbours years ago. 4. He has hitherto lived in the country. 5. He knew before I spoke. 6. You ought to have prepared before he came. 7. He gave me the things and immediately went away. 8. I am going out to buy some provisions, I shall be back immediately. 9. You must be attentive all the while. 10. He often comes here for a chat. 11. I have looked for him several times, but cannot find him. 12. Finally I agreed to what he wanted.

Transcription. Lesson 20. Part II.

\ɖi \ʌɪ /ʃɪ \khʌ. \ɕia
ˉju \ɕi

COMPOUND WORDS AND EXPRESSIONS.

15. ˉɕiao ˌchiɛn
16. ˉju ˌʃueɪ
17. /lan /chiu
18. ˌɕi·xuan
19. /thuŋ \ɖʒɪ
20. ˉju \ɕi
21. ˌwaŋ /chiu
22. /thuŋ /ɕyə
23. /chiu ˌʧhaŋ
24. xɑo /ʝi·liɑo
25. \jyn·ɖuŋ
26. ˧ȷ̊yn ˌɖueɪ
27. ˧soˌi
28. \ɹən·g̊ia
29. ˉɖzɯ·ɕɪŋ
    ˉʧhɣ
30. ˉʝi \liɛ
31. \ju /chi

CONVERSATION.

ˌʝia. ˉɕiɛn·ʃʌŋ meɪ \ʃɪ·ɖɪ /ʃɪ·xou ɖzɔ /ʃə·mə ˉɕiao·chiɛn nɪ ?

\i. /ʧhu·liɑo ˉju ˌʃueɪ, ʃɪ ɖa /lan /chiu·ɖɪ /ʃɪ·xou ɖzueɪ ˉɖɔ.

ˌʝia ni ˌɕi·xuan ɖa /lan /chiu ma ? /thuŋ \ɖʒɪ, ˌwɔ ʝɛ \aɪ na·g̊ə
ˉju·ɕi. \b̥u·g̊uɔ ˉȷ̊ɪn·laɪ ˉthiɛn·chi thaɪ \ʌ, \ɖao·ʃɪ ɖa ˌwaŋ
chiu·ɖɪ /ʃɪ·xou ˉɖɔ.

\i. \ʃɪ, ˌwaŋ·chiu \b̥u·ɕiaŋ /lan·chiu \na·mə ˉʝi·liɛ, ʝɛ ˌxən ju
i \sɯ. ni \ɖao /ʃə·mə \ɖi·faŋ chy ˌɖa nɪ ?

ˌʝia. ˌwɔ·ɖɪ /thuŋ·ɕyə *ˉɖʒaŋ·ʝi ˉʝia·li ju g̊ə ˌɕiao xua /jyan,
ˉxua·jyan \xou·miɛn ˌju khuaɪ khuŋ \ɖi, ˉthɑ ʝiu ɖzaɪ
\na·li \ɖzao·liɑo ˉi·g̊ə /chiu ˌʧhaŋ, ˌwɔ b̥u ˌɖuan ɖao ˉthɑ
na·li \chy.

\i. \na xɑo /ʝi·lə. ˉju·ɕi ʃɪ ˌxən jao ȷ̊ɪn·ɖɪ \ʃɪ ; /ju·chɪ ʃɪ ɖzaɪ
\ɕia·thiɛn, \ʌ·ʃɪ b̥u \jyn·ɖuŋ \jyn·ɖuŋ, ɖzueɪ /ɹuŋ·i ʃʌŋ
\b̥ɪŋ. ˌwɔ ɖzaɪ ˉȷ̊yn \ɖueɪ·li·ɖɪ /ʃɪ·xou, ˉthiɛn thiɛn ˌɖzao
ʧhən, chi ˌma ɖao ˉɕiaŋ·ɕia \chy. \na ʃɪ g̊ə ˌxən ˌxɑo·ɖɪ
\jyn·ɖuŋ, \ɕiɛn \ɖzaɪ \ɖʒu ɖzaɪ /ʧhʌŋˌli, ˉi·laɪ, li ˉɕiaŋ·ɕia
xən ˌjyan, \ʌɪ·laɪ, \ɖzɯ ˌʝi /ju ˌmeɪ·ju ˌma, ˌsɔ·i /ʝiu
b̥u /nʌŋ b̥u \ɖzɔ ɕiɛ \b̥iɛ·ɖɪ \jyn·ɖuŋ lə.

ˌʝia. ˌwɔ zən ˌɕi·xuan khan /ɹən·ʝia chi ˌma, khʌ·ʃɪ wɔ /ɖzɯ·ʝi
b̥u /xueɪ, wɔ \ɖʒɪ xueɪ chi ˉɖzɯ·ɕɪŋ ˉʧhɣ. ˌɖʌŋ·ɖzɔ ju
ˉʝi·xueɪ ˌwɔ·mən ˉi·thuŋ ɕia ˉɕiaŋ, ni ˉʝiao g̊eɪ ˌwɔ chi ˌma b̥a.

Translation. Lesson 20. Part II.

Sport.

COMPOUND WORDS AND EXPRESSIONS.

15. game, recreation.
16. swim.
17. basket-ball.
18. like, to.
19. of one mind.
20. sport.
21. tennis.
22. schoolmates.
23. tennis-court.
24. excellent.
25. exercise, athletics.
26. army.
27. therefore.
28. people.
29. bicycle.
30. exciting, stimulating
31. still, more, specially.

CONVERSATION.

A. When you have nothing else to do what games do you play?

B. Except when I swim I generally play basket-ball.

A. You like basket-ball? We are of one mind, I like it too. But just now, while it is hot, I spend more of my time in playing tennis.

B. Yes, tennis is not so violent as basket-ball, and it is an interesting game too. Where do you play it?

A. My school fellow Chang Chi has a small garden in his house. Behind the garden is a piece of waste land where he has made a tennis court.

B. Splendid! Athletics are very important. They are even more so in the summer time, for if we do not take exercise our health is bound to suffer. When I was in the army I went in for horse-riding in the country every morning. But now I live in the city it is too far, and besides I have not got a horse of my own, so I have to take other exercise.

A. I like very much to see people riding on horseback, but I do not know how to ride myself. All I can do is ride a bicycle. Sometime, when we get the chance to go into the country together you must teach me to ride.

Transcription. Lesson 21.

VOCABULARIES.

1st Tone.	2nd Tone.	3rd Tone.	4th Tone.
Pt.I.640. tʃhʌŋ	Pt.I.642. mɪŋ	Pt.I.644. lɪŋ	Pt.I.646. ʃɪ
641. tshun	643. mɪn	645. ja	647. dʒən
Pt.II.650. ʝiɛ	Pt.II.657. wən	Pt.II.662. ʝiɛn.	648. ɕiɛn
651. tshaɪ	658. dʒɪ	663. jɪn	649. neɪ
652. tha	659. chi	664. ʝɪŋ	Pt.II.666. jɛ
653. xʌŋ	660. ʃən	665. ʃuaŋ	667. li
654. ʝɪŋ	661. miɑo		668. ɹu
655. fʌŋ			669. ʝiɛ
656. ɕi			670. ḅan
			671. ḍuan
			672. ʝiu
			673. mən
			674. chy

Transcription of Part I.

`ḍi `ʌɪ/ʃɪ⁻i `khʌ. `ʃaŋ.

COMPOUND WORDS AND EXPRESSIONS.

1. ˌlɪŋ⁻ʝiao
2. ′mɪŋ⁻tʃhʌŋ
3. `dʒu·tʃhu
4. ⁻ḍuŋ ′nan
5. ⁻ḍuŋ ˌḅeɪ

EXERCISE.

1. ˌlɪŋ⁻ʝiao ˌlɪŋ⁻ʝiao. jao ˌʝɪn·ḍɪ `ḍi·faŋ ′mɪŋ·tʃhʌŋ, ⁻ḍu ʃɪ ′ʃə·mə ? 2. `ḍi·faŋ ′mɪŋ·tʃhʌŋ, ˌju·ḍɪ ʝiao `ʃɪ, ⁻ɕiaŋ, `dʒən ; ˌju·ḍɪ ʝiao `ɕiɛn, ˌju·ḍɪ ʝiao ˌʃʌŋ. 3. ˌʃʌŋ dzueɪ`da ; `ʃɪ, ⁻ɕiaŋ, `dʒən, dzueɪ ˌɕiɑo. 4. ′ɹən′mɪn·ḍɪ `dʒu·tʃhu, `da·ḍɪ ʝiao ′tʃhʌŋ, ˌɕiɑo·ḍɪ ʝiao `dʒuaŋ·tshun. 5. *⁻dʒuŋ·ġuɔ ′ġuɔ·neɪ, ḍuŋ ′nan ju ′ʃɪ⁻ḅa ˌʃʌŋ, ḍuŋ ˌḅeɪ ju ⁻ḍuŋ⁻san ˌʃʌŋ. 6. ′juan·laɪ ⁻ḍuŋ·faŋ ⁻di⁻i·ġə da ′ġuɔ `ʝiu·ʃɪ *⁻dʒuŋ·ġuɔ. 7. ḍi′chiu·ʃaŋ ju ˌwu ⁻dʒou ; *⁻dʒuŋ·ġuɔ dzaɪ *ˌja·dʒou, tshʊ `waɪ ʃɪ *⁻ou·dʒou, *⁻feɪ·dʒou, *ˌmeɪ·dʒou, *ˌxaɪ ′jaŋ⁻dʒou. 8. *ˌja·dʒou dzueɪ`da, *⁻ou·dʒou dzueɪ ˌɕiɑo.

Translation. Lesson 21.

VOCABULARY.

1st Tone.	2nd Tone.	3rd Tone.	4th Tone.
Pt.I.640. praise, weigh.	Pt.I.642. name.	Pt.I.644. lead.	Pt.I.646. market
641. village	643. people.	655. ugly.	647. market town.
Pt.II.650. meet.	Pt.II.657. literature.	Pt.II.662. survey.	648. district.
651. guess.	658. straight.	663. habit.	649. inside, within.
652. it.	659. strange.	664. to view, circumstances.	Pt.II.666. page, leaf.
653. exclamatory part.	660. spirit.	665. lively.	667. benefit.
654. spiritual.	661. to paint, to draw.		668. enter.
655. point. (of a weapon).			669. borrow
656. pity.			670. board.
			671. section.
			672. old.
			673. sad.
			674. interest.

Translation of Part I.

COMPOUND WORDS AND EXPRESSIONS.

1. may I ask ?
2. names.
3. dwelling-place.
4. South East.
5. North East.

EXERCISE.

1. Please enlighten me. What are the most important geographical terms? 2. Of geographical terms, there are the mart, village and town; and there are the county and provinces. 3. The province is the largest, whilst the mart, village, and town are small. 4. Of places where people live, large ones are called cities, small ones are called villages and hamlets. 5. In China, on the South-West are the Eighteen Provinces, and on the North-East are the Three Eastern Provinces. 6. China is really the largest country in the East. 7. The earth has five continents. China is in Asia. The others are Europe, Africa, America, and Oceania. 8. Asia is the largest, and Europe the smallest (of the continents).

Transcription. Lesson 21. Part II.

ˋdi ˋʌɪ ʹʃɪ ⁻i ˋkhʌ. ˋɕia.

ˋkhan ˌɕiao ⁻ʃuɔ.

COMPOUND WORDS AND EXPRESSIONS.

6. ˌɕiao ⁻ʃuɔ
7. ˌda ⁻khaɪ
8. ⁻san·fən·dʒɪ ⁻i
9. ⁻ʝiɛ·dʒɔ
10. ʝiɛn ʹdʒɪ·dɪ
11. ʹthɪŋ·dʒu
12. ˋbu ʹʝy
13. ⁻ʝɪŋ·chi
14. ˌbi·fʌŋ
15. ˌʃuaŋ·li
16. ˌkhʌ·ɕi
17. ⁻chiɛn ˋwan
18. ⁻tʃhu ˋban
19. ʹtʃhən·mən
20. ʹxuɔ·chi
21. ʹbaɪ·xua
22. ʹʝyə·də
23. ˋʝia·dʒɪ

CONVERSATION.

ˌʝia. ʹdʒɔ·thiɛn ˌju weɪ ʹphʌŋ·ju ˋsuŋ ğeɪ ˌwɔ ⁻i·bən ⁻ɕin ɕiao ⁻ʃuɔ. wɔ ˌda·khaɪ ʝiu ˋniɛn·liao ⁻san·fən·dʒɪ ⁻i. tʃhɪ ʹwan·liao ˌwan·fan ˌju ⁻ʝiɛ·dʒɔ ˋkhan, ʝiɛn ʹdʒɪ·dɪ bu ʹnʌŋ ʹthɪŋ·dʒu ⁻i·ğuŋ ʃɪ ˋsɯ·baɪ ˌdo ˋʝɛ, ni ⁻tshaɪ ˌdzə·mə ʹdʒɔ, wɔ ⁻i·chi ˋba tha niɛn ʹwan·lə, ni ˌɕiaŋ wɔ ʹʃə·mə ʹʃɪ·xou khan ʹwan liao·dɪ?

ˋi. ˋʝɛ·li ʃɪ ˋʌɪ ˌdiɛn lə ba!

ˌʝia. ⁻xʌŋ! ˌliaŋ·diɛn ʹʃɪ·fən! ⁻dʒən ˌxao! ˋbu·ʝy ⁻ʝɪŋ·chi, ˌbi·fʌŋ ju ˌʃuaŋ·li, ˌwɔ sɔ ˋkhan ˋɪu·liao ⁻ʃən·la!

ˋi. ˌni khan ʹwan·lə? ˌxao, ⁻ğaɪ ˋʝiɛ ğeɪ ˌwɔ la!

ˌʝia. ˌkhʌ·ɕi, ni ʹlaɪ ˌwan·lə, ˌdzao ˋʝiao ʌɪ ʹmeɪ·meɪ ʹna·chy·liao.

ˋi. ˌwɔ ɕiɛn ⁻ʃuɔ·ɕia, dʌŋ ⁻tha khan ˋwan, chiɛn ˋwan ˋʝiɛ ğeɪ ˌwɔ.

ˌʝia. ⁻i·dɪŋ. wɔ ⁻ʝɪn·laɪ ˋkhan·ɕiao ⁻ʃuɔ·dɪ ˌmɪ ⁻feɪ ʹtʃhaŋ·dɪ ˋda. ʃuɔ ⁻dʒən·dɪ, ⁻ʝɪn·laɪ tʃhu ˋban·dɪ ˌɕiao·ʃuɔ, ʹʃɪ·dzaɪ bi ʹtshuŋ ʹchiɛn ˌxao·dɪ ⁻do, ⁻ʝɪn·weɪ ⁻ɕɪn ɕiao ⁻ʃuɔ, ʃɪ ʝuŋ ʹchyan·li ʹmiao·ɕiɛ ⁻i·duan ˋʃɪ, ju ʹchɪŋ ju ˌʝɪŋ, ˋju ju ˌdʒu·i. ˋʝiu ɕiao ⁻ʃuɔ ʃɪ ju ʹtʃhaŋ, ju ʹtʃhən·mən, ⁻i·diɛn ʹxuɔ·chi meɪ ˌju; ˋkhuaŋ·chiɛ ɕiɛn ˋdzaɪ juŋ ʹbaɪ·xua ˌɕiɛ, ˌɕiɛ·də ʃʌŋ ˋduŋ ju ˋchy, ˌni ʃuɔ ˋʃɪ·bu ˋʃɪ?

ˋi. ˋʃɪ. ˌwɔ ʝɛ ʹʝyə·də ⁻ɕɪn ɕiao ⁻ʃuɔ ju ⁻i·sɯ, ⁻ʝɪn·weɪ ju ⁻i·ɕiɛ ʹwən·ɕyə ˋʃʌŋ·dɪ ˋʝia·dʒɪ.

Translation. Lesson 21. Part II.

Reading a Novel.

COMPOUND WORDS AND EXPRESSIONS.

6. a novel.
7. to open.
8. one-third.
9. continue.
10. plainly.
11. to stop.
12. the plot.
13. clever.
14. style.
15. brisk.
16. unfortunately, what a pity.
17. by all means.
18. publish.
19. sad and heavy.
20. liveliness.
21. colloquial.
22. feel.
23. price.

CONVERSATION.

A. Yesterday my friend gave me a new novel. I opened it, and read a third of it. After supper I continued reading it, and could not put it down. There were over 400 pages altogether, and would you believe it, I read it through at one go. What do think the time was when I finished it?

B. Midnight, I suppose.

A. My! It was ten past two! It was really good. The plot is remarkably clever and the style is racy. It carried me away completely.

B. You have finished it? Good; now you can lend it to me?

A. What a pity! You are too late; it has already been taken away by my second younger sister.

B. Let me bespeak it. When she has finished it, let me have it.

A. Certainly. Recently I have been reading a good deal of fiction. There is no question that the new novels are really better than the old ones, because (the authors) concentrate on a single plot. They have movement and atmosphere and they follow certain fixed ideas. The old novels are long and dull, and the scenes described are without life. Moreover, modern novelists use the spoken language to write their stories, and hence they can write more vividly and interestingly. Do you agree with me?

B. Yes, and it seems to me also that the new novels are more interesting because they are superior in literary style.

Transcription. Lesson 22.

VOCABULARIES.

	1st Tone.	2nd Tone.	3rd Tone.	4th Tone.
	Pt.I.675. thueɪ	Pt.I.677. ly	Pt.I.680. xuɔ	Pt.I.681. li
	676. la	678. lɔ	Pt.II.698. phɑo	682. chi
	Pt.II.686. xun	679. niu	699. ɟy	683. ʃou
	687. sun	Pt.II.693. ɟiɛ	700. ja	684. ɟiao
	688. ʃən	694. jɛn	701. li	685. tʃhʌŋ
	689. g̊ao	695. liɛn		Pt. II. 702. b̥i
	690. dʒu	696. tshɯ		703. xʌ
	691. ɟiaŋ	697. phɪŋ		704. mʌŋ
	692. tʃhuan			705. b̥ao
				706. nao
				707. fan
				708. liaŋ or 2nd tone when used as verb.
				709. b̥i
				710. wu
				711. fu
				712. chiɛn

Transcription of Part I.

ˋd̥i ˋʌɪ·ʃɪˋʌɪ ˋkhʌ. ˋʃaŋ.

COMPOUND WORDS AND EXPRESSIONS.

1. ˻d̥zouˋd̥uŋ
2. ˋd̥iɛn·li
3. ˋchi·li
4. ˊɹən·li
5. ˋʃou·li
6. ˻ɕiao⁻tʃhɤ
7. ˋɟ̊iao-tʃhɤ
8. ˋd̥iɛn-tʃhɤ
9. ˋchi-tʃɤ
10. ˋd̥a-tʃhɤ
11. ˻xuɔ⁻tʃhɤ
12. ⁻d̥uŋ·jaŋ⁻tʃhɤ
13. ˋɟ̊iao·dzɯ

EXERCISE.

1. ⁻tʃhɤ·d̥ɪ ˻d̥zou·d̥uŋ ˋjao·ʃɪ ˊb̥u·juŋ ˋd̥iɛn·li, ˋchi·li, ˋɟ̊iu·ʃɪ juŋ ˊɹən·li ˋʃou·li. 2. junˊɹən·li·d̥ɪ ⁻tʃhɤ ju ˻ɕiao⁻tʃhɤ, ju ⁻d̥uŋ·jaŋ⁻tʃhɤ. 3. ˻ɕiao⁻tʃhɤ ʃɪ ˋjuŋ ɹən ⁻thueɪ, ⁻d̥uŋ·jaŋ⁻tʃhɤ ʃɪ ˋjuŋ ɹən ⁻la. 4. juŋˋʃou⁻li·d̥ɪ ju ˋd̥a⁻tʃhɤ, juŋ ˻ma, ˊly, ˊlɔ·d̥zɯ, ˋxuʌ·ʃɪ ˊniu ⁻la·d̥ʒɔ. ˋju ju ˋɟ̊iao⁻tʃhɤ ʃɪ juŋ ˊlɔ·d̥zɯ ˋxuʌ·ʃɪ ˻ma ⁻la·d̥ɪ. 5. juŋ ˋd̥iɛn·liˋchi·li·d̥ɪ ⁻tʃhɤ ju ˋd̥iɛn⁻tʃhɤ ˋchi⁻tʃhɤ ; ˊxuan ju ˻xuɔ⁻tʃhɤ. 6. ˋɟ̊iao·d̥zɯ ʃɪ ˋjuŋ ɹən ˊthaɪ·d̥ɪ ; ˻ju juŋ ˻liaŋ·g̊ə ɹən ˊthaɪ·d̥ɪ, ˻ju juŋ ˊsɯ·g̊ə ɹən ˊthaɪ·d̥ɪ.

Translation. Lesson 22.

VOCABULARIES.

1st Tone.
Pt. I. 675. push.
676. pull.
Pt. II. 686. marriage.
687. grandson.
688. body.
689. high.
690. pearl.
691. river.
692. wear.

2nd Tone.
Pt. I. 677. donkey.
678. mule.
679. cow, ox.
Pt. II. 693. unite, join.
694. words.
695. join, arrange.
696. porcelain.
697. vase.

3rd Tone.
Pt. I. 680. fire.
Pt. II. 698. run.
699. raise.
700. elegant.
701. ceremony.

4th Tone.
709. jewel.
710. objects, things.
711. woman, wife.
712. inadequate.

4th Tone.
Pt. I. 681. strength.
682. steam.
683. animals.
684. sedan chair.
685. ride, cl. of sedans.
Pt. II. 702. end.
703. congratulate.
704. first senior.
705. announce.
706. bustle.
707. pattern.
708. measure (noun); or 2nd tone when used as verb.

Translation of Part I.

COMPOUND WORDS AND EXPRESSIONS.
1. moving, propelling.
2. electricity.
3. steam power.
4. man power.
5. animal power.
6. wheel-barrow.
7. travelling cart.
8. tram car.
9. motor car.
10. wagon.
11. steam train.
12. rickshaw.
13. sedan chair.

EXERCISE.

1. In the propelling of vehicles when electric and steam power are not used man power or animal power is used. 2. Vehicles for which man power is used are the barrow and the jinrickshaw. 3. Barrows are pushed, and jinrickshas pulled by men. 4. Vehicles drawn by animals are the wagon, for which the horse, donkey, mule and ox are used, and the travelling-cart, for which mules and horses are used. 5. Vehicles propelled by electricity and steam or vapour are tramcars, motor cars, in addition to the railway train.

Transcription. Lesson 22. Part II.

`ḍi `ʌɪ/ʃɪ`ʌɪ `khʌ. `ɕia.
`xʌ ˌju/ɹən ⁻ɉiɛ⁻xun.

COMPOUND WORDS AND EXPRESSIONS.

14. ˌju/ɹən
15. ⁻ɉiɛ⁻xun
16. xʌ ˌɕi
17. ḍiɛn`ḅao
18. li`khʌ
19. ˌdʒɪ ˌxao
20. `ɪʌ·nao
21. ɕin/niaŋ·dzɯ
22. ⁻ʃɪ`fan/ɕyə
    `ɕiao
23. ḅi`jɛ
24. ⁻ʃən·liaŋ
25. ˌɉy·ḍuŋ
26. /jɛn/than
27. /wən ˌɉa
28. ⁻wən·xʌ
29. `khuaɪ·xuɔ
30. ⁻ǧao⁻ɕiŋ
31. `suŋ ˌli
32. ˌli·wu
33. ⁻i`ḍueɪ
34. *⁻ɉiaŋ·ɕi
35. `xua·phiŋ
36. ⁻fu `fu
37. ǧan`khuaɪ
38. ḍao`chiɛn

CONVERSATION.

ˌɉia. *`mʌŋ⁻ɕiɛn·ʃʌŋ, ni /dzɔ·thiɛn ḍao *`waŋ ɉia xʌ ˌɕi `chy·liao ma ?

`i.  wɔ `chy·lə, ˌni ˌdzə·mə meɪ `chy ni ?

ˌɉia. wɔ ˌḅən ɕiaŋ `chy laɪ·dʒɔ, ˌi·ɉiŋ ʧhuan ˌxao liao ⁻i·ʃaŋ, /laɪ liao ⁻i·ǧə ḍiɛn`ḅao `ɉiao wɔ li`khʌ ʃaŋ *⁻thuŋ·dʒou `chy, ˌdʒɪ xao waŋ *⁻thuŋ·dʒou ˌphao ḅa ! /dzɔ·thiɛn `na·ḷi ɹən ⁻ḍɔ·ḅu⁻ḍɔ ?

`i.  `ɪʌ·nao /ɉi lə ! ⁻ʧha·ḅu⁻ḍɔ /dza·mən·ḍɪ ˌlao tnuŋ/ɕyə /chyan `chy·lə.

ˌɉia. `khan·ɉiɛn·liao ɕin`niaŋ·dzɯ meɪ ˌju ?

`i.  `khan·ɉiɛn·liao ; ⁻tha ɕiŋ *⁻sun, ʃɪ ⁻ɛa tshuŋ ˌny·dzɯ ⁻ʃɪ`fan/ɕyə `ɕiao ḅi`jɛ·ḍɪ⁻tha·ḍɪ /niɛn·ɉi /ḅu·ǧuɔ `ʌɪ·ʃɪ`ʌɪ·san `sueɪ, ⁻ʃən·liaŋ xən⁻ǧao, ˌɉy·ḍuŋ /jɛn·than ⁻ḍu xən /wən·ɉa ⁻wən·xʌ, xʌ */waŋ⁻ɕiɛn·ʃʌŋ `dʒan dzaɪ i`khuaɪ·ɪ ⁻dʒən ʃɪ ⁻dʒu /liɛn`ḅi/xʌ.

ˌɉia. */waŋ⁻ɕiɛn·ʃʌŋ xən `khuaɪ·xuɔ ḅa ?

`i. na /xuan juŋ ⁻ʃuɔ, ⁻ǧao·ɕiŋ /ɉi·lə.

ˌɉia. /thuŋ/ɕyə suŋ ˌli·ḍɪ ḅu ˌʃao ḅa ?

`i. /ɹən/ɹən ˌju ɕiɛ ˌli·wu ; ˌwɔ ǧeɪ ⁻tha·mən ˌmaɪ·liao ⁻i·ḍueɪ *⁻ɉiaŋ·ɕi /tshɯ·ḍɪ ˌɕiao xua/phiŋ.

ˌɉia. ⁻tha `ɉy·ḅeɪ ˌwan`fan meɪ ˌju nɪ ?

`i.  ɕiŋ/wan·liao ˌli, ɕin ⁻fu·fu ˌdʒɪ ǧeɪ `da·ɉia ⁻i·ɕiɛ ˌḍiɛn·ɕin /ʧha·ʃueɪ, ⁻ɉin·weɪ `khʌ·ɹən thaɪ ⁻ḍɔ, ḅu/ɹuŋ·i /ɉy·ḅeɪ `fan.

ˌɉia. ⁻dʒən ˌkhʌ·ɕi, wɔ /meɪ·chy /ʧhʌŋ. wɔ /khan ˌwɔ ḍeɪ ˌǧan `khuaɪ ǧeɪ */waŋ⁻ɕiɛn·ʃʌŋ ˌɕiɛ fʌŋ ḍao`chiɛn·ḍɪ ⁻ɕɪn, tshaɪ `ḍueɪ.

Translation. Lesson 22. Part II.
A Wedding.

COMPOUND WORDS AND EXPRESSIONS.

14. friend.
15. marry.
16. congratulate.
17. telegram.
18. immediately.
19. nothing else for it.
20. exciting, lively.
21. bride.
22. normal school.
23. to graduate.
24. stature.
25. manners.
26. conversation.
27. refined.
28. gentle.
29. happy.
30. pleased, elated.
31. to make a present.
32. presents.
33. a pair.
34. Kiangsi (a province).
35. flower vase.
36. husband and wife.
37. quickly.
38. apologize.

CONVERSATION.

A. Mr. Meng, did you go to the Wang family's wedding?

B. Yes. Why didn't you go?

A. I really meant to. I had already dressed when a telegram came requesting me to go to Tungchou at once. So there was nothing else to be done but to run up to Tungchou. Were there many people there?

B. We had a very lively time. Nearly all our old fellow students were there.

A. Did you see the bride?

B. Yes. Her name is Sun. She has just graduated at the Women Teachers' Training School. She is only twenty-two or three years old. She is very tall, and her manners and conversation are gentle and refined. When she and Mr. Wang stood together they looked a very fine pair.

A. Mr. Wang must be very happy.

B. Rather! He is extremely delighted.

A. Many of our fellow students gave presents, I suppose?

B. Everybody gave something. I gave them a pair of small Kiangsi porcelain vases.

A. Was there a dinner party in the evening?

B. When the ceremony was over, the bride and bridegroom provided refreshments. There were too many people for them to prepare a dinner.

A. What a pity I was not able to go. I think I must write to Mr. Wang and apologize.

Transcription. Lesson 23.

VOCABULARIES.

1st Tone.	2nd Tone.	3rd Tone.	4th Tone.
Pt.I.713. ɕiɛ	Pt.I.716. lin	Pt.I.718. ʝi̥a	Pt.I.723. i
714. tshɑo	717. fu	also in	724. phaŋ
715. ja	Pt.II.739. ju.	4th Tone v.	725. xaɪ
Pt.II.735. thiɛ	740. xu	734a.	726. liɛn.
736. ʃɪ	741. thuŋ	719. thi	727. phiɛn
737. b̥ao	742. i	720. g̊u	728. jɑo
738. d̥un	743. thiɑo	721. liŋ	729. khɑo
		722. jy	730. d̥ʒɪ
		Pt.II.744. waŋ	731. ʃu
		745. xueɪ	732. mɑo
			733. ʃʌŋ
			734. weɪ
			734a. [ʝi̥a v. 718].
			Pt. II. 746. d̥ʒʌŋ
			747. *sɪŋ
			748. g̊ua
			749. d̥ʒɪ
			750. ʝi̥
			751. *xan
			752. lou
			753. xuaɪ
			754. fu

Transcription of Part I.

ˋd̥i ˋʌɪˊʃɪ¯san ˋkhʌ. ˋʃaŋ.

COMPOUND WORDS AND EXPRESSIONS.

1. faŋ ˋʝi̥a
2. ˊi·tʃhu
3. ˋxaɪ·tʃhu
4. ˋjuŋ·tʃhu
5. ¯ʃən ͜ thi
6. thi ˋtshɑo
7. ¯b̥aŋ·d̥ʒu
8. ˋkhɑo·thou
9. ˋkhan·thou
10. ʃu ˊlm
11. ˋmɑo·ʃʌŋ
12. ¯khuŋ ˋchi
13. ¯chɪŋ·liaŋ
14. ¯ɕiɛˊfu
15. ˋweɪ¯ʃʌŋ
16. [͜ ja ˋphiɛn]

EXERCISE.

1. wɔ ˋkhan ni ˋd̥ʒɤ i ˋtshuɪ faŋ ˋʝi̥a, ˊd̥ɤ·liao ˊi·tʃhu, ¯ʃən·thi ʝi̥ɛn ͜ xɑo, b̥i ˊtshuŋ ˊchiɛn jɛ ˋphaŋ·liao i ˋdiɛn. 2. thi ˋtshɑo ͜ d̥ʒɪ ju ¯i·tshu, ˊmeɪ·ju ˋxaɪ·tʃhu; niɛn¯chɪŋ ˋliɛn·i ˋliɛn ¯ʃən·thi ʃɪ ˋd̥zueɪ ͜ xɑo. 3. ˋɪʌ·ʃɪ ˊna ja ˋphiɛn d̥aŋ ˋjɑo khan, ʃɪ ju·ʝi̥ˊd̥a ˋjuŋ·tʃhu·d̥ɪ. 4. ju ¯tha ¯g̊ʌg̊ʌ ¯b̥aŋ·d̥ʒu tha, ¯d̥ʒən ʃɪ ͜ ju·g̊ə ˋkhɑo·thou. 5. *͜ g̊u·lɪŋ¯ʃan·d̥ɪ ͜ g̊ɪŋ·d̥ʒɪ ¯d̥ʒən ͜ ju·g̊ə ˋkhan·thou; ʃu ˊlm ʝi̥ ˋmɑo·ʃʌŋ, ¯khuŋ·chi jɛ ¯chɪŋ·liaŋ; d̥zaɪ ¯ʃan·ʃaŋ ɕiɛˊfu jy ˋweɪ¯ʃʌŋ ˊʃɪ·d̥zaɪ ju ˋi.

Translation. Lesson 23.

VOCABULARIES.

	1st Tone.		2nd Tone.		3rd Tone.		4th Tone.
Pt.I.	713. rest.	Pt.I.	716. forest.	Pt. I.	718. false, pretend v. 734a.	Pt. I.	723. benefit.
	714. drill.		717. dog-days, hot season.		719. body.		724. fat.
	715. a crow.				720. ancient.		725. harm.
Pt.II.	735. stick on.	Pt. II.	739. post-office.		721. mountain range.		726. train, practise.
	736. lose.		740. lane, street.		722. with.		727. leaf.
	737. parcel, to wrap.		741. lane, street.	Pt. II.	744. towards, to go to.		728. medicine.
	738. honest.		742. lose.		745. to ruin.		729. depend on, lean on.
			743. twig, strip, length, (cl. of long things).				730. fine, delicate.
					4th Tone.		731. tree.
					748. hang.		732. luxuriant.
					749. to send, to cause to go		733. abundant.
					750. send.		743. protect.
					751. a surname of a river.		734a. [leisure v. 718].
					752. disclose.	Pt. II.	746. government.
					753. spoil.		747. a surname.
					754. near.		

Translation of Part I.

COMPOUND WORDS AND EXPRESSIONS.

1. grant leave.
2. benefit.
3. harm.
4. use (n).
5. body.
6. drill.
7. help.
8. something to depend upon.
9. something worth seeing.
10. a wood, forest.
11. luxuriant.
12. air.
13. clear and cool, pure.
14. rest during hot season.
15. hygiene.
16. [opium.]

EXERCISE.

1. I see you are all the better for your holiday this time; you are looking well and you have put on flesh. 2. There is nothing but good to be derived from physical exercise; and it is the very best thing for young people. 3. Opium is a most useful thing if it is regarded as medicine. 4. With his elder brother to help him he surely has someone to depend upon. 5. The scenery of Kuling Mountain is very beautiful, the woods are luxuriant, and the air is pure. To spend the summer there is excellent for one's health.

Transcription. Lesson 23. Part II.

ˇdi ˈʌɪ ʹʃɪ ˉsan ˇkhʌ. ˇɕia.
ʹjuˇ d͡ʒʌŋ ʹi̯y.

COMPOUND WORDS AND EXPRESSIONS.

17. [ʹjuˇ d͡ʒʌŋ ʹi̯y]
18. ʹjuˇphiao
19. ʹg̊uɔˇi̯iɛ
20. ˇg̊uaˇxao‧ɕɪn
21. ˇfuˇi̯ɪn
22. ʹxuʹthuŋ
23. ˉdan‧b̥ao
24. ˇkhuaɪˇɕɪn
25. ʃʌŋʹchiɛn
26. ˇb̥an‧fa
27. ‿xueɪˇxuaɪ
28. *ˉɕi‧b̥ɔ‧li‧ja
29. [ˇɕɪn‧i̯iɛn]

CONVERSATION.

‿i̯ia. *ˇsuŋˉɕiɛn‧ʃʌŋ, tshuŋˇ d͡ʒɤ‧li d̥ao *‿b̥eɪˉi̯ɪŋ‧dɪ ˇɕɪn, ˇjao this ‿i̯i‧fən ˇju‧phiao a?
ˇi. ˉsan‧fən. ˇb̥u‧t͡ʃhuˇg̊uɔ‧i̯iɛ ˇda‧g̊aɪ ˉd̥u ʃɪ ˉsan‧fən ˇphiao.
‿i̯ia. ˇg̊uaˇxao‧ɕɪn nɪ?
ˇi. ˇna, ‿wɔ khʌ ˇb̥u‧d̥ʒɪˇdao‧lə, ʹxuan‧ʃɪ d̥ao ʹjuˇ d͡ʒʌŋ ʹi̯y, chy ˇwən‧i‧ˇwən ‿xao.
‿i̯ia. fuˇi̯ɪn ju ʹjuʹi̯y ma?
ˇi. ‿ju. ˉt͡ʃhu‧liao ˇd͡ʒɤ‧g̊ə ʹxu‧thuŋ, ʃun ˇd̥aˉi̯iɛ waŋ ʹnan, ‿d̥zou b̥u‿jyan, luˉɕi i̯iuˇʃɪ.
‿i̯ia. chɪŋˇwən, d̥ao *‿b̥eɪˉi̯ɪŋˇchy‧dɪ ˇg̊uaˇxao‧ɕɪn jao ˉd̥ɔ‧ʃao ʹchiɛn?
‿b̥ɪŋ. ˉb̥a‧fən.
‿i̯ia. ˇg̊uaˇxao‧ɕɪn ‿d̥zou‧dɪ ˇkhuaɪ ma?
‿b̥ɪŋ. ʹb̥u‧ʃɪ. ˇg̊uaˇxao d̥ʒɪ ˉd̥an‧b̥ao ˇɕɪn‧i̯iɛn b̥uˇd̥ʒɪ‧jy ʹi‧ʃɪ‧liao. ʹjao‧ʃɪ ‿d̥a‧suan ˇkhuaɪ ˇd̥ao, ʹd̥eɪ an ˇkhuaɪ‧ɕɪn ‿d̥zou.
‿i̯ia. chɪŋˇwən, ‿wɔ ju ‿i̯i‧b̥ən ˉʃu, jao ˇi̯i d̥ao *ˇxan‧khou ˇchy, ‿d̥zənˇjaŋ ˇd̥zueɪ‧ʃʌŋ ʹchiɛn nɪ?
‿b̥ɪŋ. ʃʌŋ ʹchiɛn‧dɪ ˇb̥an‧fa, ʃɪ b̥a ˉʃuˉb̥ao‧xao, ˇlou‧d̥ʒɔ liaŋ ʹthou. ˇjao‧ʃɪ ˇg̊ueɪ‧d̥ʒuŋ‧dɪ ˉʃu, ˇd̥ɪŋ‧xao ʃɪ ʹchyan ‿b̥ao‧chi ʹlaɪ, ˉd̥an b̥ao‿guɔ ‿d̥zou.
‿i̯ia. ˉd̥aŋ b̥ao‿guɔ ‿d̥zou, ˉd̥aŋ‧ian ˇg̊ueɪ‧i ‿d̥iɛn.
‿b̥ɪŋ. ˇg̊ueɪˉd̥ɔ‧lə, khʌ ʃɪ ‿ni‧dɪ ˉʃu, b̥uˇd̥ʒɪ‧jy ‿xueɪˇxuaɪ liao.
‿i̯ia. ɕiɛnˇd̥zaɪ waŋ *ˇou‧d̥ʒou i̯iˇɕɪn, ʃɪ tshuŋ ‿na‧thiao ˇd̥ao d̥zou d̥ɪŋˇkhuaɪ?
‿b̥ɪŋ. ʃɪ ʹtshuŋ *ˉɕi‧b̥ɔ‧li‧ja ‿d̥zou d̥zueɪˇkhuaɪ, tshuŋˇd͡ʒɤ‧li d̥ao *ʹlyn‧d̥un‧dɪ ˇɕɪn, ‿i̯ɛ b̥u‧g̊uɔ ʹʃɪ‧chi‧b̥a ˉthiɛn i̯iu ˇd̥ao liao.

Translation. Lesson 23. Part II.

At the Post Office.

COMPOUND WORDS AND EXPRESSIONS.

17. (post-office).
18. stamp.
19. boundaries, country.
20. registered letter.
21. near.
22. lane, street.
23. insure, guarantee.
24. express letter.
25. save money.
26. way of managing.
27. spoil.
28. Siberia.
29. (a letter).

CONVERSATION.

A. Mr. Sung, how much will the postage be for a letter to Peking?

B. Three cents. Letters for the interior of this country are practically all three cents postage.

A. What about registered letters?

B. That I don't know, you had better go to the post office and enquire there.

A. Is there any post office near here?

B. Yes, when you leave this street walk along the High Street towards the South, and you will see the post office on the West side.

A. Please, how much will it cost to send a registered letter to Peking?

C. Eight cents.

A. Are registered letters delivered quickly?

C No. To register a letter only ensures its safety. If you want it to be delivered quickly, you must post it as an express letter.

A. Please, which will be the cheapset way to send a few books to Hankow?

C. The best way is to wrap them up and leave both ends open. But if they are valuable books, you should wrap them up entirely and post as a parcel.

A. A parcel would, of course, be more expensive?

C. Much more, but your books will not be spoiled.

A At present, which is the quickest route to send a letter to Europe?

C The quickest way is by Siberia. It only takes seventeen or eighteen days from here to London.

Transcription. Lesson 24.

VOCABULARIES.

1st Tone.	2nd Tone.	3rd Tone.	4th Tone.
Pt.I.755. ᶖɪŋ.	Pt.I.756. thi.	Pt.I.760. tha.	Pt.I.762. duan
Pt.II.767. dʒou.	757. tshʌŋ.	761. g̊u.	763. waŋ.
768. ɕi [also	758. xuaŋ.	Pt.II.773. tʃhu.	764. ᶖi.
2nd Tone].	759. lou.	774. dʒaŋ.	765. dzɔ.
769. dʒuan.	Pt.II.770. xuɑ.		766. miɑo.
	771. jɪn.		Pt.II.775. g̊ueɪ.
	772. xaŋ.		776. ᶖiɛ.
			777. dʒaŋ.
			778. ɕy.
			779. xueɪ.
			780. ʃɑo.

Transcription of Part I.

`di `ʌɪ´ʃɪ`sɯ `khʌ. `ʃaŋ.

COMPOUND WORDS AND EXPRESSIONS.

1. `duan·bu͜ khʌ
2. `wan·bu͜ khʌ
3. *¯ᶖɪŋ·dʒou
4. ¯g̊ɑo ͜tha
5. ´tʃhʌŋ¯xuaŋ`miɑo

EXERCISE.

1. ju `juŋ·tʃhu ᶖiu ´na·chy ba; `lun·dao ´chiɛn·ʃaŋ ´dzɑ·mən ͜lia `duan·bu·khʌ ´thi. 2. ni ¯chiɛn`wan`bu·khʌ `na·jaŋ ¯ʃuɔ tha. 3. `na·ᶖiɛn `ʃɪ ni `wan·bu·khʌ `waŋ·ᶖi. 4. *¯ᶖɪŋ·dʒou´tʃhʌŋ ¯ɕi´mən ͜li·biɛn, ͜ju gə ´ʃɪ¯san´tshʌŋ·dɪ ¯g̊ɑo ͜tha. 5. ´fan ʃɪ ¯i·dzɔ ´tʃhʌŋ, ͜li·biɛn `ᶖiu ju ¯i·dzɔ ´tʃhʌŋ·xuaŋ´miɑo. 6. *͜beɪ¯ᶖɪŋ tʃhʌŋ`neɪ ͜ju dzɔ¯dʒuŋ·g̊u`lou, ͜li·biɛn ju ¯i·gə da ¯dʒuŋ, ¯i·gə da ͜g̊u.

Translation. Lesson 24.

VOCABULARIES.

1st Tone.	2nd Tone.	3rd Tone.	4th Tone.
Pt.I.755. thorns.	756. mention, raise.	Pt.I.760. pagoda.	Pt.I.762. decide, cut off.
Pt.II.767. a surname, complete.	757. storey (of house).	761. drum.	763. forget.
768. interest on money [also 2nd Tone].	758. city-moat.	Pt.II.773. store.	764. remember.
769. special.	759. tower.	774. control.	765. seat, (cl. of hill, temple)
	Pt.II.770. China, splendour.		766. temple.
	771. silver.		Pt.II.775. chest, counter.
	772. bank, commercial firm.		776. great.
			777. account
			778. store up.
			779. bank draft.
			780. introduce.

Translation of Part I.

COMPOUND WORDS AND EXPRESSIONS.

1. certainly must not.
2. certainly must not.
3. Ching-chou (a place).
4. pagoda.
5. Temple of the the God of the Town.

EXERCISE.

1. If it is any use to you take it, but there must be no talk of money between us two. 2. Do not on any account reprove him like that. 3. Do not on any account forget that matter. 4. Inside the West Gate of Ching-chou city there is a pagoda with 13 storeys. 5. Wherever there is a city there is a temple to the City God. 6. In the city of Peking and there is a tower called the Chung Ku Lou, in which there is a large bell and a drum

Transcription. Lesson 24. Part II.

`di `ʌɹ`ʃɹ`suɪ `khʌ. `ɕia.

´jɪn´xaŋ.

COMPOUND WORDS AND EXPRESSIONS.

6. dʒaŋ`gueɪ·dɪ   9. `ʝiɛ\ʃao   12. `li·ɕi   15. `xueɪ`phiao
7. ´ʃou`ʃɹ          10. ⁻ɕiaŋ⁻daŋ  13. ´tʃhu`ɕy 16. chiɛn
8. ´jɪn´xaŋ   11. ´xuɔ\dʒaŋ 14. ˌkhʌ`khao        `phiao·dzuɪ

CONVERSATION.

ˌʝia. *⁻dʒou dʒaŋ`gueɪ·dɪ, ˌni ju ´ʃou·ʃɹ·dɪ ´jɪn´xaŋ meɪˌju, ˌgeɪ wɔ `ʝiɛ·ʃao i`ɕia ?

`i.  ˌwɔ·mən·dɪ `phu·dzuɪ `dzai \*´jɪn´tʃhʌŋ´jɪn´xaŋ ju `dʒaŋ, ni `jao·ʃɹ `khan·dʒɔ ɕiaŋ⁻daŋ, wɔ ˌkhʌ·i ´thuŋ ni `chy. ˌni ʃɹ `jao tshun ´chiɛn nɪ, ´xuan·ʃɹ ´jao `khaɪ gə xuɔ`dʒaŋ·nɪ ?

ˌʝia. wɔ ˌʃou·li ju ˌwu·liu⁻chiɛn·khuaɪ ´chiɛn, ˌda·suan ´tshun chi´laɪ, ⁻ʃʌŋ ɕiɛ `li·ɕi.

`i.  `jao·ʃɹ `dʒə·mə`jaŋ, ʝiu `bu·bi ˌʃaŋ \*´jɪn´tʃhʌŋ lə, wɔ ⁻dʒɪ·dao \*´xua ˌbeɪ ˌtʃhu·ɕy ´jɪn´xaŋ, dʒuan dzɔ ´tʃhu·ɕy·dɪ `ʃɹ·chɪŋ, ˌgeɪ·dɪ `li·chiɛn jɛ dzueɪ⁻gao.

ˌʝia. `na·gə ´jɪn´xaŋ khʌ`khao ma ?

`i.  `na ʃɹ ˌlao `dzuɪ·xao lə, ˌxən khʌ`khao. ni ˌda·suan tshun ˌʝi·niɛn nɪ ?´tshun·dɪ `ɹ·dzuɪ jyə⁻dɔ `dzuɪ·ɹan ´dɤ·dɪ `li·chiɛn jyə`da.

ˌʝia. `ʃɹ, wɔ `jao·ʃɹ ´tshun, `ʝiu bi ⁻dɔ ´tshun ɕiɛ ´ɹ·dzuɪ. wɔ `dzaɪ `wən ni, ˌni waŋ \*´jɪŋ·khou ʝi´chiɛn·dɪ ´ʃɹ·xou, ʃɹ ´ju ´juˀʝy `ban nɪ, ´xuan·ʃɹ ´ju ´jɪn´xaŋ `khaɪ·xueɪ`phiao ?

`i.  ˌwɔ·mən `ɕiaŋ´laɪ ʃɹ `khaɪ·xueɪ`phiao, ⁻jɪn·weɪ ˌwɔ·mən dʒɹ `gao·su ´jɪn´xaŋ i⁻ʃʌŋ, ⁻tha·mən ʝiu ˌgeɪ ´chyan ban ˌxao·lə, ˌkhʌ·ʃɹ ´juˀʝy `ban jɛ xən ˌʃʌŋ`ʃɹ.

ˌʝia. dʒaŋ`gueɪ·dɪ, wɔ `dʒɤ·li ˌju ˌliaŋ·dʒaŋ ´ɹən·ʝia ˌgeɪ·wɔ·dɪ ⁻dʒɹ`phiao, ni ´nʌŋ thi `xuan·i`xuan ma ?

`i.  xaɔ`ban, `ʝiao geɪ ˌwɔ ba ! ni `jao ɕiɛn´jaŋ, ´xuan·ʃɹ chiɛn `phiao·dzuɪ ?

ʝia. i`ban·i`ban ba ! `ɕiɛ·ɕiɛ !

Translation. Lesson 24. Part II.

The Bank.

COMPOUND WORDS AND EXPRESSIONS.

6. manager.
7. well acquainted.
8. bank.
9. recommend
10. suitable.
11. current account.
12. interest.
13. savings bank.
14. dependable, reliable.
15. bank-draft.
16. bank-notes.

CONVERSATION.

A. Mr. Chou, do you know any bank that you can recommend to me?

B. My shop has an account in the Silver City Bank. If you think it will suit you, I will go with you, (and introduce you). Do you wish to deposit money, or to open a current account?

A. I have $5000 or $6000, and wish to deposit them in a bank at interest

B. If so, we need not go to the Silver City. I know that the North China Savings Bank is specializing in Savings Deposits business, and gives very high interest.

A. Is it reliable?

B. It is an old established bank and very reliable. How many years do you want to keep your money there? Of course, the longer the time the more interest you get.

A. Yes. If I deposit the money at all I will deposit it for a long period. Tell me again. When you remit money to Yingkou do you send it through the post office, or do you send a bank draft?

B. We always send bank drafts, because we need only tell the bank and they do the rest. Nevertheless to remit through the post office is also very convenient.

A. I say, Mr. Manager, I have two cheques; can you cash them for me?

B. Certainly, give them to me. Will you have silver or bank notes?

A. Half and half. Thank you.

Transcription. Lesson 25.

VOCABULARIES.

1st Tone.	2nd Tone.	3rd Tone.	4th Tone.
Pt.II.785. ʄɪn.	Pt.I.781. lao.	Pt.I.782. thaŋ.	Pt.I.783. ɖaɪ.
786. ʃuaŋ.	Pt.II.791. xʌ.	Pt.II.795. ɖʒuŋ.	784. ɓaɪ.
787. ʃan.	792. ɓao.	796. niu.	Pt.II.797. ɓi.
788. sɯ.	793. lan.		798. xou.
789. ɖʒɪ.	794. ɹuŋ.		799. khu.
789a. ʄɪn.			800. mɑo.
[789b. ʃən cf. 689].			801. xan.
790. ʄi.			802. jɪŋ.

Transcription of Part I.

ˋɖi ʹʌɹ ʹʃɪ ˍwu ˋkhʌ. ˋʃaŋ.

COMPOUND WORDS AND EXPRESSIONS.

1. ˋɓaɪ·waŋ
2. ʹlɑo·ɖuŋ
3. ɠanˉɖaŋ
4. ˋɠua·niɛn
5. ˍthaŋ ˋɹʌ
6. ʹʧhuˉfeɪ

EXERCISE.

1. ˍni na ˍwɔ·mən·ɖaŋ ˋkhʌ ˋɖaɪ ma? 2. wɔ ʹɖzɔ·ɹ chy ˋɓaɪ·waŋ, ˍkhʌ·ɕi ʹnɪn ʹmeɪ·ju ɖzaɪ ʹʄia. 3. ʹlɑo·ɖuŋ ˉɕiɛn·ʃʌŋ·mən laɪ ˋkhan wɔ, ʹʃɹ·ɖzaɪ ʹɓu·ɠanˉɖaŋ. 4. tha ˉʧhu·chy ˋna·mɔ ˍjyan, wɔ ˋɓu ʹnʌŋ ɓuʹɠua·niɛn tha. 5. ˍna·ʌɹ·ɖɪ ˋxua·nɪ? ʹɖza·mən ʹwu·feɪ ʃɹ ˉi·ʄia·ɖɪ ʹɹən. 6. ˍthaŋ·ɹʌ ˉʄia·ɖʒuŋ ju ˋʃɹ, wɔ ʹɓu·xueɪ ɓu ˍɠeɪ ni ˋɕɪn·ɖɪ. 7. ʹʧhu·feɪ ˍni ʹxʌ wɔ ʹthuŋ chy, wɔ ˉi·ɖɪŋ ʹɓu ˋchy.

Translation. Lesson 25.

VOCABULARIES.

1st Tone.	2nd Tone.	3rd Tone.	4th Tone.
Pt.II.785. lapel.	Pt.I.781. to take trouble.	Pt.I.782. supposing, if	Pt.I.783. to treat [well or ill]
786. pair, double.	Pt.II.791. river.	Pt.II.795. kind.	784. to bow.
787. shirt.	792. thin.	796. button.	Pt.II.797. long-cloth.
788. silk.	793. orchid.		798. thick.
789. weave.	794. wool.		799. trousers.
789a. a napkin.			800. hat.
789b. [C. of suits of clothes, cf. 689.]			801. sweat.
790. long-cloth.			802. stiff.

Translation of Part I.

COMPOUND WORDS AND EXPRESSIONS.

1. pay respects.
2. give trouble.
3. dare to do.
4. to be anxious.
5. if.
6. apart from, unless.

EXERCISE.

1. Are you going to treat us as guests? 2. I went yesterday to call on you, but you were not at home. 3. It is too good of you to take so much trouble to come and see me. 4. I cannot help being anxious about his being so far away from home. 5. What are you saying? We belong to the same family. 6. If anything happens here I will be sure to send you word. 7. Unless you go with me I shall certainly not go.

Transcription. Lesson 25. Part II.

`di `ʌɪ´ʃɪ ˌwu `khʌ. `ɕia.

´jaŋ ´fu ⁻dʒuaŋ.

COMPOUND WORDS AND EXPRESSIONS.

7. [´jaŋ ´fu ⁻dʒuaŋ]
8. ⁻ɕia·ʝi
9. ´tʃhou·dzɯ
10. `ɓi·ʝi
11. ´liaŋ·khuaɪ
12. ˌliaŋ `lu
13. ´tʃhaŋ·jyan
14. `di·dao
15. ´khu·dzɯ
16. `ɓeɪ⁻ɕɪn
17. ⁻dan·ʝɪn
18. ⁻ʃuaŋ·ʝɪn
19. ˌniu·dzɯ
20. `mao·dzɯ
21. ˌʃou·ʝɪn
22. ´phi `daɪ
23. `xan⁻ʃan
24. `jɪŋˌlɪŋ
25. ⁻sɯ⁻dʒɪ·dɪ
26. ˌlɪŋ `daɪ
27. `fa·lan´ɹuŋ
28. `weɪ·ʃʌŋ⁻i
29. ˌɖa·thɪŋ
30. `ɖa·li ´fu

CONVERSATION.

ˌʝia. ˌwɔ jao `dzɔ i⁻ʃən ⁻ɕia·ʝi·dɪ ⁻i·ʃaŋ, ˌchɪŋ ˌɡeɪ wɔ ɕiɛ ´tshaɪ liao `khan·i`khan.

`i. ⁻ɕiɛn·ʃʌŋ ʃɪ `jao dzɔ ´tʃhou·dzɯ·dɪ, ´xuan·ʃɪ `ɓi·ʝi·dɪ ?

ˌʝia. ⁻ɕia·thiɛn ´xuan·ʃɪ tʃhuan ´tʃhou·dzɯ·dɪ ´liaŋ·khuaɪ ɕiɛ, `ʃɪ·ɓu·ʃɪ ?

`i. `ʃɪ, `ɓu·dan ´liaŋ·khuaɪ, xuan ´phiɛn·i nɪ ! ˌwɔ·mən ju ˌliaŋ `lu * ´xʌ·nan ´tʃhou, ⁻ɖu ʃɪ ˌdɪŋ·ʃɪ ɕɪŋ·dɪ ´tshaɪ·liao, ⁻i·dʒuŋ `xou·i ˌdiɛn, ⁻i·dʒuŋ `ɓao·i ˌdiɛn, ⁻ɕiɛn·ʃʌŋ jao ˌna i ˌdʒuŋ ?

ˌʝia. `xou·dɪ ⁻tʃhuan·dɪ ´tʃhaŋ·jyan, ˌkhʌ·ʃɪ ɓu ´liaŋ·khuaɪ, wɔ ´xuan·ʃɪ jao ´ɓao·dɪ ɓa !

`i. `ʃɪ, ⁻ɕiɛn·ʃʌŋ chɪŋ `khan ; `di·dao `ʃaŋ·dʌŋ * ´xʌ·nan´tʃhou !

ˌʝia. ˌxao, ni ˌɡeɪ wɔ ´liaŋ i⁻ʃən ɓa ! ˌwɔ jao ˌliaŋ·thiao `khu·dzɯ ´ɓu·jao ɓeɪ⁻ɕɪn, ⁻i·ɡuŋ ⁻dɔ·ʃao ´chiɛn ?

`i. suan ⁻ɕiɛn·ʃʌŋ ⁻san·ʃɪ·khuaɪ ´chiɛn, ⁻dʒən ɓu⁻dɔ ja ! ⁻ɕiɛn·ʃʌŋ jao ⁻dan·ʝɪn, ´xuan·ʃɪ ⁻ʃuaŋ·ʝɪn ? jao ˌʝi·ɡə ˌniu·dzm ?

ˌʝia. ˌwɔ khan ⁻dan·ʝɪn, ˌliaŋ·ɡə ˌniu·dzɯ, `ʝiu ɓu ´tshɔ.

`i. ⁻ɕiɛn·ʃʌŋ ´ɓu `khan·khan `mao·dzɯ, ˌʃou·ʝɪn, phi `daɪ, xan ⁻ʃan, `jɪŋ·lɪŋ ´ʃə·mə·dɪ ma ?

ˌʝia. ˌwɔ ɖu ˌju, ɕiɛn `dzaɪ xuan ´ɓu·juŋ. ˌni ju ⁻sɯ·dʒɪ·dɪ lɪŋ `daɪ meɪˌju ?

`i. ˌju, `ɕiɛn·ʃʌŋ ˌchɪŋ dao ´lou·ʃaŋ chy `khan·khan, ˌxao·ɓu ˌxao ? ˌwɔ·mən ɕɪn ´laɪ·dɪ `fa·lan ´ɹuŋ·dɪ `weɪ·ʃʌŋ⁻i jɛ ˌxən ˌxao.

ˌʝia. ˌwɔ ˌɖa·thɪŋ ˌɖa·thɪŋ, ⁻i·ʃən `ɖa·li ´fu jao ⁻dɔ·ʃao ´chiɛn ?

`i. ɖa `ɡaɪ ´ɡeɪ i ´ɓaɪ tʃhu ´thou ɓa !

Translation. Lesson 25. Part II.

The Tailor.

COMPOUND WORDS AND EXPRESSIONS.

7. [foreign clothes]
8. summer.
9. silk.
10. serge.
11. cool.
12. two kinds.
13. permanent, wear well.
14. real.
15. trousers.
16. waistcoat.
17. single-breasted.
18. double-breasted.
19. buttons.
20. hat.
21. handkerchief.
22. leather belt.
23. shirt.
24. collars (stiff)
25. silken.
26. necktie.
27. flannel.
28. under-wear.
29. inquire.
30. dress suit.

CONVERSATION.

A. I want a suit for summer wear, please show me some materials.

B. What would you like, silk or serge?

A. Silk is more comfortable for summer, is it not?

B. Yes. It's not only comfortable, it is cheap too. We have two kinds of Honan silk; both are very fashionable just now. One is a little bit thicker than the other; which would you like, sir?

A. The thicker one will last better, but it is too hot. I prefer the thinner one.

B. Very well. Look, sir, this is a real first-class Honan silk.

A. All right. Take my measure. I want two pairs of trousers, but no waist-coat. How much will you charge?

B. We will do it for you for 30 dollars, sir. It is really cheap. Do you want single or double breasted, and how many buttons would you like?

A. I think I would like it single-breasted, and with two buttons will do very well.

B. Will you have a look at our hats or handerkerchiefs, belts, shirts, collars, sir?

A. I have got them all, and don't want any more at present. Have you got any silk ties?

B. Yes come upstairs, will you? We have just got some very good flannel under-wear too.

A. I want to know how much a dress suit will cost.

B. **Probably a little more than $100.**

Transcription. Lesson 26.

VOCABULARIES.

1st Tone.	2nd Tone.	3rd Tone.	4th Tone.
PtI.803. ɕiu.	Pt.I.809. lɔ.	Pt.I.813. li.	Pt.I.818. jy.
804. ɕyə.	810. ɕiɛ.	814. ɡuaɪ.	819. ʝiaŋ.
805. ʧhaŋ.	811. ʃɪ.	815. thɪŋ.	820. xuɔ.
806. khʌ.	812. chiao.	816. juŋ.	821. chi.
807. ɖʐən.	Pt.II.829. thaŋ.	817. bao.	Pt.II.840. ɖaɪ.
808. ɖʐu.	830. xuaŋ.	Pt.II.837. ʝyan.	841. jɛ.
Pt.II.822. chou.	831. ɪou	838. ly.	842. la.
823. ɡən.	832. ju.	839. ɡʌ.	843. ɖʐao.
824. thiɛn.	833. xʌ.		844. ɡueɪ.
825. su.	834. ma.		845. ɖʐɪ.
826. sɯ.	835. fan.		845a. mi.
827. biao.	836. ʧhaŋ.		
828. fʌŋ.			

Transcription of Part I.

ˋɖi ˋʌɪ ˊʃɪ ˋliu ˋkhʌ. ˋʃaŋ.

COMPOUND WORDS AND EXPRESSIONS.

1. ˋmu·ʝiaŋ
2. ˌɕiao·lɔˋʝiaŋ
3. ˉɕiu·li
4. ˊfaŋˉɖuŋ
5. ˊɕiɛˋɖiɛn
6. ˊɕiɛˋphu
7. ˊdza·xuɔˋphu
8. ˊjy·chiˋphu
9. ˉɖʐənˉɖʐu
10. ˌbaoˊʃɪ

EXERCISE.

1. ˋʝiao ˋmu·ʝiaŋ ˊlaɪ, ba ˋɖʐɣ·ɡə ˉɕiaŋ·ɖʐɯ ˉkhaɪ·khaɪ. 2. ˋɖʐɣ·ba ˋjao·ʃɪ ˉkhaɪ·bu·khaɪ ˊmən, ʝiao ˌɕiao·lɔˋʝiaŋ laɪ ˉɕiu·li ˉɕiu·li. 3. ˋna·ʝiɛn ˋʃɪ ˌni xʌ ˊfaŋˉɖuŋ ʃuɔˉkhaɪ·lə ma? 4. jao ˌmaɪ ˉi·ʃuaŋ ˉɕyə·ɖʐɯ, ˌna·ɡə ˊɕiɛˋɖiɛn·ɖɪ ˌxao? dzaɪ *ˉchɪŋ·ʃɪ ˊchiao ˉɕi, waŋ ˊnan iˌɡuaɪ, ju ˉi·ɖzɔ ˊlou, lou ˌbeɪ·biɛn ˋʝiu·ʃɪ ɡə ˌthɪŋˌxao·ɖɪ ˊɕiɛˋphu. 5. ˋna·ɡə ˊdza·xuɔˋphu·ɖɪ ˋɖʐɯ·xao ʃɪ *ˌjuŋ ʧhaŋ. 6. ˌwɔ ʃaŋ ˊjy·chiˋphu chy, ˌmaɪ ˉi·khʌ ˉɖʐənˉɖʐu, ˉi·khuaɪ ˌbaoˊʃɪ.

Translation. Lesson 26.

VOCABULARIES.

1st Tone.	2nd Tone.	3rd Tone.	4th Tone.
Pt.I.803. repair.	Pt.I.809. gong.	Pt.I.813. manage	Pt.I.818. jade.
804. boots.	810. shoes.	814. turn.	819. workman
805. prosperous.	811. stone.	815. very.	820. goods.
806. c. of pearls.	812. bridge.	816. eternal.	821. utensil.
807. precious.	Pt.II.829. sugar.	817. precious.	Pt.II.840. pouch.
808. pearl.	830. yellow.	Pt.II.837. roll up.	841. leaf.
Pt.II.822. draw out.	831. soft.	838. Lü (a name), musical pipe.	842. hot, pungent.
823. root.	832. oil.	839. Ko, a surname.	843. look after.
824. add.	833. to bear.		844. cinnamon.
825. brittle.	834. hemp, numbers.		845. manufacture
826. manage	835. trouble.		845a. honey.
827. signal.	836. taste.		
828. bee.			

COMPOUND WORDS AND EXPRESSIONS.

1. carpenter.
2. locksmith.
3. repair.
4. landlord.
5. shoe-shop.
6. shoe-shop.
7. general store.
8. jewellers.
9. pearl.
10. diamond.

EXERCISE.

1. Call the carpenter to open this box. 2. This key will not open the door, call the locksmith to put it right. 3. Have you talked that matter out with the landlord? 4. Where is the best shop to buy a pair of boots? 5. To the west of Ch'ingshih Bridge, just after turning to the south there is a house, on the north of that house is an excellent shoe shop. 6. The sign of that general dealer is Yung Ch'ang. 7. I am going to the jewellers to buy a pearl and a diamond.

Transcription. Lesson 26. Part II.

ˋd̥i ˋʌɪ/ʃɪˋliu ˋkhʌ. ˋɕia.
/jɛnˋphu /xʌ ˋmaɪ/thaŋ·d̥ɪ.

COMPOUND WORDS AND EXPRESSIONS.

11. /xuaŋ·sɯ⁻jɛn 16. ˋjɛ·d̥zɯ⁻jɛn 21. jɛn/xʌ·b̥ao 26. ⁻g̊uŋ⁻sɯ
12. ˌʃuɛɪ·jɛn 17. thaɪˋla 22. /ma·fan 27. ˋmi/fʌŋ
13. ⁻t͡ʃhou·jɛn 18. lyˋsuŋ·jɛn 23. ˋd̥ʒao·g̊u 28. ⁻ʃaŋ⁻b̥iao
14. ⁻jɛnˌ˚jya·ɪ 19. /ɪou·xʌ 24. ˋg̊uɛɪ·xua
15. ˌʃuɛɪ·jɛnˋd̥aɪ 20. ⁻tsha·jɛn 25. ⁻su/thaŋ
    /ju·d̥zɯ

CONVERSATION.

ˌd̥ia. ˌchɪŋ ˌg̊eɪ wɔ ⁻i·bao *ˋxuaŋ·sɯ⁻jɛn.
ˋi.   *ˋg̊ʌ⁻ɕiɛn·ʃʌŋ, /xuan t͡ʃhou ˌʃuɛɪ·jɛn ma ? ˌju d̥iɛn ˋthaɪ
       b̥u ʃɪˋɕɪŋ liao.
ˌd̥ia. ˌwɔ ˌd̥ʒɪ·ʃɪ d̥zaɪ ˈd̥ia·li t͡ʃhou ˌʃuɛɪ·jɛn, t͡ʃhu/mən·d̥ɪ /ʃɪ·xou
       ˌd̥zuŋ·ʃɪ ⁻t͡ʃhou jɛnˌ˚jya·ɪ, ⁻jɪn·weɪ ˌʃuɛɪ·jɛnˋd̥aɪ /na·d̥ʒɔ
       b̥u⁻faŋ⁻b̥iɛn.
ˋi.   ˌni ˌd̥iɛn/d̥ʒɪ·d̥ɪ ˋb̥u·t͡ʃhɪ ˋjɛ·d̥zɯ⁻jɛn ma ?
ˌd̥ia. b̥u/ɕɪŋ, ˋna·g̊ə thaɪˋla, lyˋsuŋ·jɛn ˌwɔ ˌjɛ ˋb̥an·b̥u liao.
ˋi.   ˌkhʌ·ʃɪ ˋjɛ·d̥zɯ⁻jɛn ˌjɛ ˌju /ɪou·xʌ·d̥ɪ ja, ˋkhuaŋˌchiɛ b̥ɪ
       ⁻jɛnˌ˚jya·ɪ d̥iɛn ⁻d̥ɔ·liao.
ˌd̥ia. ˌmaɪ jɛnˋd̥aɪ b̥u ˌjɛ ʃɪ /chiɛn ma ?
ˋi.   ⁻i·g̊ən ⁻jɛnˋd̥aɪ /b̥u·ʃɪ ˌʃɪ ˌxao·ɕiɛ ˋɪ·d̥zɯ ma ? ⁻ɕiɛn·ʃʌŋ
       ˋkhan wɔ ˋd̥ʒɤ·ɕiɛ ˌɕiao jɛnˋd̥aɪ, ˌmei·g̊ə ˌd̥ʒɪˌʃao, /nʌŋ
       juŋ ⁻i·niɛn ⁻d̥ɔ.
ˌd̥ia. ⁻a! ⁻tsha·jɛn/ju·d̥zɯ, ˋd̥aɪ jɛn/xʌ·b̥ao, thaɪ /ma·fan : wɔ
       /xuan·ʃɪ t͡ʃhɪ ˌwɔ·d̥ɪ *⁻san·phao/thaɪ b̥a ! wɔ ⁻ʃuɔ, ˌni jɛ
       ˋmaɪ /thaŋ ma ?
ˋi.   ˋʃɪ, ɕɪn ⁻thiɛn·ʃaŋ·d̥ɪ; ⁻ɕiɛn·ʃʌŋ ˋd̥ʒao·g̊uˋd̥ʒao·g̊u. ⁻g̊aŋ
       ɕiaˋʃɪ·d̥ɪ *ˋg̊uɛɪ·xua su/thaŋ, ʃɪ ⁻d̥ʒən ˌxao, ⁻ɕiɛn·ʃʌŋ /t͡ʃhaŋ
       iˋkhuaɪ.
ˌd̥ia. wɔ /b̥u d̥a ˌɕi·xuan ⁻su/thaŋ, ni ˋjao·ʃɪ ju ˌg̊uɔ·d̥zɯ/thaŋ,
       ˌkhʌ·i ˌg̊eɪ wɔ i⁻b̥ao.
ˋi.   ˌxao ; g̊eɪ ⁻ɕiɛn·ʃʌŋ /na i/phɪŋ ⁻d̥zaˋjaŋ·d̥ɪ b̥a !
ˌd̥ia. ˋɕiɛnˋd̥zaɪ *⁻d̥ʒuŋ·g̊uɔ ˋd̥ʒɪ·thaŋ ⁻g̊uŋ·sɯ, ʃu ˌna·i⁻d̥ia d̥zuɛɪ
       ˋd̥a nɪ ?
ˋi.   /xuan·ʃɪ ʃu *ˌma·jy⁻ʃan b̥a ! wɔ ˌg̊eɪ·ni·d̥ɪ ˋna i/phɪŋ, ˋd̥iu·ʃɪ
       ⁻tha·mən ˋd̥zɔ·d̥ɪ ; ni ˋkhan, /phɪŋ·d̥zɯˋʃaŋ ju *ˋmi/fʌŋ
       ⁻ʃaŋ⁻b̥iao.

Translation. Lesson 26. Part II.

Tobacconist and Confectioner.

COMPOUND WORDS AND EXPRESSIONS.

11. yellow silk tobacco.
12. tobacco for water pipe.
13. to smoke.
14. cigarettes.
15. water-pipe.
16. leaf tobacco.
17. too hot.
18. Manilla tobacco, cigar.
19. mild.
20. pipe cleaner.
21. tobacco pouch.
22. troublesome.
23. take care of.
24. cinnamon flower.
25. toffee.
26. a commercial company.
27. honey bee.
28. trade mark.

CONVERSATION.

A. A packet of Yellow Silk, please.

B. You still smoke a water-pipe, Mr. Ko. It is rather out of fashion now.

A. I only smoke at home. When I go out I always smoke cigarettes as the water-pipe is troublesome to carry.

B. You do not smoke an ordinary pipe then?

A. No, it is too strong for me; a cigar is also beyond me.

B. But there are mild tobaccos, and tobacco for the pipe is much cheaper than cigarettes.

A. You can't get a pipe for nothing though, eh?

B. But a pipe will last a long time. You see, all the short pipes here will last more than a year at least.

A. Well, pipe cleaning and carrying a tobacco pouch are very troublesome. I had better stick to my Three Castles. I say, do you also sell sweets?

B. Yes, I started this branch recently. You must be my patron, sir. This Dominion Toffee, just come from the market, is really good. Taste some.

A. I don't like it very much. If you have Fruit Drops, please give me a packet.

B. Good, I will give you a bottle of Mixed Fruits.

A. At present, which is the largest Chinese sweet manufacturer?

B. I should say Ma-yü-shan. The bottle I am giving you is theirs. You see, the trade mark is Honey Bee.

Transcription. Lesson 27.

VOCABULARY.

1st Tone.	2nd Tone.	3rd Tone.	4th Tone.
Pt.I.846. ɕɪn.	Pt.I.847. phɪŋ.	Pt.I.848. chi.	Pt.I 854. weɪ.
Pt.II.855. ʝiɛn.	Pt.II.861. ʃɪ.	849. ʝiu.	Pt.II.868. fən.
856. tshan.	862. jy.	850. jaŋ.	869. dun.
857. ʝi.	863. dʒɑ.	851. ly.	
858. chi.	864. phaɪ.	852. g̊uan.	
859. thaŋ.	865. leɪ (3,4)	853. khu.	
860. ʃɑo.		Pt.II.866. ʝiɑo.	
		867. g̊uɔ.	

Transcription of Part I.

ˋdi ˋʌɪ ʹʃɪ ˉchi ˋkhʌ.   ʹʃaŋ.

COMPOUND WORDS AND EXPRESSIONS.

1. ˉchi ʹʃɪ
2. ˋʝiu ˳jaŋ
3. ˳chi ˳g̊an
4. ʹphɪŋ-ɑn
5. ˳ly ˳g̊uan
6. ˉɕɪn ˳khu

EXERCISE.

1. ni ˋkhan ˋdʒɤ·g̊ə ʹfa·dzɯ ˳dzə·mə ˋjaŋ? wɔ ˋkhan ˋweɪ·ḅi ʹɕɪŋ·d̥ə ˳liɑo. 2. tha ˋdzɯ·ʝi khʌ ˉʃuɔ ʃɪ ʹnʌŋ ɕɪŋ, chi ʹʃɪ ˋd̥ɑo ˳d̥i ʹnʌŋ·ḅu·nʌŋ ʹɕɪŋ, ˳jɛ ḅu·i ˋd̥ɪŋ. 3. tha ˋjɑo·ʃɪ ˳dzɑo ˋḅan, chi·ḅu·ʃɪ ˉg̊ʌŋ ˳xɑo ma? 4. ˋʝiu ˳jaŋ ˉɕiɛn·ʃʌŋ·d̥ɪ ˋd̥a ʹmɪŋ! chi ˳g̊an! chi ˳g̊an! 5. ʹmɪŋ·thiɛn ˋchy, ˋxuʌ·ʃɪ ˋxou·thiɛn ˋchy, ˉʝɪn·thiɛn ˳wan ʃaŋ ʹtshaɪ nʌŋ ˋd̥ɪŋ·g̊ueɪ. 6. ni ˋchy·niɛn ʝɪn ˉʝɪŋ, dzaɪ ˳na·li ˋdʒu dʒɔ·laɪ·d̥ʒɔ? dzaɪ ly ˳g̊uan·li. 7. ni ˳dzou ma? ˉi·lu phɪŋˉan! 8. ˋlu·ʃaŋ ˉɕɪn·khu ˳liɑo! Ans. xɑoˉʃuɔ! xɑoˉʃuɔ!

Translation. Lesson 27.

VOCABULARY.

1st Tone.	2nd Tone.	3rd Tone.	4th Tone.
Pt.I.846. bitter.	Pt.I.847. peace, level.	Pt.I.848. how ?	Pt.I.854. not yet
Pt.II.855. cl.of rooms.	Pt.II.861. eat food.	849. long time.	Pt.II.868. part, share.
856. meal, food.	862. fish.	850. look up to.	869. meal.
857. fowl.	863. fry.	851. traveller.	
858. infuse.	864. arrange	852. hotel.	
859. soup.	865. weary.	853. bitter.	
860. roast.		Pt.II.866. foot.	
		867. fruit.	

Translation of Part I.

COMPOUND WORDS AND EXPRESSIONS.

1. really.
2. long wished to meet you.
3. how dare I ?
4. peace.
5. hotel.
6. bitterness, you must be tired.

EXERCISE.

1. What do you think of this plan ? I do not think it will do. 2. He says himself he can do it, but truly it is not certain that he can. 3. Would it not be still better for him to have attended to it earlier ? 4. I have long wanted to make your acquaintance. *Ans.* I do not deserve such honour. 5. I have not yet decided whether I go to-morrow or the day after. 6. Where did you stay last year when you went to the capital ? 7. Are you going ? A good journey to you. 8. You must be tired after your long journey ! *Ans.* Thank you.

J

Transcription. Lesson 27. Part II.

ˋdi ˋʌɪ ʹʃɪ ˉchi ˋkhʌ. ˋɕia.
˻ly˻g̊uan.

COMPOUND WORDS AND EXPRESSIONS.

7. ˉkhuŋ-wu   11. ˉɕi-tshan   15. ˻ȷ̊iao ʹchiɛn   19. ˉʃao·niu
8. ˉd̯an-ȷ̊iɛn   12. ˉȷ̊ɪŋ-d̯ʒɪ   16. ˉchi ʹtʃha   ʹphaɪ
9. ˋd̯zaɪ ˋwaɪ   13. ˻khʌ ˻khou   17. ˻ȷ̊ia ʹjy ˉthaŋ   20. ʹlɪŋ ʹʃɪ
10. ˉd̯ʒuŋ-tshan   14. ˉkhaɪ-fa   18. ˻d̯ʒa ˻xaɪ ʹjy   21. ˻d̯iɛn ˉɕɪn
                                                                     22. ˻ʃueɪ ˻g̊uɔ

CONVERSATION.

˻ȷ̊ia.   ju ˉkhuŋ ˉwu·d̯zɯ ma? ˻wɔ jao ˋkhan·i ˋkhan.
ˋi.   ˋʃɪ, ˉɕiɛn·ʃʌŋ jao ˉd̯an ˉȷ̊iɛn nɪ, ʹxuan·ʃɪ ˋd̯a·i ˻d̯iɛn·d̯ɪ ˉwu·d̯zɯ?
˻ȷ̊ia.   ˉd̯an ˉȷ̊iɛn ȷ̊iu ˻xao.
ˋi.   ˻chɪŋ ʃaŋ ʹlou ˋkhan·khan b̯a!
˻ȷ̊ia.   ˋd̯ʒɤ iˉȷ̊iɛn jao ˉd̯ɔ·ʃao ʹchiɛn i ˉthiɛn?
ˋi.   ˻liaŋ·khuaɪ ˋb̯an chiɛn, ˋfan ʹʃɪ d̯zaɪ ˋwaɪ.
˻ȷ̊ia.   ˋjao·ʃɪ tʃhɪ ˋfan nɪ?
ˋi.   ˉi·thiɛn ˉsan·d̯un, ˉi·g̊uŋ ʃɪ ˉsan·khuaɪ ʹchiɛn.
˻ȷ̊ia.   ˋfan ʹʃɪ ˻d̯zə·mə ˋjaŋ nɪ?
ˋi.   ˋd̯ɪŋ·xao·d̯ɪ ˋfan·ʃɪ; ˉd̯ʒuŋ·tshan, ˉɕi·tshan, ʹsueɪ ˉɕiɛn ʃʌŋ·d̯ɪ ˋb̯iɛn. ˉȷ̊i, ʹjy, ʃɪ ˻meɪ·d̯un d̯u ˻ju; ˋd̯zɔ·d̯ɪ jɛ ˉȷ̊ɪŋ·d̯ʒɪ khʌ ˻khou.
˻ȷ̊ia.   ˻xao b̯a! ˻ni b̯a ʹɕɪŋ·li ˋb̯an·ȷ̊ɪn ʹlaɪ b̯a, ȷ̊iao ˋg̊ueɪ·ʃaŋ ˉkhaɪ·fa ˻ȷ̊iao·chiɛn.
ˋi.   ˋʃɪ, ˉɕiɛn·ʃʌŋ ˋjao ʃə·mə b̯u ˋjao?
˻ȷ̊ia.   ɕiɛn ˻d̯a phən ˻liɛn ˻ʃueɪ laɪ, ʹɪan·xou ˉchi xu ʹtʃha laɪ. ˻wan fan ʹʃə·mə ʹʃɪ·xou ˉkhaɪ nɪ?
ˋi.   ˉliu·d̯iɛn ˋb̯an d̯ʒuŋ. ˉɕiɛn·ʃʌŋ ˉȷ̊ɪn·thiɛn ˋʃɪ tʃhɪ ˉd̯ʒuŋ·tshan, ˋʃɪ tʃhɪ ˉɕi·tshan? ˉɕi·tshan·d̯ɪ ˉtshaɪ ʃɪ ˻ȷ̊ia·jy ˉthaŋ, ˻d̯ʒa ˻xaɪ ʹjy, ˉʃao·niu ʹphaɪ; ʹlɪŋ ʹʃɪ ʃɪ ʹjaŋ ˻d̯iɛn·ɕɪn ʹxʌ ˻ʃueɪ ˻g̊uɔ.
˻ȷ̊ia.   ˻g̊eɪ wɔ ˋjao i ˉfən ˉɕi·tshan b̯a, ˋsuŋ d̯ao ˋd̯ʒɤ·li ʹlaɪ, ˻wɔ thaɪ ˋleɪ·lə, ˋb̯u·jyan d̯ao ˋfan·thɪŋ ˋchy.
ˋi.   ˋd̯ʒɤ ʃɪ ˋd̯ʒɤ·ȷ̊iɛn ˋfaŋ·d̯zɯ·d̯ɪ ˋjao·ʃɪ, tʃhu ʹmən·d̯ɪ ʹʃɪ·xou, chɪŋ ˉchiɛn ˋwan ˋb̯a mən ˻sɔ·ʃaŋ, b̯a ˋjao·ʃɪ ˉȷ̊iao d̯ao ˋg̊ueɪ·ʃaŋ ˋchy.
˻ȷ̊ia.   wɔ ˉd̯ʒɪ·d̯ao.

Translation. Lesson 27. Part II.

The Hotel.

7. vacant room.
8. single room.
9. exclusive of.
10. Chinese food.
11. Western food.
12. delicate.
13. appetising.
14. begin.
15. porterage.
16. make tea.
17. turtle soup.
18. fried sea fish.
19. roast beef-steak.
20. the sweets, dessert.
21. cakes.
22. fruit.

CONVERSATION.

A. Have you a vacant room? I would like to see one.

B. Yes, sir; what do you want, a single room or a larger one?

A. A single room will do.

B. Please come upstairs and have a look.

A. How much do you charge for this room a day?

B. Two dollars and a half. Meals not included.

A. If I want meals?

B. Three meals a day, all together, would cost you $3.

A. What is the food like?

B. The very best. You can have Chinese or foreign as you please. We serve poultry and fish at every meal. The cooking is good and appetizing.

A. All right. Bring my luggage in, and pay the porter for me.

B. Yes, sir. Is there anything you would like now?

A. Bring some water for washing, and then some tea. What time is dinner?

B. At half past six. Which do you like to-day? Chinese dinner or foreign? The menu at the foreign dinner is turtle soup, fried fish, beef-steak, and cakes and fruits.

A. Give me a foreign dinner. Bring it here; I am too tired to go to the dining-room.

B. This is the key for this room. Please be sure to lock your room before you go out, and hand the key in at the office.

A. I know.

Transcription. Lesson 28.

VOCABULARIES.

1st Tone.	2nd Tone.	3rd Tone.	4th Tone.
Pt.I.870. tshaŋ.	Pt.I.872. lɪn.	Pt.I.875. fan.	Pt.I.876. fan.
871. phiɑo.	873. lun.	Pt.II.887. ʌɪ.	877. an.
Pt.II.878. xa [or 4th].	874. xuɑ.	888. ɕiɛn.	Pt.II.889. dʒɑo.
879. ɓɪn.	Pt.II.883. tshɯ.		890. ɕɪŋ.
880. khueɪ.	884. dʒɪ.		891. dʒɪ. (or 2, 3).
881. dzuŋ.	885. pheɪ.		892. ʃou.
882. dzɑo.	886. ʝiɛ.		893. ɖiɑo.

Transcription of Part I.

ˋɖi ˋʌɪ ⁄ʃɪ ⁻ɓa ˋkhʌ. ˋʃaŋ.

⁻ʝiaŋ ˋʃaŋ.

COMPOUND WORDS AND EXPRESSIONS.

1. ⁻ʝiaŋ ˋan
2. *ˋxan ˌkhou
3. ⁻ɕɪŋ ⁻chi
4. ⁄tʃhuan ⁻tshaŋ
5ɪ ⁄lɪn ⁄ʃɪ
6. ⁄lun ⁻tʃhuan
7. ˌfan ˋdʒʌŋ
8. ˌɕiɑo ⁄xuɑ·dzɯ
9. ˋʃu ˋʝɛ·dzɯ

CONVERSATION.

ˌʝia. *ˋfan⁻ɕiɛn·ʃʌŋ, i ⁄thuŋ ɖɑo ʝiaŋ ˋan·ʃaŋ ˋkhan·khan ˋchy ˌxɑo ɓu ˌxɑo?

ˋi. ˌxɑo wa, wɔ ˋʝiu·ʃou ˌɖɑ·thɪŋ· ˌɖɑ·thɪŋ, ˋxou·thiɛn ɖɑo ˋxan·khou, ˋchy·ɖɪ ⁄tʃhuan ⁄ʃə·mə ⁄ʃɪ·xou ⁻khaɪ. ˌwɔ ɖi⁻san ˋɖi ˋʝɪŋ·ɖaŋ xueɪ *ˋxan·khou ˋchy·la, ⁻ʝɪn·weɪ ˋɕia ⁻ɕɪŋ·chi ˌwu ˋʝiu khaɪ ⁄ɕyə·liɑo.

ˌʝia. ⁄xuan meɪ ˌɡeɪ tha ˋɖɪŋ xɑo tʃhuan ⁻tshaŋ ma? ˋʝɪŋ·ɖaŋ ˋkhuaɪ·ɕiɛ ˋɖɪŋ·a, ɕiɛn ˋdzaɪ ˋdʒʌŋ ʃɪ ˌwaŋ ˌxaɪ ˋwaɪ ɖzou ˋxuɔ·ɖɪ ⁄ʃɪ·xou, ⁄tʃhuan ⁻ɖu ʃɪ ⁄maŋ·ɖɪ, ˋkhuŋ·pha ⁄lɪn ⁄ʃɪ ˌmaɪ·ɓu·ʃaŋ ˋphiɑo.

ˋi. ˋna·mə, ⁄dza·mən ʝiu ˋɖɑo ⁄lun·tʃhuan⁻ɡuŋ⁻sɯ chy ˌɡeɪ tha ˌmaɪ ˋphiɑo. ni ˋkhan, ˌɡeɪ tha ˋɖɪŋ ˋʌɪ·ɖʌŋ ⁻tshaŋ ⁄ɕɪŋ·liɑo ɓa?

ˌʝia. ⁄ɕɪŋ·liɑo, ˌfan ˋdʒʌŋ ⁄ɓu·ʃɪ ˌjyan ˋɖɑo·ʌɪ, weɪ ⁄ʃə·mə ɓu ˌʃʌŋ ˌʝi·ɡə ⁄chiɛn nɪ!

ˋi. ni ˋkhan! ⁻ʝɪn·thiɛn ˋdʒɤ·li, ˌdzə·mə ⁄thɪŋ·ɖʒɔ ˋdʒɤ·mə ˌɕiɛ dʒɪ ⁻tʃhuan nɪ!

ˌʝia. wɔ ˌɕiaŋ ʃɪ ˌɖʌŋ ⁄tʃhɑo nɪ. khan ˋna·dʒɪ ɕiɑo ⁄xuɑ·dzɯ ⁻ɖɔ·mə ju ˋi·sɯ, ˋdzaɪˌʃueɪ·ʃaŋ ⁻phiɑo·ɖʒɔ, ˌxɑo ˌɕiaŋ ⁻i·ɡə ˌɕiɑo ʃu ˋʝɛ.

Translation. Lesson 28.

VOCABULARY.

1st Tone.	2nd Tone.	3rd Tone.	4th Tone.
Pt.I.870. cabin.	Pt.I.872. about to, near.	Pt.I.875. return.	Pt.I.876. a surname, gross.
871. to float.	873. wheel.	Pt.II.887. you.	877. bank shore.
Pt.II.878. yawn.	874. open boat.	888. danger.	Pt.II.889. visit, hasten.
879. shore.	Pt.II.883. excuse, words.		890. nature.
880. loss.	884. office.		891. substance.
881. kind, clan.	885. lose.		892. receive.
882. waste.	886. section.		893. fall.

Translation of Part I.

By the River.

COMPOUND WORDS AND EXPRESSIONS.

1. river bank.
2. Hankow.
3. week.
4. cabin.
5. near the time.
6. steamer.
7. after all.
8. boat.
9. leaf.

CONVERSATION.

A. Mr. Fan, how would it be for us to go together to the Bund, and have a look round?

B. Good! I will take the opportunity of enquiring what time the boats starts for Hankow. My third brother was to go to Hankow for the opening of school on Friday of next week.

A. Have you not booked a cabin for him yet? You had better do so quickly. Now is just the time when outward bound freight is heavy, and the boats are all crowded. I am afraid that near the time it would be impossible to book a passage.

B. In that case we will go to the Steamer Office and book a passage for him. Do you think a Second Class cabin would do?

A. Quite. After all it is only a short passage, and why not economize a little?

B. Look! How is it there are so many boats waiting?

A I think they are waiting for the tide. Look at that little boat there. How interesting it looks! It is just like a leaf floating on the water.

Transcription. Lesson 28. Part. II.

ˋd̪i ˋʌɹ/ʃɹ⁻b̪a ˋkhʌ. ˋɕia.

⁻ʃaŋˋjɛ /thanˋxua.

COMPOUND WORDS AND EXPRESSIONS.

10. *ˋxa·ʌɹ⁻b̪ɪn 13. ⁻ʧhuˌkhou 16. ˋɕɪŋˋd̪ʒɹ 19. ˋʃou/ʧhao
11. ⁻ɉ̊ɪŋˌli   14. /xaŋˋʃɹ   17. ˋxuɔˋwu   20. ˋd̪iao/mao
12. /ɉ̊iɛˋd̪ʒaŋ 15. /pheɪ/chiɛn 18. ˌb̪aoˌɕiɛn

CONVERSATION.

ˌɉ̊ia. /mɪŋ·thiɛn ni ⁻ʃaŋ *ˋxa·ʌɹ⁻b̪ɪn chy, ju /ʃə·mə ˋʃɹ ni ?

ˋi.   ⁻i·laɪ, wɔ ˋchy d̪ɪŋ ˌɕiɛ·gə /phiˋxuɔ, ˋʌɹ·laɪ, wɔ ˋchy ˋkhan·i· ˋkhan ˌwɔ·mən fənˋxao·d̪ɪ /chɪŋ·ɕɪŋ. ˌwɔ thɪŋ⁻ʃuɔ, ˋd̪zɯ tshuŋ *ˋd̪ʒao·ɉ̊ɪŋ·li /tshɯ/d̪ʒɹ iˋxou, ˋna·li·d̪ɪ ˌmaɪˋmaɪ ʃɹ ⁻i·thiɛn ˋb̪u·ɹu ⁻i·thiɛn ; ˌwu·jyə/ɉ̊iɛ ɉ̊iɛˋd̪ʒaŋ·d̪ɪ /ʃɹ·xou, ⁻tha·mən ⁻khueɪ·liao ⁻san·sɯˋwan·khuaɪ /chiɛn.

ˌɉ̊ia. ˌni·mən·d̪ɪ ⁻fən·xao ˌjɛ ʃɹ ⁻d̪ʒuan b̪an /phi·xuɔ ma ?

ˋi.   /b̪u·ʃɹ, ˋna·li jɛ ⁻b̪ao·b̪an ˋd̪a·d̪zuŋ·d̪ɪ ⁻ʧhu·khou ˋxuɔ. ˋd̪ʒɤ ʌɹ/niɛn·d̪ɪ /phi·xuɔ /meɪ·ju /ʃə·mə /xaŋ·ʃɹ, ˋjao·ʃɹ ⁻d̪ʒuan khao·d̪ʒɔ /phi·d̪zɯ, ⁻tha·mən ˋɉ̊iu ⁻g̊ʌŋ d̪eɪ pheɪ/chiɛn·lə.

ˌɉ̊ia. ˋɉ̊i·ʃɹ /phi·d̪zm /meɪ /xaŋ·ʃɹ, ˌni weɪ/ʃə·mə /xuan chy ˌmaɪ ni ?

ˋi.   ni ˋkhan, ˌwɔ·mən·d̪ɪ ⁻g̊uŋ·sɯ ʃɹ /d̪za·xuɔˋd̪iɛn·d̪ɪ ˋɕɪŋ·d̪ʒɹ, ˋg̊ʌ·jaŋ ˋxuɔ·wu ⁻d̪u d̪eɪ ˌju iˌd̪iɛn. ˋb̪u·g̊uan ˋmaɪ·d̪ə ⁻ʧhu·chy ˋmaɪ·b̪u⁻ʧhu·chy, ˌwɔ·mən ˌd̪zuŋ·d̪eɪ ˋjy·b̪eɪ. ˋd̪zaɪ ʃuɔ, /phi·xuɔ ˋd̪ao·liao g̊uŋ⁻sɯ·li, ˌwɔ·mən ˋɉ̊iu chy ˌb̪aoˌɕiɛn, ˋwan·i ˌju g̊ə ˋʃou/ʧhao ˋd̪iao/mao, xuan ˋb̪u·d̪ʒɹ·jy ⁻d̪zao d̪zaɪˌwɔ·mən ˌʃou·li.

Translation. Lesson 28. Part II.

A Conversation between two Merchants.

COMPOUND WORDS AND EXPRESSIONS.

10. Harbin.
11. manage.
12. finish an account.
13. export.
14. price.
15. lose money.
16. nature.
17. goods.
18. insurance.
19. suffer from damp.
20. to moult.

CONVERSATION.

A. What business are you going to Harbin for to-morrow?

B. Partly to arrange about some leather goods, and partly to look into matters at our branch there. I hear that since the manager Chao resigned, business has been getting worse and worse every day; when accounts were made up at the Fifth Month Festival they had lost $30,000 or $40,000.

A. Does your branch also deal chiefly in leather goods?

B. No, they also deal in export goods generally. For the last two years there has been no quotation for leather goods. If they dealt chiefly in leather goods their losses would be still heavier.

A. Since there is no quotation for leather, why are you going there to buy?

B. You see, our firm's business is general in character, and we have to stock some of all sorts of goods; no matter whether we can sell or not, we must still prepare for it. Then again, as soon as the goods are stored in our godown we insure, so that in the event of damage from damp or moulting the loss is covered.

Transcription Lesson 29.

VOCABULARIES.

1st Tone.	2nd Tone.	3rd Tone.	4th Tone.
894. a.	902. thɔ.	908. nao.	909. lɔ.
895. d̢ʒʌŋ.	903. phʌŋ.		910. d̢ʒan.
896. ɉɪŋ.	904. jɪŋ.		911. d̢u.
897. ʃən.	905. b̢ɔ.		912. ɪaŋ.
898. ʃao (or 3).	906. i.		913. ɕiao.
899. weɪ (or 2).	907. weɪ.		
900. ʃu			
901. la (or 2).			

Transcription of the Lesson.

ˋd̢i ˋʌɪ ˊʃɪ ˳ɉiu ˋkhʌ.

*ˉu ˋla ˋb̢ɔ ˊɪən ˊxʌ ˉtha·d̢ɪ ˋlɔ ˌthɔ.

COMPOUND WORDS AND EXPRESSIONS.

1. ˋɕiao ˋxua
2. ˊweɪ·chi·laɪ
3. *ˉa·la ˊb̢ɔ
4. ˋlɔ·thɔ
5. ˋd̢ʒaŋ ˊphʌŋ
6. ˳nao ˋd̢aɪ
7. ˉxuan ˊjɪŋ
8. ˊjy ˋʃɪ
9. ˊb̢ɔ·d̢ʒɯ
10. ˳nuan ˋchi
11. ˳ɉia ˋɪu
12. ˋd̢u ˋliaŋ
13. ˉʃao ˉweɪ
14. ˊi ˋd̢uŋ
15. ˊchyan ˉʃən
16. ˳xao ˋɕiaŋ
17. ˉʃu·ʃu·fu ˊfu·d̢ɪ

THE STORY.

ˊchiɛn·thiɛn ˳wɔ d̢ao *ˉd̢ʒaŋ·ɉia ˋchy, ɕiao ˊxaɪ·d̢ʒɯ·mən ˉd̢u d̢zaɪ ˉɉia ˊju·ɕi nɪ. ˉtha·mən ˋkhan·ɉiɛn·liao ˳wɔ, ɉiu ˋb̢a wɔ ˊweɪ·chi ˊlaɪ, ˋɉiao wɔ ʃuɔ ˋɕiao·xua ge̱ɪ ˉtha·mən ˉthɪŋ. wɔ ˋgao·su ˉtha mən, wɔ ˉd̢ʒən meɪ·ju ˋɕiao·xua. ˉtha·mən ˉla·d̢ʒu ˳wɔ ˋb̢u·faŋ ˳ʃou. wɔ ˊmeɪ·ju ˊfa·d̢zɯ, ˳d̢ʒɪ xao ˳ɕiaŋ·liao ˋb̢an ˉthiɛn, ge̱ɪ ˉtha·mən ˉʃuɔ·liao gə ˳lao ˋɕiao·xua.

Translation. Lesson 29.

VOCABULARIES.

1st Tone.	2nd Tone.	3rd Tone.	4th Tone.
894. exclamation	902. camel.	908. brain.	909. camel.
895. open the eyes.	903. tent.		910. usurp.
896. eye.	904. welcome.		911. measure.
897. stretch.	905. neck.		912. allow.
898. somewhat	906. move.		913. laugh.
899. small.	907. surround.		
900. comfortable.			
901. cut.			

Translation of the Lesson.

An Arab and his Camel.

COMPOUND WORDS AND EXPRESSIONS.

1. story.
2. surround.
3. Arab.
4. camel.
5. tent.
6. head.
7. welcome.
8. thereupon.
9. neck.
10. warmth.
11. if, supposing.
12. measure, consideration.
13. a little.
14. move.
15. whole body.
16. like, as if.
17. comfortably.

THE STORY.

The other day I was at the Chang home, and found the children a l there playing. When they saw me they gathered round me and asked me to tell them a story. I told them I honestly had none to tell them, but they laid hold of me, and would not let me escape; so there was no way out of it, but to think up something and tell them an old time tale :—

Once upon a time an Arab was sitting in his tent when his camel with his great eyes wide open, peeped in. Said the camel, "Master! it is very cold outside, may I put my head inside the tent?"

Lesson 29 (*Cont.*).

‿ju i′xueɪ, ⁻i·ğə *⁻a·la′b̦o·ɹən ˋdzɔ dzaɪˋdzaŋ·phʌŋ‿li·b̦iɛn, ⁻tha·dɪ ˋlɔ·thɔ dzaɪˋwaɪ·b̦iɛn, ⁻dʒʌɣ·dʒɔ ˋdɑ ‿jɛn·ʃ̞ɪŋ, ‿waŋ ‿li·miɛn ˋkhan.

ˋlɔ·thɔ ⁻ʃuɔ: ‿dʒu′ɹən na! ˋwaɪ·miɛn ⁻dʒən ‿lʌŋ, wɔ ‿khʌ·i b̦ɑ ‿wɔ·dɪ ‿nɑo·daɪ ⁻ʃən·ʃ̞ɪn′laɪ ma?

*⁻a·la′b̦o·ɹən ⁻ʃuɔ: ⁻xuan′jɪŋ, ⁻xuan′jɪŋ! chɪŋ ′ʃ̞ɪn·laɪ b̦ɑ.

′jyˋʃɪ ˋlɔ·thɔ ˋʃ̞iu b̦ɑ ′thou ⁻ʃən·ʃ̞ɪnˋchy·liɑo.

ˋğuɔ·liɑo i‿xuə·ɪ, ˋlɔ·thɔ ˋju ʃuɔ: ‿dʒu′ɹən na, wɔ ‿khʌ·i b̦ɑ ′b̦o·dzɯ ‿jɛ ˋʃən·ʃ̞ɪn′laɪ ′dʒɣ ɕiɛ nuanˋchi·ɹ b̦ɑ?

*⁻a·la′b̦o·ɹən ⁻ʃuɔ: ‿khʌ·i, ‿khʌ·i.

ˋlɔ·thɔ ˋju b̦ɑ ′b̦o·dzɯ manˋman·dɪ ⁻ʃən·ʃ̞ɪnˋchy liɑo.

ˋdʒɣ ′ʃɪ·xou, ˋlɔ·thɔ waŋ ˋsuɪ·miɛn iˋkhan, ˋju ɕiaŋ ⁻tha·dɪ ‿dʒu·ɹən ⁻ʃuɔ: ‿ʃ̞ia·ɹu‿wɔ b̦ɑ ‿wɔ·dɪ ′chiɛn‿ʃ̞iɑo ⁻ʃən·ʃ̞ɪn′laɪ, ‿jɛ ′b̦u·ğuɔ ⁻dɔ ˋdʒan·ʃaŋ ‿nɛɹ‿ɕiɑo·dɪ i·diɛn ˋdi·faŋ.

ˋdʒɣ·dzɔ ˋdʒaŋ·phʌŋ ‿b̦ən·laɪ ʃɪ ‿xɛn‿ɕiɑo·dɪ, ‿khʌ·ʃɪ ˋna·ğə *⁻a·la′b̦o·ɹən·dɪ ˋdu·liaŋ xən·da. tha ⁻thɪŋ·ʃ̞iɛn ˋlɔ·thɔ ˋdʒɣ·mən ⁻ʃuɔ, ʃ̞iu ⁻ʃɑo·weɪ waŋ ˋxou·miɛn ′i·duŋ i·diɛn, ɹaŋ ˋlɔ·thɔ b̦ɑ ′chiɛn ‿ʃ̞iɑo ⁻ʃən·ʃ̞ɪn′laɪ.

ˋdaɪ·liɑo i‿xuə·ɪ, ˋlɔ·thɔ ˋju ʃuɔ: ⁻thiən·chi ⁻dʒən ‿lʌŋ ɑ, ʃ̞iɑo ‿wɔ·dɪ ′chyan ⁻ʃən ⁻du ʃ̞ɪn′laɪ b̦ɑ!

*⁻a·la′b̦o·ɹən ⁻ʃuɔ: ⁻thiɛn·chi ′ʃ̞i·ɹan ˋdʒɣ·mə ‿lʌŋ, ′chyan ʃən ˋʃ̞ɪn·laɪ ʃɛ ‿khʌ·i.

′jyˋʃɪ ˋlɔ·thɔ ‿dzou ʃɪn ˋdʒaŋ·phʌŋ ˋchy·liɑo.

ˋlɑ·thɔ ˋkhan·tʃhu′laɪ·liɑo, ˋdʒɣ·ğə ˋdʒaŋ·phʌŋ thaɪ ‿ɕiɑo, ′ɹuŋ·b̦uˋɕia ⁻tha·mən ‿liaŋ·ğə. ⁻tha ʃuɔ: ‿dʒu′ɹən na! ‿wɔ·mən ‿xɑo·ɕiaŋ ˋb̦u·nʌŋ ⁻du dzaɪˋdʒɣ·li. ‿ni·dɪ ⁻ʃən·thi b̦i ‿wɔ·dɪ ‿ɕiɑo, ˋb̦u·ɹu ni ⁻tʃhu·chy, ˋɹaŋ ‿wɔ dzaɪˋdʒɣ·li⁻ʃu·ʃu·fu′fu·dɪ ˋdzɔ i‿xuə·ɪ.

ˋlɔ·thɔ ʃuɔ ′wan, ˋʃ̞iu b̦ɑ ⁻tha·dɪ ‿dʒu·ɹən ‿ʃ̞i⁻tʃhu·chy·liɑo.

Lesson 29 (*Cont.*).

The Arab said, "Welcome ! Welcome !"

So the camel put his head inside the tent.

After a little while, the camel said again, " Master ! May I also put my neck in, and obtain a little warmth ? The Arab said, " You may !"

So the camel slowly put his neck in. The camel then, looking all round, said to his master : " Suppose I put my forefeet inside, they will only occupy a very little more space."

Now the tent was really very small, but the Arab was large-hearted, and when he heard what the camel said, he drew back a little to make room for the camel to put in his forefeet. At length the camel said again, " It is really very cold, may my whole body come in?" The Arab said : " Seeing that the weather is so very cold, you may bring you whole body in. Then the camel walked into the tent.

The camel saw that the tent was too small for both, so he said : "Master ! It seems that we cannot both stay here. As your body is smaller than mine, you had better go out, and let me sit here comfortably for a while. So saying, the camel pushed his master out.

Transcription. Lesson 30.

VOCABULARIES.

1st Tone.	2nd Tone.	3rd Tone.	4th Tone.
914. phɔ.	920. wən.	930. fu.	941. an.
915. ɡ̊uŋ.	921. lɔ.	931. dan.	942. lɪŋ.
916. ɟi.	922. tʃhuan.	932. dʒaŋ.	943. b̥ɪŋ.
917. phi.	923. jy.	933. thuŋ.	944. jy.
918. ɟɪn.	924. jyan.	934. ɟiɛ.	945. mɪŋ.
919. dʒu.	925. ɟyə.	935. fou.	946. lɪŋ.
	926. ɡ̊ʌ.	936. ɡ̊aɪ.	947. dʒɪ.
	927. phɪŋ.	937. dao.	
	928. ɹuŋ.	938. jɪŋ.	
	929. tʃhɪ.	939. ɕiaŋ.	
		940. wən.	

Transcription of the Lesson.

`di ⁻san ′ʃɪ `khʌ.
⁻ɕɪn ′wən.

COMPOUND WORDS AND EXPRESSIONS.

1. ⁻ɕiao ⁄ ɕi
2. ⁻ɕɪn ′wən
3. `neɪ ′ɡ̊ʌ
4. ′tshuɪ `dʒɪ
5. `dʒʌŋ ‿fu
6. ′tʃhuan·tʃhu ⁄laɪ
7. ⁻ɕiu ‿dʒʌŋ
8. ′faŋ ‿ʃueɪ `an
9. ′jy `lun
10. `dʒʌŋ ‿daŋ
11. ⁻ɡ̊uŋ-ɟi
12. `xueɪ `i
13. `neɪ `wu
14. ‿dzuŋ ‿dʒaŋ
15. ′thi `i
16. `wən ′thi
17. ′chyan ‿thi
18. ‿thao `lun
19. ′ɟiɛ ‿ɡ̊uɔ
20. ′ɡ̊uɔ `wu ‿dzuŋ ‿li
21. `da ‿dzuŋ ‿thuŋ
22. ′ɡ̊uɔ `wu `xueɪ `i
23. ɟiɛ ′ɟyə
24. `ʃɪ ‿fou
25. `dʒɪ ′jy
26. ⁻ɟɪŋ `ɡ̊uɔ
27. `bao `ɡ̊ao
28. ′ɕiao ′jy ⁻ɟi -ɡ̊uan
29. ‿ɡ̊aɪ ′ɡ̊ʌ
30. ⁻phi ⁄ phɪŋ
31. ′jyan ⁻jɪn
32. ′xʌ ⁄ phɪŋ
33. ‿jɪŋ ‿ɕiaŋ
34. `waɪ ⁻ɟiao
35. `mɪŋ `lɪŋ
36. ‿wən ⁻daŋ
37. ′tʃhɪ ′dʒɪ
38. [⁻ɟɪn ′ɹuŋ]

CONVERSATION.

‿ɟia. *′lɔ ⁻ɕiɛn·ʃʌŋ, ⁻ɟɪn·thiɛn `b̥ao·ʃaŋ ju ′ʃə·mə ɟɪn `jao·di ɕɪn· ′wən meɪ ‿ju?

`i. ⁻ɟɪn·thiɛn·di ⁻ɕiao·ɕi `b̥u·da ‿xao, `neɪ ′ɡ̊ʌ jao ‿dzuŋ tshuɪ· ′dʒɪ nɪ!

‿ɟia. ′ʃɪ·ma? ‿chɪŋ `niɛn ɡ̊eɪ ‿wo ⁻thɪŋ·thɪŋ b̥a!

Translation. Lesson 30.

VOCABULARIES.

1st Tone.	2nd Tone.	3rd Tone.	4th Tone.
914. very.	920. hear.	930. residence.	941. law case.
915. attack.	921. spread out, a net.	931. party.	942. besides, another.
916. strike.	922. announce.	932. senior.	943. moreover.
917. criticise.	923. the public.	933. general, control.	944. nurture
918. gold.	924. officer.	934. explain, loosen.	945. command.
919. all.	925. decide.	935. not, or not.	946. law, command
	926. change	936. change, alter.	947. hinder.
	927. criticise.	937. on the other hand.	
	928. blend.	938. upset, shadow.	
	929. late.	939. shadow effect.	
		940. stable, secure.	

Translation of the Lesson.

News.

COMPOUND WORDS AND EXPRESSIONS.

1. news.
2. news.
3. cabinet.
4. resign.
5. government.
6. announce.
7. amend.
8. house duty question.
9. public opinion
10. political party
11. attack.
12. meet, discuss.
13. home affairs.
14. president of a department
15. propose a motion.
16. a question
17. general or full meeting.
18. discuss.
19. result, decision.
20. Premier.
21. President.
22. Cabinet meeting.
23. decide.
24. yes or no
25. as for.
26. experience.
27. announce.
28. Educational Organisation
29. revolution, reform.
30. criticise.
31. cause.
32. peacable.
33. effect.
34. foreign relations.
35. commands, mandates.
36. stable, steady.
37. suspended.
38. [financial prospects).

Transcription. Lesson 30 (*Cont.*).

ˊi. ˋȷ̊y ˋdʒʌŋ·fu ˋjao·ɹən ˊtʃhuan tʃhuˊlaɪ·dɪ ˉɕiao·ɕi, jɪn ˉɕiu dʒʌŋ ˊfaŋ·ʃueɪˋan, ˋdʒʌŋ˳fu ˉphɔ ʃou ˊjy·lun, xʌ ˊʜ̥iɛ·dɪ ˋdʒʌŋ˳daŋ·dɪ ˉɡ̊uŋ·ȷ̊i. ˊdzɔ·thien ˋneɪˊɡ̊ʌ xueɪˋi·dɪ ˊʃɪ·xou, ju ˋneɪ·wu˳dzuŋ˳dʒʌŋ thiˋi ˳dzuŋ tshɯˊdʒɪ. ˋdʒɤ·ɡ̊ə ˋwən·thi, ˉȷ̊ɪŋ ˊchyan·thi ˊɡ̊ʌˊjyan, ˳thaoˋlun· liao ˉi·dien˳d̥ə dʒuŋ. xueɪˋi·dɪ ˊȷ̊iɛ·ɡ̊uɔ ˋʃɪ: ˉɕien ju ˊɡ̊uɔˋwu˳dzuŋ˳li ˋchy ȷ̊ien ˋd̥a˳dzuŋ˳thuŋ, ˋɹan ˋxou dzaɪ ˊmɪŋ·thien·dɪ ˊɡ̊uɔ·wu xueɪˋi, ˳dzaɪ ˳ȷ̊iɛˊȷ̊yə ˋʃɪ˳ʃou ˊthi·tʃhu ˳dzuŋ ˊtshɯ·dʒɪ ˉʃu. ˋdʒɪ·jy ˳dzuŋ˳li ɕien ˳dzuŋ˳thuŋ·dɪ ˉȷ̊ɪŋ ˋɡ̊uɔ, ˋd̥ao ɕien ˋdzaɪ xuan ˊmeɪ·ju khʌˋkhao·dɪ ˋʜ̥ao ˋɡ̊ao.

  ˋlɪŋ i ˉɕiao·ɕi: ˋdʒɤ·tshɯ ˋneɪˊɡ̊ʌ tshɯˊdʒɪ, ˋʜ̥ɪŋ ʜ̥u ˉdan·ʃɪ ˉjɪn·weɪ ˊfaŋ·ʃueɪ ˋwən·thi, ˋʃaŋ·jyə·li ˋd̥ueɪ·jy ˋɡ̊ʌˋʃʌŋ ˋȷ̊iao·jy ˉȷ̊i·ɡ̊uan·dɪ ˳ɡ̊aɪˋɡ̊ʌ, ˳jɛ xən ˋʃou ˋʃɤ· xueɪˋʃaŋ·dɪ ˉphi·phɪŋ, ˋxuʌ·dʒɤ ˋdʒɤ ˳jɛ ʃɪ ˉi·ɡ̊ə ˊjyan·jɪn.

˳ȷ̊ia. ˳ni ˋkhan ˋdʒɤ·ɡ̊ə ˉɕiao·ɕi, ˊnʌŋ ˊtʃhʌŋ·liao ˋʃɪˋʃɪ ʜ̥uˊnʌŋ?

ˋi. ˳wɔ ˳ɕiaŋ ˊʃɪ·tʃhʌŋ·juˉʜ̥a·tʃhʌŋ nʌŋ ˊʃɪˋɕien, ˉjɪn·weɪ ˊfaŋ· ʃueɪ ˳ʜ̥ən·laɪ ˊmeɪ·ju ˳ɡ̊aɪ·dʒʌŋ·dɪ ˋʜ̥iˋjao.

˳ȷ̊ia. ˳wɔ ˳jɛ ʃɪ ˋdʒə·mə ˳ɕiaŋ, khʌˋʃɪ wɔ ˉɕi·waŋ ˊdʒʌŋ·fu ʜ̥a ˋdʒɤˉi ˋan ˋtʃhɤˉɕiao, ˊxʌ·phɪŋ·dɪ ˋɡ̊uɔ·chy, ʜ̥i ˊʃə·mə d̥u ˳xao.

ˋi. ˋʃɪ·dɪ. ˋdʒʌŋ·fu i ˳d̥ao, ˳ȷ̊ɪnˊɹuŋ ˋȷ̊iu jao ˋʃou ˳jɪŋ˳ɕiaŋ. ˋkhuaŋ ˳chiɛ ˋɕienˋdzaɪ ˋwaɪˉȷ̊iao, ˋdʒʌŋ dzaɪ tʃhɪ˳ȷ̊ɪn·dɪ ˊʃɪ·xou, ˳ɡ̊aɪ·xuan ˋdʒʌŋ·fu ˳jɛ ʜ̥u·ɕiaŋˊi.

˳ȷ̊ia. ˉȷ̊ɪn·thien ju ˊʃə·mə jao˳ȷ̊ɪn·dɪ ˋmɪŋ·lɪŋ ma?

ˋi. ˊmeɪ·ju nɪ. ˳wɔ ɕiaŋ ˋdʒʌŋ·fu ˋdʒʌŋ dzaɪ ʜ̥u˳wənˉdaŋ·dɪ ˊʃɪ·xou, ˉdaŋ·ɹan ˉdʒu ˋʃɪ d̥u ˊtʃhɪ·dʒɪ ˉi˳ɕiɛ.

Lesson 30 (*Cont.*).

CONVERSATION.

A. Mr. Lo, is there any important news in the paper to-day ?

B. The news is not very good ; the cabinet intends to resign.

A. Really ? Please read it to me.

B. According to information received from an important member of the Government, in view of the fact that since the bill amending the act regarding House Duty was introduced, the Government has been attacked by public opinion generally as well as by other political parties, the Home Minister at the cabinet meeting yesterday proposed that the Government resign. This proposition was discussed by the whole cabinet for more than an hour. The result was that it was decided that the Prime Minister should first interview the President and later at to-morrow's Cabinet Meeting decide whether or not to send in the resignation of the whole cabinet. As to what transpired at the interview between the Prime Minister and the President no reliable report up till now has been received.

Another message says that the threatened resignation of the Cabinet is not only because of the House Duty question, but possibly because the proposal last month to reform the Provincial Educational Organisation, has also been severely criticized by the public.

A. Do you think this report represents what will really happen ?

B. I think it is very likely because the House Duty Act does not really need amending.

B. I think so too. But I hope the Government will withdraw the bill. It is most desirable that the matter should be got over peaceably.

A. Yes, if the Government falls, it will at once affect the financial position. Moreover, at the present time our foreign relations are critical, and it would be unfortunate for a change of government to take place just now.

A. Are there any important mandates to-day ?

B. No. I think that as the Government is in such an unstable position everything will as a matter of course be in suspense.

NOTES.

Lesson 1. Part I.

Pronunciation.

1. In Part I of this Lesson there are six Initials, ḅ, m, ɹ, ʃ, x, j ; and seven Finals, i, eɪ, ɛ, ɑo, ɔ, u, ən.
2. Notice in the Tone Practice there is a marked modification of the vowel quality of the syllable sound ju in the 3rd and 4th tones. This is due to the influence of the tone. But the difference is not invariable. Many Chinese pronounce the words in these Tones in the same way as those in the 1st and 2nd Tones, and they are equally correct. This difference of vowel sound is represented in the Vocabulary and Tone Practice by the letters əu instead of u. In the Exercise, however, and hereafter the word will be represented by ju, as really belonging to the same class of sounds or phoneme as those so pronounced in the 1st and 2nd Tones.

Grammatical Construction.

3. Part I. of this lesson deals with Affirmation, Negation and Interrogation. The word ⌐ju (5)* is the Chinese word affirming existence or possession. The Negative ′meɪ (3) prefixed gives ′meɪ⌐ju (2), the denial of existence or possession. These two, the expression of Affirmation and Negation, combined together express Interrogation
Thus : ¬ju, *there is (are)* ; *I (we, you, etc.) have.*
    ′meɪ⌐ju, *there is (are) not ;* *I (we, you, etc.) have not.*
    ⌐ju′meɪ⌐ju, *is (are) there ?* *have I (we, you, etc.) ?*
That is, two alternatives are presented, and the question is asked, " Is it a case of ⌐ju, *there is ?* or of ′meɪ⌐ju, *there is not ?* "
4. The negative precedes the verb ; the English *have not* is, in Chinese, ′meɪ⌐ju, *not have.*
5. In using the question form ⌐ju′meɪ⌐ju, the noun-subject usually comes after the first ⌐ju ; but sometimes, particularly when the subject consists of more than one word, the whole of the form ⌐ju ′meɪ⌐ju may follow the subject.
6. Adjectives, except when used predicatively (see Less. 3) come before the nouns they qualify.
7. The Conjunction ⌐jɛ, *also*, comes before the verb. Note: ⌐jɛ, though it may often be translated *and*, cannot connect nouns. For

---

* Figures in brackets in ordinary type refer to the Vocabulary ; those in bold type to the Compounds.

this purpose other words are used (L. 15, N. 4).

8. The expression ˌbi ˈmɔ (1), *pen and ink*, is used as a collective noun meaning *stationery* in general.
9. The normal order of the simple sentence is: (1) Subject, (2) Conjunction or Adverb of Time or Manner, (3) Verb, (4) Object.

Chinese Characters.

10. The following Radicals (see p. ..) enter into the composition of the characters in Part I; viz.: Nos. 1, 2, 3, 4, 5, 6, 8, 18, 29, 30, 32, 38, 39, 73, 74, 79, 86, 118, 129, 203. Refer to the Table of Radicals in Vol. II. and find each Radical by its number. Learn its pronunciation and meaning, and note its formation.
11. Read the general directions on writing of Chinese Characters given in Vol. II.
12. Learn to write the Radicals numbered above by tracing them several times from the Characters given in Vol. II. Be careful to follow the order of strokes as shown in the space under each Radical.
13. Turn to the Characters in the Vocabulary, Chinese Text. Refer to the Table in Appendix II., and note their formation. They are to be identified by their numbers. Learn to write them by tracing them several times from the characters as given in the Vocabulary.

Lesson 1. Part II.

Pronunciation.

144. There are six new Initials in Part II., th, n, l, ɕ, ch, w; and three Finals, iɛn, ɑ, ʌŋ.

Grammatical Construction.

15. Part II. introduces the personal pronouns. In the 2nd person they are used sparingly, from politeness, and the term ⁻ɕiɛn-ʃʌŋ (7), *sir*, is often used instead, hence its introduction in this lesson.
16. The syllable ʹmən (12) is a sign of the plural of personal pronouns, and other words indicating persons.
17. The word ⁻ɕiɛn⁻ʃʌŋ, *a teacher*, or *gentleman*, is one of the two-word combinations used to avoid the ambiguity otherwise resulting from the paucity of sounds. It belongs to the class formed by a combination of two ideas (p.8.) and is formed by joining the words ⁻ɕiɛn (10), *before*, and ⁻ʃʌŋ (11), *born*, i.e. the one *born before* me is my *teacher*. The word is affixed to the surname to express the same idea as is expressed by the prefix *Mr.* in English, in which case ⁻ɕiɛn-ʃʌŋ always follows the surname. It is also used in the vocative case as a polite form of address, like the English *sir*.

Chinese Characters.

18. The following Radicals also enter into the composition of the characters in Part II., 10, 14, 42, 62, 64, 75, 100, 167, 169. Learn their pronunciation and meaning, and note their formation as shown in the Radical Table.
19. Learn to write the above Radicals according to the directions given in the Notes of Part I., by tracing them from the characters given in the Radical Table.
20. Turn to the characters in the Vocabulary. Note their formation and learn to write them as directed in the Notes of Part I.

Lesson 2. Part I.

Pronunciation.

1. The new Initials are s, ğ, kh ; and the Finals are an, ɪ, ɪn, uan, iu, ʌ, [ə], uaɪ.
2. Note the shortened form ˋğə (24). The original pronunciation of the word is as in the Vocabulary, but when used as a classifier it is almost invariably unstressed, and therefore shortened.
3. In the Tone Practice the four nouns previously learned are arranged with their appropriate Classifiers and four numerals, one in each tone, so as to provide Tone Practice in three-syllable phrases.
4. Note the sequences of 3rd tones. In S. 3 there are four 3rd Tones. In S. 8 there are also four, but in a different sequence as regards pitch. The difference is due to difference of stress. In the one case the first syllable of the four is stressed, and in the other the second.

Grammatical Construction.

Most nouns in Chinese have a special word associated with them, called by some Classifiers, because their primary object is said to be to classify ; by others Numeratives, or Numerary Adjuncts, because they are only used when the number is stated or implied. Their function is the same as that of such English words, as *pane*, in *a pane of glass*, or *piece* in *three pieces of music*.

6. In the Vocabulary there are four such Classifiers. The most common of them is ˋğə (24) the General Classifier. It expresses individuality, and is often used as a substitute for other Classifiers. This is a license, however, which the student should be chary of allowing himself.

7. Note the position of the Classifier in relation to the adjective (S.5, 12). It comes before the latter, and not between it and the noun. The Classifier, in fact, belongs to the numeral rather than to the noun, and therefore immediately follows the Numeral.
8. The pronoun ′nɪn (19) is a polite form of ˬni (15) used a great deal in Peking, but not much elsewhere.

Chinese Characters.

9. Note the formation of, and learn to write, the following Radicals as directed in Lesson 1 ; viz. Nos. 12, 24, 31, 40, 61, 194.
10. Note the formation of, and learn to write, the characters in the Vocabulary.

Lesson 2. Part II.

Pronunciation.

11. The new Initials are ɖ, ɖʒ ; and the Finals are iao, iɛ, ɣ.
12. Notice the ɪ, the shortened form of i, in the word ⁻ɖɪ (26), the original pronunciation of which is ⁻ɖi, but which when used as a possessive particle is shortened to ⁻ɖɪ.
13. The negative ˋbu (33) becomes ′bu before ˋʃɪ (29) and all words in the 4th Tone. Before words in either of the other tones it is ˋbu.
14. Notice that the expressions ·ʃɪ·bu·ʃɪ (3) and ′bu ˋʃɪ (2) always have the same intonation, when they come at the end of a question, i.e they are monotones in the middle position. It is a great help in mastering the tones to learn the intonation of particular phrases.

Grammatical Construction.

15. Compare ˋʃɪ (29) with ˬju (5), and note the difference in meaning between ˋʃɪ, *it is*, and ˬju, *there is*.
16. As in the case of ˬju (5) with the negative ′meɪ (3), so with ˋʃɪ (29) and the negative ′bu (33) ; ′bu is prefixed to the verb to express the idea of Negation, and the Affirmative and Negative combined form the Interrogative. Thus :
ˋʃɪ (1), *it is* ; ′bu ˋʃɪ (2), *it is not* ; ˋʃɪ·bu ˋʃɪ (3), *is it ?*
17. Note that ′bu is used with ˋʃɪ, and ′meɪ with ˬju. It will be found also that with verbs ˋbu in general is used with the present and future tenses, and ′meɪ with the perfect and past tenses.
18. The expression ·ʃɪ·bu·ʃɪ, following a direct statement, has the force of *is it not ?* (S. 16).

19. The particle ⁻dɪ (26) has various uses. The most common is as the sign of the possessive. Other uses will be pointed out later.
20. An alternative question, e.g. *is it yours or is it mine?* is expressed by joining together two alternative statements, but without the "or" (S. 18). It is of the same grammatical construction as ˌju·meɪˌju and ·ʃɪ·ḅu·ʃɪ.
21. The Demonstrative Adjectives are ˋdʒɤ (30) and ˋna (31). When used with singular nouns the appropriate Classifiers are used with them. When they occur with plural nouns, ˌɕiɛ (28) is used instead of the Classifier, except when the numeral is expressed, in which case the Classifier is used and the ˌɕiɛ omitted (L. 3, S. 21; L. 4, S. 12; L. 5, S. 8); to say ˋna·ɕiɛ ˌliaŋ·khuaɪ ˋmɔ would be incorrect.
22. The plural, ˋdʒɤˌɕiɛ, *these*, is used with the word ˊchiɛn (13), *money*, instead of the singular as in English.
23. As demonstrative pronouns ˋdʒɤ and ˋna are used alone (S. 22, 23), or occasionally with the General Classifier ˋg̊ə (L. 4, S. 10),
24. Note that ˌjɛ, *also*, comes after the subject, not before (S. 24); ˌjɛ ˋnaˌg̊uan ˌḅi would be wrong. Similarly, to say ⁻thaˌjɛ ˌju is correct, to say ˌjɛ ⁻tha ˌju would be incorrect.

Chinese Characters.

25. Note the formation of, and learn to write, the following new Radicals, Nos. 20, 21, 37, 72, 77, 106, 149, 157, 162, 163.
26. Note the formation of, and learn to write, the Characters in the Vocabulary.

Review.

27. Write out in the Phonetic Transcription as many sentences as possible of the types: ⁻wɔˌjuˌxao⁻ʃu; ˌwɔ ˊmeɪˌju ˌxao⁻ʃu; ⁻wɔ ˌjuˌxao⁻ʃu ˊmeɪˌju substituting each of the other pronouns and nouns.

Lesson 3. Part I.

Pronunciation.

1. The new Initials are ʝ̊, dz; and the Finals are aŋ, aɪ, uŋ, iaŋ, ɯ, ɛn.
2. Notice the raised 3rd Tone in ˌdʒɪˌḅi.
3. In the expression ˊthuŋ ˌdzɤ·ɪ the ˌdzɤ·ɪ is a contraction of ˌdzɯ (42) and ˊʌɪ (81), thuŋ dzɯ (4) is lit. *children of copper*, and the ʌɪ is an enclitic.
4. Notice that the phrases ˌxao·buˌxao and ˊʃə·mə, like ·ʃɪ·ḅu·ʃɪ and ·ḅu·ʃɪ, almost invariably have the same intonation. The student is recommended to practice these and all such phrases until their correct intonation becomes automatic.
5. Notice that ˋḅu before ˌxao [in the 3rd Tone] has its own etymological tone (See L. 2, N. 13).

Grammatical Construction.

6. The expression ˌdʒɿˌbi is used as a collective noun meaning stationery generally, in the same way as ˌbi ˈmɔ (L. 1).
7. A second class of two-word combinations (cf. L. 1, N. 17) is the class called Synonym Compounds (p.7.); i.e. combinations of two words with similar or cognate meanings ; e.g. ˈjɛn (43) and ˈthai (35) mean an *ink-slab* and *slab* respectively, but either of them used alone in speech would be liable to be confused with other words having the same sound, hence the use of the compound.
8. Note the compound numerals of the types 13 and 30. The difference is indicated by the relative position of the two numerals in each combination thus : /ʃɿ⁻san, (13) ; ⁻san /ʃɿ (30).
9. Adjectives when used as predicates come after the noun (cf. L. 1, N. 6) e.g., ˌxɑo⁻ʃu, *the good book ;* ⁻ʃu ˌxɑo, *the book is good.*
10. In L. 2 we had the case of the negative ˈbu used with ˈʃɿ, *to be.* In this lesson examples are given of the use of ˈbu in precisely the same way with adjectives, when used predicatively, to form both negative and interrogative sentences. Thus : ˌxɑo, *it is good ;* ˈbu ˌxɑo, *it is not good ;* ˌxɑo ˈbu ˌxɑo, *is it good ?*
11. The numeral adjective ˌʝi (40), *few*, when used as an interrogative asks the question with a small number, generally less than ten, in mind. It is followed by a classifier ; e.g., ˌʝi ˈgə, *how many ?*
12. In S. 11 the final syllable ⁻ma (48) is the sign of the direct question ; thus, for the question, *is this book good ?* you may say either ˈdʒɤ bən ⁻ʃu ˌxɑoˈbuˌxɑo or ˈdʒɤˈbən ⁻ʃu ˌxɑoˈma.
13. The most common intensive adverb is ˌxən (39). Normally it precedes the adjective it qualifies, but frequently it follows the adjective with the particle ⁻dɿ (26) or də (91) between.
14. The classifier ˈweɪ (44) is primarily the stall in which the minister stands when in attendance at court. (See the composition of the corresponding character in the Table of Characters in the Appendix) ; and thus comes to be used as a polite classifier of persons.

Chinese Characters.

15. Note the formation of, and learn to write, Radicals Nos. 11, 13, 28, 57, 60, 83, 112, 117, 120, 123, 138, 147, 168.
16. Learn the characters in the Vocabulary as directed in the preceding lessons.

Lesson 3. Part II.

Pronunciation.

17. There are no new Initials in Part II ; and only one Final, yɛn.
18. Notice that in the expression ⁻duŋ·ɕi (5), as in the case of ⁻ɕiɛn·ʃʌŋ there are two 1st tones, but the pitch of the second unstressed syllable drops, and the syllable is practically toneless.

19. Notice that in the expression ＇thuŋ ⁄ jyan (**7**), with two 2nd tones, the second syllable retains its tone but in a lower pitch, whereas in the expression ＇jaŋ ＇chiεn (**3**), also with two 2nd tones, the pitch of the second syllable remains high. The difference is due to the difference of stress. In the latter case the two syllables are stressed equally, whereas in the former the stress of the 2nd syllable, though not wholly absent, is weaker than the first.
20. In the following tone-graphs the intonation of Ss. 1, 14 and 15 is recorded. The double lines form the stave, and three pitches are shown. The student is recommended to make similar tone-graphs of the remaining sentences as he listens to the record. The graphs can be made independently of the script. They can therefore be inserted in any passage which may already be printed or written.

1. ɖʐɤ ʃɪ xɑo ʃu.   ɖʐɤ·ḅən ʃu xɑo.

14. ɖʐɤ ʃɪ ʃə·mə?   15. nɑ ʃɪ ʃə·mə ɖuŋ·ɕi?

Grammatical Construction.

21. The expression ⁻ɖuŋ·ɕi (**5**), *thing*, like ⁻ɕiεn·ʃʌŋ belongs to Class II of two-word combinations; viz: Logical Compounds (p.8.).
22. The word ＇ʃən (**50**) is the indefinite interrogative pronoun, but is seldom used alone; it is usually combined with the interrogative particle ⁻mɔ, or ⁻mə (**48**), in which case the n in ＇ʃən is lost, thus: ˌʃə·mə (**8**), *what?* Note: ˌʃə·mə never begins a sentence. *What is this?* is ˋɖʐɤ ˋʃɪ ˌʃə·mə, *this is what?*
23. A second use of the particle ⁻ɖɪ (cf. L. 2, N. 19) is as affixed to adjectives, converting them into substantives; e.g., ˌxɑo, *good;* ˌxɑo ɖɪ, *good ones*. Note: ˌju ˋɖɑ·ɖɪ, ˌju ˌɕiɑo·ɖɪ is not a question (cf. L. 2, N. 20); if it were, ˋʃɪ not ˌju would be used.
24. The word ˋji̊ɑo has various meanings which will be introduced later. Its primary meaning is *to call*, or *to name a thing*, as here.

Chinese Characters.

25. The new Radicals are Nos. 52, 53, 68, 99, 109, 146.
26. Learn the characters in the Vocabulary as previously directed.

Review.

27. Write out in the Phonetic Transcription as many sentences as possible of the types :—

(1). ˻wɔ ˻ju ˉsan˻bən ˉʃu; (2). ˋdʒɤ ·ʃɪ ˻wɔ·dɪ ʼchiɛn ·b̪u·ʃɪ? substituting in (1) the other nouns, pronouns, numerals and classifiers, and in (2) the other nouns and possessive pronouns, singular and plural.

Lesson 4. Part I.

Pronunciation.

1. The one new Initial in this Lesson is f, and the new Finals are ɪŋ, ʌɪ
2. The numerals furnish exceptionally good practice in tones. Moreover mistakes in tones are more than ordinarily noticeable in the case of numerals, and to produce them fluently, particularly in the higher denominations, is difficult. It is desirable, therefore, to give special attention to the Tone Practice in this lesson

Grammatical Construction.

3. The Numeral Adjectives ˉd̪ɔ (56) and ˻ʃɑo (63) are joined together to form the interrogative ˉd̪ɔ˻ʃɑo (1), *how many?* The expression is generally used with a larger number in mind than in the case of ˻ji̊ (40) and does not take a classifier, while ˻ji̊ does.
4. The word ʼlɪŋ (60) is literally a *fraction*. In the numerals, and in stating sums of money, it indicates a gap in the denominations, practically equivalent to the English *nought* (*a cypher*), though it does not, strictly speaking, mean a *cypher*.
5. In Chinese dollar currency there are three denominations. The dollar, ʼjyan (52), the *tenth of a dollar*, ʼmɑo (59), and *the cent* ˉfən (57). The last named literally means *a tenth*, but it is the tenth of a ʼmɑo, and therefore the hundredth of a dollar. Note: The classifier of ʼchiɛn when referring to copper cash is ˋg̊ə not ˋkhuaɪ; e.g. ˻wɔ˻ju˻ji̊ ˋg̊ə˗chiɛn, *I have a few* (*copper*) *cash*.
6. There are two words for the numeral *two*, ˋʌɪ (64) and ˻liɑŋ (41). For the cardinal numeral *two* ˻liɑŋ is used more frequently than ˋʌɪ, while for the ordinal ʌɪ is used. The latter is used always in compound numbers of the type ʼʃɪˋʌɪ, 12, and ˋʌɪʼʃɪ, 20, whilst ˻liɑŋ is never so used.

Chinese Characters.

7. The new Radicals are Nos. 26, 36, 65, 82, 173. In addition learn Nos. 8, 15, 16, 17.
8. Learn the characters in the Vocabulary as in previous Lessons.

Lesson 4. Part II.

Pronunciation.

9. There are no new Initials in Part II. of this Lesson. There is one new Final ʃui.
10. The Final ui in ′ʃui (69) and in combination with other Initials, like the sound ju (L. 1, 1) is modified by the influence of tone and becomes ueɪ in the 3rd and 4th Tones (see 88, 195). As they are really one class or phoneme the spelling eɪ is adopted for them all.
11. Notice the intonation of the phrase jɑo·bu·jɑo and bu·jɑo when concluding a sentence. Cf. L. 2, N. 14, and L. 3, N. 4.

Grammatical Construction.

12. The personal interrogative pronoun ′ʃueɪ (69), takes ⁻d̥i as the sign of the possessive, like the other personal pronouns, but does not take ′mən, the sign of the plural ; ′ʃueɪ itself is both singular and plural.
13. Ordinal numbers are formed by prefixing ʾd̥i (75) to the cardinal numerals ; thus, ⁻san, *three* ; ʾd̥i⁻san, *the third*. Of the two words for *two*, ʾʌɪ is always used for the ordinal numeral, thus ˌliaŋʾg̊ə ′ɪən, *two men ;* but ⁻d̥iʾʌɪʾg̊ə ′ɪən, *the second man*.
14. A third class of two-word combinations used to express single ideas is the combination of a verb with its object to express the idea of the verb ; thus : ˌɕiɛʾd̥zɯ (3), *to write characters*, meaning no more than is meant by the English verb *to write ;* ⁻ʃuɔʾxuɑ, *to say words ;* i.e., *to speak* (L. 5. 1).
15. Note the omission of ′ʃɪ in the numerals of the type 950 (Tone Practice vi). It may be inserted, as, ˌd̥iu·baɪˌwu·ʃɪ, or omitted as here.
16. In L. 2 and L. 3 we had examples of ʾb̥u with the verb *to be*, and with adjectives. In this lesson we have an example of its use with verbs in general ; thus ʾjɑo, *I want ;* ′buʾjɑo, *I do not want ;* ʾjɑo·b̥uʾjɑo, *do you want?*
17. The verb ʾjɑo is primarily *to want ;* it is also used as an auxiliary indicating the future tense (S. 13). Sometimes the two meanings are difficult to distinguish and can only be decided by the context, or by emphasis.
18. A third use of the particle ⁻d̥i is as joined to a verb, converting it into a relative clause ; thus : ⁻ɕiɛʾd̥zɯ, *to write characters ;* ˌɕiɛ·d̥i ʾd̥zɯ, *the characters which are written ;* ʾd̥ʐɤʾʃɪ⁻wɔˌɕiɛ·d̥i, *this is what I wrote*.
19. In S. 11 we have an example of the object of the verb at the beginning of the sentence. It occurs most often in questions and imperatives. (Cf. L. 5, S. 15, 20 ; L. 6, S. 3, 4, 5 ; L. 7, S. 21, etc.)

Chinese Characters.

20. The new Radicals are Nos. 33, 50, 128, 134, 140, 172. Learn also Nos. 19, 22, 23, 27.
21. Learn the characters in the Vocabulary as in the previous Lessons.

Review.

22. Write out in Phonetic Transcription as many sentences as possible of the type : ˋd͡ʒɣ·bən ˉʃu ˌxɑo·bu˷xɑo ? ˋd͡ʒɣ·bən ˉʃu ˌxɑo ; ˋd͡ʒɣ·bən ˉʃu ˋbu˷xɑo ; substituting the other nouns in L. 1, I. with their classifiers.

Lesson 5. Part I.

Pronunciation.

1. There are no new Initials in this Lesson ; the new Finals in Part I. are uɔ, iɑ, uɑ, ueɪ.
2. In this and subsequent Lessons, the syllables in most of the compound words and expressions are joined up with the dot-hyphen, only the tones of stressed syllables are marked, and these (except in Vocabularies) are marked in their original etymological pitch (see p. 21).
3. The adverbs *here, there* and *where ?* are arranged as an exercise in Tone Practice. The student should listen to them and repeat them several times until he can reproduce them readily with their correct intonation.
4. Notice that the pitch of the interrogative ˷nɑ (83a), in the third tone, is high when followed by ˷li (83), but in its normal position i.e. low, when followed by ʹʌɪ (81) and ˉbiɛn (77). The reason for the former is that ˷li is in the third tone ; though being unstressed its tone is lost, its etymological tone still remains in the sub-consciousness of the speaker, and the tone of the preceding syllable is raised accordingly.
5. The combinations ˋd͡ʒɣ·ʌɪ (8) and ˋnɑ·ʌɪ (9) in conversation are contracted to ˋd͡ʒɣ·ɪ and ˋnɑ·ɪ ; see Ss. 1, 7.

Grammatical Construction.

6. Note the three forms of expression for *here, there* and *where ?* respectively. The forms ˋd͡ʒɣ·li, ˋd͡zaɪˋd͡ʒɣ·li, etc., mean literally *in here*, etc., in the forms ˋd͡ʒɣ·ʌɪ, ˋd͡zaɪˋd͡ʒɣ·ʌɪ, etc., the ʹʌɪ is simply a particle added for the sake of euphony ; ˋd͡ʒɣ·biɛn, ˋd͡zaɪˋd͡ʒɣ·biɛn, etc., are literally *this side*, etc., and have the force of *over here*.
7. The forms ˋd͡zaɪˋd͡ʒɣ·li, etc., are always used when following the subject ; thus : you may say ˋd͡ʒɣ·li ˷ju ʹɪən, or ˋd͡zaɪˋd͡ʒɣ·li ˷ju ʹɪən, but never ˷ju ʹɪən ˋd͡ʒɣ·li. In the latter case the form ˷ju ʹɪən ˋd͡zaɪ ˋd͡ʒɣ·li must be used.

8. The preposition `ˋdzaɪ` (89), when used with a noun, always comes before the latter ; it has simply a locative meaning, and is generally supplemented by another word following the noun when such ideas as *in, upon, under*, are expressed. It includes the verb *to be*. S. 2 is an example of the form `ˋdzaɪ....ˌli`, *in*.
9. Note that `ˋna` in the 4th Tone (31) is demonstrative, whereas `ˌna` [83a], the same character but in the 3rd Tone, is interrogative.
10. A fourth use of the particle `⁻dɪ` (cf. L. 2, 3 and 4) is as joined to verbs with their objects to indicate the agent ; thus :
 `ˋniɛn⁻ʃu·dɪ`, *one who reads books*, or *a scholar*.
 `⁻ʃuɔˋxua·dɪ`, *one who is talking*.
 Compare English compound words ending in *er*, such as *book-keeper*. In S. 5 the `ˊɹən`, *man*, may equally well be omitted. Note : `niɛn⁻ʃu` is an intensive form of reading, i.e. study ; ordinary reading is expressed by `ˋkhan⁻ʃu` (96). [L. 6, N. 17].
11. In S. 11 the expression `⁻ɕɪn⁻fʌŋ` is a two-word combination meaning literally *a letter seal*, i.e. an envelope (see Pt. II., c. 19). Note : `⁻i·fʌŋ` `ˋɕɪn` is *a letter*, `⁻i·g̊ə` `ˋɕɪn·fʌŋ`, is *an envelope*.

Chinese Characters.

12. The new Radicals are Nos. 63, 70, 135, 145, 152, 166. Learn also Nos. 34, 35, 43, 44.
13. Learn to recognise and write the characters in the Vocabulary. Note : In this and subsequent Lessons the analysis of characters hitherto supplied will not be given. The student will find it more helpful henceforth to look up this information for himself. See Directions to the Student, in Vol. II.

Lesson 5. Part II.

Pronunciation.

14. There is one new Final in Part II.; viz. ou.
15. The word `ˊdɤ` (91), *to obtain*, when used as an auxiliary is shortened to `ˊdə` ; and when it means *must* it is modified to `deɪ`.

Grammatical Construction.

16. The words `ˋkhan·ǰiɛn` (**14**), *to see*, and `⁻thɪŋ·ǰiɛn` (**17**), *to hear*, belong to the class of synonym compounds (L.3,N.7). The cognate word `ˋǰiɛn` (97), *to perceive*, is combined with the words `ˋkhan` (96), *to look*, and `⁻thɪŋ` (90), *to listen*, to form words for *see* and *hear* in colloquial speech, and so avoid the confusion which would result if the words were used alone. The word `ˋǰiɛn` has been defined as an auxiliary verb, but the above is probably the truer explanation

17. One way of expressing the comparative is by adding ⁻i ˌdiɛn, *one point*, to the positive form of the adjective; thus: ˌxɑo, *good;* ˌxɑo⁻iˌdiɛn, *one point better*, i.e. *a little better*.
18. A fifth use of the particle ⁻dɪ (cf. L. 2, 3. and 4) is in the formation of adverbs; namely, by the reduplication of the adjective and the addition of the ⁻dɪ, thus: ˋman (100), *slow*, manˋman·dɪ (**21**), *slowly*.
19. The auxiliary verb ʹdə (91) is used to form the potential mood. It may be used alone with the main verb; thus: ⁻ʃuɔ·də, *it can be said;* or it may be used with compound verbs of the class mentioned above (N. 16), in which case it is placed between the two synonyms; ˋkhan·də·ɟiɛn, *I can see*.
20. By substituting the negative ˋbu for the ʹdə between the two synonyms, or by inserting it between the verb and the auxiliary, the idea of permissibility or feasibility expressed by ʹdə is strongly negatived; thus: ⁻ʃuɔ·bu·də, *it may not be said;* ˋkhan·bu·ɟiɛn, *I cannot see*. Note: ˋkhan·də·ɟiɛn, and ⁻thɪŋ·də·ɟiɛn, literally, are *to look* (or *listen*) *and attain to perceiving;* ˋkhan·bu·ɟiɛn and ⁻thɪŋ·bu·ɟiɛn are *to look* (or *listen*) and *not perceive;* similarly ⁻ʃuɔ·də is *it can be said* and ⁻ʃuɔ·bu·də, *it cannot be said* [cf. L. 16].
21. The complete tense is expressed by ˌliɑo (95). It is the sign of the perfect rather than of the preterite, though such distinctions are not consistently maintained in Chinese. It expresses completion of the action rather than time. The insertion of the negative ˋbu before the ˌliɑo expresses the impossibility of this completion of the action; see L. 16.
22. Verbs are often reduplicated, as ˋkhan·khan (**15**), *to look*, for emphasis according to some, but probably also to serve the same purpose as most two-word combinations, and avoid ambiguity. Note: ˋkhan ·khan is *to look*, while ˋkhan·ɟiɛn (**14**) is *to see;* ⁻thɪŋ·thɪŋ is *to listen* while ⁻thɪŋ·ɟiɛn (**17**) is *to hear*.
23. Often when the verb is reduplicated ⁻i, *one*, is inserted between the two verbs, in which case the second word has the force of a verbal noun; thus: ˋkhan·i·khan (**16**), *to look one look;* ⁻thɪŋ·i·thɪŋ, *to listen one listen*.
24. The words ˋwən (98) and ˌchɪŋ (92) must be carefully distinguished; ˋwən asks a question; ˌchɪŋ asks a favour.
25. The sign of the relative is ˌsɔ (94). It is not used in Peking so much as in other parts of Mandarin-speaking China, where S. 15 of this Exercise would quite commonly be; ˌwɔ ˌsɔ ˌɕiɛ·dɪ ˋdʒɤ·ɕie ˋdzɯ, etc., A sentence of this type is recorded in L.10, S. 24.
26. Note the following:—   ⁻thɑ ˋchy = *he is going*.
    ⁻thɑ ʹbu·chy = *he is not going*.
    ⁻thɑ ˋchy·liɑo = *he has gone*.
    ⁻thɑ ʹmeɪˋchy = *he has not gone*.
    ⁻thɑ ˋchy·buˌliɑo = *he cannot go*.

Chinese Characters.

27. The new Radicals are Nos. 41, 25, 69, 93, 174. Learn also Nos. 45, 46, 47, 48.

Review.

28. Write out in the Phonetic Transcription as many sentences as possible of the types :—
    (1) ˌni ju ˌʃi·bən ⁻ʃu ? ˌwɔ ju ⁻san·bən ⁻ʃu.
    (2) ˌni ju ⁻dɔ·ʃao ⁻ʃu ? ˌwɔ ju ˋʌɪ·ʃɪ⁻san·bən ⁻ʃu
    substituting the other suitable Nouns, Pronouns, Numerals and Classifiers.

Lesson 6. Part I.

Pronunciation.

1. The only new Initial is tʃh, and one new Final is y.
2. The exercise in Tone Practice consists of two-syllable combinations in which the first syllable is stressed and has its full etymological tone, whilst the second syllable is toneless. The latter is in each case a particle, or auxiliary, and is combined with a stressed word in each of the four tones. Notice, in the cases of ⁻na·li and ⁻dzou·liao, how the etymological tone of the second syllable though lost still influences the syllable preceding, the tone (3rd) of which is therefore raised.

Grammatical Construction.

3. Note the synonym compounds : ′mɪŋ·baɪ (1), ˋɪən·ʃɪ (5), ⁻i·sɯ (9) ˋdzɯ·ʃi (8) ; also the verb with its object : ′ʃɪ ˋdzɯ (4).
4. In the verbs dun·də (2), and ˌɕiao·də (3), the force of the auxiliary ′də (91) differs from that stated in L. 5, N. 19. Here it expresses the completion of the idea of the main verb.
5. The word ˋxueɪ, *to be able*, is expressive of acquired ability, as distinguished from natural ability, for which there is another word ′nʌŋ (see L. 7). Note : in the 3rd tone the same word has the meaning, *a time*.
6. The reflexive pronoun ˋdzɯ·ʃi (8) follows the personal pronoun, e.g., ⁻tha ˋdzɯ·ʃi ; or it may be used alone, ˋdzɯ·ʃi, meaning *oneself*.
7. The word tʃhu (119) is literally *a place* ; it is used to form abstract nouns by adding it to adjectives ; thus ˌxao (6), *excellent*, ˌxao·tʃhu, *excellence*, i.e. *good points* ; ′nan (108), *difficult*, ′nan·tʃhu, *difficulty*.

8. The word ˳geɪ (112), *for, to,* primarily means *to give,* and hence is the sign of the dative. When used with the meaning of *for,* as in this lesson, it comes before the verb; when it is used in the sense of *giving to,* it comes after the verb; e.g. wɔ˳geɪ niˇmaɪ, *I will sell it for you;* wɔˇmaɪ geɪ ni, *I will sell it to you.*

Chinese Characters.

9. The new Radicals are Nos. 49, 102, 132, 141, 180. Learn also Nos. 51, 54, 55, 56.
11. There is one new Final: yə.

Lesson 6. Part II.

Pronunciation.

12. The exercise in Tone Practice consists of two-syllable combinations in which the first syllable is fully stressed and carries its etymological Tone, and the second syllable is weak in stress—in most cases so weak as to be practically toneless, and only in one or two instances retaining something of its tone character.

Grammatical Construction.

13. The adverb ˳i·ǰɪŋ **(15)**, indicating past time, immediately precedes the verb it qualifies, and is always followed by ˳liɑo (95) after the verb.
14. The conjunction ˇjiu (134), literally *to follow,* is one of the signs of the future tense; it refers to an event immediately following upon another. When two sentences are joined by ˇǰiu, *when* is implied in the first sentence. (S. 11.)
15. The adverb ˇdzaɪ (133), *again,* looks forward to the future. It is not, as in the case of the English word *again,* used of the past. Another word ˇju (456) is used for this purpose, e.g. ˳wɔ ˇdzaɪ ⁻ʃuɔ, *I will say it again;* ⁻tha ˇju ⁻ʃuɔ, *he said again.*
16. In S. 13 is an instance of a verb, ʹmɪŋ·baɪ, functioning as an adverb, or as some explain it, as an auxiliary to the main verb ⁻thɪŋ. The student must bear in mind, what has been said elsewhere, that it is characteristic of the Chinese language that any word may function as any one of what in English are called " the parts of speech."
17. Note that ˇniɛn ⁻ʃu is *to read aloud* or *recite,* as scholars in school recite, and hence generally means *to study;* ˇkhan ⁻ʃu means simply *to read.*

Chinese Characters.

18. The new Radicals are Nos. 66, 103, 108, 124. Learn also Nos. 58, 59, 67, 71, 76, 78.
19. Note the difference between the character of c. 129, ˏi, *already*, and that of c. 113 ˏj̊i, *self*.

Review Lesson.

20. In the sentence: ˋnɑ·b̥ən ˉʃu d̥zaɪ ˋd̥ʒɤ·li, substitute :—(1) the other demonstratives including the plural; (2) the other adverbs of place including the interrogative.

Lesson 7. Part I.

Pronunciation.

1. There are no new Finals in this Lesson and no new Initials in Part I.
2. The Tone Practice in this Lesson, and in those that follow, consists of two-syllable combinations in which the first syllable may be either fully or weakly stressed, but in which the second syllable is fully stressed. The student is recommended to give special attention to the practice of these phrases. The complete series includes all the Finals in stressed positions, and each final in all four tones. Mastery of a correct pronunciation of these will go a long way towards the mastery of Chinese tones.
3. There are many final particles used in Mandarin which carry no meaning, but are simply euphonic endings. The syllable ˉlɑ or ˉlə is one of these.

Grammatical Construction.

4. Notice the apparently redundant use of ˏliɑo (95) and ˏlə, in the second sentence of S. 1. The ˏliɑo here expresses the perfect tense of the verb ʹlaɪ (144), while ˏlə rather completes the sentence, or may be regarded simply as a euphonic ending.
5. The ɑ (141) in S. 4 is an honorific particle used in polite forms of address. The words ˋg̊ueɪ (150), *honourable*, and ˋj̊iɛn (151), *humble*, are also applied to the one addressed, in the one case, and to oneself in the other, as forms of politeness. In S. 6, the word ˋb̥i (152) is used in place of ˋj̊iɛn, with a similar meaning.

Chinese Characters.

6. The new Radicals are Nos. 90, 130, 154, 170. Learn also Nos. 80, 81, 84, 87, 88, 89.

Lesson 7. Part II.

Pronunciation.

7. There is one new Initial, ph.

Grammatical Construction.

8. Note that ⁻ɖuŋ (46) and ⁻ɕi (47), which were introduced in Less. 3 as a compound word meaning *thing*, are here used in their primary meanings of *East* and *West* respectively.
9. The word nʌŋ (165), *to be able*, expresses natural ability, as distinguished from xueɪ (115) which expresses acquired ability (cf. L. 6).
10. The enclitic particles, ˌɖzɯ (42) and ′ʌɪ (81), both primarily mean *son*. They are added to many nouns, and so help to differentiate these words from others of similar sounds. In this use they imply individuality, or the concrete.
11. Notice the different ways of expressing the imperative. In Ss. 16, 23, the simplest form is used; the verbs ′laɪ (144), *to come*, and ˋchy (170), *to go*, are used as auxiliaries with the verb ′na (162), *to carry in the hand*, the object of the verb coming betwen them; thus: ′na ′phan·ɖzɯ ′laɪ, *carrying a plate come*; i.e. *bring a plate*.
12. The above idiom is often modified by the use of ⁻ba̭ (Ss. 17, 18, 24), the same word as ˌba̭, the classifier of knives, forks, spoons and other articles which are handled, but in the 1st Tone, in which it has the force of an instrumental verb meaning *to take hold of with the hand*. The object of the verb comes after the ⁻ba̭, and before the ′na·laɪ or ′na·chy, as in S. 19, 21, which literally are :—*Take hold of....and bring*, or *take hold of....and take away*. In the 4th Tone the same word means a *handle*.
13. Sometimes the auxiliary ˌliao is inserted between the ′na and ˋchy, as in S. 17, which literally is : *Take hold of those few plates and having carried them, go.*
14 Note that tʃha (157), *fork*, takes the enclitic ɖzɯ, but that tʃha (160), *tea*, does not.
15. In Ss. 19, 21, the word ˋjao (71), *to want*, with or without the negative ˋbu, is used with the force of the imperative.
16. Note : ⁻i·g̭ə ′tʃha·wan is *a tea-cup*; ⁻i·wan ′tʃha is *a cup of tea*.

Chinese Characters.

17. The new Radicals are Nos. 133, 137. Learn also Nos. 91, 92, 94, 95, 96, 97, 98, 101.

[Note.—In the five lessons preceding, Review exercises have been recommended. The student will now be in a position to devise these for himself].

Lesson 8. Part I.

Pronunciation.

1. There are no new Initials in this Lesson; and only one new Final in Part I., uaŋ.
2. Note the Third Tone in ˌkhʌ·i is raised throughout the Exercise. It is because the i is in the 3rd Tone, and, though unstressed and therefore toneless, it nevertheless affects the tone of the syllable preceding.

Grammatical Construction.

3. The expression ˌkhʌ·i, *may* or *can*, is used both as a subjunctive and as an imperative, just as in English the phrase *you can do so and so* is often used with the force of a command.
4. The word ⁻ǰiaŋ, *about to*, is used to express the immediate future. It may be used alone (S. 11) or with the auxiliary verb ˋjao (L.15, S.3)
5. The English prepositions *upon* and *below* are expressed by the words ˋʃaŋ and ˋɕia, but they follow the noun instead of preceding it as in English. They are often used in conjunction with the preposition ˋd̪zaɪ (see L. 5, N. 6, 7).
6. The word ˋʃaŋ is also used as an adjective, as in ˋʃaŋ·faŋ, *an upper room*, and as a verb (259a), as in ˌʃaŋ⁻ǰiɛ (L. 10, S. 18).
7. The preposition ʹphaŋ·biɛn, *by the side of*, also follows its noun, and is used in conjunction with ˋd̪zaɪ, which precedes the noun.
8. Note the difference between ˌd̪i·ɕia and ˋd̪i·ɕia. The former is *underneath*, and the latter is *on the ground*, ˌd̪i meaning *below*, and ˋd̪i *the ground* or *the earth*.
9. The verb ˋd̪ao (184), *to arrive*, (cf. S. 11), is used as a preposition in conjunction with a large class of verbs implying some point to be reached, e.g. ˌd̪zou·d̪ao, *to go to* ; ˋsuŋ·d̪ao, *to escort to*.
10. Note the use of ⁻d̪ɪ (26) following the preposition ˋʃaŋ (S. 7) forming an adjectival clause. The phrase literally is: *the knives and forks of the on-the-table*; that is, *the knives and forks which are on the table*.
11. Ordinarily the addition of ⁻d̪ɪ (26) to an adjective converts the latter into a noun (L. 3, N. 23). When the adjective is preceded by an adverb, however, the ⁻d̪ɪ is added to the former without changing its adjectival function. Either ˌwɔ ˌju ˋd̪a ʹfaŋ·d̪zɯ, or ˌwɔ ˌju ˌxən ˋd̪a·d̪ɪ ʹfaŋ·d̪zɯ, is correct, whereas ˌwɔ ˌju ˌxən ˋd̪a ʹfaŋ·d̪zɯ is not good, and ˌwɔ ˌju ˋd̪a·d̪ɪ ʹfaŋ·d̪zɯ is positively incorrect.

Chinese Characters.

12. The new Radicals are Nos. 131, 151. Learn also Nos. 91, 92, 94 to 98, 101.

Lesson 8. Part II.

Pronunciation.

13. There is one new Final, uan, in Part II.

Grammatical Construction.

14. Note the use of ⁻wən (123) in S. 16 with the meaning of *warm* which is its primary meaning. The meaning (*practice*) in L. 6, S. 12 is secondary.
15. Note the future perfect tense in S. 14. The past tense would be ′laɪ·dɪ xən ˋkhuaɪ.
16. The word ′xuan (194) is also read ′xaɪ and ′xan. It has various uses: In S. 17 it means *yet* ; in S. 19 it may mean either *still* or *more* ; in S. 20 it means *still*.
17. Note the two expressions for *ready* : ˌxɑo·lə, *good*, and ′dʌ·lə, *obtained*. (Ss. 17, 23, 24).

Lesson 9. Part I.

Pronunciation.

1. There is one Initial in Part I of this Lesson, viz. tʃh.

Grammatical Construction.

2. The Adjectives ˌxɑo (6) and ′nan (108), are also used as adverbs, as in Ss. 2, 16, 22, 26. The word ˌxɑo is also used as a verb, but in the 4th tone, meaning *to like, to be fond of*, e.g. ⁻thɑ ˋxɑo ʃuɔˋxuɑ, *he is fond of talking*, but ˌxɑo⁻ ʃuɔ, *it is kindly said*.
3. The word ⁻dʒɪ·dɑo (1), *to know*, is more commonly used in some parts of the country, and ˌɕiɑo·də (L. 6, 3) in others.
4. The expression ′xʌ·ʃɪ (2) is literally *in agreement with the pattern*, hence *suitable*.
5. The most common expression for probability in Pekinese is ˋdɑ·ğaɪ ˋdɑ·ğaɪ is literally *the great whole* ; hence *on the whole, probably*.
6. The present participle ′dʒɔ (206) is used with ˋdʌ (91) as an auxiliary verb to express the carrying into effect the action of the principal verb ; or with ˋbu (33) to express the opposite idea. Thus in S. 6, juŋ·də·dʒɔ is *can use*, i.e. *need*, and juŋ·bu·dʒɔ is *cannot use* ; i.e. *do not need*, the two together forming the interrogative *do you need ?*
7. Note the two expressions for *will it do ?* ˌkhʌ·i bu ˌkhʌ·i (L.8, S.1) and ′ɕiŋ·bu′ɕiŋ. The first expresses the idea, *Is it permissible ?* and the second, *Is it workable ? Will it go ?*

L

8. The particle ⁻nɪ is the sign of a question. It is used when the question cannot be answered by *yes* or *no ;* see S. 17. It is also used as a note of exclamation to express surprise, indignation, perplexity or impatience. Thus in S. 11 it expressed uncertainty, and in S. 19 it implies an element of surprise.

Chinese Characters.

9. The new Radicals are Nos. 181, 185. Learn also Nos. 150, 153, 155, 156, 158, 159, 160, 161, 164, 165.
10. Note that ′d̥iɛ (S. 12) takes the enclitic ˌdzɯ, whereas ˌwan does not.

Lesson 9. Part II.

Pronunciation.

11. In Part II. there is one new Final, un.
12. Notice the contraction of d̥zən (227) to d̥zə in d̥zə·mə (13), and the shortening of ɤ to ə in d̥ʒə·mə (19). Note that ⁻fɑ, *method*, is in the 1st Tone though the same character as ˌfɑ, *law*.

Grammatical Construction.

13. The Classifier ʽǰiɛn (233) primarily means *to divide*. It is used as the classifier of words implying separate wholes.
14. The interrogative weɪ′ʃə·mə (18), *why ?* is literally *for what ?* It usually follows the subject (S. 19).
15. The interrogative particle ⁻mɔ or ⁻mə (48) is used as a modal particle with d̥ʒɤ, ʽnɑ and ˌd̥zən, meaning, in combination with these words, respectively, *in such a way as this, in such a way as that*, and *in what way ?*
16. There are three expressions for *in this way*, ʽd̥ʒɤ·jaŋ (24), ʽd̥ʒɤ·mə (19), and ʽd̥ʒɤ·mə·jaŋ ; and for *in that way*, ʽnɑ·jaŋ (25), ʽnɑ·mə (20), and ʽnɑ·mə·ʽjaŋ.
17. The numerical adjective ⁻d̥ɔ (56), *many*, is used interrogatively in conjunction with the modal particle ⁻mɔ (48), and thus acquires the meaning *how much?*
18. The words ⁻fɑ (223a) and ʽt͡ʃhu (119) are used as noun-suffixes. They are added to verbs and adjectives to form nouns. (S. 21).
19. The word ⁻d̥aŋ (223) has many uses. Primarily it means *suitable, fitting ;* and this meaning can be discerned in most of the combinations in which it occurs. The two expressions in which we find it in this lesson belong to the class already explained as synonym compounds (cf. L. 13, N. 8 ; L. 25, N.1).

Chinese Characters.

20. There are no new Radicals in Part II. Learn Nos. 171, 175 to 179, 182, 183, 186 to 189.

Lesson 10. Part I.

Pronunciation.

There are no new Initials or Finals in this Lesson. In the foregoing vocabularies all the Initials, as explained in the Notes on Chinese Sounds, are included; and all the Finals except two, yn and iuŋ. In the Tone Practice, however, all the Finals are given in each of the four tones, so that these ten lessons furnish a complete system of drill in the pronunciation of Mandarin.

Grammatical Construction.

1. The most common expression for similarity, or sameness, is ⁻i˙jaŋ (3), *of one sort*, and for its opposite, ˙bu·i·jaŋ, *not of one sort*.
2. There are many ways of expressing the idea of approximation, most of them in the negative form. The most common are those given in this lesson, viz.:—˙ḫu˙li (6), ˙ḫu·ḍa˙li (7), ˙tʃha·ḫu˙li (4) ⁻tʃha·ḫu⁻ḍo (5).
3. Note in S. 1 the difference between ⁻ǧuan·ʃaŋ, ˙ḫi·ʃaŋ and ˌsɔ·ʃaŋ; ⁻ǧuan (237) is the primitive wooden bolt of a Chinese door, and ⁻ǧuan·ʃaŋ is to pass the bolt into its socket; ˙ḫi·ʃaŋ is simply to push the door to, and ˌsɔ·ʃaŋ is to lock it with a padlock. There is nothing in the construction of a Chinese door by which a door may be fastened in such a way that it can be reopened by simply turning a handle without the use of a key. The expression ⁻ǧuan·ʃaŋ, however, is generally used to express this idea where the European type of door has been imported.
4. The Chinese mile, li (249) is about a third of the English mile (S. 5, etc.)

Chinese Characters.

5. There is one new Radical, No. 193. Learn also Nos. 190-193, 195-202.

Lesson 10. Part II.

Grammatical Construction.

6. The word ˙ʃaŋ, *on, above*, is also used in the 3rd tone, ˌʃaŋ, as a verb meaning *to go towards* (S. 18). See L.8, N.6.
7. The imperative mood is often expressed by the particle ˙ḅa (266)

at the end of the sentence or clause (S. 28).

8. The suffix ʻthou (211) is added to many nouns implying mass or pointedness. In this lesson it is added to the word *a tree*, and the two words together mean the material *wood*.

Chinese Characters.

Learn the remainder of the Radicals, viz.: Nos. 204-214.

Lesson 11.

1. Note that ˋjiao, *to compare*, the etymological tone of which is the 4th Tone, becomes 3rd Tone when used with ˍbi, and the tone of the latter is consequently raised.
2. In S. 27 in the phrase ˉdɔ·mən ˋda the mən is the Interrogative (v. 48) usually in this connection pronounced mə, but often as here pronounced mən.
3. The general terms to express comparison are ˍbi, (277), ˍbiˍjiao (**6**) and ˍjiaoˍbi. The most common is the single word ˍbi, the meaning of which is *compared with*, but which is generally best expressed by the English word *than ;* Ss. 1, 7, 13.
4. Note the difference between ˍbiˍjiao and ˍjiaoˍbi. The former is *to compare*, S. 12 ; and the latter is *compared with*, S. 2.
5. The Chinese preference for the negative is seen in the mode of expressing the comparative degree, the most common terms for which are ˋbuʻɹu (**8**) and ˍgan·buˋʃaŋ (**9**). The former literally is *not like*, i.e. *not equal to* (S. 4, 5) ; and the latter, *cannot catch up*, that is *not so good as* (S. 6).
6. Positive modes of expressing the comparative are by the use of ˋgʌŋ (283), *more* (S. 8), and ʻchiaŋ (271), *excellent* (S. 7). The former, however, often means a degree stronger than the comparative ; e.g. ˋdʒɤ ɕiɛ ˉxua bi duŋˉjyan·dzɯ·dɪ ˉxua ˍxao, ˉɕi ʻjyan·dzɯ·dɪ ˉxua ˋgʌŋ ˍxao, would be, *these flowers are better than those in the East garden, but those in the West garden are better still*.
7. The progressive comparative of the type *the more the better*, is expressed in Chinese by the use of the words ˋjyə (300) (S.31), and ˋjyə·fa (**23**) or ˋjyə·fa·dɪ (S. 32).
8. Note the new meaning of ˍsɔ (94), here used as Classifier of houses.
9. The superlative is often expressed by the word ˍʃu, which literally means *subject to*, and indicates that all the other members of a class are subject to the one singled out as the best of the class (S. 30). Four other words used to express the superlative are given in this lesson, viz.: ˋdɪŋ (293), which literally is *the summit*, i.e. *tip-top* (S.28) ˋdʒɪ (298), *the end, extreme*, i.e. *the limit* (S. 26) ; and ˋdzueɪ (301), *extreme, the most* (S. 27).
10. The expression ˍbiˍtshɯ (**20**) is literally *that and this*, used metaphorically for *you and me*, hence *mutually*.

Lesson 12.

1. There is one new Final, iuŋ.
2. Note the Compound No. 7 with the unusual lower 3rd tone preceding a 3rd tone.
3. Note specially and practice the intonation on the Record of ′nan ⁻ny‿lɑo`ʃɑo in S. 4.
4. The passive voice is expressed by the use of the auxiliary words `ƀeɪ (339) and `ɉiɑo (53) or `ɉiɑo (136), the two latter being used interchangeably. The auxiliary follows the subject of the verb, and is followed by the word indicating the agent. E.g. `nɑ·ɕiɛ ⁻ɉiɑ·xuɔ ɖu `ƀeɪ ɹən ′nɑ·chy·lə, *those tools have been taken away by somebody.* For an example of the use of `ɉiɑo see L. 21, N. 5.
5. The prepositions *before* and *after*, referring to place, are ′chiɛn (327) and `hou (340). They are sometimes joined to the suffixes thou, ƀiɛn, etc. Like those in previous lessons they are in Chinese really post-positions; i.e. they follow the noun. Examples: `dzaɪ `dɑ·mən ′chiɛn ju ‿ɉi·g̊ə ′ɹən jɑo`ɉiɛn ni, *in front of the main gate there are some people wanting to see you;* ′faŋ·dzɯ `xou·ƀiɛn ju ⁻i·g̊ə ⁻xuɑ·jyan, *behind the house there is a flower-garden.*

Lesson 13.

1. The general term for time is ′ʃɪ·xou (1), and the common expression for *at that time* is `nɑ·g̊ə ′ʃɪ·xou or `nɑ ′ʃɪ·xou, and for *when?* or *at what time?* is ′ʃə·mə ′ʃɪ·xou. Two other terms, however, are used for *when?* ‿ɉi·ʃɪ (2) (S. 16) and ⁻ɖɔ·dzan (3) (S. 26), the latter less frequently in Pekinese.
2. Note:—In speaking of days, weeks, months and years, Chinese always put the higher denominations first.
3. For past or precedent time the word ⁻ɕiɛn (10) is most commonly used but ′chiɛn (327), the word for *before* referring to place, is also used in the time sense in such phrases as ′chiɛn·thiɛn (9), *the day before yesterday*, in which the word *yesterday* is understood. Other terms for past and precedent time are ɖzɑo (368), *early*, and ′tshuŋ ′chiɛn (29a), *formerly* (cf. L. 20, N. 1).
4. Present time in the general sense is expressed by `ɕiɛn·dzaɪ (13a), *now*, and ′ɹu·ɉɪn, *now*. The word ⁻ɉɪn (347), *now*, is prefixed to ′niɛn (309), *year*, and ⁻thiɛn (345) or `ɹ (355), *day*, to introduce the present year or to-day, but not with `jyə (374), *month*, for which the word ‿ƀən (21) is used. The word ‿ƀən is also used with ′niɛn. Its primary meaning is *a root*, hence *origin* as in ‿ƀən·laɪ (L. 9). Hence it comes to mean something originating with or peculiar to myself; thus ƀən′g̊uɔ, *my country;* ƀən`ʧhu, *this place;* ƀən`jyə, *this month.*

5. Future or subsequent time is expressed by ˋxou (340), *after*, the same word as for *after* as referring to place. N.B. ˋxou (340) is a different word from ˋxou (356) though in the same tone. The meaning of the latter is *time*. See the corresponding characters in the Chinese Text.
6. Note that in such phrases as *the 3rd year, the 3rd day*, no classifier is used, and ˋdi (75) the sign of the ordinal may or may not be used, thus: ⁻san niɛn, *three years*, may also be *the year three ;* di ⁻san niɛn is *the third year ;* i.e. from some specific point of time. In the case of the month, however, the classifier is used both with the ordinal and when stating a number of months: ⁻san·gə ˋjyə, *three months*, di ⁻san·gə ˋjyə, *the third month*. But the expression ⁻san jyə, *the month three*, is also used and without the ordinal ˋdi, as in the case of ʹniɛn, *year;* e.g. ˊmɪn·guɔ ˋsɯ·niɛn ˌwu·jyə, *the fifth month of the fourth year of the Republic.*
7. Note the use of ʹtshaɪ (351), ⁻faŋ·tshaɪ (4) and ⁻gaŋ·tshaɪ (5) in Ss. 9, 8 and 15, respectively, as expressing time immediately preceding the present.
8. Note the use of daŋ⁻tʃhu (6) in S. 7 to express the beginning of a specific period of time. The word ⁻daŋ (223) primarily means *ought, what is right* or *fitting* (L. 9, N. 19); but it has various other uses. Here it has the meaning of *at the time of.* (Cf. L. 25, N.1.)
9. The expression ⁻ɕɪŋ·chi (24), *a week*, literally is the star-time period, analogous to the year as the sun period, and the month as the moon period.
10. The word ⁻tʃhu (343), *beginning*, is placed before the numeral indicating the day of the month when it is one of the first ten days; thus: ⁻san jyə tʃhu ⁻san, *the 3rd day of the 3rd month.*
11. The frequently recurring expression ˋlaɪ·dɪ is a participial noun, *coming.*

Lesson 14.

1. The Conditional Mood is expressed most commonly by ɪʌ (389), ˋɪʌ·ʃɪ or ˋjaɔ·ʃɪ (1), *if*, followed by ˋʝiu (134), *then*, ˋbi (391) or ˋbi·ɕy (2), *must*, ˋʝiu ˋbi, *then must*, or other correlative expressions. (Ss. 1, 8.)
2. In L. 9, N. 5 it was stated that probability is expressed by the term ˋda·gaɪ. Another word expressing probability in lesser degree is ˌɕy (400) or ˌjɛ·ɕy, *perhaps*. (Ss. 19, 20.)
3. The simple imperative is expressed in various ways, as shown in previous lessons, (L. 7, 8 and 10). Emphatic imperative, certainty, or necessity, is expressed by 2, 3, 4, 5, 6, in the Vocabulary of Compound Words. They may be used interchangeably.
4. The idea of exclusion or exception is expressed by ʹtʃhu (395) and ʹtʃhu·liaɔ (24) (Ss. 27, 28 and 33).
5. Alternatives are expressed by ˋxuɔ (410) or ˋxuɔ·ʃɪ (S. 18).

6. In Ss. 13 and 14 are examples of the use of the auxiliary ˌliɑo (95) preceded by ˋbu (33) to express the impossibility of completing the action of the main verb, as explained in L. 5, N. 21.
7. For the use of ˋji·ɹan in S. 31 see L. 15, N. 8.

Lesson 15.

1. Note the new Final, yn.
2. The distributive adjectives are ˋgʌ (430), *each*, ˌmeɪ (426), *every*. When the latter is used as applied to events it is combined with fʌŋ (411), see S. 6. The English word *every* is often expressed by reduplicating the noun which is in that case followed by ⁻du, *all;* e.g. ⁻thɑ·mən ʹɹən·ɹən ⁻du jɑo ʹlaɪ, *they are all coming.*
3. The word *all* is expressed in various ways; the most common is by du (78), see S. 17. Another expression is ˌluŋˌdzuŋ (14), see S. 15. The former follows the noun, the latter precedes it. Another word is ˋdʒuŋ (431) but used in conjunction with ⁻du. The former before and the latter after the noun (S. 7). A fourth term is ˎfan (420), see S. 8.
4. The most common connectives are ʹxʌ (422), *with*, and ʹthuŋ (421), *together with*. Sometimes they are used in combination, as in S. 9, the former preceding the noun and the latter the verb. The ʹxʌ is used to connect things as well as persons, but the ʹthuŋ is used to connect persons only. The ʹthuŋ, however, is not so common used alone as ʹxʌ. The ʹxʌ is often followed by iˋkhuaɪ·ʌɹ, lit.: *one piece.*
5. It will be noticed in this lesson that the word ɹan (437) is combined with many words to form adverbs and conjunctions. The word primarily signifies affirmation; in the classical language it is *yes*, then it comes to have the force of an adversative, *but, however*. As an adverbial suffix it signifies *manner*.
6. The concessive conjunction *although* is expressed by ⁻sueɪ (440) and ⁻sueɪ·ɹan (17) followed by ʹxuan·ʃɹ (23) or ˋchyə-ʃɹ (27), see S. 19
7. The following are adversative conjunctions in common use : ˌkhʌ·ʃɹ, *but* (L. 14, **10**) ; ˋdan·ʃɹ (**24**), (336), and ˌdʒɹ·ʃɹ (**26**), (334), *but, only;* ʹxuan (**23**), *yet, still*, (194) ; ʹɹan·ʌɹ (**25**), *but*, ʹɹʌŋ·ɹan (**22**), *still;* ˋchyə·ʃɹ (**27**), *but, nevertheless*. They generally begin a clause or sentence or follow immediately after the subject.
8. The causal conjunction *since* or *seeing that* is ˋǰi·ɹan (**19**). It is often used as a sign of the perfect tense. It precedes the verb in a subordinate clause, and is followed by a principal verb in the main clause ; e.g. ni ˋǰi·ɹan ˋnɑ·mə ⁻ʃuɔ, ˌwo ǰiu ˋchy, *as you speak in that way I will go.*
9. Suddenness is most commonly expressed by ⁻xu·ɹan (**20**).
10. Certainty is expressed by the terms ˋbi·ɹan (**18**,) ˊgu·ɹan (**21**) ˌguɔ·ɹan, ʹʃɹ·dzaɪ (L. 15) and iˋdɪŋ (L. 16). Each has its own

particular shade of meaning which the student will gather by practice.

11. Learn the following sentences on the model of S. 28, substituting `ˋdzɯ·ɹan, *naturally, of course*,..........ˋḍan·ʃɪ, *but*, and ˉsueɪ·ɹan, *although*,..........ˋchyə·ʃɪ, *still*, for ˋgu·ɹan, *undoubtedly*,..........˷khʌ·ʃɪ, *but* :—

ˋna ˋdzɯ·ɹan ʃɪ˷xao ˋʃɪ, ˋḍan·ʃɪ ˷xən nan ˋḅan, *that is, of course, a good thing, but very difficult*.

ˋna ˉsueɪ·ɹan ʃɪ ˷xao ˋʃɪ, ˋchyə·ʃɪ ˷xən nan ˋḅan. *although that is a good thing, it is very difficult*.

Lesson 16.

1. Note the tone of mu (457) in mu·ɕia (5), see S. 7.
2. S. 1-7 in Part I. are examples of the use of ˋḅu (33) as negativing possibility. When used in this sense it comes between the verb and its auxiliary. Instances of its use with ʹḍə (91) were given in L. 5. Here, further instances are given of its use with the prepositions and auxiliaries ˋḍao (184), ˋḍuŋ (455), ˷liao (95), ʹʝi (449), and ˷chi·laɪ (L. 13, Pt. I.). When a fact or intention, is simply negatived the negative precedes both the verb and its auxiliary, e.g. ˉtha bu˷chi·laɪ, *he will not get up* ; ˉtha ˷chi·ḅu ʹlaɪ, *he cannot get up*
3. Note the use of ˉiˋḍɪŋ (3) to express certainty. For other modes of expression v. L. 15, N. 10, and L. 18, N. 2.
4. The particle ˷liao (95), the sign of the complete tense, and ʹʝi (449), *to reach*, are used as auxiliaries to express the possibility of completion. Their most frequent use is in the negative. When used in the affirmative they are preceded by ḍə (91), (cf. L. 5) ; e.g. ˋḅan·ḍə˷liao, *it can be managed* ; ˋḅan·ḅu˷liao, *it cannot be managed* ; ʹlaɪ·ḍəʹʝi, *to be able to* ; ʹlaɪ·ḅuʹʝi, *to be unable to*.
5. The preposition ˋḍao and the auxiliary ˋḍuŋ are used with verbs expressing movement, e.g. ˷dzou·ḍao, *to arrive* ; ˷dzou·ḅuˋḍao, *unable to arrive* ; ʹnɔ·ḍuŋ, *to move (a thing)* ; ʹnɔ·ḅuˋḍuŋ, *unable to move (a thing)*.
6. Note the contracted dzə·mɔ for ˷dzən·mɔ and ˋdʒə·mɔ for ˋdʒɤ·mɔ in Part II.
7. The compound expression ˷chi·laɪ (L. 13, Pt. I.), *to arise*, is used as an auxiliary implying inceptive action ; ˷ɕiaŋ·chiʹlaɪ, *to recall*, i.e. to think up (something) ; ˷ɕiaŋ·ḅu˷chi·laɪ, *unable to recall*.
8. ˋju (456), *again*, refers to past time, or to circumstances already existing, as distinguished from dzaɪ (133), which refers to future time.
9. The adverb ʹʌɪ·chiɛ (1), *moreover, further*, introducing a new statement, is usually followed by ˋju (456), *again*.
10. In addition to the forms mentioned in L.15, N.6, the idea of concession is expressed by the forms ʹɹən·phɪŋ (8), *to allow, let (him)* ʹsueɪˋḅiɛn (7), *to follow one's convenience* ; ˷dʒɪ˷guan ˋchy (6 *to be free to go* (lit. *only determine the going*).

11. The words ˌʝia (476a), ˋi (487a), ˌbɩŋ (476b) ˉdɩŋ (463b), are the first four of the Ten Celestial Stems which are used in conjunction with the Twelve Horary Branches to denote the years of the Chinese Saxagenary Cycle. They are also used, as here, in the same way as the letters A, B, C, D, etc., of the English Alphabet are used, viz.: to denote the different speakers in a dialogue. (See any Chinese-English Dictionary.)
12. The pronoun ʹdza·(468) is a polite form of *we*, and includes the one or more spoken to, in contradistinction from ˌwɔ·mən (L. 1), which though used loosely, strictly speaking refers only to the speaker and those associated with him, to the exclusion of those addressed.
13. Note that thi, *instead of*, is sometimes used in place of ğeɪ (112), *for* (L.6, N. 8).
14. Euphony is one of the most marked features of the Chinese language. It often determines grammatical construction as well as the position of the accent in the sentence. It also produces a large number of final particles which have no meaning, but are used simply as euphonious endings to sentences or paragraphs. It is difficult to determine by rule their use and selection. Two occur in the conversation in this Lesson, na and ba; and several others will be found in the following lessons. It will be noticed that the choice is sometimes affected by the sound of the words preceding; thus, ˌna·ɪ·na.

Lesson 17.

1. Sentences 1 to 4 are examples of reduplication of double expressions in adverbs (S. 1, 2) and verbs (S. 3, 4); see L. 5, N. 18, 22, for reduplication of single words.
2. The expression ˋdzaɪˉsan (3) literally, *again three (times)*, means *an indefinite number of times, repeatedly*.
3. ˋdao ̣di (4); lit. *to the end* (S. 5).
4. Notice the use and position of the intensives ʝi (490), *extremely* (S. 6) and ˌʝɪn (491), *utmost* (S. 7),
5. The idea of totality is expressed by ˌman (492), *full* (S. 8, 9) meaning *the whole of* the thing referred to; thus: ˌmanˉthiɛn; ˌmanˉwu·dzɯ, *the whole of the sky; the whole of the room*.
6. Note the phrase ʹwu·lun·ɪuʹxʌ (12) and (13). It literally is: *without discussing as to what*; hence, *in any case*.
7. Note the euphonic ending, ja.

Lesson 18.

1. Note the different modes, simple and intensive, of expressing the optative: ˋjyan·i, *a willing mind* (S. 1); ˌxən·buʹnʌŋ, *to hate being*

2. *unable* (S. 4); ⁻ba·buʹdɤ (S. 5), with the same meaning as ⌄xən·bu ʹnʌŋ, though not easy to explain.
2. Sentences 2 and 6 furnish two further modes of expressing certainty or assurance (cf. L. 16, N. 3); ⌄dʒun (534), see S. 6, *surely*; ⁻gan ⌄bao (S. 2), *not afraid to guarantee*; and ⌄dʒun⌄bao, *to grant a guarantee* (L. 19).
3. Note: ʹda·jɪŋ (4), see S. 2, means simple consent, while ⁻jɪŋ·ɕy (S. 9) means *to promise*.
4. Satisfaction is expressed by ˋdʒuŋˋi (5), which literally is, *to hit the target in one's mind, to get to the spot*.
5. Note the phrase ˋna·gə ʹdʒu·i (S. 7), literally, *to take a master purpose*, i.e. *make a decision*. Note: dʒu (354) in the expression ʹdʒu·i is in the 2nd tone: ʹdʒu, not ⌄dʒu, which is its etymological tone.
6. For ⌄da·suan in S. 10 see (15) in Part II.
7. Emphatic assent to a statement is expressed by the phrase khʌʹbu·ʃɪ (see Dialogue) or khʌʹbu·ʃɪ·ma, literally, *could it be otherwise?*
8. Note the phrase ʹjy.........dʒɪˋwaɪ, *except*. ʹjy (548) is the same meaning as ˋdzaɪ (89), *at* or *in*. The phrase literally is: *at the outside of*.
9. Note the two uses of ⁻da (542); daʹtʃhuan, *to take a passage*; da⁻ɕɪn, *to receive a letter*.

Lesson 19.

1. The numeral ⁻i (49), *one*, is prefixed to several words to express the idea of *one whole, all together* e.g. ⁻iˋguŋ, *the whole of*; ⁻iˋkhuaɪ, *in one piece, together*; ⁻iˋchie, *all*; ⁻iʹthuŋ, *together with*; See MacGillivray's Vocabulary for a very full list of such phrases.
2. The word ʹchyan, without the ⁻i, *and the expression* ʹchyan⌄thi, *the whole body*, are also used to express totality.
3. The most common adverbial numerals are ˋtshuɪ and ʹxueɪ, thus: ⁻iˋtshuɪ (Pt. II.), *once*, ⌄ju i·xueɪ, *once upon a time* (L. 29).
4. Note the phrase ⌄ju ʃɪ⌄ju: (*as to the question whether*) *there is, it is* (*a case of*) *there is*.

Lesson 20.

1. In Ss. 1 to 5 are examples of various ways of expressing past time cf. L. 13, N. 3.
2. Instantaneous action is most commonly expressed by ˋliʹʃɪ (8), *immediately*. Other expressions are used, of which one, ˋliˋkhʌ, is in L. 22, Pt. II. Often ˋjiu (134) alone is used, as in S. 8, with the same meaning.

3. Frequent action is expressed by ˌlyˋtshɯ (12), *many times;* continuous action by ˊʃɪˋkhʌ (9), *every section of time,* constantly repeated action by ˊtʃhaŋ (348) (Ss. 9, 10, 11). The term for unbroken time is bu ˋduan (v. Pt.II.).
4. A common term to express the end of a period of time is ˋmɔ·mɔ ˌliao (S. 12), which is used more strictly in the time sense than ˋdaoˌdi (L. 17, S. 5) is.
5. Another adversative conjunction (L. 15, N. 7) is ˋbu·ğuɔ or ˋbu ğuɔ·ʃɪ, *no more than* i.e. *only.*
6. ˊji, the intensive adverb in the phrase xao ˊji·lə, (Pt. II.) may follow the word it qualifies, as here, or precede it in the form ji˳xao; cf. L. 23, S. 3, where ˊ ̥ji occurs with the adjective ˋda.
7. ˊju·chi, *still more,* is similar in meaning to ˋğʌŋ (L. 11, N. 6), ˋjyə⁻fa (L. 11, N. 7) and ˊʌɪ·chiɛ (L. 16, N. 9).
8. Cause or reason is commonly expressed by ˌsɔˌi, *that by reason of which,* a combination of the relative ˌsɔ (L. 5, N. 25) and ˌi, *to use, by means of.*

Lesson 21.

1. ˌlɪŋ⁻ ̥jiao, *to receive instruction,* is a polite way of asking a question.
2. ⁻iˋchi, *at one breath,* i.e. *without pause,* is another of the class of adverbial numerals mentioned in L. 19, N. 1.
3. ⁻chiɛnˋwan, *a thousand times ten thousand,* is another mode of the intensive (cf. L. 24).
4. ˋɪu liao ⁻ʃən la, literally is *entered my spirit.*
5. In ˋ ̥jiao ˋʌɪˋmeɪ·meɪ ˋna·chy·liao, *taken away by my second younger sister,* ˋ ̥jiao is the sign of the passive (L. 12, N.4).
6. In ˋ ̥jɪn·laɪ, *recently,* ɪn (253) is *near* and laɪ (144) *come,* i.e. *come from the near (past).*

Lesson 22.

1. Notice the long substantival clause in Pt. II.: ʃɪ⁻ɕɪn tshuŋ......biˋjɛ·dɪ. The verbal clause ⁻tshuŋ......biˋjɛ is converted into a substantival clause by the dɪ in the same way as the verb ˌɕiɛ, *to write,* is converted into a substantive ˌɕiɛ·dɪ, *what is written* (cf. L. 4, N. 8).
2. As has been seen in preceding lessons reduplication in Chinese serves more than one purpose. To those previously cited must be added the very common mode of expressing the distributed universal: ˊɪən ˊɪən (see L. 15, N. 2) means *all men, one by one.* Cf. ˋğʌ ˊɪən, *each,* and ˌmeɪ, *every.*
3. Note the force of ˊtʃhaŋ in the sentence ˌwɔ ˊmeɪ·chy ˊtʃhaŋ, *I did not complete my going.*

Lesson 23.

1. Notice the suffix `ˋtʃhu` in S. 2 added to `⁻i` and `ˋxaɪ`. Cf. L. 9, N. 18.
2. Notice the use of the classifier `ˋg̊ə` without a numeral (S. 4). It is equivalent to the indefinite article *a* or *an*, the numeral *one* being understood.
3. Note the use of `˳khʌ` in the sentence, `ˋna ˳wɔ khʌ ˋb̥u·d̥ʒɪˋd̥ao·lə`, It has the same force as the English word *however* (cf. L. 27, N. 2).
4. Notice the adjectival clause formed by d̥ɪ in the last sentence of Part II., `tshuŋˋd̥ʒɤ·li·d̥ao..... *ʹlun·d̥un·d̥ɪ`. The d̥ɪ governs the whole clause from tshuŋ.

Lesson 24.

1. The emphatic negative imperative is expressed by the phrases `ˋd̥uan·b̥u˳khʌ`, *you positively must not* (S. 1), `ˋwan·b̥u˳khʌ`, *you ten thousand times must not* (S. 3), and `⁻chiɛn ˋwan·b̥u˳khʌ`, *you a thousand times ten thousand times must not* (S. 2).
2. Note the form `ʹfan·ʃɪ`, *all that are*, or *whatever is a* ....
3. `⁻iˋɕia`, is *one place*.
4. `⁻ɕiaŋ⁻d̥aŋ`, *suitable*; lit. *in relation (to the circumstances of the case) right*.

Lesson 25.

1. The word `⁻d̥aŋ` has occurred in earlier lessons in two different senses. Here in S. 1 it occurs in a different sense again, viz.: *to fill the place of, to act as;* thus, `ʹna......⁻d̥aŋ` means *to take*, or *regard ......as in the place of* (cf. L. 9, N. 16; L. 13, N. 8). Similarly in S. 3, `ˋb̥u·ğan⁻d̥aŋ` means *I dare not accept that position*.
2. The Chinese language is fond of double negatives. In this exercise (S. 4, 5, 6) we have three examples; `ˋbu·nʌŋˋb̥u`, `ʹwu·feɪ`, and `b̥uˋxueɪ·b̥u`. The expression `ʹtʃhu·feɪ` (S.7.), *unless*, a combination of *to exclude*, and *not*, is of the same nature.
3. The use of `ˋɪʌ` in the Conditional Mood was explained in L. 14, N.1. Here (S. 6) it is used in combination with `˳thaŋ`, *if*.

Lesson 27.

1. Uncertainty is expressed by prefixing a negative to terms expressing certainty; thus in S. 1 `ˋweɪ`, *not yet*, is prefixed to `ˋb̥i`, *certainly* (L. 14, N. 3) and in S. 2 `ˋb̥u` is prefixed to `iˋd̥ɪŋ` (L. 16, N. 2).

2. The use of ˌkhʌ·ʃɪ, *but*, has already been explained (L. 15, N. 7). Here the word ˌkhʌ alone is used in the sense of *however*, as explained in L. 23, N. 3, in which sense it does not, like ˌkhʌ·ʃɪ, begin the sentence, but follows after the subject (S. 2).
3. The word ˌchi, *how?* is used to express surprise, protest or emphatic assertion; thus: ˌchi·ɡan, *how dare I* (S. 4), i.e. in protest that the remark in question is too complementary; ˌchi ʼbu·ʃɪ ⁻ɡʌŋ ˌxao ma? (S. 3), an emphatic assertion.
4. Note the splitting up of the expression ʼsueɪˋbiɛn, (L. 16, N. 10) by the insertion of the words ⁻ɕiɛn·ʃʌŋ·d̦ɪ.

Lesson 28.

1. For the expression ⁻iʼthuŋ see L. 19, N. 1.
2. Notice the use of ˋna·mə without ˋjaŋ (L. 9, N. 15). It is sometimes used with the particle ʼd̦ʐɔ and sometimes with the particle d̦ɪ, thus: ˋna·məʼd̦ʐɔ, ˋma·mə·d̦ɪ. The demonstrative ˋd̦ʐɤ is used in exactly the same way either with ⁻mə alone or with ⁻mə and ʼd̦ʐɔ, ⁻d̦ɪ or ˋjaŋ.
3. The phrase ˌfanˋd̦ʐʌŋ, literally is: *whether upside down or upright*, i.e. *in any case.*
4. The phrase ⁻i⁻thiɛn ˋbu·ɪu ⁻i·thiɛn, *worse and worse each day*, literally is: *one day worse than one day.*
5. Notice the use of ʼd̦ə and ˋbu (see L. 5, N. 19, 20) in the phrase ˋbu·ɡuan ˋmaɪ·d̦ə⁻tʃhu·chy, &c., *no matter whether they can be sold or not.* ˋmaɪ tʃhuˋchy is *to sell outwards;* the insertion of ʼd̦ə and ˋbu express possibility and the reverse, respectively.
6. The expressive phrase ˋwan⁻i, *one in ten thousand*, is of frequent use to express a most improbable contingency.
7. Notice the causal conjunction ˋʝi·ʃɪ (cf. L. 15, N. 8).

Lesson 29.

1. Note the phrase ˌju iʼxueɪ, *once upon a time*, lit.: *there was one time*, and the phrases ʼɡuɔ·liɑo iˌxueɪ, *after a time* (N.B. The ˌxueɪ is a different word in each case, see the Chinese Text.) and d̦zɔ iˌxueɪ, *sit for a while.* For iˌxueɪ see L. 19, N. 3.
The following table will illustrate the uses of the word ʼxueɪ and the similar word ˋtshɯ.

iʼxueɪ	⁻iˋtshɯ	*once.*
⁻san·xueɪ	⁻sanˋtshɯ	*three times.*
ˋʃaŋ·xueɪ	ˋʃaŋˋtshɯ	*last time.*
ˋd̦ʐɤ·iʼxueɪ	ˋd̦ʐɤ·iˋtshɯ	*this time.*
ˋɕiɑʼxueɪ	ˋɕiɑˋtshɯ	*next time.*
ˌmeiʼxueɪ	ˌmeiˋtshɯ	*every time.*

2. A very common auxiliary is ⁻tʃhu𐞰laɪ, *to come out*. It denotes successful completion of the action of the main verb; thus: ˋsuan 𐞰tʃhu·laɪ, *to reckon (a thing) out;* ˋkhan𐞰tʃhu·laɪ, *to look to the point of seeing (a thing);* ˋdzɔ𐞰tʃhu⁻laɪ, *to finish making*.
3. In the phrase 𐞰ɹuŋ·ḅuˋɕia, *too small*, ɕia is the auxiliary completing the action of the main verb, 𐞰ɹuŋ, *to contain;* the insertion of the ⁻ḅu negatives the possibility of such completion.

Lesson 30.

1. The character for ˏdʒaŋ *senior* (932)—see Vocabulary in the Chinese Text—also means *long*, in which case it is aspirated and in the 2nd tone: 𐞰tʃhaŋ.

LINGUAPHONE
CONVERSATIONAL COURSES

for beginners and advanced students are now ready in
ENGLISH, FRENCH, GERMAN, SPANISH, ITALIAN, RUSSIAN, DUTCH, AFRIKAANS, IRISH, ESPERANTO, CHINESE and PERSIAN.

Each course consists of 30 interesting conversational and descriptive lessons, supplied with all the necessary text books in an attractive carrying case.

LINGUAPHONE
TRAVEL COURSES

in **ENGLISH, FRENCH and ITALIAN.**

Each course consists of 30 interesting and instructive talks contained on 15 double-sided 10-inch records. They take you for a tour through Great Britain, France or Italy accompanied by a guide who describes to you, clearly and interestingly, the principal objects of interest in each place visited, and talks to you about the Art, Music, History Geography, etc., of his country. Supplied complete with text-book in an attractive carrying case.

LINGUAPHONE
LITERARY COURSES

are available in
ENGLISH, FRENCH, ITALIAN and GERMAN.

Each course consists of 20 extracts, in prose and poetry, from the works of the most famous writers in each language. Ten double-sided 12 inch records. complete with text-book in an attractive carrying-case. There is also a Literary Course in Esperanto—consisting of 5 double-sided 12 inch records supplied with text in an attractive Album.

For further particulars write to :

THE LINGUAPHONE INSTITUTE,

24-27, High Holborn, London, W.C.1.

TWO UNIQUE RECORDS
Spoken by
BERNARD SHAW
"Spoken English & Broken English"

These interesting records were specially made for the benefit of Linguaphone students by the great writer Bernard Shaw. He wrote for the purpose a special article entitled "Spoken English and Broken English," and he has recorded the speech on two twelve-inch double-sided records, which have been autographed by him.

Apart from the educational value of such records as an example of English, spoken by one of the most famous exponents of that language, their significance as a lasting record of the great writer's voice and of his views on spoken English, expressed in his inimitable Shavian style, will be fully appreciated.

It is the first time in the history of the world that the voice of a writer of Mr. Shaw's calibre has been recorded, and every enthusiast for the writings of the famous man will welcome the opportunity of hearing him speak.

Set of two 12-in. Double-Sided Records with booklet containing full text. Autographed. Complete in Album.

LINGUAPHONE SONGS
in FRENCH and ENGLISH.

The Linguaphone set of songs consists of 5 double-sided 10-inch records of favourite songs, including characteristic nursery rhymes, folk songs, marching songs, etc. The records are accompanied by a delightfully illustrated book of words, and are supplied in an album.

As one of the principal objects of these songs has been to teach pronunciation, special attention has been paid to enunciation. These songs are a source of continual delight to students, whether in the home or in class.

For further particulars, write to :

THE LINGUAPHONE INSTITUTE,
24-27, High Holborn, London, W.C.1.

Dative: one to whom something is given said or done

Optative: expressing desire or wish.

Genitive: indicating possession or origin - source

Expletive: added to fill out sentence, give emphasis

北京大学中国语言学研究中心

早期北京话珍稀文献集成

主编 刘云

——西人北京话教科书汇编

分卷主编 翟赟 郭利霞 陈颖

言 语 声 片

［英］爱德华·丹尼森·罗斯 主编

老舍 等编著

卷二

北京大学出版社
PEKING UNIVERSITY PRESS

Linguaphone Oriental Language Courses.

General Editor: Sir E. DENISON ROSS, C.I.E., Ph.D., Director, School of Oriental Studies, University of London.

Phonetic Editor: A. LLOYD JAMES, M.A., Reader in Phonetics, School of Oriental Studies, University of London.

CHINESE

by

J. PERCY BRUCE, M.A., D.Lit., Professor of Chinese,
School of Oriental Studies, University of London.

E. DORA EDWARDS, M.A., Lecturer in Chinese,
School of Oriental Studies, University of London.

C. C. SHU, Lecturer in Chinese, School of Oriental Studies,
University of London.

Spoken by
C. C. SHU, Lecturer in Chinese, School of Oriental Studies,
University of London.

With Phonetic Transcription in the Alphabet of the International Phonetic Association.

VOL. II
First Edition.

THE LINGUAPHONE INSTITUTE,
24-27, HIGH HOLBORN, LONDON, W.C.1,
ENGLAND.

Printed in Great Britain by
The Linguaphone Institute,
24-27, High Holborn, London, W.C.1.

(BB1230) Chinese 901

VOL. II.

THE CHINESE TEXT.

CONTENTS.

Directions to the Student	7
Chinese Sounds I	10
Chinese Sounds II	13
Chinese Text of Lessons 1—30	16—134

Directions to the Student.

[NOTE.—The Chinese Text of *Chinese Sounds*, Parts I and II, is given for reference only, and is not intended to be learned. It will be useful also in the case of a student going to a part of the country where a somewhat different form of Mandarin is spoken, in which case a Chinese teacher can be asked to read the text from the Chinese character, and the student can note the variations in pronunciation.]

1. When Lesson I has been mastered orally turn to the Chinese Text. Follow the directions given in the following paragraphs and in the Notes, learning to recognise and write the assigned Radicals first, and then the characters in the Vocabulary.*

NOTE.—The Chinese Characters will be found much less difficult to learn if the order here suggested is followed. The oral work should always be a lesson ahead of the written.

2. With regard to the recognition of characters many students find what is called the analytic method helpful; i.e., by analyzing any given character into its component elements, and noting its historical developments, the meaning of the character is impressed upon the memory. Others, however, find this only an additional burden upon the memory, and prefer to learn the characters as they are without regard to their component parts.

3. Those to whom the analytic method appeals will find the archaic forms with the Remarks in the Table of Radicals, Appendix I, and the analysis of the characters in Lessons 1-4 given in Appendix II, helpful.

4. From Lesson 5 onwards only the numbers of those Radicals which have not previously occurred are given. In the case of those which he has already learned it will be good practice for the student to recognise them for himself in their new combinations.

5. The Phonetics will be easily found in Soothill's *Pocket Dictionary*. Look up the character under its Romanized Spelling in Part II among the small characters. The number given is the number of the Phonetic in Part I. For further analysis and archaic forms see Wilder & Ingram's *Analysis of Chinese Characters*. Another Pocket Dictionary which will be found useful and complementary to Soothill's is Fenn's *Five Thousand Dictionary* in which the Radical of each character is given.

6. With a view to the use of dictionaries later the student will do well to learn to discover the Radical of a given character for himself. In doing so, although absolute consistency cannot be assured, the following general rules will be helpful:—

---

* The Romanized spelling in the Chinese Vocabularies and in the Appendices is according to Wade's system as used in most Dictionaries.

(1) Nearly all characters, when not Radicals themselves, are composed of two parts, either side by side or one above the other.

(2) When the two parts are side by side the Radical is generally on the left; except Nos. 18, 19, 59, 67, 76, 79, 163, which are generally on the right.

(3) When one part of the character is above the other the lower part is generally the Radical, except Nos. 8, 14, 40, 87, 116, 118, 122, 140, which are usually above.

7. In the writing of characters two things are important viz: their form and the order in which the strokes forming them are written.

8. With regard to form the student will find it most satisfactory to trace with pencil or ordinary pen the characters as given in the Radical Table (Appendix I) and in the Vocabularies. In tracing each character he need not trouble himself about the difference in the thickness and thinness of the strokes, which can only be reproduced with the brush-pen and is not essential, especially in these days when every up-to-date Chinese writes with a fountain pen or pencil. The points which are essential to a well-formed character are the correct balance of the several parts and the proper direction of the strokes.

9. Chinese authorities give the character *yung*, eternal

as furnishing the best example of the elementary strokes used in writing. These strokes are:— 1, the *dot* on the top (R. 3); 2, the *horizontal stroke* (R. 1); 3, the *perpendicular stroke with a hook* at the bottom (R. 6); 4, on the left hand side, a downward *stroke to the left* (R. 4); with which is joined another horizontal; 5, on the right-hand side, a downward *stroke to the right*, above which is another stroke to the left. Other strokes, or modifications of the above are:—6, the *straight* (without the hook) either tapering or thickened at the bottom; *perpendicular* (R. 2) and 7, the *spike* a tapering slant stroke written upwards from left to right. Note carefully the difference between 5 and 7 from the point of view of the direction of the stroke. Further interesting particulars and their manner of writing will be found in a small but useful book by F. W. Baller entitled *The A.B.C. of Chinese Writing*, and a more exhaustive treatment in *How to write Chinese*, by J. Dyer Ball.

10. It may seem that the order in which the strokes of a character are written is unimportant. That is not the case. Apart from the fact that the order of writing will imperceptibly affect the direction of the strokes, the most elementary knowledge of Psychology will teach us that to learn to write the strokes in a certain order will prove a very material aid to memory, and if they are always written in the same order it may as well be the correct order.

This order is given in a parallel column in the two Tables of the Appendix. Two general rules will serve as a guide :—

(1) Top strokes, or the top part of the character, to be written before the bottom strokes, or bottom part of the character.

(2) Left-hand strokes, or left-hand part of the character, to be written before the bottom strokes, or bottom part of the character.

Other rules, supplementary to, or qualifying the above are :—

(3) The base line, if any, to be written last of all.

(4) Horizontals before perpendiculars.

(5) A surrounding square, with the exception of the base line, to be written first.

(6) Perpendiculars, when they have other elements on their two sides, are written first ; when they pass through the rest of the character they are written last.

The student will notice examples of these rules as he writes the Radicals and characters in the Vocabularies.

11. When the student has learned both to recognize and write the characters in the Vocabulary he should write out the Exercise in character from the Transcription. By the time he has finished this he will find that the characters are fairly well fixed in his memory. His next and final step will be to write the exercise in character from the Translation.

Chinese Sounds, Part I.

發音練習上

1. 首音 INITIALS.

1. 罷
2. 怕
3. 大
4. 榻
5. 固
6. 庫
7. 罵
8. 怒
9. 臘
10. 父
11. 訴
12. 入
13. 恕
14. 戲
15. 戶
16. 在
17. 菜
18. 住
19. 處
20. 記
21. 氣
22. 物
23. 訝

2. 尾音 FINALS.

1. 必
2. 律
3. 訓
4. 信
5. 命
6. 費
7. 稅
8. 業
9. 滅
10. 面
11. 飯
12. 換
13. 卷
14. 賣
15. 快
16. 詐
17. 放
18. 掛
19. 曠
20. 下
21. 項
22. 鬧
23. 妙
24. 課
25. 逆
26. 二
27. 末
28. 貨
29. 獸
30. 這
31. 度
32. 順
33. 凍
34. 六
35. 兄
36. 四
37. 悶
38. 月
39. 志
40. 日

3 四聲 THE FOUR TONES.

[A Single Sound-Syllables in the Four Tones.]

i.	低	敵	底	地
ii.	梯	提	體	替
iii.	居	局	舉	句
iv.	媽	麻	馬	罵
v.	嚷	瓤	攘	讓
vi.	哥	格	葛	各
vii.	遮	摺	者	哲
viii.	疵	慈	此	次
ix.	吩	焚	粉	忿
x.	吃	持	尺	赤

[B. Tones in Relation to Stress.]

i. 風光　山河　鄉長　公斷
　　紅花　群臣　連屬　抬轎
　　想家　老娘　兩廣　寶貴
　　放心　掙錢　快走　害怕

ii. 綠的　木頭　走了　拿去
　　打發　利錢　手筆　玫瑰

[C. Tones Modified by Position.]

i. 王先生說,他明天許走。

他兄弟說,他也許走。

他們若是走,我也許走。

ii. 不多　不能　不好

不是　不大　不用

Chinese Sounds, Part II.

發音練音 下

1. 伊索寓言

酸葡萄

一個很餓的狐狸路過一座葡萄園看見許多又熟又好看的葡萄高高兒的在架上垂着。他就往起跳,可是直到他都跳乏了,一個葡萄還是沒吃着。到末末了,他說啦,誰愛要誰要,我反正不管了,這不過是些沒熟的酸葡萄。

紅樓夢 第二十五回

ii.

這日飯後看了兩篇書,又同紫鵑等作了一會針線,總悶悶不舒,一同步行出來看庭前纔逬出的新笋,不覺出了院門,來到園中四望無人,惟見花光鳥語,信步便往怡紅院來,只見幾個丫頭舀水都還好麼黛玉道我正忘了,多發人送兩瓶茶葉與姑娘,可帖子請的鳳姐道,我前日打個黛玉笑道,今兒齊全,誰下進來,都笑道這不又來了兩鳳姐寶釵都在這裏。一見他見房內笑聲,原來是李宮裁、在迴廊上看畫眉洗澡呢。聽謝想着寶玉道我嘗了,不好。

不知別人嘗了怎麼樣，寶釵道，味倒好，只是沒甚顏色。鳳姐道，那是暹羅國貢的，我嘗了也不覺甚好，還不如我們常吃的呢。黛玉道，我吃着好，不知你們的脾胃是怎麼樣的。寶玉道，你說好把我的都拿了去吃吧。鳳姐道，我那裏還多着呢。黛玉道，我叫了頭取去。鳳姐道，不用我打發人送來。我明日還有一事求你，一同叫人送來。林黛玉聽了他笑道，你們聽聽，這是吃了他家一點子茶葉，就使喚起人來了。

Chinese Text. Lesson 1. Part I.

第一課 上

VOCABULARIES.

1st Tone	2nd Tone	3rd Tone	4th Tone
1. 書 shu	2. 人 jên	4. 筆 pi	8. 墨 mo
	3. 沒 mei	5. 有 yu	
		6. 好 hao	
		7. 也 yeh	

COMPOUND WORDS AND EXPRESSIONS.

1. 筆墨　　2. 沒有　　3. 有沒有

TONE PRACTICE.

	i.	ii.	iii.	iv.	v.	vi.
1st Tone	書	逼	蒿	噎	憂	摸
2nd Tone	熟	鼻	毫	爺	油	饢
3rd Tone	屬	筆	好	也	有	抹
4th Tone	樹	敝	號	夜	右	墨

EXERCISE.

1. 有書,有人,有筆,有墨。
2. 沒有書,沒有人,沒有筆,沒有墨。
3. 有書沒有,有人沒有,有筆沒有,有墨沒有。
4. 有筆墨沒有,沒有。
5. 有好書,也有好筆好墨。
6. 好人有沒有,有。

7. 有書沒有,有書。
8. 有筆沒有,沒有筆。
9. 有墨沒有,沒有。
10. 筆墨有沒有,有筆沒有墨。
11. 有好書沒有,有。
12. 有好筆沒有,有好筆,也有好墨。
13. 有好人沒有,有好人。
14. 好筆墨有沒有,好筆墨有。

B

Chinese Text. Lesson I. Part II.

第一課 下

VOCABULARIES.

	1st Tone		2nd Tone		3rd Tone	4th Tone
9.	他 t'a	12.	們 mên	14.	我 wo	
10.	先 hsien	13.	錢 ch'ien	15.	你 ni	
11.	生 shêng			16.	李 li	

COMPOUND WORDS AND EXPRESSIONS.

4. 我們　5. 你們　6. 他們　7. 先生

TONE PRACTICE.

	vii.	viii.	ix.	x.
1st Tone	先	生	謙	呢
2nd Tone	開	繩	錢	泥
3rd Tone	險	省	淺	你
4th Tone	線	聖	欠	溺

EXERCISE.

15. 我有書,先生有沒有。
16. 李先生沒有好墨。
17. 你有墨,他有沒有。
18. 你們有書,他們沒有。
19. 我們沒有錢,你們有沒有。
20. 他們有好墨,沒有好筆。

21. 他有筆墨,先生有沒有。我有筆墨。
22. 你有筆,他有沒有。 他沒有筆。
23. 李先生有好筆沒有。 李先生有好筆,沒有好墨。
24. 你有好墨沒有。 有,先生有沒有。
25. 他們有書,你們有沒有。 我們有好書。
26. 你們有墨,他們有沒有。 他們沒有好墨。
27. 我們有錢,你們有沒有。 我們有錢。
28. 我們有書,有筆,有墨,他們有沒有。他們有好書,也有好筆,好墨。

Chinese Text. Lesson 2. Part I.
第 二 課　上

VOCABULARIES.

1st Tone	2nd Tone	3rd Tone	4th Tone
17. 三 san	18. 十 shih	20. 五 wu	23. 六 liu
	19. 您 nin	21. 本 pên	24. 個 ko
		22. 管 kuan	25. 塊 k'uai

TONE PRACTICE.

i.	ii.	iii.	iv.
三本書	十本書	五本書	六本書
三個人	十個人	五個人	六個人
三管筆	十管筆	五管筆	六管筆
三塊墨	十塊墨	五塊墨	六塊墨

EXERCISE.

1. 有三個人。
2. 有十管筆。
3. 我有五本書。
4. 他有六管筆。
5. 李先生有三塊好墨。
6. 他們有六塊錢。

7. 先生有書沒有。我有三本書。
8. 他有筆沒有。他有五管筆。
9. 您有墨沒有。我有六塊墨。
10. 他有沒有。他有好筆,好墨。
11. 您有錢沒有。我有三塊錢。
12. 你們有筆沒有。我們有六管好筆。
13. 他們五個人有書沒有。他們有十本書。

Chinese Text. Lesson 2. Part II.

第 二 課 下

VOCABULARIES.

1st Tone	2nd Tone	3rd Tone	4th Tone
26. 的 ti		27. 小 hsiao	29. 是 shih
		28. 些 hsieh	30. 這 chê
			31. 那 na
			32. 大 ta
			33. 不 pu

COMPOUND WORDS AND EXPRESSIONS.

1. 是   2. 不是   3. 是不是

TONE PRACTICE.

v.	vi.	vii.	viii.
我的	我們的	這本書	那些書
你的	你們的	這個人	那些人
他的	他們的	那管筆	這些筆
		那塊墨	這些墨

EXERCISE.

14. 這是筆,那是墨。
15. 這不是筆,那不是墨。
16. 這是我的錢,是不是。
17. 那是你們的書不是。
18. 這些錢是你的,是我的。
19. 不是我的,也不是你的,是他的。

20. 這個人有墨沒有。有。
21. 那個人有沒有。那個人也有。
22. 這是好墨不是。是是好墨。
23. 這是李先生的筆不是。不是,是我的筆。
24. 那管筆是他的不是。不是,那管筆也是我的。
25. 他們有小筆沒有。他們有小筆,也有大筆。

Chinese Text. Lesson 3. Part I.

第 三 課　上

VOCABULARIES.

1st Tone	2nd Tone	3rd Tone	4th Tone
34. 張 chang	35. 台 t'ai	38. 紙 chih	43. 硯 yen
(麼) mo	36. 銅 t'ung	39. 很 hên	44. 位 wei
	37. 洋 yang	40. 幾 chi	
		41. 兩 liang	
		42. 子 tzŭ	
		(少)† shao	

COMPOUND WORDS AND EXPRESSIONS.

1. 紙筆　2. 硯台　3. 洋錢　4. 銅子

TONE PRACTICE.

i.	ii.	iii.	iv.
三十張紙	五十塊錢	六十個人	我有五管筆
十三張紙	十五塊錢	十六個人	你的筆很好
			他的紙很少

* This word is recorded in the Vocabulary of Part II.
† This word is recorded in the Vocabulary of Lesson 4, Part I.

EXERCISE.

1. 這是好書。這本書好。
2. 他是好人。那個人好。
3. 我有好筆。我的筆好。
4. 這是好墨。這塊墨好。
5. 這個大,那個小。
6. 這塊硯台很小,那兩塊也不大。
7. 我的筆好,他的筆不好,您的好不好。
8. 這些紙筆很好。
9. 這位先生有十五本書,那位先生有五十本。
10. 他的墨好不好。他的墨很不好。
11. 那幾張紙好麼。那幾張紙不很好。
12. 先生的硯台大,是不是。是,很大。
13. 您有錢没有。我有洋錢,也有銅子。

Chinese Text. Lesson 3. Part II.

第三課 下

VOCABULARIES.

1st Tone	2nd Tone	3rd Tone	4th Tone
45. 箱 hsiang	50. 甚(什) shên		53. 叫(叫) chiao
46. 東 tung	51. 盒 ho		
47. 西 hsi	52. 元 yüan		
48. 麽 mo			
49. 一 i			

COMPOUND WORDS AND EXPRESSIONS.

5. 東西 6. 一些 7. 銅元 8. 甚麽

TONE PRACTICE.

v.	vi.	vii.
三十三	三十五	三十六
五十三	五十五	五十六
六十三	六十五	六十六

EXERCISE.

14. 這是甚麼。
15. 那是甚麼東西。
16. 那一些箱子有大的,有小的。
17. 這幾張紙有好的,有不好的。
18. 我有六十三元錢,也有一些銅元。
19. 這一些東西是甚麼。這一些東西是書。
20. 那些東西叫甚麼。那些東西叫紙筆。
21. 這個盒子好不好。好,那兩個大的也好。
22. 那些墨有好的麼。有三十五塊好的,有五十六塊不好的。

Chinese Text. Lesson 4. Part I.

第四課 上

VOCABULARIES.

1st Tone	2nd Tone	3rd Tone	4th Tone
54. 七 ch'i	59. 毛 mao	61. 九 chiu	64. 二 erh
55. 八 pa	60. 零 ling	62. 百 pai	65. 四 ssu
56. 多 to		63. 少 shao	
57. 分 fên			
58. 枝 chih			

COMPOUND WORDS AND EXPRESSIONS.

1. 多少

TONE PRACTICE.

i. 一 二 三 四 五 六 七 八 九 十

ii. 三百七十八
　　五百八十三
　　四百八十五

iii. 七百五十四
　　九百五十九
　　六百九十五

iv. 八百四十五
　　五百二十六
　　二百六十四

EXERCISE.

1. 有多少人。
2. 先生有幾管筆。
3. 他們有四十五本書,七十八管筆,二十九塊墨。
4. 張先生有八百五十四元錢。
5. 我有十塊三毛六分錢。
6. 有五百零七個人。
7. 你有幾枝筆。我有四枝。
8. 張先生有多少書。有一百零六本書。
9. 這位有多少錢。他有八塊零三分洋錢。

Chinese Text. Lesson 4. Part II.
第四課 下

VOCABULARIES.

1st Tone	2nd Tone	3rd Tone	4th Tone
66. 千 ch'ien	69. 誰 shui	70. 寫 hsieh	71. 要 yào
67. 聲 shêng			72. 字 tzǔ
68. 鉛 ch'ien			73. 萬 wan
			74. 吊 tiao
			75. 第 ti

COMPOUND WORDS AND EXPRESSIONS.

2. 誰的   3. 寫字   4. 鉛筆

TONE PRACTICE.

v.
三千七百五十九
五千九百四十六
六千四百七十八

vi.
四萬五千九百五
八萬四千二百六
九萬三千七百八

EXERCISE.

10. 不要這個,要那個。
11. 這個鉛筆要不要。
12. 這兩位先生是誰。
13. 我要寫字。
14. 這枝筆是誰的。
15. 有五萬三千七百元。
16. 張先生有八千五百零七吊錢。
17. 書是第一聲,錢是第二聲,筆是第三聲,墨是第四聲。
18. 你要甚麼。我要紙筆寫字。
19. 要錢不要。不要錢,我有一些。
20. 那位先生是誰。那是張先生。
21. 這是誰的錢。那是我的錢。
22. 那些字是先生寫的麼。不是我寫的,是李先生寫的。

Chinese Text. Lesson 5. Part I.
第五課 上

VOCABULARIES.

1st Tone	2nd Tone	3rd Tone	4th Tone
76. 說 shuo	81. 兒 erh	83. 裏 (裡) li	84. 信 hsin
77. 邊 pien	82. 房 fang	83a. (那) [na]	85. 念 nien
78. 都 tu			86. 話 hua
79. 家 chia			87. 外 wai
80. 封 fêng			88. 對 tui
			89. 在 tsai

COMPOUND WORDS AND EXPRESSIONS.

1. 念書
2. 說話
3. 外邊
4. 裏邊
5. 這裏
6. 那裏
7. 那裏
8. 這兒
9. 那兒
10. 那兒
11. 這邊
12. 那邊
13. 那邊

TONE PRACTICE.

i.	ii.	iii.
在這裏	在那'裏	在'那裏
在這兒	在那'兒	在'那兒
在這邊	在那'邊	在'那邊

EXERCISE.

1. 那幾位先生都在這兒。
2. 李先生在書房裏寫信。
3. 張先生在家念書。
4. 在外邊有一些人說話。
5. 這是一位念書的人。
6. 裏邊說話的是誰。
7. 我寫的那封信在那兒。
8. 那三位先生在這邊麼。他們不在這邊,都在那邊。
9. 我的鉛筆在那裏。你的鉛筆在那裏。
10. 我說的話對不對。先生說的話都對。
11. 有信封沒有。有,在這裏。

Chinese Text. Lesson 5. Part II.

第五課 下

VOCABULARIES.

1st Tone	2nd Tone	3rd Tone	4th Tone
90. 聽 t'ing	91. 得 tê	92. 請 ch'ing	96. 看 k'an
		93. 點 tien	97. 見 chien
		94. 所 so	98. 問 wên
		95. 了 liao	99. 快 k'uai
			100. 慢 man
			101. 夠 (向多)(彀) kou
			102. 告 kao
			103. 訴 su

COMPOUND WORDS AND EXPRESSIONS.

14. 看見 17. 聽見 20. 快一點 23. (看得見)
15. 看看 18. 告訴 21. 慢慢的 24. (聽得見)
16. 看一看 19. 信封 22. 快快的

TONE PRACTICE.

iv.
交 書
交 錢
交 筆
交 墨

v.
拿 書
拿 錢
拿 筆
拿 墨

vi.
買 書
買 錢
買 筆
買 墨

vii.
賣 書
賣 錢
賣 筆
賣 墨

EXERCISE.

12. 看得見看不見。看得見。
13. 聽見了麼。沒聽見。
14. 你要看不要看。我要看。
15. 我寫的這些字請先生們看一看。
16. 請先生慢慢的説。
17. 請先生快一點念。
18. 他告訴我,那些書不夠。
19. 我寫的那些字你看見了麼。看見了。
20. 我的話你聽得見聽不見。聽不見。
21. 請問這是甚麼字。我看看,這是告字。
22. 這些錢夠不夠。夠了。
23. 裏邊有人沒有。我問一問。

Chinese Text. Lesson 6. Part I.

第六課　上

VOCABULARIES.

1st Tone	2nd Tone	3rd Tone	4th Tone
104. 思 ssǔ	106. 明 ming	110. 懂 tung	114. 認 jèn
105. 心 hsin	107. 白 pai	111. 曉 hsiao	115. 會 hui
	108. 難 nan'	112. 給 kei	116. 意 i
	109. 識 shih	113. 己 chi	117. 句 chü
			118. 自 tzǔ
			119. 處 ch'u

COMPOUND WORDS AND EXPRESSIONS.

1. 明白
2. 懂得
3. 曉得
4. 識字
5. 認識
6. 認得
7. 些個
8. 自己
9. 意思
10. 難處

TONE PRACTICE.

i.	ii.	iii.	iv.	v.
他的	家裏	說了	刀子	多麼
白的	城裏	來了	房子	甚麼
有的	那裏	走了	李子	怎麼
是的	那裏	見了	帽子	這麼

EXERCISE.

1. 明白不明白。懂得不懂得。曉得不曉得。
2. 這是甚麼意思。我不曉得。
3. 這個字你會寫不會寫。
4. 這句話你懂不懂。我懂得。
5. 這些字你認識不認識。認識些個。
6. 那個人識字不識字。他識字不少。
7. 那位先生你認得麼。
8. 他自己說,他不明白你的意思。
9. 你不明白他心裏的難處,我給你說一說。

Chinese Text. Lesson 6. Part II.

第六課下

VOCABULARIES.

1st Tone	2nd Tone	3rd Tone	4th Tone
120. 清 ch'ing	124. 完 wan	127. 楚 ch'u	130. 校 hsiao
121. 音 yin	125. 學 hsüeh	128. 口 k'ou	131. 課 k'o
122. 經 ching	126. 習 hsi	129. 已	132. 徧(遍) pien
123. 溫 wên			133. 再 tsai
			134. 就 chiu
			135. 正 chêng
			136. 教 chiao

COMPOUND WORDS AND EXPRESSIONS.

11. 聲音   13. 學生   15. 已經   17. 學校
12. 清楚   14. 口音   16. 兩徧   18. 溫習

TONE PRACTICE.

vi.	vii.	viii.	ix.
先生	舒服	清楚	聽見
明天	難為	來往	零碎
北邊	裏頭	想你	子粒
意思	硯台	自己	告訴

EXERCISE.

10. 這本書有三十課。我已經學了好幾課。
11. 看完了這一課,就看第七課。
12. 這一課很難學,那一課也得溫習溫習。
13. 你說的話我沒聽明白,請再說一徧。
14. 你寫完那些字,我要看一看。
15. 那位學生的口音很正。
16. 他的聲音很好,說的話也清楚。
17. 先生已經教了幾課。
18. 那個學校的學生很多先生也不少。

Chinese Text. Lesson 7. Part I.

第七課　上

VOCABULARIES.

1st Tone		2nd Tone		3rd Tone		4th Tone	
137	官 kuan	143	國 kuo	145	獎 chiang	147	坐 tso
138	中 chung	144	來 lai	146	等 têng	148	過 kuo
139	英 ying					149	姓 hsing
140	廳 t'ing					150	貴 kuei
141	啊 ah					151	賤 chien
142	啦 la					152	敝 pi
						153	客 k'o

COMPOUND WORDS AND EXPRESSIONS.

1. 中國   3. 官話   5. 好聽   7. 客廳
2. 英國   4. 好看   6. 客人   8. 過獎

TONE PRACTICE.

i.	ii.	iii.	iv.
到家	下霜	最高	太多
發芽	很忙	馬槽	中國
騎馬	過獎	太小	是我
說話	一樣	還要	請坐

EXERCISE.

1. 來客了。來了客啦。客來了。
2. 請在客廳裏坐一坐。
3. 先生貴姓。賤姓李。
4. 李先生好啊。好,先生好。
5. 請坐,請坐。
6. 貴國是那國。敝國是英國。
7. 先生會說中國話麽。不大會。
8. 先生的官話很好。過獎過獎。
9. 英國的書貴,中國的書賤一點。
10. 來了兩位客人要見你。
11. 請他們在客廳裏等一等。
12. 那位學生姓甚麽。他姓張。

Chinese Text. Lesson 7. Part II.
第七課 下

VOCABULARIES.

1st Tone	2nd Tone	3rd Tone	4th Tone
154. 屋 wu	160. 茶 ch'a	166. 碗(盌) wan	169. 放 fang
155. 擱 ko	161. 碟 tieh	167. 把 pa	170. 去 ch'ü
156. 喝 ho	162. 拿 na	168. 伙 huo	
157. 义 ch'a	163. 盤 p'an		
158. 刀 tao	164. 杓 shao		
159. 傢 chia	165. 能 nêng		

COMPOUND WORDS AND EXPRESSIONS.

9. 拿來　　11. 拿了去　　13. 傢伙
10. 拿去　　12. 茶碗

TONE PRACTICE.

v.	vi.	vii.	viii.
大 洲	春 秋	莊 村	上 東
從 頭	五 福	五 倫	貧 窮
好 走	過 午	允 准	攏 總
高 壽	書 舖	不 順	輕 重

EXERCISE.

13. 能不能。不能。 能。
14. 你能去不能去。 不能去。
15. 在那個學校能不能學中國話。能學。
16. 拿三個盤子來。
17. 把這幾個碟子拿了去。
18. 把這些碗放在西屋裏。
19. 把那些茶碗都要拿來。
20. 杓子义子拿來了麼。都拿來了。
21. 這幾把刀子不要擱在這兒,都要拿去。
22. 看完了這一課,我就喝茶。
23. 拿兩碗茶去,擱在客廳裏。
24. 把這些傢伙放在東屋裏。

Chinese Text. Lesson 8. Part I.

第八課 上

VOCABULARIES.

1st Tone	2nd Tone	3rd Tone	4th Tone
171. 棹(桌) cho	174. 牀 chuang	178. 椅 i	182. 上 shang
172. 將 chiang	175. 旁 p'ang	179. 可 k'o	183. 下 hsia
173. 方 fang	176. 壺 hu	180. 以 i	184. 到 tao
	177. 廚 ch'u	181. 底 ti	185. 地 ti
			186. 撤 ch'ê
			187. 臥 wo

COMPOUND WORDS AND EXPRESSIONS.

1. 上房
2. 廚房
3. 臥房
4. 旁邊
5. 底下
6. 地下
7. 將要
8. 可以
9. 廚子
10. 地方
11. 茶壺
12. 放下
13. 撤去
14. 來到

TONE PRACTICE.

i.	ii.	iii.	iv.	v.
青苔	縣官	酒杯	到期	不吃
纔來	東南	門楣	不離	正直
好歹	飯碗	南北	鉛筆	買紙
兩塊	吃飯	小妹	天地	實事

EXERCISE.

1. 可以不可以。不可以。可以。
2. 這些東西要擱在甚麼地方。
3. 上房裏有三張棹子,棹子旁邊有六把椅子。
4. 拿一把茶壺來,放在棹子上。
5. 這些東西可以放下。
6. 把牀底下的東西都要拿來。
7. 棹子上的刀子叉子可以撤去。
8. 臥房的椅子好坐。
9. 那些東西可以放在地下麼。不可以。
10. 把這些傢伙擱在廚房裏,可以不可以。可以的。
11. 那兩位先生將來到。
12. 他有很大的房子,我的房子不大。

Chinese Text. Lesson 8. Part II.
第八課下

VOCABULARIES.

1st Tone	2nd Tone	3rd Tone	4th Tone
188. 吃 (喫) ch'ih	193. 涼 liang	195. 水 shui	199. 飯 fan
189. 乾 kan	194. 還 huan	196. 洗 hsi	200. 淨 ching
190. 開 k'ai		197. 臉 lien	201. 熱 jé
191. 師 shih		198. 板 pan	202. 傅 fu
192. 擦 ts'a			203. 凳 teng

COMPOUND WORDS AND EXPRESSIONS.

15. 吃飯　17. 師傅　19. 板凳
16. 飯廳　18. 大師傅　20. 乾淨

TONE PRACTICE.

vi.
八音
飛禽
要緊
寫信

vii.
好聽
七情
山頂
天命

viii.
上街
碗碟
生鐵
一切

ix.
好天
洋錢
一點
一片

EXERCISE.

13. 拿熱水來,我要洗臉。
14. 開水快來了。
15. 涼水已經拿來了。
16. 拿一壺溫水來。
17. 飯好了。　飯還沒好。
18. 茶涼了,拿熱的來。
19. 先生還吃不吃。還吃。不吃了。
20. 還有開水,你要不要。還要。不要了。
21. 把這些盤子洗一洗。
22. 這些板凳不乾淨,可以擦一擦。
23. 可以問問廚子,飯得了麼。還沒得。
24. 大師傅説,飯得了,請先生吃飯。

Chinese Text. Lesson 9. Part I.
第九課 上

VOCABULARIES.

1st Tone	2nd Tone	3rd Tone	4th Tone
204 知 chih	205 答 t'ao	213 掃 sao	216 式 shih
	206 着 cho	214 箒 chou	217 道 tao
	207 留 liu	215 使 shih	218 概 kai
	208 合 ho		219 錯 ts'o
	209 行 hsing		220 用 yung
	210 從 ts'ung		
	211 頭 t'ou		
	212 王 wang		

COMPOUND WORDS AND EXPRESSIONS.

1. 知道
2. 合式
3. 從頭
4. 答箒
5. 用着
6. 用不着
7. 大概

TONE PRACTICE.

i.	ii.	iii.	iv.
必須	國君	補缺	大全
騎驢	黑雲	大學	本源
下雨	不允	下雪	挑選
同去	古訓	滿月	馬圈

EXERCISE.
1. 知道不知道。不知道。知道。
2. 這些傢伙不好使。
3. 這些盤子合式不合式。
4. 不用那些碗了,可以拿去。
5. 你說的不清楚,可以從頭再說。
6. 這些書你用得着用不着。
7. 拿笤箒來,掃掃這個屋子。
8. 不錯,那些書都在書房裏。
9. 這管筆行不行。不行,拿好的來。
10. 你要的那些傢伙都在廚房裏,你知道不知道。我知道了。
11. 王先生在書房裏麼。我不知道,大概在那裏呢。
12. 飯廳裏有碟子碗麼。大概有。

Chinese Text. Lesson 9. Part II.

第九課 下

VOCABULARIES.

221 呢 ni	224 情 ch'ing	227 怎 tsen	231 辦 pan
222 因 yin	225 忙 mang	228 緊 chin	232 為 wei
223 當 tang	226 原 yüan	229 法 fa	233 件 chien
223a (法) [fa]		230 妥 t'o	234 事 shih
			235 順 shun
			236 樣 yang

COMPOUND WORDS AND EXPRESSIONS.

8. 小心
9. 因為
10. 原來
11. 本來
12. 事情
13. 怎麼
14. 怎麼樣
15. 要緊
16. 好處
17. 辦法
18. 為甚麼
19. 這麼
20. 那麼
21. 多麼
22. 妥當
23. 順當
24. 這樣
25. 那樣

EXERCISE.

13. 這是為甚麼。那是為甚麼。
14. 那個不要緊。
15. 裏頭有難處,要小心辦。
16. 那件事情很順當,好辦。
17. 這件事情要緊,你怎麼辦呢。
18. 那件事他辦的怎麼樣。
19. 你為甚麼那樣辦呢。
20. 那件事你辦的很妥當。
21. 那個辦法沒有好處。
22. 這件事本來很難辦。
23. 他為甚麼不去。因為他很忙。
24. 那個箱子多麼大。就是這麼大。
25. 我沒去,因為他沒叫我去。
26. 原來這件事情不好辦。

Chinese Text. Lesson 10. Part I.
第十課 上

VOCABULARIES.

1st Tone	2nd Tone	3rd Tone	4th Tone
237. 關 kuan	243. 門 mên	247. 北 pei	251. 閉 pi
238. 相 hsiang	244. 南 nan	248. 鎖 so	252. 路 lu
239. 京 ching	245. 離 li	249. 里 li	253. 近 chin
240. 通 t'ung	246. 隔 ko	250. 遠 yüan	254. 住 chu
241. 州 chou			255. 差 ch'a
242. 車 ch'ê			

COMPOUND WORDS AND EXPRESSIONS.

1. 開開
2. 關上
3. 一樣
4. 差不離
5. 差不多
6. 不離
7. 不大離
8. 相隔
9. 北京
9a. 南京
10. 通州

TONE PRACTICE.

i.	ii.	iii.	iv.
捐資	坐車	認真	颱風
恩慈	車轍	各人	不能
不死	難捨	六本	天冷
寫字	貫徹	發悶	下剩

EXERCISE.

1. 開開門。關上門。閉上門。鎖上門。
2. 那兩個茶碗不一樣。
3. 這兩個人的意思差不多一樣。
4. 這個地方離那個地方多麼遠。
5. 從這裏到那裏不遠,有六十多里地。
6. 那個地方很近,是不是。不錯,離這裏不過八里路。
7. 從北京到通州不甚麼遠。
8. 他說的不離。
9. 那個人的意思不大離。
10. 那兩個地方相隔多麼遠。
11. 張先生是坐車來的。
12. 他們住在甚麼地方。
13. 先生貴處。敝處是南京。
14. 你的辦法和他的辦法差不離一樣。

Chinese Text. Lesson 10. Part II.
第十課下

VOCABULARIES.

1st Tone	2nd Tone	3rd Tone	4th Tone
256. 街 chieh	258. 實 shih	259. 買 mai	260. 賣 mai
257. 商 shang		259a. (上) (shang)	261. 鋪(舖) p'u
			262. 木 mu
			263. 做(作) tso
			264. 價 chia
			265. 店 tien
			266. 吧(罷) pa
			267. 界 chieh

COMPOUND WORDS AND EXPRESSIONS.

11. 買賣
12. 飯店
13. 洋錢
14. 價錢
15. 實在
16. 木頭

EXERCISE.

15. 買不買。賣不賣。
16. 他是做買賣的人。
17. 他是商界的人。
18. 你上那兒去。上街去。
19. 上街去做甚麼呢。買東西去。
20. 這個地方的買賣很大。
21. 大街上的舖子很多。
22. 他要的價錢很大。
23. 那個房子實在好,買的很貴麼。
24. 他所賣的那張牀是木頭的。
25. 那兩把椅子也是木頭做的。
26. 那一個茶碗是一塊三毛錢買的。
27. 大街上的飯店很貴。
28. 小心罷,不要辦錯了。
29. 他不買,因為沒有錢。

Chinese Text. Lesson 11. Part I.

第十一課 上

VOCABULARIES.

1st Tone	2nd Tone	3rd Tone	4th Tone
268. 窗 ch'uang	271. 強 ch'iang	277. 比 pi	280. 戶 hu
269. 花 hua	272. 別 pieh	278. 趕 (趕) kan	281. 架 chia
270. 真 chên	273. 如 ju	279. 傘 san	282. 鑰 yao
	274. 匙 shih / chih	279a. 所 so	283. 更 kêng
	275. 園 yüan		284. 較 chiao
	276. 盆 p'ên		

COMPOUND WORDS AND EXPRESSIONS.

1. 鑰匙
2. 書架子
3. 窗戶
4. 花園
5. 花盆
6. 比較
7. 較比
8. 不如
9. 趕不上
9a. [實在]

EXERCISE.

1. 這個箱子比那個箱子大。
2. 這個鑰匙較比那個鑰匙好使。
3. 這件事較比那件事更不好辦。
4. 東屋西屋都不如北屋好。
5. 那個書架子還不如不買好。
6. 西邊的窗戶趕不上東邊的大。
7. 這個法子比那個法子強。
8. 這些花好,西園子的花更好。
9. 小心罷,別錯了。
10. 那把傘真好,買罷。
11. 那個人很實在。
12. 那兩所房子,那一所好,你可以比較比較。
13. 南街上的房子比北街上的大。
14. 東邊的花園好看,裏邊的花很多。
15. 我看這個園子沒有那個好。
16. 這一個書架子比那一個大的多了。

Chinese Text. Lesson 11. Part II.
第十一課 下

VOCABULARIES.

1st Tone	2nd Tone	3rd Tone	4th Tone
285. 出 ch'u	288. 朋 p'êng	289. 友 yu	296. 進 chin
286. 發 fa		290. 走 tsou	297. 怕 p'a
287. 幫(帮) pang		291. 恐 k'ung	298. 至 chih
		292. 屬 shu	299. 太 t'ai
		293. 頂 ting	300. 越 yüeh
		294. 彼 pi	301. 最 tsui
		295. 此 tz'u	302. 助 chu

COMPOUND WORDS AND EXPRESSIONS.

10. 進來
11. 出去
12. 進去
13. 出來
14. 拿進來
15. 拿出來
16. 拿進去
17. 拿出去
18. 朋友
19. 相好
20. 彼此
21. 幫助
22. 恐怕
23. 越發

EXERCISE.

17. 他們都出去了。
18. 請李先生進來。
19. 那幾本書拿進去了。
20. 張先生在屋裏,就要出來。
21. 那是他自己做的事。
22. 那件事恐怕他自己不能辦,你得幫助他。
23. 他要上北京去,就快走了。
24. 我的朋友來了。
25. 那兩個人彼此很相好。
26. 他至多給六十塊錢。
27. 那幾個盒子最大的多麼大。
28. 那個法子頂好,可以那樣辦。
29. 這兩把椅子太大。
30. 那些個盒子屬那一個小的好。
31. 你去給我買一張棹子越小越好。
32. 恐怕那件事越發的不好辦了。
33. 還是走大道好,小道真難走。
34. 至少得去三個人。
35. 來了一些人,他們都進去啦。

Chinese Text. Lesson 12. Part I.

第十二課 上

VOCABULARIES.

1st Tone	2nd Tone	3rd Tone	4th Tone
303. 親 ch'in	308. 男 nan	312. 女 nü	316. 紀 chi
304. 兄 hsiung	309. 年 nien	313. 姐 chieh	317. 歲 (歲) sui
305. 莊 (庄) chuang	310. 閣 ko	314. 母 mu	318. 妹 mei
306. 稼 chia	311. 活 huo	315. 老 lao	319. 父 fu
307. 哥 ko			320. 弟 ti
			321. 戚 ch'i
			322. 種 chung
			322a. [少] shao

COMPOUND WORDS AND EXPRESSIONS.

1. 父親
2. 母親
3. 父母
4. 哥哥
5. 兄弟
6. 弟兄
7. 姐姐
8. 妹妹
9. 姐妹
10. 太太
11. 年紀
12. 出閣
13. 親戚

EXERCISE.

1. 李太太在家麼。在家。
2. 父母還在麼。還在。
3. 他的弟兄姐妹都在家。
4. 在他家裏男女老少有二十口人。
5. 我的父親叫我去。
6. 他的母親年紀很大。
7. 有一位老太太來了。
8. 我的妹妹家去了。
9. 你的哥哥上那兜去了。
10. 他的父母還在麼。他的父母都不在了。
11. 你的兄弟多麼大年紀。他是二十三歲。
12. 我有弟兄三個,還有三個姐妹。
13. 他的大哥做買賣,他的二哥種地,他自己是教書。
14. 他的姐妹出了閣沒有。
15. 他的姐姐出了閣,他兩個妹妹還沒有。
16. 李老三的親戚來了,可是快走了。

Chinese Text. Lesson 12. Part II.

第十二課 下

VOCABULARIES.

1st Tone	2nd Tone	3rd Tone	4th Tone
323. 光 kuang	327. 前 ch'ien	333. 眼 yen	336. 但 tan
324. 單 tan	328. 孩 hai	334. 只 chih	337. 透 t'ou
325. 姑 ku	329. 娘 niang	335. 守 shou	338. 顧 ku
326. 閨 kuei	330. 爺 yeh		339. 背 pei
	331. 叔 shu		340. 後 hou
	332. 才 ts'ai		341. 孝 hsiao
			342. 幹 kan

COMPOUND WORDS AND EXPRESSIONS.

14. 透光
15. 眼前
16. 背後
17. 孝順
18. 趕緊的
19. 本分
20. 大爺
21. 少爺
22. 閨女
23. 姑娘
24. 出門
25. 門口
26. 別的
27. 才幹

EXERCISE.

17. 這個窗戶不透光。
18. 光你自己來了麼。
19. 我光知道他出了門。
20. 不可單顧眼前不顧背後。
21. 他單買這一樣,不買別的。
22. 能辦不能辦,那單看他的才幹怎麼樣。
23. 他來到門口,就又走了。
24. 那件事要趕緊的辦。
25. 他有兩個少爺還有三個閨女。
26. 這些老娘們從很遠的來。
27. 李大爺的姑娘將要出閣。
28. 他的父母都是年紀很大,有八十多歲。
29. 我的二叔光有一個孩子,還是一個姑娘。
30. 他的孩子是很孝順實在守本分。
31. 這個孩子幾歲。今年五歲。
32. 不但是那樣,他還說他不能去。
33. 我的錢不夠,只有十幾塊。

Chinese Text. Lesson 13. Part I.

第十三課　上

VOCABULARIES.

1st Tone	2nd Tone	3rd Tone	4th Tone
343. 初 ch'u	348. 常 ch'ang	352. 起 ch'i	355. 日 jih
344. 啥 tsan	349. 昨 tso	353. 左 tso	356. 候 hou
345. 天 t'ien	350. 時 shih	354. 主 chu	357. 現 hsien
346. 剛 kang	351. 纔 ts'ai		358. 右 yu
347. 今 chin			

COMPOUND WORDS AND EXPRESSIONS.

1. 時候
2. 幾時
3. 多啥
4. 方纔
5. 剛纔
6. 當初
7. 今天
8. 昨天
9. 前天
10. 明天
11. 後天
12. 大前天
13. 大後天
13a. [現在]
13b. [起來]

EXERCISE.

1. 他是先來的,我是後來的。
2. 他是昨天來的,我是前天來的。
3. 明天你甚麼時候起來。
4. 大後天他要回來。
5. 後天我去把那些書拿回來。
6. 你今天甚麼時候走。
7. 當初他説要,現在不要了。
8. 李先生方纔出去了。
9. 你來的時候他纔來。
10. 我是大前天來的。
11. 他是買賣人,他常來這兒做買賣。
12. 那個地方很遠,恐怕後天回不來。
13. 主人坐在右邊,客人坐在左邊。
14. 他已經走了兩天,這就快到了。
15. 我剛纔説的話,你聽明白了麼。
16. 他幾時回來。再等三天就回來了。

Chinese Text. Lesson 13. Part II
第十三課 下

VOCABULARIES.

1st Tone	2nd Tone	3rd Tone	4th Tone
359. 黑 hei	364. 晨 ch'ên	365. 午 wu	369. 夜 yeh
360. 規 kuei		366. 晌 shang	370. 定 ting
361. 鐘 chung		367. 晚 wan	371. 切 ch'ieh
362. 星 hsing		368. 早 tsao	372. 半 pan
363. 期 ch'i		368a. 冷 lêng	373. 刻 k'o
			374. 月 yüeh
			375. 臘 la

COMPOUND WORDS AND EXPRESSIONS.

14. 早晨
15. 晌午
16. 晚上
17. 上半天
18. 下半天
19. 過晌
20. 白天
21. 夜裏
22. 明年
23. 前年
24. 星期
25. 正月
26. 臘月
27. 上月
28. 定規
29. 一切
29a. [從前]

EXERCISE.

17. 今天他來的早,我晚了。
18. 早晨起來的時候很涼。
19. 白天很熱,晚上纔涼一點,夜裏很冷。
20. 他七點鐘起來,八點半鐘吃早飯。
21. 十二點三刻吃晌飯,晚上八點吃晚飯。
22. 上月他上北邊去了,到八月纔能回來。
23. 我是前年來的,明年要回去。
24. 李先生是正月來的,臘月要走。
25. 到星期三晌午我就走。
26. 各人要自己定規多喒走。
27. 他來的很晚,天已經黑了。
28. 現在去很難,再等一個星期我可以去。
29. 他做的事都好。
30. 過晌他要上街,晚上回來。
31. 明天上半天他就來。
32. 今天下半天我要走。

Chinese Text. Lesson 14. Part I.

第十四課 上

VOCABULARIES.

1st Tone	2nd Tone	3rd Tone	4th Tone
376. 須 hsü	385. 抬 t'ai	388. 總 tsung	389. 若 jo
377. 應 ying	386. 沉 ch'ên		390. 務 wu
378. 該 kai	387. 無 wu		391. 必 pi
379. 搬 pan			392. 送 sung
380. 端 tuan			393. 重 chung
381. 挑 t'iao			
382. 輕 ch'ing			
383. 非 fei (also 4th)			
384. 擔 tan			

COMPOUND WORDS AND EXPRESSIONS.

1. 若是
2. 必須
3. 必要
4. 必得
5. 務必
6. 總得
7. 一擔
8. 應該
9. 擔當
10. 可是
11. 無非

EXERCISE.

1. 他若是不去,你必須自己去。
2. 他不能很晚了,趕晌午必能來到。
3. 李先生來的時候,你必得告訴我。
4. 要把西屋裏的傢伙搬到東屋裏去。
5. 叫兩個人把那張棹子抬到上房去。
6. 把這封信送給張先生。
7. 拿三碗茶,端到客廳裏去。
8. 若不使這個,就必要使那個。
9. 請他明天務必早來。
10. 叫人挑一擔水來。
11. 那是好事,應該那樣辦。
12. 你總得小心,那件事很難辦。
13. 這個擔子很沉,恐怕你挑不了。
14. 那個事情很大,我擔當不了。
15. 你不應該做那樣的事。
16. 我應該早去,可是很忙,去不了。
17. 無非是他不分輕重就是了。

Chinese Text. Lesson 14. Part II.
第十四課 下

VOCABULARIES.

1st Tone	2nd Tone	3rd Tone	4th Tone
394. 支 chih	395. 除 ch'u	397. 枉 wang	402. 算 suan
	396. 存 ts'un	398. 儉 chien	403. 賬 chang
		399. 省 shêng	404. 數 shu
		400. 許 hsü	405. 費 fei
		401. 手 shou	406. 收 shou
		401a. (數) shu	407. 換 huan
			408. 欠 ch'ien
			409. 票 p'iao
			410. 或 huo

COMPOUND WORDS AND EXPRESSIONS.

12. 或是
13. 許多
14. 算賬
15. 下存
16. 下欠
17. 淨存
18. 淨欠
19. 儉省
20. 枉費
21. 數數
22. 算算
23. 支去
24. 除了
25. 賬本子
26. 現錢
27. 支票
27a. [既然]

EXERCISE.

18. 或是你去,或是我去,都不甚麼要緊。
19. 那個辦法也許行。
20. 明天他許來,可也許不來。
21. 有許多人在街上賣東西。
22. 來吧,可以和我算賬。 23. 下存多少錢。
24. 下欠多少錢。 25. 淨存多少錢。
26. 手裏存多少錢。
27. 除支下存二百三十塊洋錢。
28. 除支下欠四十四塊五毛。
29. 本月我們花錢花的少一點。
30. 我算得對不對。 不大對,可以再數一遍。
31. 你的錢既然不多,你應該儉省一點不可枉費。
32. 收的錢可以數數,支出的錢可以算算。
33. 除了這些賬本子,都可以拿去。
34. 拿這個票去換現錢。
35. 可以說說你要支多少錢,我可以給你開個支票。

Chinese Text. Lesson 15. Part I.

第十五課 上

VOCABULARIES.

1st Tone	2nd Tone	3rd Tone	4th Tone
411. 風 fêng	417. 雹 pao	423. 雨 yü	428. 氣 ch'i
412. 颶 kua	418. 雲 yün	424. 雪 hsueh	429. 凍 tung
413. 霜 shuang	419. 逢 fêng	425. 攏 lung	430. 各 ko
414. 陰 yin	420. 凡 fan	426. 每 mei	431. 眾 chung
415. 晴 ch'ing	421. 同 t'ung	427. 彩 ts'ai	432. 散 san
416. 冰 ping	422. 和 ho		

COMPOUND WORDS AND EXPRESSIONS.

1. 天氣
2. 陰天
3. 下雨
4. 晴天
5. 凍冰
6. 颶風
7. 下霜
8. 冰凉
9. 雲彩
10. 每逢
11. 同心
12. 合意
13. 大家
14. 攏總
15. 應當
16. 一塊兒

EXERCISE.

1. 各人有各人的難處。
2. 他每天出去辦事。
3. 今日陰天,將要下雨。
4. 上年臘月下了雹子。
5. 前天下大雪。
6. 每逢去的時候,他總有難處。
7. 眾人都是同心合意。
8. 凡事大家同心是很要緊的。
9. 你應當等他來和你同去。
10. 你是叫他和你一塊兒去麼。
11. 晴了天啦。
12. 今天沒凍冰。
13. 昨天颳大風。
14. 今天清晨下了霜。
15. 攏總有多少人在那裏。
16. 這些水冰涼,可以換熱的來。
17. 雲彩都散開了。
18. 今年的天氣很順當。

Chinese Text. Lesson 15. Part II.

第十五課 下

VOCABULARIES.

1st Tone	2nd Tone	3rd Tone	4th Tone
433. 春 ch'un	437. 然 jan	441. 暖 nuan	442. 季 chi
434. 秋 ch'iu	438. 仍 jêng		443. 夏 hsia
435. 冬 tung	439. 而 êrh		444. 却 ch'üeh
436. 忽 hu	440. 雖 sui		445. 既 chi
			446. 固 ku

COMPOUND WORDS AND EXPRESSIONS.

17. 雖然
18. 必然
19. 既然
20. 忽然
21. 固然
22. 仍然
23. 還是
24. 但是
25. 然而
26. 只是
27. 却是
28. 起行
29. 然後
30. 雨水
31. 春天
32. 夏天
33. 秋天
34. 冬天
35. 南京

EXERCISE.

19. 雖然很貴,我還是要買。 20. 他雖然説是去,然而道上不好走,沒法去。 21. 我説那個事不如不辦好,可是他仍然要辦。 22. 那個辦法不必然好。 23. 李先生有意上南京去,但是現在有事,走不了。 24. 你既然有那個意思,為甚麼不早説呢。 25. 他剛要起行,忽然有人來叫他,沒走了。 26. 那個房子固然是好,只是我買不起。 27. 他現在要見你,然後他再見王先生。 28. 那固然是好事,可是很難辦。 29. 我本來昨天要給他寫信,可是忘了。 30. 一年有四季,就是春夏秋冬。 31. 冬天很冷,夏天很熱。 32. 春天秋天都是不冷不熱。 33. 春天秋天雨很少,夏天的雨水很多。 34. 冬天下雪下雹子,夏天也有時候下雹子。 35. 今天風很大,却是不冷。

Chinese Text. Lesson 16.

第 十 六 課

VOCABULARIES.

1st Tone	2nd Tone	3rd Tone	4th Tone
	PART I.	PART I.	PART I.
	447. 挪 no	453. 想 hsiang	455. 動 tung
	448. 泥 ni	454. 且 ch'ieh	456. 又 yu
PART II.	449. 及 chi		457. 目 mu
459. 工 kung	450. 隨 sui	PART II.	458. 便 pien
460. 夫 fu	451. 任 jên	473. 找 chao	
461. 她 t'a	452. 憑 p'ing	474. 馬 ma	PART II.
462. 山 shan		475. 敢 mu	477. 喂 wei
463. 空 k'ung	PART II.	476. 打 ta	478. 電 tien
463a. 哪 na	464. 局 chü	476a. 甲 chia	479. 志 chih
463b. 丁 ting	465. 宅 chai	476b. 丙 ping	480. 據 chü
	466. 倫 lun		481. 易 i
	467. 陽 yang		482. 續 hsü
	468. 咱 tsa		483. 複 fu
	469. 談 t'an		484. 睡 shui
	470. 容 jung		485. 覺 chüeh
	471. 全 ch'üan		486. 湊 ts'ou
	472. 雜 tsa		487. 願 yüan
	472a. 詳 hsiang		487a. 乙 i

Text of Part I.

第十六課 上

COMPOUND WORDS AND EXPRESSIONS.

1. 而且
2. 年輕
3. 一定
4. 見識
5. 目下
6. 只管
7. 隨便
8. 任憑

EXERCISE.

1. 一天怕他趕不到。
2. 這些傢伙很沉,我自己挪不動。
3. 今天道上泥很多,車子走不了。
4. 三天一定來不及。
5. 他是年輕而且那件事情又很難他自己一定辦不了。
6. 一個人的見識總有看不到的地方。
7. 我目下想不起來。
8. 你想去,只管去。
9. 不用等着我們,各人隨便罷。
10. 任憑他怎麼說我不去。

Chinese Text. Lesson 16. Part II.

第十六課 下
打電話

COMPOUND WORDS AND EXPRESSIONS.

9. 咱們　13. 地畝　17. 手續　21. 願意

10. 夫人　14. 容易　18. 非常　22. 湊手

11. 談談　15. 一來　19. 複雜　23. 詳細

12. 近來　16. 二來　20. 打電話　24. 工夫

CONVERSATION.

甲　喂，西局一五六二。
乙　有人叫，等一等。
甲　喂，這是西城方宅嗎。
丙　是，找那一位。
甲　張子良要和方志倫先生說話。
丙　是，等一等。
丁　喂，子良麼我是志倫。你在那兒哪。
甲　我在正陽門大街買東西哪。我說，昨天咱們談的那件事你辦了沒有。
丁　我昨天晚上到馬先生那裏去了。他沒在家我和他的夫人談了一談，據她說近來地畝的事情很不容易辦呢。
甲　怎麼呢。
丁　一來是西山的空地差不多全賣給各學校了。二來是買地的手續非常的複雜。昨天我快睡覺的時候，馬先生給我打電。他也是這麼說。他說，你若是不忙，他很願意慢慢的替你找一找。你若是現在就要，可是實在沒有湊手的地。
甲　志倫，你今天下半天到我家來，我們再詳細談一談，好不好。你大概有工夫吧。
丁　好吧，下半天見。

Chinese Text. Lesson 17.

第十七課

VOCABULARIES.

1st Tone	2nd Tone	3rd Tone	4th Tone
PART I.	PART I.	PART I.	PART I.
488. 烟 yen	489. 回 hui	491. 儘 chin	493. 試 shih
PART II.	490. 極 chi	492. 滿 man	494. 驗 yen
496. 蕉 chiao	PART II.	PART II.	495. 議 i
497. 斤 chin	506. 何 ho	515. 港 kang	PART II.
498. 哇 wa	507. 成 ch'êng	516. 海 hai	517. 況 k'uang
499. 捐 chüan	508. 梨 li		518. 運 yün
500. 香 hsiang	509. 頻 p'in		519. 稅 shui
501. 呀 ya	510. 由 yu		520. 罐 kuan
502. 功 kung	511. 龍 lung		521. 荔 li
503. 嗎 ma	512. 桃 t'ao		522. 餞 chien
504. 公 kung	513. 棠 t'ang		523. 預 yü
505. 新 hsin	514. 熟 shu, shou		524. 備 pei
			525. 謝 hsieh

Text of Part I.

第十七課　上

COMPOUND WORDS AND EXPRESSIONS.

1. 試驗
2. 商議
3. 再三
4. 到底
5. 方便

EXERCISE.

1. 我實實在在的説吧。
2. 説的明明白白的纔好。
3. 你若是不信可以試驗試驗。
4. 現在還有我的父親我必得回家去商議商議纔能定規。
5. 我再三問他到底沒問出來。
6. 我們在那裏極方便。
7. 王先生在後街上儘東頭住。
8. 滿天都是黑雲彩是要下雨的樣子。
9. 滿屋子都是烟。

Chinese Text.   Lesson 17.   Part II.

第十七課 下
賣水果

COMPOUND WORDS AND EXPRESSIONS.

6. 香蕉　11. 熟透了　16. 公道　22. 荔枝
7. 況且　12. 無論　17. 白梨　23. 大蜜桃
8. 運費　13. 如何　18. 蘋果　24. 海棠
9. 稅捐　14. 湊合　19. 罐頭　25. 預備
10. 從前　15. 成功　20. 香港　26. [水果
　　　　　　　　　21. 龍眼

CONVERSATION.

甲 請問,這個香蕉賣多少錢一斤呢.
乙 二毛錢一斤,先生。
甲 香蕉是不錯可是二毛錢一斤有點太貴了。況且現在正是香蕉賤的時候。
乙 先生你不知道哇,現在的運費和稅捐都比從前重了。我們也沒有法子不賣貴一點。再說這是熟透了的香蕉。
甲 無論如何也不應當這麼貴呀。
乙 好吧,先生多買一些,我賤賣一點,兩湊合買賣不是就成功了嗎。給先生三斤吧,算你一毛八分一斤,這公道不公道。
甲 好,就是這麼辦吧。你真會做買賣呀。
乙 還要別的嗎,先生。我的大白梨和山東蘋果都是頂好的東西,價錢也不貴,各樣的罐頭都是新由香港來的,荔枝,龍眼和大蜜桃都有。
甲 你有自己做的蜜餞海棠沒有。
乙 對不起我們現在不預備那個,因為天氣還太熱,擱不住。
甲 好,再見吧。
乙 謝謝先生。

Chinese Text. Lesson 18.

第十八課

VOCABULARIES.

1st Tone

PART I.
- 526. 巴 pa
- 527. 歡 huan

PART II.
- 538. 哈 ha
- 539. 之 chih
- 540. 歐 ou
- 541. 洲 chou
- 542. 搭 ta
- 543. 催 ts'ui
- 544. 機 chi
- 545. 安 an

2nd Tone

PART I.
- 528. 答 ta
- 529. 勻 yün

PART II.
- 546. 吳 wu
- 547. 什 shih
- 548. 於 yü
- 549. 讀 tu
- 550. 形 hsing
- 551. 船 ch'uan
- 552. 希 hsi
- 553. 營 ying
- 554. 伯 po

3rd Tone

PART I.
- 530. 敢 kan
- 531. 保 pao
- 532. 討 t'ao
- 533. 喜 hsi
- 534. 準 chun

PART II.
- 555. 美 mei

4th Tone

PART I.
- 535. 畫 hua
- 536. 恨 hên
- 537. 面 mien

PART II.
- 556. 社 shê
- 557. 富 fu
- 558. 裕 yü
- 559. 望 wang
- 560. 業 yeh
- 561. 敗 pai
- 561a. 遇 yü

Text of Part I.

第十八課 上

COMPOUND WORDS AND EXPRESSIONS.

1. 主意   3. 放心   5. 中意
2. 回答   4. 答應

EXERCISE.

1. 他回答說,他很願意去。
2. 放心罷,我敢保他不能不答應。
3. 這張畫我看着很中意。
4. 我實在想你,恨不能常見面纔好。
5. 他巴不得討你們大家的喜歡。
6. 他準去,就是現在勻不出工夫來。
7. 我自己不能定規,請你替我拿個主意。
8. 那個人老沒有主意,竟靠着他夫人辦事。
9. 他昨天應許了,可是今天早晨見了那個朋友,他又不肯了。
10. 我打算學幾句英文,不知道先生每天能勻一點工夫來教我不能。

Chinese Text. Lesson 18. Part II.

第十八課 下
遇友

COMPOUND WORDS AND EXPRESSIONS.

6. 知識
7. 讀書
8. 社會
9. 情形
10. 搭船
11. 富裕
12. 希望
13. 以後
14. 機會
15. 打算
16. 事業
17. 經營
18. 本着
19. 經驗
20. 成敗
21. 營商
22. 便飯
23. 下午
24. 方便
25. 請安
26. [遇友]
27. [伯母]

CONVERSATION.

甲　哈哈,吳先生什麼時候回來的。
乙　我昨天纔回來的,我們有五年沒見了。
甲　可不是,在美國這麼幾年一定得了不少的新知識吧。
乙　不敢說,不過於讀書之外,常到各處去看看,多少明白一些社會上的情形。
甲　也到歐洲去了嗎。
乙　沒有呢。本想回國的時候搭船到歐洲去,後來因為手裏不富裕,又搭着老母親寫信催我快回家,所以就沒得去。希望以後有機會再去吧。
甲　機會一定有。現在打算作些什麼事業呢。
乙　打算經營個小買賣,本着這幾年在外國得來的經驗試一試,成敗不敢說。
甲　營商是好事。我說,幾時有工夫到家裏吃個便飯呢,老太太很想看看你。
乙　明天下午六點鐘方便不方便,我正想去給伯母請安。
甲　好,就這麼辦,明天見。
乙　明天見。

Chinese Text. Lesson 19.

第十九課

VOCABULARIES.

1st Tone	2nd Tone	3rd Tone	4th Tone
PART I.	**PART I.**	**PART I.**	**PART I.**
562. 衣 i	568. 裁 ts'ai	581. 紫 tz'ŭ	585. 號 hao
563. 興 hsing	569. 縫 iêng	582. 淺 ch'ien	586. 緞 tuan
564. 深 shên	570. 服 fu	583. 襖 ao	587. 布 pu
565. 粗 tsʻu	571. 顏 yen	584. 准 chun	588. 料 liao
566. 裳 shang	572. 宜 i	**PART II.**	589. 色 sê
567. 跟 kên	573. 綢 ch'ou	597. 火 huo	**PART II.**
PART II.	574. 紅 hung	598. 擠 chi	599. 站 chan
590. 津 chin	575. 齊 ch'i		600. 倍 pei
591. 加 chia	576. 藍 lan		601. 共 kung
592. 豐 fêng	577. 材 ts'ai		602. 特 t'ê
593. 擁 yung	578. 皮 p'i		603. 次 tz'ŭ
	579. 棉 mien		604. 奉 fêng
	580. 夾 chia		605. 略 lüeh
	PART II.		606. 帶 tai
	594. 停 t'ing		607. 磅 pang
	595. 搖 yao		
	596. 鈴 ling		

Text of Part I.

第十九課 上

COMPOUND WORDS AND EXPRESSIONS.

1. 裁縫　5. 顏色　9. 材料　13. 夾衣裳
2. 字號　6. 時興　10. 兄台　14. 單衣裳
3. 衣服　7. 齊全　11. 皮襖　15. 準保
4. 衣裳　8. 上等　12. 棉襖　16. 便宜

EXERCISE.

　　前街有個裁縫舖,字號是同和。他做的衣服樣子和顏色都很時興。
　　他的綢緞有紅的,有紫的,有青的,淺的深的都很齊全。他的藍布無論是粗的是細的,都是上等材料。
　　兄台要買皮襖棉襖或是夾衣裳單衣裳,跟他買準保便宜。

Chinese Text. Lesson 19. Part II.

第十九課 下
火車站

COMPOUND WORDS AND EXPRESSIONS.

17. [火車站]
18. 天津
19. 一倍
20. 一共
21. 大洋
22. 現洋
23. 站臺
24. 開車
25. 豐台
26. 特別
27. 快車
28. 奉天
29. 通車
30. 略為
31. 擁擠
32. 慢車
33. 行李
34. 過磅
35. 飯車

CONVERSATION.

甲　天津的三等票多少錢。
乙　一塊七毛五。
甲　二等呢。
乙　多加一倍。
甲　請給我兩張二等票,一共是,
乙　七塊大洋。
甲　這是一張十塊錢的票子,請找給我三塊現洋吧。
甲　請問到天津去的車在那個站臺開。
丙　在第三站台。
甲　什麼時候開車。
丙　三點十五分,現在已經是三點八分了。
甲　車都在那裏停呢。
丙　只在豐台停五分鐘,因為這是特別快車。
甲　夜裏有由天津回來的快車沒有。
丙　有一次是由奉天下來的通車,不過車上略為擁擠一點,不如坐八點二十分的慢車,車上人既不多,到京的時候也不很晚。
甲　我們的行李用過磅不用。
丙　這麼小的箱子你們可以自己帶着,不用打行李票了。
甲　車上有飯車沒有。
丙　有是有,可是現在已經過了開飯的時候了,你們頂好在站台上買些點心帶着。
甲　啊,搖鈴了,快上車吧。

Chinese Text. Lesson 20.

第二十課

VOCABULARIES.

1st Tone	2nd Tone	3rd Tone	4th Tone
PART I.	**PART I.**	**PART I.**	**PART I.**
608. 鄉 hsiang	610. 鄰 lin	612. 倆 lia	615. 向 hsiang
609. 交 chiao	611. 城 ch'êng	613. 舍 shê.	616. 立 li
PART II.	**PART II.**	614. 屢 lü	617. 菜 ts'ai
619. 消 hsiao	622. 游 yu	**PART II.**	618. 末 mo
620. 激 chi	623. 籃 lan	628. 遣 ch'ien	**PART II.**
621. 軍 chün	624. 球 ch'iu	629. 場 ch'ang	632. 濟 chi
	625. 尤 yu	630. 網 wang	633. 戲 hsi
	626. 其 ch'i	631. 短 tuan	634. 作 tso.
	627. 騎 ch'i		635. 愛 ai
			636. 像 hsiang
			637. 烈 lieh
			638. 病 ping
			639. 隊 tui

Text of Part I.

第二十課 上

COMPOUND WORDS AND EXPRESSIONS.

1. 從來
2. 先前
3. 鄉下
4. 早年
5. 鄰舍
6. 向來
7. 早已
8. 立時
9. 時刻
10. 留心
11. 談心
12. 屢次
13. 老是
14. 末末了

EXERCISE.

1. 我從來沒去過。
2. 他先前住在鄉下。
3. 我們倆早年做過鄰舍。
4. 他向來住在城裏。
5. 我還沒說,他早已知道了。
6. 在他沒來以前,你應該預備好。
7. 他把東西交給我,立時就回去了。
8. 我出去買一點菜,就回來。
9. 你要時刻留心。
10. 他常常上這裏來談心。
11. 我屢次找他,老是找不着。
12. 末末了,我答應了他。

Chinese Text. Lesson 20. Part II.

第二十課 下
游戲

COMPOUND WORDS AND EXPRESSIONS.

15. 消遣
16. 游水
17. 籃球
18. 喜歡
19. 同志
20. 游戲
21. 網球
22. 同學
23. 球場
24. 好極了
25. 運動
26. 軍隊
27. 所以
28. 人家
29. 自行車
30. 激烈
31. 尤其

CONVERSATION.

甲　先生沒事的時候作什麼消遣呢。
乙　除了游水,是打籃球的時候最多。
甲　你喜歡打籃球嗎。同志,我也愛那個游戲。不過近來天氣太熱,倒是打網球的時候多。
乙　是,網球不像籃球那麼激烈,也很有意思。你到什麼地方去打呢。
甲　我的同學張濟家裏有個小花園,花園後面有塊空地,他就在那裏造了一個球場。我不短到他那裏去。
乙　那好極了。游戲是很要緊的事,尤其是在夏天,若是不運動運動,最容易生病。我在軍隊裏的時候天天早晨騎馬到鄉下去。那是很好的運動。現在住在城裏,一來離鄉下很遠,二來自己又沒有馬,所以就不能不作些別的運動了。
甲　我很喜歡看人家騎馬,可是我自己不會,我只會騎自行車。等著有機會我們一同下鄉,你教給我騎馬吧。

Chinese Text. Lesson 21.

第二十一課

VOCABULARIES.

1st Tone	2nd Tone	3rd Tone	4th Tone
PART I.	**PART I.**	**PART I.**	**PART I.**
640. 稱 ch'êng	642. 名 ming	644. 領 ling	646. 市 shih
641. 村 ts'un	643. 民 min	645. 亞 ya	647. 鎮 chên
PART II.	**PART II.**	**PART II.**	648. 縣 hsien
650. 接 chieh	657. 文 wên	662. 簡 chien	649. 内 nei
651. 精 ts'ai	658. 直 chih	663. 癮 yin	**PART II.**
652. 牠 t'a	659. 奇 ch'i	664. 景 ching	666. 頁 yeh
653. 哼 hêng	660. 神 shên	665. 爽 shuang	667. 利 li
654. 精 ching	661. 描 miao		668. 入 ju
655. 鋒 fêng			669. 借 chieh
656. 惜 hsi			670. 版 pan
			671. 段 tuan
			672. 舊 chiu
			673. 悶 mên
			674. 趣 ch'ü

Text of Part I.

第二十一課 上

COMPOUND WORDS AND EXPRESSIONS.

1. 領教 3. 住處 5. 東北
2. 名稱 4. 東南

EXERCISE.

1. 領教領教要緊的地方名稱都是甚麼。
2. 地方名稱,有的叫市,鄉鎮,有的叫縣,有的叫省。
3. 省最大,市,鄉,鎮最小。
4. 人民的住處,大的叫城,小的叫莊村。
5. 中國國內,東南有十八省,東北有東三省。
6. 原來東方第一個大國就是中國。
7. 地球上有五洲,中國在亞洲,此外是歐洲,非洲,美洲,海洋洲。
8. 亞洲最大,歐洲最小。

Chinese Text. Lesson 21. Part II.

第二十一課 下
看小説

COMPOUND WORDS AND EXPRESSIONS.

6. 小説
7. 打開
8. 三分之一
9. 接着
10. 簡直的
11. 停住
12. 布局
13. 精奇
14. 筆鋒
15. 爽利
16. 可惜
17. 千萬
18. 出版
19. 沈悶
20. 活氣
21. 白話
22. 覺得
23. 價值

CONVERSATION.

甲　昨天有位朋友送給我一本新小說我打開就念了三分之一。吃完了晚飯又接著看簡直的不能停住。一共是四百多頁,你猜怎麼着,我一氣把牠念完了。你想我什麼時候看完了的。

乙　夜裏十二點了吧。

甲　哼,兩點十分。真好,布局精奇,筆鋒又爽利,我所看入了神啦。

乙　你看完了,好該借給我啦。

甲　可惜,你來晚了,早叫二妹妹拿去了。

乙　我先說下,等她看完千萬借給我。

甲　一定。我近來看小說的癮非常的大。說真的近來出版的小說實在比從前好的多。因為新小說是用全力描寫一段事,有情有景,又有主義。舊小說是又長又沈悶,一點活氣沒有。況且現在用白話寫,寫得生動有趣,你說是不是。

乙　是,我也覺得新小說有意思,因為有一些文學上的價值。

Chinese Text. Lesson 22.
第二十二課

VOCABULARIES.

1st Tone	2nd Tone	3rd Tone	4th Tone
PART I.	**PART I.**	**PART I.**	**PART I.**
675 推 t'ui	677 驢 lü	680 火 huo	681 力 li
676 拉 la	678 騾 lo	**PART II.**	682 汽 ch'i
PART II.	679 牛 niu	698 跑 p'ao	683 獸 shou
686 婚 hun	**PART II.**	699 舉 chü	684 轎 chiao
687 孫 sun	693 結 chieh	700 雅 ya	685 乘 ch'êng
688 身 shên	694 言 yen	701 禮 li	**PART II.**
689 高 kao	695 聯 lien		702 畢 pi
690 珠 chu	696 磁 tz'u		703 賀 ho
691 江 chiang	697 瓶 p'ing		704 孟 mêng
692 穿 ch'uan			705 報 pao
			706 鬧 nao
			707 範 fan
			708 量 liang
			709 壁 pi
			710 物 wu
			711 婦 fu
			712 歉 ch'ien chien

Text of Part I.

第二十二課 上

COMPOUND WORDS AND EXPRESSIONS.

1. 走動　5. 獸力　9. 汽車　13. 轎子
2. 電力　6. 小車　10. 大車
3. 汽力　7. 轎車　11. 火車
4. 人力　8. 電車　12. 東洋車

EXERCISE.

1. 車的走動,要是不用電力,汽力,就是用人力,獸力。
2. 用人力的車有小車,有東洋車。
3. 小車是用人推,東洋車是用人拉。
4. 用獸力的有大車,用馬驢騾子,或是牛拉着,又有轎車是用騾子,或是馬拉的。
5. 用電力汽力的車,有電車汽車,還有火車。
6. 轎子是用人抬的,有用兩個人抬的,有用四個人抬的。

Chinese Text. Lesson 22. Part II.

第二十二課 下

賀友人結婚

COMPOUND WORDS AND EXPRESSIONS.

- 14. 友人
- 15. 結婚
- 16. 賀喜
- 17. 電報
- 18. 立刻
- 19. 只好
- 20. 熱鬧
- 21. 新娘子
- 22. 師範學校
- 23. 畢業
- 24. 身量
- 25. 舉動
- 26. 言談
- 27. 文雅
- 28. 溫和
- 29. 快活
- 30. 高興
- 31. 送禮
- 32. 禮物
- 33. 一對
- 34. 江西
- 35. 花瓶
- 36. 夫婦
- 37. 趕快
- 38. 道歉

CONVERSATION.

甲　孟先生,你昨天到王家賀喜去了嗎。
乙、我去了,你怎麼沒去呢。
甲　我本想去來着,已經穿好了衣裳,來了一個電報叫我立刻上通州去,只好往通州跑吧。昨天那裏人多不多。
乙、熱鬧極了,差不多咱們的老同學全去了。
甲　看見了新娘子沒有。
乙、看見了,她姓孫,是新從女子師範學校畢業的。她的年紀不過二十二三歲,身量很高,舉動言談都很文雅温和。和王先生站在一塊,真是珠聯璧合。
甲　王先生很快活吧。
乙、那還用說,高興極了。
甲　同學送禮的不少吧。
乙、人人有些禮物,我給他們買了一對江西磁的小花瓶。
甲　他預備晚飯沒有呢。
乙、行完了禮,新夫婦只給大家一些點心茶水,因為客人太多,不容易預備飯。
甲　真可惜我沒去成。我看我得趕快給王先生寫封道歉的信纔對。

Chinese Text. Lesson 23.

第二十三課

VOCABULARIES.

1st Tone

PART I.
713. 歇 hsieh
714. 操 ts'ao
715. 鴉 ya

PART II.
735. 貼 t'ieh
736. 失 shih
737. 包 pao
738. 敦 tun

2nd Tone

PART I.
716. 林 lin
717. 伏 fu

PART II.
739. 郵 yu
740. 糊 hu
741. 衕 t'ung
742. 遺 i
743. 條 t'iao

3rd Tone

PART I.
718. 假 chia
719. 體 t'i
720. 古 ku
721. 嶺 ling
722. 與 yü

PART II.
744. 往 wang
745. 毀 hui

4th Tone

PART I.
723. 益 i
724. 胖 p'ang
725. 害 hai
726. 練 lien
727. 片 p'ien
728. 藥 yao
729. 靠 k'ao
730. 緻 chih
731. 樹 shu
732. 茂 mao
733. 盛 shêng
734. 衛 wei
734a. [假] chia [v. 718]

PART II.
746. 政 chêng
747. 宋 sung
748. 掛 kua
749. 致 chih
750. 寄 chi
751. 漢 han
752. 露 lu, lou
753. 壞 huai
754. 附 fu

Text of Part I.

第二十三課 上

COMPOUND WORDS AND EXPRESSIONS.

1. 放假
2. 益處
3. 害處
4. 用處
5. 身體
6. 體操
7. 幫助
8. 靠頭
9. 看頭
10. 樹林
11. 茂盛
12. 空氣
13. 清涼
14. 歇伏
15. 衛生
16. 鴉片

EXERCISE.

1. 我看你這一次放假得了益處,身體見好比從前也胖了一點。
2. 體操只有益處沒有害處,年輕練一練身體是最好。
3. 若是拿鴉片當藥看,是有極大用處的。
4. 有他哥哥幫助他,真是有個靠頭。
5. 古嶺山的景緻真有個看頭,樹林極茂盛,空氣也清涼,在山上歇伏,與衛生實在有益

Chinese Text. Lesson 23. Part II.

第二十三課 下
郵政局

COMPOUND WORDS AND EXPRESSIONS.

17. [郵政局] 20. 掛號信 23. 擔保 26. 辦法
18. 郵票   21. 附近   24. 快信 27. 毀壞
19. 國界   22. 衚衕   25. 省錢 28. 西伯利亞
                                   29. [信件]

CONVERSATION.

甲　宋先生,從這裏到北京的信要貼幾分郵票呀。
乙　三分。不出國界大概都是三分票。
甲　掛號信呢。
乙　那我可就不知道了,還是到郵政局去問一問好。
甲　附近有郵局嗎。
乙　有,出了這個衙衙,順大街往南走不遠路西就是。

甲　請問,到北京去的掛號信要多少錢。
丙　八分。
甲　掛號信走的快嗎。
丙　不是,掛號只擔保信件不致於遺失了,要是打算快到,得按快信走。
甲　請問我有幾本書要寄到漢口去,怎樣最省錢呢。
丙　省錢的辦法是把書包好,露著兩頭,要是貴重的書,頂好是全包起來當包裹走。
甲　當包裹走當然貴一點。
丙　貴多了。可是你的書不致於毀壞了。
甲　現在往歐洲寄信是從那條道走頂快。
丙　是從西伯利亞走最快,從這裏到倫敦的信也不過十七八天就到了。

Chinese Text. Lesson 24.

第二十四課

VOCABULARIES.

1st Tone

PART I.
755. 荆 ching

PART II.
767. 周 chou
768. 息 hsi [also 2nd Tone]
769. 專 chuan

2nd Tone

PART I.
756. 提 t'i
757. 層 ts'êng
758. 隍 huang
759. 樓 lou

PART II.
770. 華 hua
771. 銀 yin
772. 行 hang
[§ 209.]

3rd Tone

PART I.
760. 塔 t'a
761. 鼓 ku

PART II.
773. 儲 ch'u
774. 掌 chang

4th Tone

PART I.
762. 斷 tuan
763. 忘 wang
764. 記 chi
765. 座 tso
766. 廟 miao

PART II.
775. 櫃 kuei
776. 介 chieh
777. 賬 chang
778. 蓄 hsü
779. 滙 huei
780. 紹 shao

Text of Part I.
第二十四課 上

COMPOUND WORDS AND EXPRESSIONS.

1. 斷不可
2. 萬不可
3. 荊州
4. 高塔
5. 城隍廟

EXERCISE.
1. 有用處就拿去吧。論到錢上咱們倆斷不可提。
2. 你千萬不可那樣說他。
3. 那件事你萬不可忘記。
4. 荊州城西門裏邊有個十三層的高塔。
5. 凡是一座城裏邊就有一座城隍廟。
6. 北京城內有座鐘鼓樓裏邊有一個大鐘一個大鼓。

Chinese Text. Lesson 24. Part II.

第二十四課 下
銀 行

COMPOUND WORDS AND EXPRESSIONS.

6. 掌櫃的　9. 介紹　12. 利息　15. 滙票

7. 熟識　10. 相當　13. 儲蓄　16. 錢票子

8. 銀行　11. 活賬　14. 可靠

CONVERSATION.

甲　周掌櫃的,你有熟識的銀行沒有,給我介紹一下。

乙　我們的舖子在銀城銀行有賬,你要是看着相當我可以同你去。你是要存錢呢還是開個活賬呢。

甲　我手裏有五六千塊錢,打算存起來生些利息。

乙　要是這麼樣,就不必上銀城了,我知道華北儲蓄銀行專作儲蓄的事情,給的利錢也最高。

甲　那個銀行可靠嗎。

乙　那是老字號了,很可靠你打算存幾年呢。存的日子越多,自然得的利錢越大。

甲　是,我要是存就必多存些日子。我再問你,你往營口寄錢的時候,是由郵局辦呢還是由銀行開滙票。

乙　我們向來是開滙票,因為我們只告訴銀行一聲,他們就給全辦好了。可是郵局辦也很省事。

甲　掌櫃的,我這裏有兩張人家給我的支票,你能替換一換嗎。

乙　好辦,交給我吧。你要現洋還是錢票子。

甲　一半一半吧。謝謝。

Chinese Text. Lesson 25.

第二十五課

VOCABULARIES.

1st Tone	2nd Tone	3rd Tone	4th Tone
	PART I.	PART I.	PART I.
	781. 勞 lao	782. 倘 t'ang	783. 待 tai
			784. 拜 pai
PART II.	PART II.	PART II.	
785. 襟 chin	791. 河 ho	795. 種 chung	PART II.
786. 雙 shuang	792. 薄 po, pao	796. 鈕 niu	797. 啤 pi
787. 衫 shan	793. 蘭 lan		798. 厚 hou
788. 絲 ssŭ	794. 絨 jung		799. 褲 k'u
789. 織 chih			800. 帽 mao
789a. 巾 chin			801. 汗 han
789b. [身] [cf. 689] [shên]			802. 硬 ying
790. 嘰 chi			

Text of Part I.

第二十五課 上

COMPOUND WORDS AND EXPRESSIONS.

1. 拜望
2. 勞動
3. 敢當
4. 掛念
5. 倘若
6. 除非

EXERCISE.

1. 你拿我們當客待嗎。
2. 我昨日去拜望可惜您沒有在家。
3. 勞動先生們來看我實在不敢當。
4. 他出去那麼遠我不能不掛念他。
5. 那兒的話呢咱們無非是一家的人。
6. 倘若家中有事我不會不給你信的。
7. 除非你和我同去我一定不去。

Chinese Text. Lesson 25. Part II.

第二十五課 下

洋服莊

COMPOUND WORDS AND EXPRESSIONS.

7. [洋服莊]
8. 夏季
9. 綢子
10. 嗶嘰
11. 涼快
12. 雨路
13. 長遠
14. 地道
15. 褲子
16. 背心
17. 單襟
18. 雙襟
19. 鈕子
20. 帽子
21. 手巾
22. 皮帶
23. 汗衫
24. 硬領
25. 絲織的
26. 領帶
27. 法蘭絨
28. 衛生衣
29. 打聽
30. 大禮服

CONVERSATION.

甲　我要做一身夏季的衣裳,請給我些材料看一看。

乙,　先生是要做綢子的還是嗶嘰的。

甲,　夏天還是穿綢子的涼快些,是不是。

乙,　是,不但涼快,還便宜呢,我們有兩路河南綢,都是頂時興的材料,一種厚一點,一種薄一點,先生要那一種。

甲,　厚的穿得長遠,可是不涼快,我還是要薄的吧。

乙,　是,先生請看,地道上等河南綢。

甲,　好,你給我量一身吧。我要兩條褲子,不要背心,一共多少錢。

乙,　算先生三十塊錢真不多呀。先生要單襟,還是雙襟,要幾個鈕子。

甲,　我看單襟兩個鈕子就不錯。

乙,　先生不看看帽子,手巾,皮帶,汗衫,硬領什麼的嗎。

甲,　我都有現在還不用。你有絲織的領帶沒有。

乙,　有,先生請到樓上去看看,好不好,我們新來的法蘭絨的衛生衣也很好。

甲,　我打聽打聽,一身大禮服要多少錢。

乙,　大概得一百出頭吧。

Chinese Text. Lesson 26.

第二十六課

VOCABULARIES.

1st Tone	2nd Tone	3rd Tone	4th Tone
PART I.	**PART I.**	**PART I.**	**PART I.**
803. 修 hsiu	809. 鑼 lo	813. 理 li	818. 玉 yü
804. 靴 hsüeh	810. 鞋 hsieh	814. 拐 kuai	819. 匠 chiang
805. 昌 ch'ang	811. 石 shih	815. 挺 t'ing	820. 貨 huo
806. 顆 k'o	812. 橋 ch'iao	816. 永 yung	821. 器 ch'i
807. 珍 chên	**PART II.**	817. 寶 pao	**PART II.**
808. 珠 chu	829. 糖 t'ang	**PART II.**	840. 袋 tai
PART II.	830. 黃 huang	837. 捲 chüan	841. 葉 yeh
822. 抽 ch'ou	831. 柔 jou	838. 呂 lü	842. 辣 la
823. 根 kên	832. 油 yu	839. 葛 ko	843. 照 chao
824. 添 t'ien	833. 荷 ho		844. 桂 kuei
825. 酥 su	834. 麻 ma		845. 製 chih
826. 司 ssu	835. 煩 fan		845a. 蜜 mi
827. 標 piao	836. 嘗 ch'ang		
828. 蜂 fêng			

Text of Part I.

第二十六課 上

COMPOUND WORDS AND EXPRESSIONS.

1. 木匠　　4. 房東　　7. 雜貨舖　10. 寶石
2. 小鑼匠　5. 鞋店　　8. 玉器舖
3. 修理　　6. 鞋舖　　9. 珍珠

EXERCISE.
1. 叫木匠來把這個箱子開開。
2. 這把鑰匙開不開門,叫小鑼匠來修理修理。
3. 那件事你和房東說開了嗎。
4. 要買一雙靴子,那個鞋店的好。在青石橋西往南一拐,有一座樓,樓北邊就是個挺好的鞋舖。
5. 那個雜貨舖的字號是永昌。
6. 我上玉器舖去,買一顆珍珠一塊寶石。

Chinese Text. Lesson 26. Part II.

第二十六課 下
烟舖和賣糖的

COMPOUND WORDS AND EXPRESSIONS.

11. 黃絲烟
12. 水烟
13. 抽烟
14. 烟捲兒
15. 水烟袋
16. 葉子烟
17. 太辣
18. 呂宋烟
19. 柔和
20. 擦烟油子
21. 烟荷包
22. 麻煩
23. 照顧
24. 桂花
25. 酥糖
26. 公司
27. 蜜蜂
28. 商標

CONVERSATION.

甲　請給我一包黃絲烟。
乙　葛先生還抽水烟嗎,有點太不時興了。
甲　我只是在家裏吃水烟,出門的時候總是抽烟捲兒,因為水烟袋拿着不方便。
乙　你簡直的不吃葉子烟嗎。
甲　不行,那個太辣,呂宋烟我也辦不了。
乙　可是葉子烟也有柔和的呀,況且比烟捲賤多了。
甲　買烟袋不也是錢嗎。
乙　一根烟袋不是使好些日子嗎,先生看我這些小烟袋,每個至少能用一年多。
甲　啊擦烟油子,帶烟荷包太麻煩,我還是吃我的三礮臺吧。我說你也賣糖嗎。
乙　是新添上的,先生照顧照顧剛下市的桂花酥糖是真好,先生嘗一塊。
甲　我不大喜歡酥糖,你要是有菓子糖可以給我一包。
乙　好,給先生拿一瓶雜樣的吧。
甲　現在中國製糖公司屬那一家最大呢。
乙　還是屬馬玉山吧,我給你的那一瓶就是他們做的,你看瓶子上有蜜蜂商標。

Chinese Text. Lesson 27.

第二十七課

VOCABULARIES.

1st Tone	2nd Tone	3rd Tone	4th Tone
PART I.	**PART I.**	**PART I.**	**PART I.**
846. 辛 hsin	847. 平 p'ing	848. 豈 ch'i	854. 未 wei
		849. 久 chiu	
PART II.	**PART II.**		**PART II.**
855. 間 chien	861. 食 shih	850. 仰 yang	868. 份 fên
856. 餐 ts'an	862. 魚 yü	851. 旅 lü	869. 頓 tun
857. 鷄 chi	863. 炸 cha	852. 舘 kuan	
858. 沏 ch'i	864. 排 p'ai	853. 苦 k'u	
859. 湯 t'ang	865. 累 lei		
860. 燒 shao		**PART II.**	
		866. 脚 chüeh / chiao	
		867. 菓 kuo	

Text of Part I.

第二十七課 上

COMPOUND WORDS AND EXPRESSIONS.

1. 其實　　3. 豈敢　　5. 旅館
2. 久仰　　4. 平安　　6. 辛苦

EXERCISE.

1. 你看這個法子怎麼樣。我看未必行得了。
2. 他自己可說是能行,其實到底能不能行也不一定。
3. 他要是早辦豈不是更好嗎。
4. 久仰先生的大名。豈敢豈敢。
5. 明天去或是後天去,今天晚上纔能定規。
6. 你去年進京在那裏住着來着。在旅館裏。
7. 你走嗎。一路平安。
8. 路上辛苦了。好說,好說。

Chinese Text. Lesson 27. Part II.

第二十七課 下
旅館

COMPOUND WORDS AND EXPRESSIONS.

7. 空屋　11. 西餐　15. 脚錢　19. 燒牛排
8. 單間　12. 精緻　16. 沏茶　20. 零食
9. 在外　13. 可口　17. 甲魚湯　21. 點心
10. 中餐　14. 開發　18. 炸海魚　22. 水果

CONVERSATION.

甲　有空屋子嗎,我要看一看。
乙　是先生要單間呢,還是大一點的屋子。
甲　單間就好。
乙　請上樓看看吧。
甲　這一間要多少錢一天。
乙　兩塊半錢,飯食在外。
甲　要是吃飯呢。
乙　一天三頓一共是三塊錢。
甲　飯食怎麼樣呢。
乙　頂好的飯食,中餐西餐隨先生的便,雞魚是每頓都有,做得也精緻可口。
甲　好吧,你把行李搬進來吧,叫櫃上開發腳錢。
乙　是先生要什麼不要。
甲　先打盆臉水來,然後沏壺茶來,晚飯什麼時候開呢。
乙　六點半鐘。先生今天是吃中餐是吃西餐。西餐的菜是甲魚湯,炸海魚,燒牛排,零食是洋點心和水果。
甲　給我要一份西餐吧,送到這裏來,我太累了,不願到飯廳去。
乙　這是這間房的鑰匙,出門的時候請千萬把門鎖上,把鑰匙交到櫃上去。
甲　我知道。

Chinese Text. Lesson 28.

第二十八課

VOCABULARIES.

1st Tone	2nd Tone	3rd Tone	4th Tone
PART I.	**PART I.**	**PART I.**	**PART I.**
870. 艙 ts'ang	872. 臨 lin	875. 反 fan	876. 范 fan
871. 漂 p'iao	873. 輪 lun	**PART II.**	877. 岸 an
PART II.	874. 划 hua	887. 爾 erh	**PART II.**
878. 哈 ha	**PART II.**	888. 險 hsien	889. 趙 chao
879. 濱 pin	883. 辭 tz'ŭ		890. 性 hsing
880. 虧 k'uei	884. 職 chih		891. 質 chih
881. 宗 tsung	885. 賠 p'ei		892. 受 shou
882. 糟 tsao	886. 節 chieh		893. 掉 tiao

Text of Part I.

第二十八課 上
江 上

COMPOUND WORDS AND EXPRESSIONS.

1. 江岸
2. 漢口
3. 星期
4. 船艙
5. 臨時
6. 輪船
7. 反正
8. 小划子
9. 樹葉子

CONVERSATION.

甲　范先生,一同到江岸上看看去,好不好。
乙　好哇,我就手打聽打聽後天到漢口去的船什麼時候開。我的三弟應當回漢口去啦,因為下星期五就開學了。
甲　還沒給他定好船艙嗎。應當快些定啊,現在正是往海外走貨的時候,船都是忙的,恐怕臨時買不上票。
乙　那麼咱們就到輪船公司去給他買票,你看給他定二等艙行了吧。
甲　行了,反正不是遠道兒,為什麼不省幾個錢呢。
乙　你看今天這裏怎麼停着這麼些支船呢。
甲　我想是等潮呢。看那支小划子多麼有意思,在水上漂着,好像一個小樹葉。

Chinese Text. Lesson 28. Part II.

第二十八課 下

商業談話

COMPOUND WORDS AND EXPRESSIONS.

10. 哈爾濱   13. 出口   16. 性質   19. 受潮

11. 經理   14. 行市   17. 貨物   20. 掉毛

12. 結賬   15. 賠錢   18. 保險

CONVERSATION.

甲. 明天你上哈爾濱去有什麼事呢。

乙. 一來我去定些皮貨,二來我去看一看我們分號的情形。我聽說,自從趙經理辭職以後,那裏的買賣是一天不如一天。五月節結賬的時候,他們虧了三四萬塊錢。

甲. 你們的分號也是專辦皮貨嗎。

乙. 不是,那裏也包辦大宗的出口貨。這二年的皮貨沒有什麼行市,要是專靠着皮子,他們就更得賠錢了。

甲. 既是皮子沒行市,你為什麼還去買呢。

乙. 你看,我們的公司是雜貨店的性質,各樣貨物都得有一點。不管賣得出去賣不出去,我們總得預備。再說皮貨到了公司裏,我們就去保險,萬一有個受潮掉毛還不至於糟在我們手裏。

Chinese Text. Lesson 29.

第二十九課

VOCABULARIES.

1st Tone	2nd Tone	3rd Tone	4th Tone
894. 阿 ah	902. 駝 t'o	908. 腦 nao	909. 駱 lo
895. 睜 chêng	903. 棚 p'êng		910. 佔 chan
896. 睛 ching	904. 迎 ying		911. 度 tu
897. 伸 shên	905. 脖 po		912. 讓 jang
898. 稍 shao	906. 移 i		913. 笑 hsiao
899. 微 wei	907. 圍 wei		
900. 舒 shu			
901. 剌 la			

Text of the Lesson.

第二十九課

阿剌伯人和他的駱駝

COMPOUND WORDS AND EXPRESSIONS.

1. 笑話
2. 圍起來
3. 阿剌伯
4. 駱駝
5. 帳棚
6. 腦袋
7. 歡迎
8. 於是
9. 脖子
10. 暖氣
11. 假如
12. 度量
13. 稍微
14. 移動
15. 全身
16. 好像
17. 舒舒服服的

The Story.

前天我到張家去,小孩子們都在家游戲呢。他們看見了我,就把我圍起來,叫我說笑話給他們聽。我告訴他們我真沒有笑話,他們拉住我不放手。我沒法子,只好想了半天,給他們說了個老笑話。
有一回,一個阿剌伯人坐在帳棚裏邊,他的駱駝在外邊睜着大眼睛往裏面看。
駱駝說,主人哪,外面真冷,我可以把我的腦袋伸進來嗎。
阿剌伯人說,歡迎歡迎,請進來吧。
於是駱駝就把頭伸進去了。
過了一會兒,駱駝又說,主人哪,我可以把脖子也伸進來,得些暖氣兒吧。
阿剌伯人說可以,可以。
駱駝又把脖子慢慢的伸進去了。
這時候,駱駝往四面一看,又向牠的主人說,假如我把我的前脚伸進來,也不過多佔上很小的一點地方。
這座帳棚本來是很小的,可是那個阿剌伯人的度量很大。他聽見駱駝這麼說,就稍微往後面移動一點,讓駱駝把前脚伸進來。
待了一會兒,駱駝又說,天氣真冷呀,叫我的全身都進來吧。
阿剌伯人說,天氣既然這麼冷,全身進來也可以。

於是駱駝走進帳棚去了。

駱駝看出來了，這個帳棚太小，容不下他們兩個。牠說主人哪，我們好像不能都在這裏，你的身體比我的小，不如你出去，讓我在這裏舒舒服服的坐一會兒。

駱駝說完，就把牠的主人擠出去了。

Chinese Text. Lesson 30.

第三十課

VOCABULARIES.

1st Tone
914. 頗 p'o
915. 攻 kung
916. 擊 chi
917. 批 p'i
918. 金 chin
919. 諸 chu

2nd Tone
920. 聞 wên
921. 羅 lo
922. 傳 chuan, ch'uan
923. 輿 yü
924. 員 yüan
925. 決 chüeh
926. 革 ko
927. 評 p'ing
928. 融 yung, jung
929. 遲 ch'ih

3rd Tone
930. 府 fu
931. 黨 tang
932. 長 chang
933. 統 t'ung
934. 解 chieh
935. 否 fou
936. 改 kai
937. 倒 tao
938. 影 ying
939. 響 hsiang
940. 穩 wên

4th Tone
941. 宗 an
942. 另 ling
943. 并 ping
944. 育 yü
945. 命 ming
946. 令 ling
947. 滯 chih

Text of the Lesson.

第三十課

新聞

COMPOUND WORDS AND EXPRESSIONS.

1. 消息
2. 新聞
3. 內閣
4. 辭職
5. 政府
6. 傳出來
7. 修正
8. 房稅案
9. 輿論
10. 政黨
11. 攻擊
12. 會議
13. 內務
14. 總長
15. 提議
16. 問題
17. 全體會議
18. 討論
19. 結果
20. 國務總理
21. 大總統
22. 國務會議
23. 解決
24. 是否
25. 至於
26. 經過
27. 報告
28. 教育機關
29. 改革
30. 批評
31. 原因
32. 和平
33. 影響
34. 外交
35. 命令
36. 穩當
37. 遲滯
38. [金融]

CONVERSATION.

甲　羅先生，今天報上有什麼緊要的新聞沒有。

乙　今天的消息不大好，內閣要總辭職呢。

甲　是嗎。請念給我聽聽吧。

乙　據政府要人傳出來的消息，因修正房稅案，政府頗受輿論和別的政黨的攻擊，昨天內閣會議的時候，由內務總長提議總辭職。這個問題經全體閣員討論了一點多鐘。會議的結果是先由國務總理去見大總統，然後在明天的國務會議再解決，是否提出總辭職書。至於總理見總統的經過，到現在還沒有可靠的報告。
另一消息，這次內閣辭職，并不單是因為房稅問題，上月裏對於各省教育機關的改革，也很受社會上的批評，或者這也是一個原因。

甲　你看這個消息能成了事實不能。

乙　我想十成有八成能實現，因為房稅本來沒有改的必要。

甲　我也是這麼想，可是我希望政府把這一案撤消，和平的過去，比什麼都好。

乙　是的，政府一倒，金融就要受影響。況且現在外交正在吃緊的時候，改換政府也不相宜。

甲　今天有什麼要緊的命令嗎。

乙. 沒有呢,我想政府正在不穩當的時候,當然諸事都遲滯一些。

APPENDIX I.

THE RADICALS.

In the following Table the Radicals with their pronunciation and meanings are arranged in the order of their numbers, which is according to the number of strokes in each radical, and the order followed in all Chinese and Foreign dictionaries.

The class of formation to which the character belongs (see Introduction, Vol. I, p. 9) and remarks on the significance of their composition are given in parallel columns.

The modern forms of the characters with the ancient forms (commonly known as the Seal characters) are given on pp. 165-179).

It is not intended that the information should all be learned, but simply read and noted as an aid to memory. It is desirable, however, that the student should be able to recognize and write each radical, know its sound and meaning, and, in the case of those most commonly used, its number.

The references are :—

    W.—Wieger, *Chinese Characters*.

    I.—Wilder & Ingram, *Analysis of Chinese Characters*.

    C.—Chalfant, *Early Chinese Writing*.

    K.—Karlgren, *Sound and Symbol in Chinese*.

    S.—Soothill, *General Pocket Dictionary*.

No.	Wade's Spelling.	Meaning.	Class of Formation.	Remarks.
		ONE		STROKE.
1.	I[1]	One		Symbol of Heaven, primordial unity, the ultimate reality, and other symbolical meanings. [W., 1, A; I., 19.] Older forms were vertical [C., Plate 29.].
2.	Kun[3]	Downstroke		Various symbolical meanings to be referred to as they occur in later combinations. [W., 6, A; I., 57.]
3.	Chu[3]	Dot		The modern form is due to the use of a brush in writing. Various symbolical meanings. [W., 4, A.]
4.	P'ieh[4]	Stroke to left		Symbol of motion; also means *to diminish*. [W., 7, A; 18, M; I., 176.]
5.	I[4]	One, bent		The ancient form represents a seedling springing up. [W., 9, A; I., 137.]
6.	Chüeh	A hook		Various symbolical meanings. [W., 6, 3]
		TWO		STROKES.
7.	Êrh[4]	Two		Older forms were vertical [C, 391] Symbolical of earth, of two extremes, and other ideas. [W., 2, A; I., 20.] Also an old form of the character *shang*[4], *high*, [W., 2, G.]
8.	T'ou[2]	A Cover		In ancient characters this form is used for No. 11, [q.v.]
9.	Jên[2]	Man		One who stands upright on two legs [W 25 A I 3]

No.	Wade's Spelling.	Meaning.	Class of Formation.	Remarks.
10.	Jên²	Man		The legs of a man. [W., 29, A; I., 27.]
11.	Ju⁴	Enter		Represents a plant with its roots *entering* the earth. In composition of ancient characters the seal form of No. 8 is used. [W., 15, A; I.,35.]
12.	Pa¹	Eight		Originally *to divide into two parts*. *Eight* is a number divisible into two unities, viz.: fours or squares. [W., 18, A; I., 569.]
13.	Chiung³	Borders		Representing border lines and the intervening waste. [W., 34, A; I., 468.]
14.	Mi⁴	To cover		A line that falls at both ends. [W., 34, H.]
15.	Ping¹	Ice		A picture of lines formed on the surface of water at the moment of freezing. [W., 17, A; I., 138.]
16.	Chi¹	Bench		Picture of a *stool*. [W., 20, A; I., 775.]
17.	K'an³	Receptacle		Representing a hole in the earth]W., 38, A; I., 46.]
18.	Tao¹	Knife		A *knife-blade* with curved handle. [W., 34, H; I., 37.]
19.	Li⁴	Strength		A nerve with its sheath; by extension *strength*. W., 53, A; I., 179.]
20.	Pao¹	Wrap		A man bending to *enfold* an object. [W., 54, A; I., 80.]
21.	Pi³	Ladle		A *spoon*. But also an inverted man, hence, *to turn*, *hua*. [W., 26, A; I., 491.]

No.	Wade's Spelling.	Meaning.	Class of Formation.	Remarks.
22.	Fang¹	Basket		A log hollowed out. [W., 51, A; I., 925.]
23.	Hsi³	Box		The horizontal stroke represents the cover of the *box*. [W., 10, A.]
24.	Shih²	Ten		Symbol of extension in two dimensions, and of the five cardinal points (including centre). The number that includes all numbers. [W., 24, A., I., 59.]
25.	Pu³	To divine		The perpendicular and horizontal veins developed by heat in the shell of the tortoise in the process of *divining*. [W. 56, A; I., 14.]
26.	Chieh²	A seal		The right half of the ancient character *ch'ing¹*, meaning two pieces of wood or jade which tallied, the right hand one of which was given to an official on his appointment. [W., 55, A, B; I., 42.]
27.	Han⁴	Cliff		The surface and slope of a *cliff*. [W., 59, A; I., 841.]
28.	Ssŭ¹	Private		Primarily a *cocoon*. The old form represents a silkworm curling itself up in its cocoon. [W., 89, A; I., 89.]
29.	Yu⁴	The right hand, again		A hand with the number of fingers reduced to three. Cf. R. 64 which has five fingers. The left hand is in the reverse position. In R. 55 both hands are combined. [W., 43, B; I., 43.]

No.	Wade's Spelling.	Meaning.	Class of Formation.	Remarks.
		THREE		**STROKES.**
30.	K'ou³	Mouth	A	Representation of the *mouth* ; see older form in Wieger. [W., 72, A ; I., 17.]
31.	Hui² or Wei²	Enclosure	A	To be distinguished from R. 30. [W., 76, A.]
32.	T'u³	Earth, Ground	A	The top line represents the surface, the bottom line the subsoil, the perpendicular the thing growing. [W., 81, A ; I., 13.] An older form represents a sprout springing up out of the ground [C., 80.]
33.	Shih⁴	Scholar	B	Primarily means *a thing*. It is composed of R. 1. *one*, and R. 24, *ten* : the numbers *one* to *ten* comprehend all things. By extension *a sage* or *scholar*. [W., 24, C ; I., 69.]
34.	Chih³	Step forward	A	A combination of R. 9 and a curved stroke to the right meaning *to follow* ; i.e. a *man* caught up by one *following* him. [W., 31, B.]
35.	Sui¹	Walk slowly	A	R. 9 with a hooked stroke passing through it, thus representing a *man walking on slowly* in spite of obstacles. [W., 31, C.]
36.	Hsi²	Evening	A	Represents the moon rising. [W., 64, A ; I., 14.]
37.	Ta⁴	Great	A	A grown man standing ; hence adult stature, *great*. [W., 60, A ; I., 54.]

No.	Wade's Spelling.	Meaning.	Class of Formation.	Remarks.
38.	Nü³	Woman	A	The figure of a woman. For older and simpler forms, see Chalfant. [W., 67, A; I., 16; C., 24.]
39.	Tzŭ³	Child, son	A	Infant with legs swathed. Older forms show legs free, for which see Chalfant. [W., 94, A; I., 1; C., C., 26.]
40.	Mien²	Roof	A	See Chalfant for older and more realistic representations. [W., 36, A; I., 1; C., 141.]
41.	Ts'un⁴	Inch, finger joint	A	The short stroke, acc. to Wieger, represents the pulse which is one inch distant from the hand; or, acc. to Chalfant, and more probably, the *joint* of the finger. See older forms in which the stroke is inside the hand instead of outside. [W., 45, B; I., 69; C., 43; cf. also Williams' Dictionary.]
42.	Hsiao³	Small	A	The vertical stroke represents an *object*, or, acc. to Chalfant, a *stick*. The two strokes on either side are the R. 12 with the meaning *to divide*; hence, an *object*, or *stick*, *divided* and therefore *small*. Note the older forms in Chalfant. [W., 18, H; I., 627; C., 285.]
43.	Wang¹	Crooked, lame	A	A man with his right leg bent. [W., 61, C; I., 98.]

No.	Wade's Spelling.	Meaning.	Class of Formation.	Remarks.
44.	Shih¹	Corpse	A	A spirit seated. In ancient times a living descendant impersonated the dead ancestor in sitting posture at ancestral worship. [W., 32, A; I., 449.]
45.	Ch'ê⁴	A sprout	A	Represents a root, the shoot and two leaves. [W., 78, A.]
46.	Shan¹	Hill	A	See the older forms in Chalfant [W, 80, A; I., 857; C., 93.]
47.	Chu'an¹	Streams	A	The curved strokes in the ancient form represented flowing water. One such stroke was used for a *rivulet*, two for a *stream* 30 miles long, and three for a large *river*. [W., 80, A; I., 598; C., 85.]
48.	Kung¹	Work	A	Represents the ancient carpenter's square. [W., 82, A; I., 89.]
49.	Chi³	Self	A	The most ancient form [see W and I] represents the woof of the web on the loom, with the shuttle. The meaning was originally *succession*. The modern meaning *self* is derived [W., 84, A; I., 129, cf. 191]
50.	Chin¹	Napkin	A	A cloth suspended from the girdle. The centre stroke represents the suspension, the square figure formed by the other two strokes represents the cloth itself. [W., 35, A; I., 143.]

No.	Wade's Spelling.	Meaning.	Class of Formation.	Remarks.
51.	Kan[1]	Shield	A	Represents a *pestle*; hence, to grind, destroy, oppose. [W., 102, A; I., 110.]
52.	Yao[1]	Minute	A	Fine thread, acc. to Wieger, obtained from two cocoons [cf R. 28]; but see Chalfant. [W., 90, A; I., 24; C., 330.]
53.	Yen[3]	A cover	A	Half of a roof [see R. 40] open on one side; hence, a *shed*. [W., 59, I; I., 132; C., 143.]
54.	Yin[3]	Move on	A	The ancient form is as in Wieger, but see Chalfant, who gives a form representing a man walking. [W., vol. II, p. 61; C., 315.]
55.	Kung[3]	Hands joined	A	Two hands [cf. R. 29] joined together in the position adopted by one person in presenting something to another. [W., 47, D; I., 175, 247.]
56.	I[4]	A dart	A	Probably picture of a *dart* [cf. R. 62]; but origin doubtful. [W., 71, A; I., 576.]
57.	Kung[1]	A bow	A	See Chalfant for older pictorial forms. [W., 87, A; I., 55; C., 211.]
58.	Chi[4]	Boar's snout	A	The second form is the older. The top stroke represents the flat nose, the bottom stroke the neck, and the projection at the top the tusk. See the ancient forms for *pig* or *boar* in Chalfant [C., 18], and note the relation of the snout to the picture as a whole. [W., 68, A; C., 18.]

No.	Wade's Spelling.	Meaning.	Class of Formation.	Remarks.
59.	Shan¹	Feathers, Hair	A	Pictorial, but used only in combination. [W., 62, A ; C., 62.]
60.	Ch'ih⁴	Step to left	A	A man's successive three steps. [W., 63, A ; C., 311.]
		FOUR		**STROKES.**
61.	Hsin¹	Heart	A	Representing the *heart* with ventricles and aorta. See older forms in Chalfant. [W., 107, A; I., 18; C., 41.]
62.	Ko¹	Halberd, spear	A	A hook on the top, a crossbar, and a sword-knot hanging. See older forms in Chalfant. [W., 71, F ; I., 2 ; C., 213.]
63.	Hu⁴	Door	A	One leaf of a pair of double doors. [W., 129, A ; I., 5,480 ; C., 191.]
64.	Shou³	Hand	A	The hand with five fingers [cf. R. 29]. [W., 48, A ; I., 53.]
65.	Chih¹	Branch	B	The *right hand*, the lower part of the ideograph [R. 29.], holding a *branch*, the upper part of the ideograph. [W., 43, C ; I., 950.]
66.	P'u³	To tap, to rap	B	The *right hand* holding a *rod ;* cf. R. 25, *to divine*, hence *diviner's rod*. [W., 43, D ; I., 17.]
67.	Wen²	Literature	B	Blended lines as in writing, like the veins of bamboo. [W., 61, F ; I., 427 ; C., 279.]
68.	Tou³	A peck	A	Originally, acc. to older forms, *a dipper,;* see Chalfant. [W., 98, B ; I., 117 ; C., 160.]

(145)

No.	Wade's Spelling.	Meaning.	Class of Formation.	Remarks.
69.	Chin¹	Axe	A	See older forms in Chalfant. [W., 128, A ; I., 419 ; C., 205.]
70.	Fang¹	Square	A	Ancient forms [see Wieger] represent the four regions of the earth's surface. [W., 117, A ; I., 503.]
71.	Wu²	Not	A	The top stroke represents an obstacle. The remainder of the ideograph represents a man bending his leg in a vain effort to resist the obstacle ; hence *in vain, not*. [W., 61, C ; I., 507.]
72.	Jih⁴	Sun. Day	A	Older forms are a circle with a dot in the centre ; see Chalfant. [W., 143, A ; I., 12 ; C., 71.]
73.	Yüeh⁴	Say	A	The *mouth* [R. 30] exhaling *breath*, represented by angle stroke at the top. [W., 73, A ; I. 9]
74.	Yüeh⁴	Moon	A	The moon's crescent. See older forms in Chalfant which are still more realistic. [W., 64, G ; I., 43 ; C., 72.]
75.	Mu⁴	Tree. Wood	A	A tree with its branches and roots. [W., 119, A ; I., 22 ; C, 97.]
76.	Ch'ien⁴	Exhale. Owe	A	A man (the lower part) *breathing out air* (the upper part) ; hence, *to yawn*, and by extension to be deficient in strength, *to owe*, [W., 99, A ; I., 273, 571.]

No.	Wade's Spelling.	Meaning.	Class of Formation.	Remarks.
77.	Chih³	To stop	A	Represents a foot : heel on the left, toes on the right, and ankle on the top. Hence *to march*, and then *to stop*, but possibly represents a sprout impeded in its growth ; V.C. [W., 112, A ; I., 10 ; C., 110.]
78.	Tai³	Bad	A	Remains of a skeleton (see W. for older forms) ; hence, *death, evil*. [W., 118, C ; I., 711.]
79.	Shu¹	Kill	B	The *right hand* (R. 29) making a jerky motion (the upper part) ; hence, *to strike*. [W., 22, D ; I., 71.]
80.	Wu²	Do not	A	A woman placed under lock and bar (the horizontal stroke) ; hence, *to prohibit*. [W., 67, K.]
81.	Pi³	Compare	B	Two men standing together comparing heights. [W., 27, I ; I., 966 ; C., 282.]
82.	Mao²	Hair. Plumage	A	Picture of *plumage*. [W., 100, A ; I., 254.]
83.	Shih⁴	Clan. Family		A floating plant that ramifies and grows ; hence a wandering tribe, *family*. [W., 114, A ; I., 8.]
84.	Ch'i⁴	Vapour. Breath. Air	A	Vapour rising from the ground ; cf. C. 137 for the form of *ch'i, steam, vapour*. [W., 98, A ; I., 47 ; C., 136.]
85.	Shui³	Water	A	Ripples on a small stream (the centre stroke). See older forms. [W., 12, B ; I., 79 ; C., 84.]

(147)

No.	Wade's Spelling.	Remarks.	Class of Formation.	Remarks.
86.	Huo³	Fire	A	Flames ascending; see C. for older forms. [W., 126, A; I., 169; C., 81.]
87.	Chao³	Claws	A	The right hand pressing upon the ground; hence, *paws, claws*. [W., 49, A; I., 281, 673; C., 44.]
88.	Fu⁴	Father	A	The right hand (R. 29) holding a rod, the symbol of authority. [W., 43, G; I., 317.]
89.	Yao²	Intertwine	A	Pictorial. [W., 39, G.]
90.	Ch'iang²	Frame	A	The left half of a tree (v. R. 75); hence, a *frame, bed*. [W., 127, B.]
91.	P'ien⁴	A strip	A	The right half of a tree; v. R. 75. [W., 127, A.]
92.	Ya²	Tooth	A	Represents the grinding surface of teeth meeting together. [W., 147, A; I., 97; C., 51.]
93.	Niu²	Ox	A	Represents a horned animal; see ancient forms in C. [W., 132, A; I., 50; C., 5.]
94.	Ch'üan³	Dog	A	See Chalfant for older form representing an animal with curled tail. [W., 134, A; I., 424; C., 7.]
		FIVE		**STROKES.**
95.	Hsüan²	Dark	A	Composed of R. 11, the upper part, and R. 52, the lower part. Represents *fine thread*, R. 52, dipped *into*, R. 11, dark green or black dye. [W., 91, A.]

No.	Wade's Spelling.	Meaning.	Class of Formation.	Remarks.
96.	Yü⁴	Jade	A	Chalfant gives a string of three jade beads as the old form of *wang*, a king (C. 234). There seems to be a close connection between the two ideographs. [W., 53, A; I., 124; C., 234.]
97.	Kua¹	Melon	A	Represents a melon hanging between tendrils. [W., 162, A.]
98.	Wa³	Tile	A	Older forms suggest tiles overlapping in Chinese fashion. [W., 145, A; I., 558; C., 196.]
99.	Kan¹	Sweet	A	Something (the stroke in the middle) palatable held in the mouth, R. 30; see older forms in Chalfant. [W., 73, B; I., 23; C., 342.]
100.	Shêng¹	Grow. Produce	A	Represents a growing plant. [W., 79, F; I., 14; C., 109.]
101.	Yung⁴	To use	A	The perpendicular with the horizontal stroke near the top represents an arrow piercing a target represented by the rest of the ideograph; hence, capacity, to use. [W., 109, B; I., 225.]
102.	T'ien²	Field	A	Land divided into plots. [W., 149, A; I., 82; C., 184.]
103.	P'i³	A piece of cloth		A borrowed character from an ancient form *shu* meaning *the foot in motion*. The curve which is superimposed on R. 77 (q.v.) represents the motion. [W., 112, C.]

No.	Wade's Spelling.	Meaning.	Class of Formation.	Remarks.
104.	Ni⁴	Disease		A man lying (the horizontal stroke) on a bed (the left hand portion is R. 90) in sickness. [W., 127, C; I., 437, 593.]
105.	Po⁴	Back to back. Opposed		Two feet (R. 77) in opposite directions; hence, mutually opposed. [W., 112, H; I, 214.]
106.	Pai²	White	A	The sun (R. 72) rising; the dawn when the sky becomes bright with white light [W., 88, A; I., 6.], but acc. to Chalfant depicts the white of the eye [C., Plate XLII.]
107.	P'i²	Skin. To flay		There are three portions in the ideograph. On the left is the *skin*, on the top a *knife*, and below, the *hand* that *flays* the *skin* with a *knife* [W., 42, H; I., 224.]
108.	Min³	Dish		Picture of an ancient dish with pedestal. [W., 157, A; I., 648; C., 155.]
109.	Mu⁴	Eye		See older forms in Chalfant, one of which represents the socket of the eye with two eyelids and pupil. [W., 158, A; I., 102, 547; C., 31.]
110.	Mao²	Lance		A three-pronged halberd. [W., 95, C; I., 897; C., 220.]
111.	Shih⁴	Arrow		An arrow with barbed point at the top and feathers at the bottom. [W., 131, A; I., 100; C., 212.]

No.	Wade's Spelling.	Meaning.	Class of Formation.	Remarks.
112.	Shih²	Stone		A piece of rock fallen from a cliff. [W., 59, D; I., 42; C., 96.]
113.	Shih⁴	Reveal		The two horizontal strokes are an old form of *shang⁴, high* (v. R. 7), hence used for heaven. The vertical strokes represent the three celestial luminaries, sun, moon and stars, suspended from heaven, which show the will of Heaven to men. [W., 3, D; I., 164; C., 353.]
114.	Jou²³⁴	Track. Footprint		The hind legs and tail of an animal; hence, the trail which it leaves. [W., 23, C.]
115.	Ho²	Growing grain		A plant (cf. R. 75) with an ear of corn hanging to one side. [W., 121, A; I., 556; C., 118.]
116.	Hsüeh⁴	Cave		A *roof* (R. 40) combined with R. 12, which originally meant *to divide, to separate,* hence, *to remove.* The old form thus represents the empty space after the earth is removed from under the roof. [W., 37, A; I., 97; C., 194.]
117.	Li⁴	To stand		Represents a man standing on the ground; see Chalfant. [W., 60, H; I, 216 C., 320.]

No	Wade's Spelling.	Meaning.	Class of Formation.	Remarks.
		SIX		**STROKES.**
118.	Chu²	Bamboo		*Bamboo* twigs pendant; contrast R. 140 in which the *sprouts* point upwards. [W., 77, B; I., 7; C., 117.]
119.	Mi³	Rice		Modification of older form composed of nine dots in the form of a square and representing shelled grains of *rice*. [W., 122, A; I., 47, 658; C., 124.]
120.	Mi⁴	Silk		The lower part represents the twisting of the threads obtained from the two cocoons; cf. R. 52. [W., 92, A; I., 8; C., 134.]
121.	Fou³	Earthenware vessel		Older form in Chalfant represents "a *wine-jar* with sealed lid secured by cords." [W., 130, C; I., 264; C., 158.]
122.	Wang³	Net.		A *net* with its meshes; see older form in Chalfant. [W., 39, C; I., 38; C., 165.]
123.	Yang²	Sheep		Represents a *ram* with horns, legs and tail; see older form in Chalfant in which the horns are curved. [W., 103, A; I., 253; C., 6.]
124.	Yü³	Wings		A pair of wings with feathers. [W., 62, E; I., 583; C., 45.]

No.	Wade's Spelling.	Meaning.	Class of Formation.	Remarks.
125.	Lao[3]	Old		Composed of *hair* (R. 82), *man* (R. 9) and a primitive meaning *to turn* or *change* (cf. W., 30, D; I., 20, 491.); hence, a man whose hair is changing to white. [W., 30, E; I., 209.]
126.	Êrh[2]	And yet		Modern meaning is derived. Originally the beard and whiskers. [W., 164, A; 635; C, 38; I.
127.	Lei[3]	Plough		A harrow made of wood (R. 75). The upper part represents the prongs. [W., 120, E; I., 601.]
128.	Êrh[3]	Ear		Picture of the external ear. [W., 146, A; I., 71; C., 32.]
129.	Yü[4]	Pen		A *stylus* (the perpendicular stroke) held in the *hand* (R. 29), to write letters (the horizontal stroke) on a tablet (the curve at the bottom). [W., 169, A; I., 7; C., 202.]
130.	Jou[4]	Flesh		Pieces of dried flesh (W., 17, G) wrapped in a bundle (R. 20). [W., 65, A; I., 133; C., 54.]
131.	Ch'ên[2]	Statesman		Origin obscure. Possibly represents some insignia of office; see older forms in Chalfant. [W., 82, E; I., 120; C., 239.]
132.	Tzŭ[4]	From, Self		Representing the nose. [W., 159, A; I., 104; C., 269.]

No.	Wade's Spelling.	Meaning	Class of Formation.	Remarks.
133.	Chih⁴	To reach		The bottom horizontal stroke represents the ground; the upper part a bird with wings and tail outspread alighting on the ground. [W., 133, B; I., 88.]
134.	Chiu⁴	Mortar	A	See older forms. A vessel, or earlier a hole in the ground, containing grain. [W., 139, A; I., 479; C., 200.]
135.	Shê²	Tongue	A	Below is the *mouth* (v. R. 30); the remainder represents the tongue protruding. [W, 102, C; I., 73; C., 56.]
136.	Ch'uan³	Contradict	B	Composed of *sui* (R. 35, q.v.) and the inverted form of the same back to back; hence, *opposition, contradiction*. [W., 31, E; I., 321.]
137.	Chou¹	Boat	A	Picture of a boat showing high curved prow and deck with compartments below. [W., 66, A; I., 108; C., 170.]
138.	Kên⁴	Defiant. Limit	B	Composed of *hua, to turn* (v. W., 26, A) and *mu, the eye* (R. 109). To turn suddenly and look a man in the face; hence, *defiant*, [W., 26, L; I. 158.]
139.	Sê⁴	Colour	B	Composed of R. 9 and R. 26. "The *colour* of the face corresponds to the feelings of the heart as the seal to the stamp that produces it." [W., 28, D.]

No.	Wade's Spelling.	Meaning.	Class of Formation.	Remarks.
140.	Ts'ao[3]	Grass. Herbs		Two *sprouts*, see R. 45. [W., 78, B; I., 22; C., 104.]
141.	Hu[1]	Tiger	A	This, the seal form, is said to represent a tiger's stripes but older forms are pictures of the tiger itself; see Chalfant. [W. 135, A; I., 258; C., 2.,]
142.	Ch'ung[2]	Worm. Snake. Insect	A	"A worm with its convolutions." [W., 110, A; I., 232; C., 11.]
143.	Hsüeh[3]	Blood	A	Represents *blood* (the stroke in a sacrificial *dish*; v. R. 108. [W., 157, D; C., 11.]
144.	Hsing[2]	Go. Do.	B	Composed of *ch'ih*, a *step with the left foot* (R. 60) and *ch'u*, a step with the right foot (W., 63, B); thus footprints of one walking, see Chalfant.[W., 63, C; I., 161; C., 317.]
145.	I[1]	Clothes	A	Upper garment with sleeves at top, and at the bottom the robe waving. [W., 16, A; I., 51; C., 166.]
146.	Hsi[1]	West	A	The original R. 146 was *hsia*, meaning *a cover*. An older form as given by Chalfant represents a bird sitting on its nest at sunset [W., 41, C, D; I, 26; C., 122.]

No.	Wade's Spelling.	Meaning.	Class of Formation.	Remarks.
		SEVEN		STROKES.
147.	Chien⁴	To see	A	Eye emitting light; see older forms in Chalfant. [W., 158, C; I., 85; C., 267.]
148.	Chio² Chiao³	Horn	A	Oldest forms are pictures of a horn. [W., 142, B; I., 250; C., 50.]
149.	Yen²	Words	B	See older forms in Chalfant which picture *words*, the upper part, issuing from the *mouth* (R. 30). [W., 73, C; I., 10; C., 276.]
150.	Ku³	Valley	B	The R. 12 with the meaning *to separate* repeated, one form being superimposed on the other to represent a gorge; below is R. 30, a *mouth* representing a water-course. [W., 18, E; I., 579.]
151.	Tou⁴	Bean	A	Originally a sacrificial dish in which meat (the horizontal stroke) was served; see Chalfant for actual form as seen in exhumed vessel. The modern meaning, *bean*, is borrowed. [W., 165, A; I., 105; C., 156.]
152.	Shih⁴	Pig	A	The *pig* with head, four legs and tail. Older forms are in the horizontal position; see Chalfant. [W., 69, A; I., 221; C., 18.]
153.	Chai⁴	Reptile	A	Acc. to Chalfant, the *unicorn*; acc. to Wieger, feline animals. [W., 166, A; C., 16.]

No.	Wade's Spelling.	Meaning.	Class of Formation.	Remarks.
154.	Pei⁴	Valuable	A	A cowrie shell with the feelers of the living inmate. Older forms show the bi-valve; see Chalfant. [W., 161, A; I., 38; C., 132.]
155.	Ch'ih⁴	Red. Flesh colour. To flush	B	Composed of *ta⁴, great*, or *a man standing* (W., 60, G.), and R. 86, *fire;* thus it represents the *flushing* of the face with shame or anger. [W., 60, N; I., 542.]
156.	Tsou³	Walk	A	A man (cf. R. 155) *bending* (the upper part) in order to walk more quickly, and then *stopping,* (see R. 77). [W., 112, A, D; I., 146; C., 315.]
157.	Tsu²	Foot	A	A foot at rest (cf. R. 77). The circle signifies stillness. [W., 112, B; I., 299, 484; C., 37.]
158.	Shên¹	Body	A	A man (the top part), R. 9, with trunk and legs (the lower part). [W., 148, A; I., 291; C., 28.]
159.	Ch'ê¹	Cart	A	A cart, turned on its side for convenience in modern writing. If turned the other way the present perpendicular is seen to be the axle, the two horizontals the wheels, and the centre part the body. But see older forms in Chalfant showing shaft for pair of horses. [W., 167, A; I., 136; C., 206.]

No.	Wade's Spelling.	Meaning.	Class of Formation	Remarks.
160.	Hsin[1]	Bitter	B	Composed of *shang*[4], *above* (the two strokes at the top), and *jên*[3], *to offend* (W., 102, F). Thus, to offend one's superior; hence, *bitterness*. Chalfant, however, says the origin is obscure. [W., 102, H; I., 274; C., 343.]
161.	Ch'ên[2]	Time	B	The modern meaning is borrowed. [W., 30, B; I., 122.]
162.	Cho[1]	To go step by step	A	Composed of R. 60 and R. 77; to *step* forward with the left foot and then *stop*. [W., 112, E; I., 10; C., 312.]
163.	I[4]	City	B	"An *enclosure* (R. 31) and *seal* (R. 26); hence, official seat, *city*." [W., 74, C; I., 11; C., 249.] Note: the abbreviated form is always on the right of the character of which it is the radical.
164.	Yu[3]	Wine jar	A	An ancient jar for preserving fermented liquor. [W., 41, G; I., 422; C., 172.]
165.	Pien[4]	Differentiate	A	The print of a beast's claws outspread by which the track is *distinguished*. [W., 123, A; I., 801; C., 348.]
166.	Li[3]	Village. Mile	B	Composed of a *field* (R. 102) and *earth* (R. 32). [W., 149, D; I., 82; C., 348.]

No.	Wade's Spelling.	Meaning.	Class of Formaton.	Remarks.
		EIGHT		**STROKES**
167.	Chin¹	Gold. Metal		The upper part *chin¹, now*, is a phonetic. The lower part is *earth*, R. 32, with two strokes representing nuggets of gold. [W., 14, T ; I., 13.] But see older forms in Chalfant [C., 32.]
168.	Ch'-ang²	Long	A	Locks of hair so *long* that they must be tied by a band (the horizontal stroke) and a brooch (the small part below). [W., 113, A ; I., 55.]
169.	Mên²	Door		Two leaves of a *door*. Older forms show pivots and bolt as seen in the ordinary house door in China to-day. [W., 129, C ; I., 5 ; C., 169.]
170.	Fou⁴	Mound	A	A *cliff* (R. 27). with successive layers of earth. [W., 86, A ; I., 493 ; C., 193.] Note : the abbreviated form is always on the left of the character of which it is the radical.
171.	Tai⁴	To reach	B	A *hand* grasping the tail of a fleeing animal. [W., 44, E ; C , Plate XLVII.]
172.	Chui¹	Birds		See older forms showing picture of a short-tailed bird. [W., 168, A ; I., 21 ; C., 13.]
173.	Yü³	Rain		See older forms in Chalfant representing falling *rain drops* under the vaulted heaven ; altered later to conform to the character for *heaven*. [W., 1, b ;125, B ; I., 61; C., 89.]

No.	Wade's Spelling.	Meaning.	Class of Formation.	Remarks.
174.	Ch'-ing¹	Nature-colour		Composed of *tan¹, cinnabar, red* [W., 115, D] and R. 100. It has a series of meanings, viz: the earth colour red, the green of vegetation, and the blue of the sky; i.e. nature-colour [W., 79, F; I., 63; C., Plate XLVII.]
175.	Fei¹	Not	A	Back to back; hence, opposed, negation. cf. R. 105. [W., 170, A; I., 276; C., 386.]
		NINE		STROKES
176.	Mien⁴	Face	A	The head (see R. 185 in W., 160, A; and C., 29) set in an outline of the face; see older forms in Chalfant showing 2 eyes and nose. [W., 160, B; I., 486; C., 30.]
177.	Ko²	Hides	A	The raw hide of a sheep (R. 123 contracted) stretched on a frame (the 2 horizontal strokes) with two hands (see older form in Wieger) scraping it. [W., 105, A; I., 163.]
178.	Wei²	Thongs. Leather	A	Older form in Chalfant is a picture of knotted cords. [W., 31, G; I., 772; C., 197.]
179.	Chiu³	Leeks	A	Growing leeks with their leaves. [W., 170, B.; C., 116.]

No.	Wade's Spelling.	Meaning.	Class of Formation.	Remarks.
180.	Yin¹	Sound	B	*Speech* (R. 149) issuing from the *mouth* (R. 30) in a single utterance (the short stroke in R. 30). [W., 73, E; I., 39; C., 277.]
181.	Yeh⁴	Head	A	A *head* (R. 185) upon a *man* (R. 10). [W., 160, C; I., 105.]
182.	Fêng¹	Wind	A	Origin vague; see alternative form in W. and I. [W., 21, B; I., 365.]
183.	Fei¹	To fly	A	A bird flying, see older forms in Chalfant [W., 11, A; I., 612; C., 63.]
184.	Shih²	Eat	B	Composed of *hsiang¹*, *boiled grain* (W., 26, L) and *chi²*, *collected* (W., 14, A); i.e. grain collected or mingled for food. [W., 26, M; I., 75.]
185.	Shou³	Head	A	Outline of face or head with hair above. [W., 160, A; I., 101; C., 29.]
186..	Hsiang¹	Fragrance	B	Sweetness (R. 99) of millet (R. 202). [W., 73, B; I., 587.]
	TEN		**STROKES**	
187.	Ma³	Horse	A	The picture of a horse with its head, mane, legs and tail. [W., 137, A; I., 261; C., 4.]
188.	Ku³	Bones	B	Composed of *kua²*, *a skeleton* (W., 118, A), and R. 130, *flesh*. [W., 118, A; I., 292.]

No.	Wade's Spelling.	Meaning.	Class of Formation.	Remarks.
189.	Kao¹	High	A	Older forms represent a tower over a city gate. [W., 75, B; I., 142; C., 305.]
190.	Piao¹	Long hair	B	Composed of *long* (R. 168) and *locks of hair* (R. 59). [W., 113, B; I., 626; C., 40.]
191.	Tou⁴	Strife	B	The ancient primitive *chü²*, *to seize*, duplicated, the two forms facing each other; hence, *to strive*. [W., 11, I; I., 688; C., Plate XLVIII.]
192.	Ch'-ang⁴	Sacrificial wine. Aromatic herbs.	A	A wine-cup containing grain with the ladle below. [W., 26, C; C., 370.]
193.	Li⁴ or ko⁴	Tripod Cauldron	A	Older forms represent a tripod such as is used in temples. [W., 155, A; I., 536; C., 373.]
194.	Kuei³	A spirit	A	Picture of a vanishing demon with head and legs; the appendage represents the swirl caused by the vanishing movement [W., 40, C; I., 447; C., 354.]
		ELEVEN		**STROKES**
195.	Yü²	Fish	A	Older forms are pictures of the fish with head, body, fins, scales and tail. [W. 142, A; I., 284; C., 8.
196.	Niao³	Bird	A	Picture of a long-tailed bird. [W., 138, A; I., 628; C., 12.]

No.	Wade's Spelling.	Meaning.	Class of Formation.	Remarks.
197.	Lu³	Salt	A	Four grains of rock-salt and *west* (R. 146) from whence it came; or, picture of an earthen vessel (see older forms) for evaporating salt. [W., 41, D; I., 294; C., 133.]
198.	Lu¹	Deer	A	A deer with horns, head and feet. [W., 136, A; I., 844; C., 3.]
99.	Mai⁴	Wheat	B	Composed of *sui¹*, to advance (R. 35) and *lai²*, to come. The latter (W., 13, C; I., 64) represents a plant with ears of corn suspended. The meaning *come* is borrowed. [W., 13, C; I., 405.]
200.	Ma²	Hemp.	A	Represents *p'ai*, *hemp* (W., 79, H) prepared and stored under *cover* (R.53) [W., 79, H; I., 24.]
		TWELVE		**STROKES**
201.	Hu-ang²	Yellow		The colour of loess soil. Composed of *fields* (R. 102), and an old form of *kuang¹*, *light* (W., 24, J) [W., 171, A; I., 207.]
202.	Shu³	Glutinous millet		The millet from which wine is produced. Composed of *grain*, (R. 115), *to enter* (R. 12, cf. R. 8), and *water* (R. 85); i.e. grain which put into water produces wine. [W., 121, I.]

No.	Wade's Spelling.	Meaning.	Class of Formation.	Remarks.
203.	Hei[1]	Black. Soot		The lower part consists of R. 86, *fire*, reduplicated, which causes the deposit of soot, and the upper part is the opening through which the smoke escapes and in which the soot is deposited. [W., 40, D; I., 178.]
204.	Chih[3]	Embroider		The top part is a contracted form of a primitive *tsao*[2], meaning *foliage*, (W., 102, I). The lower part is a piece of *cloth* (W., 35, F). Hence, a piece of cloth *embroidered* with a foliage pattern. [W., 35, G, C., 180.]
		THIRTEEN		**STROKES**
205.	Min[3]	Toad		Pictorial; see older form in Chalfant. [W., 108, c; C., 9.] Cf. R. 213.
206.	Ying[3]	Tripod		Tripod incense burner. See older forms in Chalfant. [W., 127, D; C, 364.]
207.	Ku[3]	Drum		The left-hand part is the original primitive, *chou*[1], *a drum*. The right hand represents a *hand* (R. 29) holding a rod. [W, 165, C; I., 684.]
208.	Shu[3]	Rat		Head, whiskers and tail of a rodent. Note the older form in Wieger and Chalfant. [W., 139, B; C., 21.]

No.	Wade's Spelling.	Meaning.	Class of Formation.	Remarks.
209.	Pi³	Nose		The upper part represents a nose; see older form in Chalfant. The lower part is pi^4, *to agree*, used as a phonetic. [W., 40, C; C., 33.]
210.	Ch'i²	Level. Even		Ears of corn of *even* height. [W., 174, A; I., 455; C., 119.]
211.	Ch'ih³	Front teeth		The lower part is the original; viz: a mouth showing teeth. The upper part is *chih*, R. 77, added later as a phonetic. [W., 175, A; C., 52.]
212.	Lung²	Dragon		See older form in Wieger. [W., 140, A; I,. 286.]
213.	Kuei¹	Tortoise		Showing head, claws, shell and tail; see older forms in Chalfant. [W., 108, B; C., 10] Cf. R. 205.
214.	Yo⁴	Flute		Composed of chi^2 (W., 14, A), *union* (the upper-part), bamboos strung together (the lower part), and three mouths between. Thus, a union of bamboos strung together and their apertures. [W., 14, H.]

No.	Modern Form.	Order of Writing.	Ancient Form.	No.	Modern Form.	Order of Writing.	Ancient Form.
	ONE STROKE.			8	亠	ヽ一	人
1	一		一	9	人	ノ乀 / 亻	儿
2	丨		丨	10	儿	丿乚	〣
3	丶		丶	11	入	ノ乀	人
4	丿		丿	12	八	ノ乀	八
5	乙		㇆	13	冂	丨𠃌	冂
6	亅		✓	14	冖	丶一	冂
	TWO STROKES			15	冫	㇀丶	仌
7	二	一一	二				

No.	Modern Form.	Order of Writing.	Ancient Form.	No.	Modern Form.	Order of Writing.	Ancient Form.
16	几	几	几	24	十	一丨	十
17	凵	凵	凵	25	卜	丨丶	卜
18	刀	刀 刂	刀 刂	26	卩 巳	𠃍丨 乚	弓 乙
19	力	𠂉	𠠵	27	厂	丿	厂
20	勹	勹	勹	28	厶	厶	ㄖ
21	匕	匕	匕	29	又	八	彐
22	匚	匚	匚				
23	匸	乚 丂					

THREE STROKES.

| 30 | 口 | 冂一 | 日 |

No.	Modern Form	Order of Writing.	Ancient Form.	No.	Modern Form	Order of Writing.	Ancient Form.
31	口		口	39	子		
32	土		土		孑		
33	士		士	40	宀		
34	夂			41	寸		
35	夊			42	小		
36	夕			43	尢		
37	大				尣		
38	女			44	尸		

No.	Modern Form.	Order of Writing.	Ancient Form.	No.	Modern Form.	Order of Writing.	Ancient Form.
45	屮		屮	53	广		广
46	山		山	54	叉		叉
47	巛 川	巛 川	川	55	廾		廾
48	工		工	56	弋		弋
49	己		弓	57	弓		弓
50	巾		巾	58	彐 彑		彐 彑
51	干		干				
52	幺		幺	59	彡		彡

No.	Modern Form	Order of Writing	Ancient Form	No.	Modern Form	Order of Writing	Ancient Form
60	彳			65	支		
				66	攴 攵		
FOUR STROKES.				67	文		
61	心 忄 小			68	斗		
				69	斤		
62	戈						
63	戶			70	方		
64	手 扌			71	无 旡		

No.	Modern Form.	Order of Writing.	Ancient Form.	No.	Modern Form.	Order of Writing.	Ancient Form.
72	日	丨フ二	日	80	母	ㄣフ一	母
73	曰	丨フ二	曰		母	ㄣフ二	
74	月	丿仁	月	81	比	比	比
75	木	一小八	木	82	毛	𠂉乚	毛
76	欠	𠂉人	欠	83	氏	氏	氏
77	止	𠂉二	止	84	气	气	气
78	歹	一歹	歺	85	水	氺 氵	水
	歺	一歺					
79	殳	几又	殳	86	火 灬	火 灬	火

No.	Modern Form.	Order of Writing.	Ancient Form.	No.	Modern Form.	Order of Writing.	Ancient Form.
					FIVE STROKES.		
87	爪		爪	95	玄		
88	父			96	玉 王		王
89	爻			97	瓜		瓜
90	爿			98	瓦		瓦
91	片		片	99	甘		甘
92	牙			100	生		生
93	牛 牜		牛	101	用		用
94	犬 犭			102	田		田
				103	疋		疋

No.	Modern Form.	Order of Writing.	Ancient Form.	No.	Modern Form.	Order of Writing.	Ancient Form.
104	疒			112	石		
105	癶			113	示 ⺬		
106	白						
107	皮			114	内		
108	皿			115	禾		
109	目 四			116	穴		
				117	立		
110	矛						

SIX STROKES.

118	竹 ⺮		
111	矢						

No.	Modern Form.	Order of Writing.	Ancient Form.	No.	Modern Form.	Order of Writing.	Ancient Form.
119	米		米	126	而		而
120	糸		糸	127	耒		耒
121	缶		缶	128	耳		耳
122	网 四 罒		网 冈	129	聿		聿
123	羊		羊	130	肉 月		肉
124	羽		羽	131	臣		臣
125	老		老	132	自		自

No.	Modern Form	Order of Writing	Ancient Form	No.	Modern Form	Order of Writing	Ancient Form
133	至			141	虍		
134	白			142	虫		
135	舌			143	血		
136	舛			144	行		
137	舟			145	衣 衤		
138	艮			146	西		
139	色						
140	艸						

SEVEN STROKES

| 147 | 見 | | |

175

No.	Modern Form.	Order of Writing.	Ancient Form.	No.	Modern Form.	Order of Writing.	Ancient Form.
148	角			157	足		
149	言			158	身		
150	谷			159	車		
151	豆			160	辛		
152	豕			161	辰		
153	豸			162	辵		
154	貝				之		
155	赤			163	邑		
156	走				阝		

No.	Modern Form.	Order of Writing.	Ancient Form.	No.	Modern Form.	Order of Writing.	Ancient Form.
164	酉		酉	171	隶		隶
165	采		采	172	隹		隹
166	里		里	173	雨		雨

EIGHT STROKES.

				174	青		青
				175	非		非
167	金		金				
168	長		長				

NINE STROKES.

169	門		門	176	面		面
170	阜		阜	177	革		革

No.	Modern Form.	Order of Writing.	Ancient Form.	No.	Modern Form.	Order of Writing.	Ancient Form.
178	韋			186	香		
179	韭				**TEN STROKES**		
180	音			187	馬		
181	頁			188	骨		
182	風			189	高		
183	飛			190	髟		
184	食			191	鬥		
				192	鬯		
185	首			193	鬲		

No.	Modern Form.	Order of Writing.	Ancient Form.	No.	Modern Form.	Order of Writing.	Ancient Form.
194	鬼					**TWELVE STROKES.**	
				201	黃		
	ELEVEN STROKES.			202	黍		
195	魚			203	黑		
196	鳥			204	黹		
197	鹵					**THIRTEEN STROKES.**	
198	鹿			205	黽		
199	麥			206	鼎		
200	麻			207	鼓		

No.	Modern Form	Order of Writing	Ancient Form	No.	Modern Form	Order of Writing	Ancient Form
208	鼠			212	龍		
209	鼻			213	龜		
210	齊			214	龠		
211	齒						

APPENDIX II.

ANALYSIS OF CHARACTERS IN LESSONS 1 TO 4.

No.	Wade's Spelling.	No. of Radical.	No. of Phonetic in Soothill.	Class of Formation.*	Remarks.
		LESSON I.			PART I.
1.	Shu¹	73	669	B	The yüeh⁴, to say, here is a contracted form chê³ meaning sentences. The phonetic yü⁴ is a pen; hence, to write sentences. [W., 159, B; I., 9.]
2.	Jên²	9	429	A	See Table of Radicals in all cases where the character is itself a Radical.
3.	Mei². Mo²Mu²	85	536 (R.79)	B	Diving into the water. [W., 76, I; I., 79.]
4.	Pi³	118	669 (R.129)	B	Pen with bamboo handle: the modern brush-pen. [I.7.]
5.	Yu³	74	184	B	The moon and the right hand. The original meaning is the moon's phases presenting the appearance of being partly covered by the hand. To be and to have are borrowed meanings. [W., 46, H; I., 43.]
6.	Hao³	38	552	B	Wife and child; i.e., what is good and what one loves. [I., 90].
7.	Yeh³	5	301		The modern meaning is borrowed. [W., 107, B; I. 4.]
8.	Mo⁴. Mei⁴	32	83	B	Lampblack and earth mixed to make the cakes of Chinese ink. [W., 40, D; I. 382.]
		LESSON I.			PART II.
9.	T'a¹	9	301	B	Man with also; i.e. the other man. [W., 107, B; I. 4.]
10.	Hsien¹	10	39	B	The upper part is chih¹, a small plant issuing from the ground; hence, to grow, to advance. Thus, combined with R. 10, the two legs of a man, the whole character means to advance with the feet, to be first. [W., 79, B; I., 27.]
11.	Shêng¹	100	41	A	

* Refer to the Radical in Table I (Vol. I, . 9) and to the Phonetic in Soothill's Dictionary.

No.	Wade's Spelling.	No. of Radical.	No. of Phonetic in Soothill.	Class of Formation.	Remarks
12.	Mên²	9	635 (R.169)	C	[W., 129, C ; I., 5.] Note.—In the case of characters in Class C there is usually no further signification beyond the combination of Radical and Phonetic.
13.	Ch'ien⁴	167	332	C	[I. 13.]
14.	Wo³	64	338	B	The *hand* grasping a *spear*, suggestive of egoism. See older form in Chalfant. [I., 2 ; C., 307.]
15.	Ni³	9	121		Composed of *man* (R. 9) and *erh³*, which has the borrowed meaning of *you*. [W., 18, O ; I., 3.]
16.	Li³	75	484	B	The *offspring* or fruit of a *tree*. [W., 119, K ; I., 360.]
	LESSON II.				PART I.
17.	San¹	1	1	A	Symbolical of the Three Powers: Heaven, Earth and Man. [W., 3, A ; I., p. xi.]
18.	Shih²	24	13	A	See Table of Radicals.
19.	Nin²	61	121	C	[I., 892.]
20.	Wu³	7	726	B	Originally two lines intersecting diagonally making with the point of intersection *five* points. This was enclosed between the two strokes of R. 7 symbolical of the *Yin* and the *Yang*, the five points symbolizing the so-called Five Elements. [W., 39, A ; I., 30.] Still older forms were composed of five horizontal or vertical lines [C., 394.].
21.	Pên³	75	485	C	The stroke in the lower part represents the ground from which the *tree* is growing and below which is the root. [W., 120 A ; I., 36].

No.	Wade's Spelling.	No. of Radical.	No. of Phonetic in Soothill.	Class of Formation	Remarks.
22.	Kuan³	118	751	C	[W., 86, C; I., 481.]
23.	Liu⁴	12	80	B	The old form is a modification, by the addition of a dot, of *four*, the next even number preceding; [I., 31] but see Chalfant [W., 42, A; C., 395.]
24.	Ko⁴	9	703	C	[W., 24, F; I., 28.]
25.	K'uai⁴	32	808 (R. 194)	C	[I., 215.]
		LESSON II.			**PART II.**
26.	Ti¹,⁴	106	231	B	The meaning *possessive* is borrowed, The original meaning is a *target*. [W., 54, H; 88, A; I., 6.]
27.	Hsiao³	42	121	A	See Table of Radicals.
28.	Hsieh³	7	129	B	*Tz'ŭ³*, *this*, and a *second* (R. 7); hence, *these*. [W., 112, A; I., 20.]
29.	Shih⁴	72	139	B	The old form, the meaning of which was *right*, was composed of *jih⁴*, *sun*, and *chêng⁴*, *correct, exact;* the sun exactly on the meridian is *straight* or *right*. [W., 112, I; I., 12.]
30.	Chê⁴	162	740 (R. 149)	B	Originally *to go to meet* someone. The modern meaning is borrowed. [I., 10.]
31.	Na⁴	163	143	B	Meaning borrowed. The word originally was composed of *jan³*, *fur* (W., 116, A) and *i⁴*, *city*. *Na⁴* was the name of a city in Ssŭch'uan whose inhabitants wore furs. [W., 116, B; I., 11.]
32.	Ta⁴	37	451	A	See Table of Radicals.
33.	Pu⁴	1	120	A	Meaning borrowed. [W., 133, A; I., 19.]

(185)

No.	Wade's Spelling.	No. of Radical.	No. of Phonetic in Soothill.	Class of Formation.	Remarks.
		LESSON III.			PART I.
34.	Chang¹	57	353 (R.168)	C	[W., 113, A; I. 55.]
35.	T'ai²	30	718	B	An abbreviated form. The full form *t'ai²*, *a terrace* (see S., 885; I., 580), is composed of *chih⁴*, *to reach* (R. 133), *kao¹*, *high*, contracted, and an ancient form of R. 32, here used with the meaning of *summit*: a high place on the summit of which birds alight. [W, 75, B; I, 580]
36.	T'ung²	167	580	C	[W., 34, I I, 249]
37.	Yang²	85	151 (R. 123)	C	[W., 103, A; I., 253.]
38.	Chih³	120	348 R. 83)	C	[W., 114, A; I., 8.]
39.	Hên³	60	359 (R. 138)	C	[W., 26, L; I., 223.]
40.	Chi³	52	346	B	Composed of *shu⁴*, *a guard* (i.e. *men*, R. 9, with *spears*, R. 62) and R. 52, *little*, repeated (hence *very minute*): sentry are attentive to *small* things. [W., 90, D; I., 34.]
41.	Liang³	11	562	A	Meaning *two* is borrowed. The original meaning is *ounce*; it represents scales in equilibrium with two characters *ju⁴* (R. 11) suspended representing the things weighed. [W., 35, I; I., 35.]
42.	Tzŭ³	39	112	A	See Table of Radicals.
43.	Yen⁴	112	865 (R. 147)	C	[W., 158, C.]
44.	Wei⁴	9	84 (R. 117)	B	The position, or stall, at court in in which the *minister* (R. 9) stands *upright* (R. 117); hence, *position*, *dignity*. [W., 60, H; I., 216.]

No.	Wade's Spelling.	No. of Radical.	No of Phonetic in Soothill.	Class of Formation	Remarks.
			LESSON III.		PART II.
45.	Hsiang¹	118	847	C	[W., 158, B ; I., 106.]
46.	Tung¹	75	504	A	The *sun* (R. 72) low in the heavens and so shining below the top of the *tree*. [W., 120, K ; I., 22.]
47.	Hsi¹	146	775 (R. 146)	A	See Table of Radicals.
48.	Mo¹	200	494	B	Originally meant *vegetable fibre*, and composed of R. 200, *hemp*, and R. 52, *floss silk*, contracted. [W., 90, A ; I., 24.]
49.	I¹	1	1 (R.1)	A	
50.	Shên²	99	104 (R. 99)	B	Composed of R. 99, *sweet*, and *p'i*, meaning *a pair ;* hence, *affection for one's mate*, and so *superlative very*. [W., 73, B ; I., 23.]
51.	Ho².-Hê²	108	708	C	[W., 14, B ; I., 236.]
52.	Yüan²	10	388	B	The two strokes at the top are R. 7 used for *shang*⁴, *upon*. That which is *upon* a *man*, i.e., *the head, origin, principle*. [W., 29, H ; I., 93.]
53.	Chiao⁴	30	23 (R.68)	C	[W., 98, B : I., 117.]
			LESSON IV.		PART I.
54.	Ch'i¹	1	326		Present form has no significance. Old form was composed of seven lines. [W., 33, A ; I., 32 ; C., 396.]
55.	Pa¹	12	392 (R. 12.)	A	See Table of Radicals.
56.	To¹	36	269	A	Signifies reduplication ; hence, *many*. [W., 64 ; I., 184.]
57.	Fên¹	18	395	B	A *knife* that *divides*, the old meaning of R. 12. [W., 18, B ; I., 181.]
58.	Chih¹	75	539	C	[I., 815.]
59.	Mao²	82	375 (R. 82)	A	See Table of Radicals.
60.	Ling²	173	438	C	[W., 14, I ; I.. 61.]

No.	Wade's Spelling.	No. of Radical.	No. of Phonetic in Soothill.	Class of Formation.	Remarks.
61.	Chiu[3]	5	302		Present form has no significance. Original form was composed of nine lines. [W., 23, A ; I., 33 ; C., 398.]
62.	Pai[3]	106	805	C	[W., 88, B ; I., 58.]
63.	Shao[3]	42	122		
64.	Êrh[4]	7	1		See Table of Radicals.
65.	Ssŭ[4]	31	773		See old forms in Chalfant, composed of four lines. [W., 42. A ; I., 29 ; C., 393.]
		LESSON IV.			PART II.
66.	Ch'ien[1]	24	24	C	[W., 24, D ; I., 59 ; C., 403.]
67.	Shêng[1]	128	404	C	The phonetic has more than phonetic significance. It is composed of R. 79, *to strike*, and a primitive with the meaning *musical stone:* the effect on the *ear* of striking musical stones is *sound*. [W., 173, A ; I., 71.]
68.	Ch'ien[1]	167	719	C	[W., 22, D.]
69.	Shui[2]	149	52	C	[W., 168, A ; I., 21.]
70.	Hsieh[3]	40	688	C	[W., 138, C ; I., 41.]
71.	Yao[4]	146	776		Meaning borrowed. [W., 50, N ; I., 16.]
72.	Tzŭ[4]	39	112	C	[W., 94, A ; I., 1.]
73.	Wan[4]	140	576	A	Meaning borrowed. [W., 23, H ; I., 60.]
74.	Tiao[4]	30	557	B	Originally composed of *man* (vertical stroke) and *bow* (R. 57) which is carried over the shoulder; hence, *suspend*. [W., 28, H ; I., 266.]
75.	Ti[4]	118	249	C	[W., 87,E ; I., 86.]

CHINESE INDEX.

190

1 一
一 49
七 54
三 17
下 183
上 182, 259a
不 33
且 454
丙 476b
並 943

2 丨
中 138

3 丶
主 354

4 丿
久 849
之 539
乘 684

5 乙
乙 487a
九 61
也 7
乾 189

6 亅
了 95
事 234

7 二
二 64
五 20
些 28
亞 645

8 亠
交 609
京 239

9 人
人 2
介 776
今 347
什 50, 547
仍 438
他 9
以 180
令 946
伙 168
份 868
任 451

伏 717
件 233
仰 850
你 15
住 254
作 44
位 263, 634
伸 897
但 336
何 506
估 910
伯 554
使 215
來 144
便 458
信 84
保 531
修 803
倆 612
倘 782
條 743
倍 600
倫 466
倒 937
候 356

們 12
個 24
傢 159
做 263
假 718
停 594
傘 279
傳 202
催 922
備 543
傢 524
儉 636
價 398
儘 264
儲 491
儲 773

10 儿
元 52
兄 304
先 10
光 323
兒 81

11 入
入 668

內 649
全 471
兩 41

12 八
八 55
六 23
公 504
共 601
其 626

13 冂
同 421
再 133

14 冖

15 冫
冬 435
決 925
冰 416
況 517
冷 368a
准 584
凍 429
凉 193

16 几
凡 420

凳 203

17 凵

18 刀
刀 158
分 57
切 371
划 874
初 343
刺 667
別 272
到 184
剌 901
刻 373
前 327
剛 346

19 力
力 680
功 502
加 591
助 302
務 390
動 455
勞 781

20 勹
勹 529
包 737

21 匕
匕 247
匙 274

22 匚
匠 819

23 匸

24 十
十 18
千 66
午 365
半 372
南 244

25 卜

26 卩
却 444
卿 608

27 厂
厚 798
原 226

28 厶
去 170

29 又
又 456
叉 157
及 449
友 289
反 875
叔 331
受 892

30 口
口 128
可 179
司 826
右 358
另 942
句 117
只 334
古 720
台 35
向 615
各 430
名 642
合 208

吃 188
吊 74
否 935
叫 53
告 102
吳 546
呂 838
吧 266
咱 468
周 767
呀 501
命 945
和 422
呢 221
哈 538/878
哪 463a
哇 498
哼 653
唪 836
員 924
啊 141
哥 307
問 98
啦 142
商 257

唫 344
單 324
喝 156
喜 533
喂 477
喫 188
嗎 503
嘗 836
譏 790
嘩 797
器 821

31 囗
四 65
回 489
因 222
固 446
國 143
園 275
圓 906a

32 土
地 185
在 89
坐 147
城 611
場 629

塔 760
塊 25
報 705
墨 8
壞 753

33 士
壺 176

34 夂

35 夂
夏 443

36 夕
外 87
多 56
夜 369
夠 } 101
够 }

37 大
大 32
太 299
天 345
夫 460
失 736

夾 580
奉 604
奇 659
獎 145

38 女
女 312
好 6
如 273
她 461
妥 230
姑 325
姐 313
妹 318
姓 149
要 71
娘 329
婚 686
婦 711

39 子
子 42
字 72
存 396
孝 341
孟 704

李 442	將 172	嶺 721	幫 287	**57 弓**	**弓**	快 99	忠 763
孩 328	專 769			弟 320		志	忽 479
孫 687	對 88	**47 巛**	**51 干**	張 34		忘	怪 436
學 125		州 241	平 847	強 271		怕	念 890
			年 309			思	怎 297
40 宀	**42 小**	**48 工**	幷 943	**58 彑**		恨	恐 85
宅 465	小 27	工 459	幹 342			情	惜 104
守 335	少 63/322a	左 353		**59 彡**		您	悶 227
安 545		差 255	**52 幺**	形 550		意	愛 536
宋 747	**43 尢**		幾 40	彩 427		想	慢 291
完 124	尤 625	**49 己**		影 938		憑	懂 224
官 137	就 134	己 113	**53 广**			應	768
定 370		已 129	庄 305	**60 彳**			656
宗 881	**44 尸**	巴 526	底 181	往 744			19
宜 572	局 464		店 265	彼 294			673
家 79	屋 154	**50 巾**	府 930	待 783			116
客 153	屢 614	巾 789a	度 911	很 39			635
富 557	魯 757	市 646	座 765	後 340			453
容 470	屬 292	布 587	尉 177	從 210			100
害 725		希 552	朝 766	得 91			452
寄 750	**45 屮**	帖 735	廳 140	徧 132			110
實 258	山	郗 287		微 899			377
寫 70	**46 山**	師 191	**54 廴**				
寶 817	山 462	帶 606		**61 心**			
	出 285	常 348	**55 廾**	心 105			
41 寸	岸 877	帳 777		必 391			
封 80	歲 317	帽 800	**56 弋**	忙 225			
			式 216			**62 戈**	
						成 507	

我 14	梃 815	攏 425	新 505	景 664	李 16
或 410	掃 213	**65 支**	斷 762	暖 441	東 46
戚 321	接 650	支 394	**70 方**	曉 111	牀 174
戲 633	掛 748	**66 攴**	方 173	**73 曰**	板 198
63 戶	掉 893	收 406	於 548	更 283	林 716
戶 280	排 864	攻 915	旁 175	書 1	枉 397
房 82	捫 595	改 936	旅 851	最 301	枝 58
所 94	描 661	放 169	**71 无**	會 115	柔 831
64 手 扌	換 407	攺 746	旡 445	**74 月**	架 281
手 扌 401	褪 756	教 136	**72 日**	月 374	桌 171
才 332	掌 774	敗 561	日 355	有 5	案 512
打 476	捲 837	敝 152	早 368	朋 288	根 941
扠 473	搭 542	敢 530	昌 805	服 570	桂 823
把 167	搽 192	敦 738	易 481	望 559	校 845
扰 917	搬 379	散 432	明 106	期 363	椅 130
拉 676	推 675	數 401a/404	是 29	**75 木**	棚 178
抬 385	攄 480	**67 文**	昨 349	木 262	棟 903
拐 814	撤 186	文 657	星 362	本 21	極 171
抽 822	擔 384	**68 斗**	春 433	未 854	棃 490
拜 784	標 714	斗	時 350	末 618	棠 508
挑 381	擁 593	**69 斤**	駒 366	材 577	棉 513
揶 447	擦 192	斤 497	晨 364	村 641	概 579
捐 499	擊 916	所 279a	晚 367	杓 164	業 218
拿 162	擱 155		晴 415		楚 560
	擠 598				127

樓 759	80 毋	油 832	激 620	爾 887	球 624
標 827	毋 314	活 311	濱 879	90 爿	壁 709
樣 236	每 426	洲 541	濟 632	91 片	97 瓜
樹 731	81 比	洋 37		片 727	98 瓦
機 544	比 277	洗 196	86 火 灬	版 see 198	瓶 698
橋 812	82 毛	津 590	火 597	92 牙	99 甘
櫃 175	毛 59	消 619	炸 863	93 牛	甚 50
76 欠	83 氏	海 516	烟 488	牛 679	100 生
欠 408	氏 643	淨 200	烈 637	牠 652	生 11
次 603	84 气	清 120	無 387	物 710	101 用
歇 713	气	涼 193	然 437	特 602	用 220
歎 712	氣 428	港 515	煩 835	94 犬 犭	102 田
歡 527	85 水 氵	添 824	照 843	猜 651	由 510
77 止		淺	熟	獸 682	甲 476a
正 135	水 195	深	燒 514	95 立	男 308
此 295	永 816	滿 564	熱 860		界 267
歲 317	江 691	滙 492	營 201	96 玉	留 207
78 歹	汗 801	湊 779	553	王 212	畝 475
	沒 3	溫 486	87 爪 爫	玉 818	畢 694
79 殳	汽 681	游 123	為 232	珍 807	署 605
段 671	沉 386	湯 622	88 父	珠 690	畫 535
穀 101	法 229	準 859	父 319	理 813	當 223
毀 745	泥 448	漢 534	爺 330	現 357	
	沏 858	漂 751	89 爻		
	河 791	滯 947	爽 665		

103 疋	广	看 96	神 660	118 竹	絫 865	罗 921
104 广		省 399	票 409	笑 913	紹 780	羊
病 638		相 238	禮 702	第 75	織 794	123 羊
癮 663		眞 270		筈 205	統 933	美 555
105 癶		眼 333	114 肉	筆 4	紫 581	着 206
登 203		眾 431	115 禾	等 146	給 112	124 羽
癸 286		睛 896	秋 434	答 528	結 693	習 126
106 白		睜 895	移 906	節 886	經 122	125 老
白 107		睡 484	稍 898	算 402	絲 788	老 315
百 62			稅 519	管 22	綱 630	126 而
的 26	110 矛		稼 306	箔 214	綢 573	而 439
107 皮	111 矢		稱 640	箱 45	縣 648	127 耒
皮 578	知 204		種 322	簡 662	練 726	128 耳
108 皿	短 631		穗 795	籃 624	緞 586	聞 920
盂 276	112 石		穩 940	119 米	縫 569	聯 696
益 723	石 811		116 穴	料 588	緊 228	聲 67
盛 733	硯 43		空 463	粗 565	緻 730	職 884
盒 51	硬 802		穿 692	精 654	總 388	聽 90
盤 163	碟 161		窗 268	糖 829	織 789	129 聿
109 目	碗 166		117 立	糟 882	續 482	130 肉 月
目 457	磁 697		立 616	120 糸	纔 351	育 944
直 658	磅 607		站 599	紀 316	121 缶	胖 724
	113 示 礻		端 380	紅 574	罐 520	背 339
	社 556			紙 38	122 网 罒	
					罷 266	

150 谷		148 角		145 衣			136 舛	131 臣
議 495	親 303	角 解 934	行 772	衣 562	蓄 778	舘 852	能 165	
讀 549	覺 485		街 256	衫 787	範 707		脚 866	
讓 912		149 言	衕 741	袋 840	荔 521	137 舟	脖 905	
151 豆		言 695	御 740	裁 568	葛 839	船 551	腦 908	
豈 848		討 532	衛 734	裕 558	萬 73	艙 870	臉 197	
豐 592		記 764		裡 83	藥 728		臘 375	
152 豕		許 400		裏 83	蕉 496	138 艮		臥 187
		訴 103		製 846	薄 792	色 589		臨 872
153 豸		評 927		裳 566	藍 576			132 自
		話 86		複 483	蘋 509	139 色		自 118
154 貝		該 378		褲 779	蘭 793	色		
貨 820		詳 472a		襖 583				133 至
費 405		試 493		襪 785	140 艸			至 298
貴 150		說 76			花 269			致 749
買 259		認 114		146 西	范 876			
賀 703		請 92		西 47	茂 732			134 臼
質 891		課 131			苦 853			與 722
賤 151		談 469		147 見	英 139			興 563
賬 403		誰 69		見 97	若 160			舉 700
賠 885		諸 919		規 360	茶 755			舊 672
賣 260		謝 525			荊 833			
		識 109			荷 305			135 舌
155 赤					莊 770			舍 613
					華 617			舒 900
156 走					菜 867			鋪 261
走 290					葉 841			

| 157 足 | 158 身 | 159 車 | 160 辛 | 161 辰 | 162 辵 | 163 邑 | 164 酉 | 165 釆 | 166 里 | 167 金 | 168 長 | 169 門 | 170 阝 | 171 隶 | 172 隹 | 173 雨 | 174 青 | 175 非 | 176 面 | 177 革 | 178 韋 | 179 韭 | 180 音 | 181 頁 |

起 352
趕 278
越 300
趙 889
趕 278
趣 674

跑 699
路 252
跟 567

身 688

車 242
軍 621
較 284
輕 382
輪 873
輿 923
轎 683

辛 846
辣 842

辦 231
辯 883

近 253
迎 904
送 392
這 30
通 240
逢 337
過 419
進 148
運 296
遇 518
道 561a
遍 217
遠 132
遣 250
還 628
遲 194
遺 929
邊 742
邊 77

那 {31,83a}
都 78
郵 739
鄰 610

鐘 361
鑰 282
鑼 809
鎮 647

酥 825

長 932

門 243
開 251
閉 190
閒 326
閣 310
關 237

金 918
鈕 796
鉛 68
鈴 596
銀 771
銅 36
鋒 655
錢 13
錯 219
鎖 248

附 754
阿 894
除 395
陰 414
陽 467
隊 639
陸 758
隔 246
隨 450
險 888

雅 701
雖 440
雙 786
雜 472
難 857
離 245
難 108

雨 423
雪 424
雲 418
零 60
電 478
雷 417
霜 413
露 752

青 383

非 729

面 537

革 926
靴 804
鞋 810

韋

韭

音 121
響 939

頂 666
頂 293
須 376
順 235
頓 869
預 523
頗 914
領 694
頭 211
顯 806
顏 571

願487	185 首香	188 骨	196 鳥	202 黍	208 鼠
顧338	186 香500	體719	鴉715	203 黑	209 鼻齊
182 風	187 馬	189 高	197 鹵鹿麥麻	黑點黨359 93 931	210 齊575
風411	馬駝駱騎驃驗驢474 902 910 627 678 494 677	高689	198	204 黹黽鼎鼓	211 齒龍
颷412		190 髟	199		212 龍511
183 飛		191 鬥	200 麻麽834 48	205	213 龜
184 食		鬧706	201 黃黃830	206	214 龠
食飯餐餞861 199 856 522		194 鬼魚		207 鼓761	
		195 魚862			

ENGLISH INDEX.

A

ability 342, 12^{27}
able 115, 165, 179, 8^8
about to 172, 872, 8^7
above 182
abundant 733
according to 452, 480
account 403, 777
account-book 14^{25}
account, current 24^{11}
acre 475
add 824
add to 591
add up 14^{21}
adjust 575
affairs 234, 9^{12}, 18^{16}
affairs, classifier of 233
after 340
after all 17^4, 20^{14}, 28^7
afternoon 13^{18,19}, 18^{23}
afterwards 618, 15^{29}, 18^{13}, 20^{14}
again 133, 483
again and again 17^3
age 12^{11}
ago, two days 13^{12}
air 428, 23^{12}
all 78, 420, 431, 471 601, 919, 15^{13}
all 13^{29}
all the more 300, 11^{23}
all together 15^{14}
allow, 470, 584, 912, 16^8
already 129, 6^{15}, 20^7
also, and 7, 16^1, 449, 456
alter 936
although 440, 15^{17}
altogether 15^{16}, 19^{20}
amend 30^7
ancient 720
and, also 7, 450, 456
and, yet 430
animals 683
animal-power 22^5
announce 705, 922, 30^6, 30^{27}
another 942, 12^{26}
answer 18^3
anxious, to be 25^4
apart from 25^6
apartments, woman's 310
apologise 22^{38}
appetising 27^{13}
apple 509
apple, a small 17^{22}
Arab 29^3
ardent 637
arena 629
arise 352, 563
army 20^{26}
arrange 69^5, 864
arrive 184, 8^{14}
artisan, title of 8^{17}
as for 30^{25}
as if 29^{16}
as, like 273
as quickly as possible 12^{18}
ask 98
ask, may I ? 21^1
assent 18^4
at 89, 548
at, to be 89
at last 618
at liberty to 16^8
at once 20^8
at present 16^5
at the beginning 13^6
athletics 20^{25}
attack 915, 30^{11}
attain 449
aunt 325
autumn 434, 15^{33}
available 16^{22}

B

back (n.) 339
baggage 19^{33}
balance to credit 14^{15}
balance to debit 14^{16}
ball 624
banana 496, 17^6
bank 772, 24^8
bank-draft 779, 24^{15}
bank-note 24^{16}
bank-note, cheque 409
bank, shore 877
basin 276
basket 623
basket ball 20^{17}
be (to) 29
bear (to) 833
bear, endure 14^9
beat (to) 476
beautiful 555
beautiful (to hear) 7^5
beautiful (to see) 7^4
because 232, 99
bedroom 8^3
bee 828
beef-steak, roast 27^{19}
before 10, 327
beforehand 523
begin 27^{14}
beginning 343
beginning, at the 13^6
beginning, from the 9^3
behind 12^{16}
bell 361, 596
belong to 292
below 181, 183, 8^5
belt, leather 25^{22}
benefit 667, 723
benefit, a 9^{16}, 23^2
beside 8^4
besides 942
bicycle 20^{29}
bitter 846 853
bitterness 27^6
black 359
blend 928
blow to 412
blow (to) (wind) 15^6
blue 576
board 198, 670
boat 551, 28^8
boat, open 874
body 688, 719, 23^5
body, the whole 29^{15}
boil (to) 190
bolt (to) 237
book 1
book-shelves 11^2
boots 804
born 11
borrow 669
boundaries of a country 23^{19}
bow 784
bowl 166
box 45
box (small) 51
brain 908
branch 58
branch, a ; pay 394
bride 22^{21}
bridge 812
bring 7^9
bring in 11^{14}
bring out 11^{15}
brisk 21^{15}
brittle 825
brittle-toffee 26^{25}
broom 205, 214, 9^4
brother, elder 304, 307, 12^4
brother, eminent 19^{10}
brother, younger 320, 12^5
brothers 12^6
business, must 390
bustle 706
busy 225
but 334, 336, 444, 14^{10}, 15^{25}
but still 15^{23}, 15^{27}
button 796, 25^{19}
buy 259
by all means 21^{17}
by, from 510

C

cabin 870, 28^4
cabinet 30^3
cabinet meeting 30^{22}
cake, classifier of ink 25
cakes 27^{21}
call (to) 53
camel 902, 909, 29^4
capital, the 239
car, dining 19^{35}
car, restaurant 19^{35}
careful 20^{10}
careful, be 9^8, 16^{23}
carpenter 26^1
carry 606
carry (on a pole) 381
carry (on shoulder) 384
carry (people on shoulders) 385
cart 22^7
case (law) 941
cash, 13, 3^4
cash, string of 74
catty 497
cause, a 222, 30^{31}
cause to go (to) 749
cent 57
ceremony 701
certain 446, 16^3
certainly 15^{21}
certainly may not 24^{1,2}
change 926, 936
characters (written) 72
chair 178
chat (to) 469, 16^{11}
cheap 151, 19^{16}
cheque 14^{27}
cheque, bank-note 409
chest 775
Chiang-hsi (province) 22^{34}

(200)

(201)

child 328
China 7¹, 770
Chinese food 27¹⁰
Ching-Chow 24³
cigar 26¹⁸
cigarettes 26¹⁴
cinnamon 844
cinnamon flower 26²⁴
circumstances 664, 18⁹
city 241, 611
city-moat 758
class, first 19⁸
classifier of affairs 233
classifier of books 21
classifier of chairs, knives, jugs, etc. 167
classifier, general 24
classifier of hills and temples 765
classifier of ink 25
classifier of letters 80
classifier of long things 743
classifier of paper 34
classifier of pearls 806
classifier of pens 22
classifier of pencils 58
classifier of persons 44
classifier of rooms 855
classifier of sedans 685
clean 8²⁰
clean a pipe 26²⁰
clear 106, 127, 415, 12¹⁴
clear and cool 23¹³
clear away (to) 186, 8¹³
clear sky 15⁴
clever 21¹³
close (to) 251
cloth 587
cloth, a 789a
clothes 19³,⁴, 562, 566, 570
clothes, lined 19¹³
clothes, unlined 19¹⁴
clouds 15⁹, 418, 427
coarse 565
coat, fur 19¹¹
coat, quilted 583
coat, wadded 19¹²
cold 368a

collars 25²⁴
collect (to) 17¹⁴, 425, 486
collectively 601
College, Teachers' Training 22²²
colloquial 21²¹
colour 19⁵, 571
come 144
come in 11¹⁰
come out 11¹³
comfits 522
comfortable 29¹⁷, 900
command 945
commands 30³⁵
commerce 257
company 639
company, a 26²⁶
compare 11⁶
compare 11⁶, 277, 284
compared with 11⁷
complete 19⁷, 507, 767
complimentary, over 7⁸
condition 18⁹
congratulate 22¹⁶, 703
constantly 348
consult 17²
continent 541
continue 21⁹, 482
contribute 499
control 774, 933
convenient 17⁵, 18²⁴, 458
conversation 22²⁶
converse (to) 20¹¹
cook, a 8⁹, 8¹⁸
cool 25¹¹, 193
copper 36
copper cash 3⁴⁷,
coppers 58
correct 88, 135, 223
cottage 613
cotton 579
couch 174
count (to); number, a 404
counter, a 775
country 20³, 608
cow 679
credit balance 14¹⁵
credit, nett balance to 14¹⁷
criticise 30³⁰, 917, 927
crow, a 715
crowd (to) 593
crowded 19³¹

cups 7¹²
current account 24¹¹
customs duty 17⁹
cut 568, 901
cut off 762
cut out 568

D

danger 888
dare 530
dare to do 25³
dark 414
dative, sign of 112
daughter 12²²
day after to-morrow, the 13¹¹
day before yesterday, the 13⁹
day, heaven 345
day, sun 355
daytime 13²⁰
dear 150
debit balance 14¹⁶
debit, nett balance to 14¹⁸
decide 13²⁸, 30²³ 762, 925
deduct 14²⁴
deduct, exclude 395
deep 564
define 605
delicate 27¹², 730
depart (to) 290
depend on 729
depend upon, something to 23⁸
dependable 24¹⁴
dessert 27²⁰
destroy 561
detail 472a
detail, in 16²³
determination 479
diamond 26¹⁰
different 255
different, not very 10⁴,⁵
difficult 108
difficulty 6¹⁰
dining-car 19³⁵
dining-room 8¹⁶
disclose 752
discuss 17², 30¹², 30¹⁸, 495
dissipate 619
distant 250
distant from 245
distinct 6¹²
district 241, 648
divan 174
divide equally 529
do 209, 263, 634

do not 272
do, unable to 11⁹
dog-days 717
dollar 52
dollars 3⁸, 10¹³, 19²¹
donkey 677
door 243, 280
doorway 12²⁵
double 19¹⁹, 483, 786
double (to) 600
double-breasted 25¹⁸
double-lined 580
down 183
dragon 511
draw (to) 535
draw out 822
draw (pictures) 661
dress-suit 25³⁰
drill 23⁶, 714
drink (to) 156
drum 761
dry 189
dull day 15²
duty 12¹⁹
duty, customs 17⁹
duty, tax 519
dwell 254
dwelling-place 21³

E

each 430
early 368
earth 185
east 46
easy 16¹⁴, 481
eat 8¹⁵, 188, 861
economical 14¹⁹
educated 6⁴
educational organisation 30²⁸
effect 30³³, 939
eight 55
elated 22³⁰
elder brother 12⁴, 304, 307
elder sister 12⁷, 313
electric 478
electricity 22²
11 a.m.—1 p.m. 365
employ 215
employment 18¹⁶
empty 463
enclitic particle (son) 42, 81
endure, bear 14⁹
England 7²
enough 101
ensure 23²³
enter 296, 668
envelope, an 5¹⁹

equal 529
escort, send, take 392
especially 20³¹
estate 560
eternal 816
Europe 540
even (adj.) 529, 575
evening 13¹⁶
evening, late 367
every 426
every time 15¹⁰
exactly 534
examine 494
excellent 20²⁴, 271
exchange 407
exciting 20³⁰
exclamatory particle 477, 498, 501, 653, 894
exclude, deduct 395
excuse 883
exercise 20²⁵
experience 16⁴, 18⁶, 18¹⁹, 30²⁶
explain 934
expletive particle 538
export 28¹³
express letter 23²⁴
express train 19²⁷, 19²⁹
extent, to this 9¹⁹
extent, to that 9²⁰
extreme 491
extremely 299
eye 333, 457, 896

F

face 197, 537
fall 893
fall of frost 15⁷
false 718
far out, not very 10⁷
farmhouse 305
fashionable 19⁶
fat 724
father 12¹, 319, 330
father's elder brother 554
favourable 235
fear 11²²
fear (to) 291, 297
feel 21²², 485
feelings 224
female 312
Fêng-t'ai 19²⁵
Fêng-'tien 19²⁸
few 40, 63
field 629
filial 341

fine 730
finish (to) 124, 266
finish an account 28¹²
finish work 17¹⁵
fire 597, 680
first (surname) 704
first class 19⁸
first month 13²⁵
first stem 476a
firstly 16¹⁵
fish 862
fish, fried 27¹⁸
five 20
fixed 370
flannel 25²⁷
flourishing 139, 592
flower 269
flower garden 11⁴
flower pot 11⁵
flower vase 22³⁵
follow 450, 451, 567
follow convenience 16⁷
food 199, 861, 856
food, Chinese 27¹⁰
food, ordinary 18²²
food, Western 27¹¹
foot 866
ford 590
foreign 37
foreign relations 30³⁴
foreign tailor 25⁷
forest 23¹⁰, 716
forget 763
fork 157
form 550
formerly 17¹⁰, 20¹, 20², 20⁶
former years, in 20⁴
four 65
fowl 857
fraction 60
fragrant 500
frame 281
freeze 15⁵, 429
freightage 17⁸
frequently 20¹², 614
fried fish 27¹⁸
friend 288, 289
friend 11¹⁸, 22¹⁴
friend, to meet a 18²⁶
friendly 11¹⁹
from 210, 567
from, by 510
frost, fall of 15⁷
frost (white) 413
fruit 17²⁶, 27²², 866
fry 863
full 492
fur-coat 19¹¹

furniture 7¹³
future auxiliary 71

G

game 20¹⁵
garden 275
garden, flower 11⁴
general 240, 933
general meeting 30¹⁷
general store 26⁷
genitive, sign of 539
gentle 22²⁸
girl 12²³, 326
give 112, 609
go 170, 209, 290
go in 11¹²
go out 11¹¹, 12²⁴, 285
go to, 259a, 744
God of town, Temple of 24⁵
gold 918
gong 809
good 6
goods 820, 28¹⁷
government 30⁵, 30¹⁰, 746
graduate (to) 22²³
grandson 687
grant 584
grant leave 23¹
grasp (to) 159a
great 776
greet 18²⁵
gross 876
ground, on the 8⁶
group 639
guarantee 19¹⁵
guarantee (to) 23²³
guard (to) 335
guess 651
guest 7⁶, 153
guest hall 7⁷

H

habit 663
hail 417
half 372
hall 140
hand 401
handkerchief 25²¹
hang (to) 748
Hankow 28²
happy 22²⁹, 527, 533
Harbin 28¹⁰
harm 23³, 725
harvest 317
hasten 889
hat 25²⁰, 800
hate 536

have 5
he 9
he, his 626
head 29⁶, 211
hear 5¹⁷, 920
heart 105
heaven 345
heavy 386, 393
help 11²¹, 23⁷, 287, 302
help (to) 632
hemp 834
hence, two days 13¹³
her 626
here 5⁵, ⁸, ¹¹
high 689
hill 462
hinder 947
holiday 734a
home 79
Home Affairs 30¹³
honest 738
honey 845a
honey bee 26²⁷
honey-peaches 17²³
Hong-Kong 17²⁰
honorific particle 141
honourable 150
hope 18¹², 552, 559
horse 474
host 354
hot 201, 842
hot, too 26¹⁷
hot season 717
hotel 10¹², 27⁵, 852
house 82
House Duty question 30⁸
how 9¹³, 17¹³, 227
how ? 848
how dare I ? 27³
how many ? 4¹, 40
how much 4¹, 9²¹
how much less 17⁷
how much more 17⁷
humble 151
hundred 62
husband 16¹⁰, 460
husband and wife 22³⁶
hygiene 23¹⁵

I

I 14
ice 416
ice-cold 15⁸
idea 6⁹
if 14¹, 25⁵, 389, 782
ill, illness 638
immediately 20⁸, 22¹⁸

(203)

imperative particle 266
implements 7¹³
important 9¹⁵
in, 83, 548
in detail 16²³
in former years 20⁴
in front 12¹⁵
in that way 9²⁰
in the night 13²¹
inadequate 712
incessantly 20⁹
incorrect 219
infuse 858
infuse tea 27¹⁶
ink 8
inkslab 3², 43
inn 265
inquire 25²⁹
inside 5⁴, 83, 649
insurance 28¹⁸
interest 24¹², 674, 768
interrogative particle 48, 221, 463a, 503
introduce 780
is it not so ? 2³
is there ? 1³
it 652
it is 29
it, its 626

J

jade 818
jar, pot 520
jewel 709
jewellers 26⁸
join 693, 696
join, to 482
jug 176
just 17¹⁶
just (adj.) 504
just now 13⁴,⁵, 346, 351

K

keep, to 207
keep, preserve 396
kettle 176
key 11¹, 274, 282
Kiang-hsi (province) 22³⁴
kind 795, 881
kind, a 236
kingdom 143
kitchen 8², 177
knife 158

know 9¹, 111, 204

L

lady 12¹⁰
lagoon 515
land 13
landlord 26⁴
lane 23²², 740, 741
lapel 785
large 32
last, at 618
last month 13²⁷
late 929
laugh 913
late, evening 367
law 229, 946
lead 606, 644
lead (n.) 68
lead-pencil 4⁴
leaf 28⁹, 727, 841
lean on 729
learn 125
leather belt 25²²
leave, to grant 23¹
left (hand) 353
leisure 16²⁴, 734a
length 743
length of time 344
less, how much 17⁷
lesson 131
lest 11²²
letter 84, 23²⁹
letters, classifier of 80
letter, express 23²⁴
letter, registered 23²⁰
liberty to, at 16⁸
lichi 521, 17²²
light (adj.) 382
light (n.) 323
like 636
like (to) 18⁵, 20¹⁸
like, as 273
like, as if 29¹⁶
lined, double 580
listen 90
literature 657
little, a 29¹³, 93
live, to 254
lively 21²⁰, 22²⁰, 656
lock 248
locksmith 26²
longcloth 790, 797
long time 849
long wished to meet you 27²
look (to) 96
look and see 5¹⁵
look, to have a 5¹⁶

look after 843
look up to 850
loosen 934
lord 354
lose, 736, 742, 885
lose money 28¹⁵
loss 880
love 635
luggage 19³³
luggage, to weigh 19³⁴
lung-yen fruit 17²¹
luxuriant 23¹¹, 732

M

machine 544
make 263, 634
make mind easy 18³
make tea 27¹⁶
make up (to) 486
male 308
man 2
man-power 22⁴
manage 28¹¹, 231, 813, 826
management, method of 9¹⁷
manager 24⁶
managing, way of 23²⁶
mandarin, a 137
Mandarin language 7³
manners 22²⁵
manufacture 845
many 56
many, very 14¹³
market 646
market-town 647
marry 12¹², 22¹⁵
marriage 686
master 354
material 588
material (n.) 577
materials 19⁹
matter, no 17¹²
may 8⁸
meal 856, 868
meaning 6⁹, 116
means, by all 21¹⁷
measure 708, 911
medicine 728
meet 17¹⁴, 30¹², 419, 561a, 650
meet a friend, to 18²⁶
meeting, a general, 30¹⁷
mention 756
merely 14¹¹
merit 502

method 16¹⁷, 223a
middle 138
mild 26¹⁹
mile (Chinese) 249
military 621
mind 105
mind, of one 15¹¹, 20¹⁹
miscellaneous 16¹⁹, 472
money 13
money, ready 14²⁶
money, silver 19²²
moon, month 374
more 517
more, how much 17⁷
moreover 454, 517, 943
moreover, also 16¹
morning 13¹⁴, 13¹⁷, 364
most 298, 301
mother 12², 314, 329
motor-car 22⁹
moult. 28²⁰
mountain range 721
mouth 128
move 29¹⁴, 447, 455, 906
moving 22¹
Mr. 1⁷
mud 448
mule 678
musical pipe 838
must 14²,³,⁴,⁵,⁶, 15¹⁸, 376, 388, 391
must, business 390
must, ought 14⁸
mutual 11²⁰, 238

N

name 21², 642
name, a 585
name (to) 53
name of a river (Han) 751
Nanking 10⁹ᵃ, 15³⁵
napkin 789a
nature 28¹⁶, 890
near 23²¹, 253, 754
near the time 28⁵
neck, 29⁹, 905
needed 9⁵
needed, not 9⁶
neighbour 20⁵, 610
net 630, 921
net-ball 20²¹
nett balance to credit 14¹⁷

nett balance to debit 14^{18}
nevertheless 15^{22}
new 505
news 30^{1,2}
next year 13^{22}
night 369
night, in the 13^{21}
nine 61
no 2^2
no matter 17^{12}
noon 13^{15}, 366
north 247
Normal School 22^{22}
north-east 21^5
not 3, 33, 383, 387
not as good as 11^8
not equal to 11^8
not far wrong 10^6
not included 27^9
not, or not 935
not very different 10^{4,5}
not very far wrong 10^7
not yet 854
nothing else for it 22^{19}
novel 21^6
now 347, 357
number, count (to) 404
numbness 834
nurture 944

O

obedient 12^{17}
objects 710
obtain 91
occasions, on all 20^{13}
office 464, 884
officer 924
official 137
of one mind 15^{11}, 20^{19}
often 20^{12}
oil 832
old 315, 672
on the ground 8^6
on the other hand 937
once, at 20^8
one 49
one-third 21^8
only 323, 324, 334, 336
only (but) 15^{24}, 15^{26}
open 10^1, 21^7, 190
open the eyes 895
opinion 18^1
opinion, public 30^9

opium 23^{16}
opportunity 18^{14}
optative, sign of 526
or not 935
or, whether 410
orchid 793
ordinal, sign of 75
ordinary food 18^{22}
origin 226
originally 9^{10}, 9^{11}
ought 377, 378
ought, must 14^8
outline 605
outside 5^3, 87
overcoat 583
over-complimentary 7^8
overtake, unable to 11^9
owe 408
ox 679

P

page 666
pagoda 24^4, 760
paint (to) 661
pair 786
pair, a 22^{33}
paper 38
paper, classifier of 34
parcel 737
parents 12^3
part 868
participle, present auxiliary 206
particle, enclitic 81 42
particle, euphonic 463a
particle, exclamatory 477, 653
particle, expletive 538
particle, final 498, 501
particle, honorific 141
particle, imperative 266
particle, interrogative 48, 221, 503
party 931
party, government 30^{10}
pass (to) 148
past 122
past auxiliary 95, 142

pattern 216, 707
pay (to); branch 394
pay respects 25^1
pay, send 14^{23}
peace 27^4, 545, 847
peaceable 30^{32}
peach 512
pear 508, 7^{17}
pear, a kind of 513
pearl 26^9, 690, 808
pearl, classifier of 806
Peking 10^9
pen 4
pen, classifier of 22, 58
pen and ink 1^1
pencil 4^4
pencil, classifier of 58
penetrate 240, 337
perceive 97
perfectly ripe 17^{11}
perhaps promise 400
permit (to) 534
people 20^{28}, 643
person 2
person, classifier of 44
picture 535
piece (classifier of ink) 25
pity 656
pity, what a 21^{16}
place, a 8^{10}, 119, 173
place (to) 155, 169
plainly 21^{10}
plan 553
plant (to) 306
plate 163
plate, small 161
plum 16
plural, sign of 12, 28
point, a 93
point (of a weapon) 655
polish (to) 192
porcelain 696
porterage 27^{15}
position (classifier of persons) 44
possessive, sign o 26
post-office 23^{17}, 739
pot, jar 520,
potential auxiliary 91
pouch 26^{21}, 840
pound (weight) 607
practice 726

practise (to) 6^{18}, 123, 126
praise 640
praise (to) 145
precious 807, 817
premier 30^{20}
prepare 17^{25}, 524
present, at 16^5
present participle 206
present, to make a 22^{31}
presents 22^{32}
preserve, keep 396
president 30^{21}
president of a department 30^{14}
pretend 718
previously 20^7
price 10^{14}, 264
price 21^{23}
prince 212
probably 9^7, 218
process 16^{17}
profession 560
promise, perhaps 400
pronunciation 6^{14}
propelling 22^1
propose a motion 30^{15}
prosperous 805
protect 531, 734
platform, station 19^{23}
play 633
pleasant to hear 7^5
pleased 22^{30}
plot 21^{12}
public 504
public, the 923
public opinion 30^9
publish 21^{18}
pull 676
pungent 842
pupil 6^{13}
pure 23^{13}, 120 200,
purple 581
purpose, with one 15^{12}
pursue 278
push 598, 675
put down 8^{12}, 169
put forth 286

Q

quarter 373
question 30^{16}
quick 99
quickly 5^{22}, 22^{37} 99,

quickly, a little more 5^{20}
quality, finest 19^8
quilted coat 583

R

rain (n.) 15^{30}, 423
rain (to) 15^3
raise 699, 756
ramble 622
rather 19^{30}
read (to) 5^1
read 18^7, 85, 549
ready cash 14^{26}
real 25^{14}, 258
really 10^{15}, 27^1
reason 217
receive 406, 604, 892
recently 16^{12}
reckon 18^{15}, 402
reckon accounts (to) 14^{14}
reckon up 14^{22}
recognise $6^{5,6}$, 109, 114
recommend 24^9
record 316
recreation 20^{15}
red 574
refined 22^{27}
regard (to), 338
registered letter 23^{20}
rejoice 527
relate 103
related 303
relations 12^{13}, 321
relationships 466
relative, sign of 94
reliable 24^{14}
remember 764
remove 379
repair 26^3, 803
repeatedly 17^3, 614
reply 18^2, 18^4, 528
request 92
residence 465, 930
resign 30^4
rest 613, 713
rest during hot season 23^{14}
restaurant 10^{12}
restaurant-car 19^{35}
result 30^{19}
return 489, 875
review (to) 123
revolution 30^{29}
rice 199
rich 557
rickshaw 22^{12}
ride 627, 685

right 223
right (hand) 358
ripe 17^{11}, 514
rise (to) 352
river 691, 791
river-bank 28^1
road 252
roast 860
roast beef-steak 27^{19}
roll up 837
room, a 82, 154
room, single 27^8
room, upper 8^1
room, vacant 27^7
rooms, classifier of 855
rooms, woman's 310
root (classifier of books) 21
root (classifier of cigarettes, etc.) 823
rouse 620
rub (to) 192
ruin 561, 745
rule 360
run 698

S

sad 673
sad and heavy 21^{19}
salute 18^{25}
same, the 10^3
satin 586
satisfactory 9^{22}, 230
saucer 161
save money 23^{25}
savings (bank) 24^{13}
say 76, 217
scatter 432
scheme 553
scholar 6^{13}
school 6^{17}
school-house 130
schoolmates 20^{22}
sea 516
seal (to) (classifier of letters) 80
season 442
season, time 350
seat 765
second stem 487a
secondly 16^{16}
section 671
sections 886
secure (adj.), 940
sedan 22^{13}
sedan-chair 684
sedan, classifier of 685
see 5^{14}

seed, to sow, 322
seeing, something worth 23^9
seek 473, 532
self 6^8, 113, 118
sell 260
send 628, 749, 750
send, pay 14^{23}
send, take, escort 392
senior 932
sentence 117
separate 10^8, 246
serge 25^{10}
servant, head 8^{17}
servant, title of 8^{17}
set time 363
set up in business 18^{21}
seven 54
several 3^6
sew 569
shadow 939
shake 595
shallow 582
share 868
she 9, 461, 626
sheet (classifier of paper) 34
shirt 25^{23}, 787
shoes 810
shoe shop $26^{5,6}$
shop 261, 265
shop sign 19^2
shore 877, 879
short 631
shut 10^2, 237
Siberia 23^{28}
side 77, 175
sign 19^2
sign, a 585
sign of completed action 95
sign of dative 112
sign of genetive 539
sign of optative 526
sign of ordinal 75
sign of possessive 26
sign of relative 94
signal 827
silk 25^9, 573, 788
silken 25^{25}
silver 771
simply 16^6
since 15^{19}, 445
single-breasted 25^{17}
single room 27^8
sir 1^7
sister, elder 12^7, 313
sister, younger 12^8, 318
sisters 12^9

sit 147
six 23
skin 578
slab 35
sleep 484
sleep (to) 187
slice (to) 371
slight 582
slow 100
slowly 5^{21}, 100
slow train 19^{32}
small 27, 899
smoke 488
smoke (to) 26^{13}
smoothly 9^{23}
snow 424
society 18^8, 556
soft 831
some 6^7, 28
something to depend upon 23^8
somewhat 898
son 12^{21}, 42, 81
sort, a 236
sound 67, 121
soup 859
soup, turtle 27^{18}
south 244
south-east 21^4
sow 306
sow seed (to) 322
sparing 398
speak 5^3
special 19^{26}, 620, 769
spend 405
spirit 660
spiritual 654
splendour 770
spoil 23^3, 23^{27}
spoon 164
sport 20^{20}
spread out 921
spring 15^{31}, 433
stable 30^{36}
stable (adj.) 940
stamp 23^{18}
stand 616
stand (to) 599
star 362
start 19^{24}
state, a 143
station 19^{17}
station platform 19^{23}
stationery 1^1, 3^1
stature 22^{24}
steady 30^{36}
steam 682
steam-power 22^3
steamer 28^6
stems, 1st of the ten 476a

stems, 2nd of the ten ten 487a
stems, 3rd of the 476b
stems, 4th of the ten 463b
stick on 735
stiff 802
still 194, 438
still more 20³¹, 283, 625
stimulate 620
stimulating 20³⁰
stone 811
stool 8¹⁹, 198, 203
stop 21¹¹ 594
store (to) 773
store, general 26⁷
store up 778
storey 757
story 29¹
straight 658
strange 659
street 23²², 256, 740, 741
strength 681
stretch 897
strike 916
strike (to) 476
string of cash 74
strip, a 743
student 6¹³
style 21¹⁴
substance 891
succeed 482
success and failure 18²⁰
suddenly 15²⁰, 436
suffer from damp 28¹⁹
sugar 829
suitable 9², 24¹⁰, 572
summer 25⁸, 15³², 443
sun 467
sun, day 355
superintend 202
supposing 29¹¹ 782
surname 149
surname (Chow) 767
surname (Fan) 876
surname (Ko) 830
surname (Li) 16
surname (Sung) 747
surname (Wang) 212
surplus 399 558
surplus wealth 18¹¹
surround 29², 907
survey 662

suspend 74
suspended 30³⁷
sweat 801
sweep (to) 213
swim 20¹⁶, 622

T

table 171
tailor 19¹
tailor, foreign 25⁷
take 162
take as a basis 18¹⁸
take away 7¹⁰,¹¹
take care of 26²³
take, escort, send 392
take in 11¹⁶
take out 11¹⁷
take passage 18¹⁰, 542
talent 332
taste 836
tax, duty 519
tea 160
tea-cup 7¹²
tea, infuse 27¹⁶
tea-pot 8¹¹
teach (to) 136
teacher 8¹⁷, 191, 202
Teachers' Training College 22²²
telegram 22¹⁷
telephone (to) 16²⁰
tell 102
tell (to) 5¹⁸
temple 766
Temple of the Town God 24⁵
ten 18
ten cents 59
ten thousand 73
tennis 20²¹
tennis-court 20²³
tent 29⁵, 903
tenth 57
terrace 35
test 17¹, 493
thank 525
that 31, 294, 626
then 134
there 5⁶,⁹,¹²
there is, are 5
there is not 1²
therefore 20²⁷
thereupon 29⁸
they 1⁶
thick 798
thin 792
thing 3⁵, 547, 710
think 453
third stem 476b

this 30, 295, 626
thorns 755
thought 6⁹, 104
thousand 66
three 17
through, to go 240
through train 19²⁹
thus 9²⁴
Tien ts'in 19¹⁸
ties 25²⁶
time 13¹, 356
time, a 132, 603
time, length of 344
time, season 350
tinned goods 71¹⁸
title of servant or artisan 8¹⁸
tobacco leaf 26¹⁶
tobacco for water-pipe 26¹²
to-day 13⁷
together 421
to-morrow 13¹⁰
to-morrow, the day after 13¹¹
tone 67
tools 7¹³, 159, 168
towards 615, 744
tower 759
town 611
trade 10¹¹
trade (to) 18¹⁷
trade-mark 26²⁸
train (steam) 22¹¹
traveller 851
treat 783
tree 731, 262
trouble 835
trouble (to) 781
troublesome 26²²
trousers 25¹⁵, 799
true 270
try (to) 17¹, 493
tube (classifier of pens) 22
T'ung-chow 10¹⁰
turn 814
turtle soup 27¹⁷
twelfth month 13²⁶
twice 6¹⁶
twig 743
two 612
two 41, 64
two days ago 13¹²
two days hence 13¹³
two kinds 25¹²

U

ugly 645
umbrella 279
unable to do 11⁹

unable to overtake 11⁹
uncle 12²⁰, 331, 902
under 181
underneath 8⁵
understand 6¹,²,³, 110, 111
underwear 25²⁸
unfortunately 21¹⁶
unite 693
unless 25⁶
unusual 16¹⁸
unworthy 152
upon 182
upper room 8¹
up-to-date 19⁶
urge 543
urgent 228
use (n.) 23⁴
use (to) 180, 220
useless 397
usurp 910
utensil 821
utensils 7¹³, 159, 168
train, express 19²⁷,²⁹
train, fast 19²⁷
train, slow 19³²
train, (to) 726
tram 22⁸
transport 518

V

vacant 463
vacant room 27⁷
vacation 734
vase 22³⁵, 697
vegetable 617
vehicle 242
very 39, 50, 293, 490, 564, 815, 914
very many 14¹³
view 664
village 641
visit 889
voice 6 ¹¹
volume (classifier of books) 21

W

wadded coat 19¹²
wagon 22¹⁰
waistcoat 25¹⁶
wait 146
walk (to), 290
want 71
warm 123, 441
warmth 29¹⁰
wash (to) 196

wool 794
words 86, 694, 883
waste 882
wasteful 14^{20}
water 195
water-pipe 26^{15}
way, in what 9^{14}
way, in this 9^{19}, 9^{24}
way, in that 9^{20}, 9^{25}
we 1^4, 16^9, 468
wear 692
wear well 25^{13}
weary 865
weather 15^1
weave 789
week 13^{24}, 28^3
weigh 640
weigh luggage (to) 19^{34}
welcome 29^7, 904
well-acquainted 24^7
west 47

Western food 27^{11}
what 50, 506
what ? 3^8
wheel 873
wheel-barrow 22^6
when 13^2,^{3}
where ? 5^7,^{10},^{13}, 83a
whether, or 14^{12}, 410
white 107
who 69
whole body 29^{15}
whose 4^2
why ? 9^{18}
wife 711
will (n.) 479
willing 487
wind 411
wind blowing 15^6
window 11^3, 268
winter 15^{34}, 375, 435
wish 487

wish (to) 16^{21}
with 208, 422, 722
within 649
woman 329, 711
woman, young 12^{23}
women's rooms 310
wood 10^{16}, 262
woods 23^{10}
word (written) 72
write 4^3, 70
work 459
workman 819
world 267
worth seeing, something 23^9
wrap 737

Y

yawn 878
yellow 830

yellow silk tobacco 26^{11}
year 309, 317
year before last, the 13^{23}
years, in former 20^4
yes 2^1, 29
yes and no 30^{24}
yesterday 13^8, 349
yesterday, the day before 13^9
yet 194
yet, and 439
you 15, 887
you (plur.) 1^5
you (polite) 19
young 16^2
young woman 12^{23}
younger brother 12^5, 320
younger sister 12^8, 318

LINGUAPHONE CONVERSATIONAL COURSES.

For beginners and advanced students are now ready in

ENGLISH, FRENCH, GERMAN, SPANISH, ITALIAN, RUSSIAN, DUTCH, SWEDISH, AFRIKAANS, IRISH, ESPERANTO, CHINESE AND PERSIAN.

Each course consists of 30 interesting conversational and descriptive lessons, supplied with all the necessary text-books in an attractive carrying-case.

LINGUAPHONE TRAVEL COURSES

in ENGLISH, FRENCH and ITALIAN.

Each course consists of 30 interesting and instructive talks contained on 15 double-sided 10-inch records. They take you for a tour through Great Britain, France or Italy accompanied by a guide who describes to you, clearly and interestingly, the principal objects of interest in each place visited, and talks to you about the Art, Music, History, Geography, etc., of his country. Supplied complete with text-book in an attractive carrying-case.

LINGUAPHONE LITERARY COURSES

are available in

ENGLISH, FRENCH, ITALIAN and GERMAN.

Each course consists of 20 extracts, in prose and poetry, from the works of the most famous writers in each language. Ten double-sided 12-inch records, complete with text-book in an attractive carrying-case. There is also a Literary Course in Esperanto—consisting of 5 double-sided 12-inch records supplied with text in an attractive Album.

For further particulars, write to:

THE LINGUAPHONE INSTITUTE,
24-27, High Holborn, London. W.C.1.

扫码听录音

"早期北京话珍本典籍校释与研究"
丛书总目录

早期北京话珍稀文献集成

（一）日本北京话教科书汇编
《燕京妇语》等八种　　　　　　　四声联珠
华语跬步　　　　　　　　　　　　官话指南·改订官话指南
亚细亚言语集　　　　　　　　　　京华事略·北京纪闻
北京风土编·北京事情·北京风俗问答
伊苏普喻言·今古奇观·搜奇新编

（二）朝鲜日据时期汉语会话书汇编
改正增补汉语独学　　　　　　　　修正独习汉语指南
高等官话华语精选　　　　　　　　官话华语教范
速修汉语自通　　　　　　　　　　无先生速修中国语自通
速修汉语大成　　　　　　　　　　官话标准：短期速修中国语自通
中语大全　　　　　　　　　　　　"内鲜满"最速成中国语自通

（三）西人北京话教科书汇编
寻津录　　　　　　　　　　　　　北京话语音读本
语言自迩集　　　　　　　　　　　语言自迩集（第二版）
官话类编　　　　　　　　　　　　言语声片
华语入门　　　　　　　　　　　　华英文义津逮
汉英北京官话词汇　　　　　　　　北京官话：汉语初阶
汉语口语初级读本·北京儿歌

（四）清代满汉合璧文献萃编
清文启蒙　　　　　　　　　　　清话问答四十条
一百条·清语易言　　　　　　　　清文指要
续编兼汉清文指要　　　　　　　　庸言知旨
满汉成语对待　　　　　　　　　　清文接字·字法举一歌
重刻清文虚字指南编
（五）清代官话正音文献
正音撮要　　　　　　　　　　　　正音咀华
（六）十全福
（七）清末民初京味儿小说书系
新鲜滋味　　　　　　　　　　　　过新年
小额　　　　　　　　　　　　　　北京
春阿氏　　　　　　　　　　　　　花鞋成老
评讲聊斋　　　　　　　　　　　　讲演聊斋
（八）清末民初京味儿时评书系
益世余谭——民国初年北京生活百态
益世余墨——民国初年北京生活百态

早期北京话研究书系
早期北京话语法研究
早期北京话语法演变专题研究
早期北京话语气词研究
晚清民国时期南北官话语法差异研究
基于清后期至民国初期北京话文献语料的个案研究
高本汉《北京话语音读本》整理与研究
北京话语音演变研究
文化语言学视域下的北京地名研究
语言自迩集——19世纪中期的北京话（第二版）
清末民初北京话语词汇释